Also by Joan Gould

Spirals: A Journey to
the Center of a Woman's Life

Spinning Straw
into Gold

Spinning Straw into Gold

What Fairy Tales Reveal
About the Transformations
in a Woman's Life

Joan Gould

RANDOM HOUSE TRADE PAPERBACKS
NEW YORK

Published in the United States by Random House Trade Paperbacks,
an imprint of The Random House Publishing Group,
a division of Random House, Inc., New York.

RANDOM HOUSE TRADE PAPERBACKS and colophon are registered
trademarks of Random House, Inc.

Originally published in hardcover in the United States by Random House,
an imprint of the Random House Publishing Group,
a division of Random House, Inc., in 2005.

LIBRARY OF CONGRESS CATALOGING-IN-PUBLICATION DATA
Gould, Joan
Spinning straw into gold:
what fairy tales reveal about the transformations in a woman's life
Joan Gould.
p.   cm.
ISBN 978-0-8129-7545-1
1. Fairy tales—History and criticism. 2. Symbolism in fairy tales.
3. Psychoanalysis and fairy tales. 4. Women—Folklore.
5. Women—Mythology. I. Title.
GR550.G68 2005
398'.352'082—dc22   2004051085

www.atrandom.com

Book design by Dana Leigh Blanchette

To Arnold
my sustainer

Contents

❦

PART 2
Matron
The Age of Attachment

187

⚛

Introduction

Spinning Straw into Gold

"What's your favorite fairy tale?" I like to ask friends and acquaintances.

Most women answer "Cinderella" without thinking, while men pause, look bemused, say, "I can't remember any. Would 'Peter Pan' count?"

After a few minutes of reflection, however, most people dredge up some images that come to the surface charged with significance, even if the plot line has been forgotten. The choice (which may not turn out to be "Cinderella," after all) gives a glimpse into the speaker's soul, even if its relevance remains hidden. So many images fill the classic fairy tales that they are bound to hold a dozen different shades of meaning for a dozen readers, which makes interpreting a fairy tale for somebody else as tempting and risky as disentangling his or her dream.

"Rumpelstiltskin," one woman said to me, an uncommon answer. "We were poor, so I didn't have many toys when I was little, and I thought how wonderful it would be to take a bag of straw and spin it into gold so I could buy all the toys I wanted."

"Rumpelstiltskin," said another woman, younger. "I saw myself as the heroine who was threatened with death if she didn't spin straw into gold, and so she promised a dwarf that if he would spin the straw for her she would give him her firstborn child. That's my secret fear—my feeling that my baby isn't really mine. I didn't make him, I may not deserve him, and he may not be mine to keep. Someday I may have to ransom him from fate."

"The dwarf, not the Queen, is the pivot of the story," a male psychiatrist said. "His feeling that his name, which is his identity, must be kept secret, or else he'll be revealed to the world as the hunchbacked, shriveled, ridiculous creature he knows himself to be. And if that happens, he'll disappear."

THIS IS A BOOK ABOUT WOMEN, specifically about fairy tales and the way they illuminate the metamorphoses at each stage of a woman's life: those shifts in consciousness as well as biology that propel women from one level of being to another. We are born to be changed, the stories tell us; we are always on the move from one transformation to the next, whether we want to be transformed or not.

In folklore, there are a few male Cinderella figures ("The Ugly Duckling") and male Sleeping Beauties, but in general the hero, bent on conquests, wants nothing so much as to remain himself once he reaches adulthood, simply growing more powerful and widely known. The heroine, on the other hand, is a shape-shifter, living a life of transformation in a body that passes through inevitable metamorphoses. A teenage girl longs for curves in order to be seen as a fertile maiden. A fertile maiden wants to become a lover or wife. (She may change her partner later on, but not the step she has taken, which has carried her from one level of existence to another.) A wife wants the big belly that carries her future child. A new mother expects her breasts to become fountains of milk. But the crone, past her child-feeding years, becomes flat and barren as a prepubescent girl again.

Maybe this is why the witch builds a gingerbread house in the woods, to feed her flesh on the vigor of two hungry children so that she can start her cycle all over again.

WHAT, THEN, IS TRANSFORMATION? All we know for sure is that it's a process that can't be stopped or reversed once it has started. It's a constant transit from the known to the unknown, including death as well as birth. In everyday life, we rely on the pleasingly deceptive fantasy that we will always be whatever we are now, while fairy tales strip away this illusion, or narcotic, and point us toward the underlying truth. To be fully alive and aware of our human fate, we must do our best to wake up to the transformations—which mean the transience—of our lives.

But one thing transformation is not: It's not a magic wand that turns a poor girl's rags to riches. That particular trick can be done by winning the state lottery, which is good luck indeed, but only external. True transformation, which is never reversible, happens internally and involves pain—it involves rising (or falling) from one level of consciousness to the next, gaining a new sense of where we are in our lives and what must come next.

In the German version of the Cinderella story, for instance, the kitchen drudge can have anything she wants from the gift-giving tree that grows on top of her mother's grave, but she doesn't think to ask for a golden gown until her haughty stepsisters leave for the ball. But why not, when she was never meant to be a kitchen maid in the first place? She was, and is, the heir to her father's house; her stepsisters are only intruders.

Transformation takes place only when Cinderella sheds her perception of herself as an Ash Girl along with her rags, and this is the moment of change: not when a man kneels down to fit the slipper onto her foot, but when she recognizes that she has turned into the princess she was always meant to be. Her new approval of herself—which every woman must develop if men are to share her confidence in her desirability—makes the rest of the night possible.

What we think of as magic, as Iona and Peter Opie point out in their book *The Classic Fairy Tales,* is simply this ability to bring to term what was latent in our nature from the beginning, to recognize what was always there even though we couldn't see it, perhaps because the people around us didn't want us to see it.

Wicked or foolish females, by contrast, are those who fail to develop, so that their consciousness does not match their current stage of life: Snow White's stepmother can't bear to see that time has moved on. Her daughter has grown more beautiful than she is, while she herself has aged. The witch in "Rapunzel" can't acknowledge that the heroine should be released from the tower, now that she has outgrown it. The proof of how much time has passed is that her hair reaches the ground.

In real life, all of us know Sleeping Beauties who fall asleep during puberty and fail to wake up until they find themselves married to the wrong man. We know grown women (my mother was one of them) who spend their entire lives thinking of themselves as girls—in fact, as persecuted girls like Cinderella, forced to sit forever in the ashes and do the dirty work while the undeservedly happy women around them pass their time by going to balls.

Fairy tales tell us that a day comes when we are due to wake up to a new reality, come to life again transformed, echoing Snow White as we exclaim, "Oh, heavens, where am I?" with a sense of wonder at how far we've come, along with a twinge of nostalgia for the person we used to call "me" but for whom we no longer have a name. This is why several stories in this book deal with protagonists who fall asleep in the middle of their adventure, or die a short-term death and cannot wake up until their inner transformation is complete. When they open their eyes, they find a Prince hovering over them, which makes us think at first that the Prince's presence, or kiss, has saved them, but it's also possible that after their new consciousness has fully ripened, the time comes around for them to live with a higher sense of self, and so the Prince appears.

THERE IS, or there used to be, a misconception among women that fairy-tale heroines are pretty but helpless victims who do nothing but wait to be rescued by heroes. "Look at Cinderella," the critics say. But if Cinderella is supposed to be a passive heroine, longing to escape from her abusive home, why did she run away from the Prince three nights in a row after dancing with him at the ball?

Fairy tales are female lore by and large, handed down by women from one generation to the next, so they tend to show heroines wide open to receiving and transmitting magic, or taking vigorous action. In these stories, sisters rescue brothers far more often than brothers save sisters. Daughters rescue fathers or lovers rather than the reverse:

Beauty goes into the Beast's castle, prepared to sacrifice her life in order to save her father. Her father is saved, but she survives and transforms the Beast as well as herself, turning the monster into a princely husband.

Hansel may be the one who scatters bread crumbs to mark the way home from the forest (men are usually pathfinders), but it's Gretel who saves her brother's life by pushing the witch into her own oven.

Gerda goes off in heroic pursuit of her playmate Kay in Hans Christian Andersen's story "The Snow Queen," just as Meg Murry sets off to find her brother and father in Madeleine L'Engle's *A*

Wrinkle in Time. Psyche descends to the Underworld to win back her lover, Cupid.

Rather than maintaining a fixed form, fairy tales change from one country, century, or social group to another. The more patriarchal and stratified the society, the more clearly the heroine is expected to rely on the hero to save her. In a fairy tale written for the French court at the end of the seventeenth century, Bluebeard's last wife can do nothing but pray that her brothers will gallop down the road to rescue her before her murderous husband chops off her head. But in "Fitcher's Bird," a more archaic version of the same plot, the country-bred heroine disposes of the tyrant and his whole family with poetically ghoulish touches.

The most patriarchal of all tale-tellers is Walt Disney, the chief mythographer of our time, whose fairy-tale films are so popular that they have practically obliterated their sources. With him, the focus of the story shifts from the heroine's transformation to the hero's courage, as hero and witch do battle for possession of the girl. Romance takes over. The girl's best hope for survival is that "Some day my Prince will come."

BEGIN LOW AND END HIGH is the usual path for fairy tales. "Rumpelstiltskin," from the brothers Grimm, begins with a poor miller who possesses a single treasure, a daughter who is as beautiful as the morning and as clever as she is beautiful. So proud is the miller of this girl that when he meets the King one day he cannot stop himself from boasting that his daughter can spin straw into gold.

Her supposed talent excites the interest of the King, who is exceedingly fond of money, so he orders the girl brought to the palace the next day. When she arrives, he shows her into a room containing bushels of straw and a spinning wheel, and tells her the straw must be spun into gold before morning if she values her life. After that he leaves the room, locking the door behind him.

What can the girl do but weep? Her father's boasts are no fault of hers but they will cost both of them her life. As she weeps, the door opens—never mind the fact that it's locked—and in hobbles a rickety dwarf who looks the situation over and asks, "What will you give me if I spin this straw into gold?"

"My necklace," the girl answers. The little man sits down at the wheel, which whirs merrily until the straw is spun.

The next morning, when the King sees what he sees, he becomes even greedier, and so he orders a larger heap of straw to be laid at the feet of the miller's daughter. Again the dwarf appears and asks why she weeps and what she will pay him to perform her task. This time she takes the ring from her finger and gives it to him.

By the third day, the King is beside himself with delight. He installs the miller's daughter in a bigger room filled with straw, and announces that if she succeeds only once more she will become his Queen, but if she fails her head will be chopped off.

The dwarf returns as soon as she is alone. "But I have nothing left to give you," the poor girl says amidst her tears. "Then promise me your firstborn child when you become Queen," the manikin proposes. What choice does she have? If she's beheaded the next day she will never bear a child, nor will she sit on a throne.

The wheel whirs, the gold is spun, the room is filled with it by morning, and the miller's daughter is crowned Queen. Not long afterward, another more remarkable transformation is under way—a female feat that requires nine months instead of a few hours of turning a wheel and results in treasure of another sort. At the end of that time, the Queen gives birth to a baby.

In her joy, the new mother forgets her promise, but the dwarf soon shows up to remind her. She offers him all the riches of the kingdom in exchange for her child; she salts her pleas with tears bitterer than those she shed when she thought she would lose her head. At last the dwarf relents. "I will give you three days' grace," he says. "If, during that time, you can tell me my name, you shall keep the child."

On the first of the dark nights after the dwarf's challenge, the Queen lies awake making a list of all the names she knows, which she rattles off to her visitor in the morning. "Caspar, Melchior, Balthazar," she says, along with hundreds of more likely guesses, but none proves to be the answer. On the second day, she reels off the most far-fetched nicknames she can think of—Spindleshanks, Sourpickle, Stoopnagle, and so forth. "No," says the dwarf. "No, no, and again most assuredly no."

Meanwhile, the Queen's personal messengers are scouring the kingdom for names that no one in the palace has ever heard.

On the third day, just before the dwarf's hour, one of the messengers returns and reports that as he was roaming through the forest "where the fox and the hare bid each other good night," he saw a fire burning in front of a hut, and a little man dancing around it as he sang:

> *"The first day I brew, the second I bake,*
> *The third day the young Queen's child I'll take.*
> *She'll never learn from her guessing game*
> *That Rumpelstiltskin is my name."*

The Queen manages to contain herself while she confronts the dwarf. "Is your name Tom?" she asks. "No." "Then it must be Dick. No, it's not Dick? Then how about Harry?" "No, no." "Then perhaps it's Rumpelstiltskin?"

"The devil told you that!" the little man shrieks, and stamps so hard in his fury that his whole leg is driven into the ground, right up to his crotch.

The Queen has beaten him. With the preternatural alertness of a new parent, she has sent her wits, her intuition (which the story embodies as messengers), out to pry the lifesaving secret from the forest. As soon as she is mature enough to be a mother (which in fairy tales is another word for *queen*), her consciousness deepens. She takes possession of her life and her child.

As for the dwarf, in his frenzy to pull his leg loose he tears himself in two, which is the last that anyone hears of him.

THE MESSAGE WE ARE left with is the message of all fairy tales and, in fact, all religions: When we are locked in a room alone with a spinning wheel and nothing more promising than straw to work with; when we cannot try any harder or work more skillfully at our present paltry level of being (in fact, our efforts may be what's balking us if we think we can force something new into existence); when life seems to hold no promise for tomorrow but loss or death; a locked door—inside us, or out—opens by itself. A curious-looking little man hobbles in and sits down at the wheel to summon what we lack out of the dross that lies under our feet, beneath notice. Straw is transformed into gold again. We grow closer to what we hoped to be.

SO HERE WE HAVE IT: two different kinds of transformation at work. The dwarf's magic exists outside the known world in a land where the fox and the hare bid each other good night. His mastery of the spinning wheel is as aberrational as those courteous farewells between predator and prey, since women, not men, are supposed to be spinners. He blurs the line between sexes as thoroughly as the line between species. He blurs the distinction between good and evil, since he saves the heroine's life and yet threatens to kidnap her child. He transforms more than straw. As one of the few fairy godfathers on record (for which he gets no thanks), he turns the maiden into a Queen and the wife into a true mother, while at the same time he is possessed, like all demons, by the lust to capture a human soul.

The Queen's magic, on the other hand, is female and human. Sitting alone, locked in the middle of her marriage with nothing but the most ordinary material at hand, she does what every woman does, or attempts to do. She spins a child, though not without the help of a masculine spirit.

Spinning is a metaphor for transformation, and transformation is woman's work. The woman of the house spins flax or wool into yarn, which she makes into clothes; then turns old clothes into rags, rags into quilts or rugs, and quilts or rugs into art. She turns, or used to turn, grain into flour and flour into bread, which becomes part of her family's flesh. In her highest moments, like the Queen, she transforms a drop of protoplasm into a new human being in the heated oven that is her womb; turns the food that she herself eats into milk that flows from her breasts; and transforms the wild creatures she gives birth to into more or less civilized members of society.

In her minor moments she nags, which is the means toward a lower form of transformation. Anyone or anything close to her, from a living room to a lover, she has to trim into better shape. If she stops nagging, that can be a danger signal, implying that she no longer cares enough for those around her, at least not in the way she used to, or else they have grown beyond her reach.

Since woman's magic is a metaphor for natural growth, fairy tales about heroines differ intrinsically from those about heroes. In stories, a hero has a single choice—conquer or die—but a heroine has no choice at all. She has to survive, that's nature's mandate for her, survive and reproduce, at least until her child-rearing years are over. To do that, she transforms herself into whatever the moment demands.

The heroine changes from seal maiden or mermaid to human being, shedding her skin to reveal her legs and the package that lies between them. She goes to sleep as an adolescent girl and awakens as an ardent woman when the right man or moment arrives. If she can't escape from an unbearable situation, she metamorphoses downward instead of up, like Daphne, who turns into a tree when pursued by the god Apollo, who is intent on raping her.

Or she slips in and out of clothes instead of skins. "Cinderella" is a story no more than six pages long in which the heroine changes her clothes nine times, each time an outer manifestation of what's going on inside her. In fairy tales as in life, a change of clothing or house is never trivial. It's an external sign of transformation, which is one of the chief themes of this work.

———

THIS BOOK CONCENTRATES ON the classic European fairy tales and a couple of well-known myths (I have added some details of my own invention), along with novels and movies that are reworkings of the same themes. *Jane Eyre, The African Queen, Gone with the Wind, Lady Chatterley's Lover, A Little Princess, My Fair Lady, Pretty Woman,* owe at least part of their popularity to the fact that they re-state transformations found in ancient tales and make them relevant to our lives today.

Familiarity is a large part of the usefulness of these tales. They can be considered the dreams we dream in common, altering from one era or country or individual to the next, even reversing their message (nowadays the Beast is regarded as a seductive outcast instead of a monster), but keeping intact the images that haunt us.

For years, my own favorite story was the Greek myth of Persephone and her mother, Demeter. I thought this was because I was fascinated by the mysteries of the dead and by Queen Persephone, who ruled over them. Then one day, when my mother was old and sick and bitter, and I was telling her this myth to pass the time, I realized that wasn't the reason for my preference at all. I was captivated by the story of a mother goddess so in love with her daughter that she defied the gods and made the whole world suffer for her loss when Persephone was stolen from her. It was more than I thought my mother would do for me.

I look back at this myth now for a different reason: After Persephone was released from the Underworld, something happened to transform her mother, Demeter. Something unexpected had better happen to a mother after her daughter marries and settles down or else she withers, and I, for one, need to find out more about this late blooming. I don't know these stories as well as they know me, I've discovered.

Now that I think about it, Persephone was never lost, except to her mother's sight. She had moved on to another level, and her mother had to do the same. Only if we remain conscious of the transformations we've gone through so far can we learn to forgive our younger selves, or our family, or the gods for what we failed to understand years ago when our vision was more focused but also more limited than it is today. "Just like mother" is a phrase that changes meaning as we age.

THE THREE SECTIONS of this book correspond to three stages in a woman's life, three transformations in body, psyche, and role: Maiden, Matron, and Crone. In the past, we used to think of these phases as Single, Married, and Widow, but our lives are no longer so sharply divided into segments now that we have single mothers by the millions; unwed couples who live together for years; unmarried career women who would scarcely call themselves "maidens"; divorcées who are as avid to go to the royal ball as Cinderella ever was; and grandmothers who take on the role of mothers in order to care for their grandchildren.

Despite the blurred boundaries, the categories still speak to us about the problems encountered at each stage:

Part One, *Maiden,* deals with the transformation from puberty to maturity during the years before marriage.

Part Two, *Matron,* spans a woman's years as wife and mother, when she herself has been transformed into a transformer.

In Part Three, the *Crone* survives alone, often after her husband has died or disappeared and her children have left home.

Maiden, Matron, Crone. In many parts of the ancient world, the Goddess was seen in three forms: as a nubile virgin, a fertile mother, and an old woman—in other words as the creator, nourisher, and destroyer of life on earth. The beginning, middle, and end.

In apparent accord with women's lives, the moon moves through cycles that seem to be images of transformation in a higher sphere, a monthly calendar of change. The crescent moon, barely visible at first, grows more luminous every night. The full moon draws the waters below it with maximum force, bringing in nutrients from the deep twice a day. The waning moon is gradually swallowed by shadow.

And after the waning come those dark nights which, oddly enough, we call "new moon," as if acknowledging that every ending is also a beginning.

PART 1

⁂

Maiden

The Age of Attraction

"Snow White"
"Cinderella"
"Sleeping Beauty"
"Beauty and the Beast"

In the first section of this book, the heroine faces her primary task: She must separate from her parents and home. Of course, a hero must also leave home before his adventures can begin, which seems natural to us, but the young woman has a purpose that is hidden even from her. She leaves one home only to find or found another.

This is what distinguishes a child from a marriageable maiden as definitively as sexual maturity—this break with the family, which remains difficult even in modern times, when single women are no longer expected to live with their parents. While the heroine may lay the blame for the separation on her murderous stepmother ("Snow White"), or on her loyal need to serve her father ("Beauty and the Beast"), her body is what forces her to leave childhood behind, as her body will dictate so many of the passages of her story.

Whether a woman recognizes her motive or not, the goal of romance may not be marriage so much as motherhood, which requires shelter for her unborn children. The Prince may be chiefly a means to that end.

The maiden's story isn't a simple trajectory from virginity to marriage, however. When assaulted by sexual knowledge for the first time, a girl plunges into a period of blackness, which is required in order to let her emotions catch up with her body.

Sleeping Beauty sleeps. Cinderella waits, and while she waits she works her way through the darkness of depression. Snow White both works and sleeps before she is ready to open her eyes and find a Prince leaning over her. Beauty leaves the Beast to visit her ailing father, promising to return in a week, but once she is back in her childhood home she falls into a mindless trance that makes her forget her promise.

In most of the stories, although the girl never suspects the truth, it's Nature as the Terrible Mother, taking the form of wicked step-mother, witch, or thirteenth fairy, who is the agent of growth, propelling the girl out of maidenhood and forward into sexuality, which is something the Good Mother—who wants her child to remain a child forever—could never do.

CHAPTER 1

Snow White:

Breaking Away from Mother

The youngest heroine in this book, at least the youngest emotionally, is a girl who hasn't yet completed her first transformation of consciousness: puberty, which eventually produces an independent sexual woman from a dependent child. Snow White's body has begun to change by the time her story is under way—we know this from the violence of her stepmother's reactions to her beauty—but her self-awareness hasn't taken into account the biological upheaval starting to take place inside her.

Adolescence involves a break with the past, as well as a thrust toward the future. Without any choice, either too soon or too late to suit her, a girl loses the flat, lean body that she took for granted and finds that she has become a sexual creature, obscurely desired or threatened from all sides. At this stage, she must learn to see herself as separate from her background, her parents, and her home, with as few recriminations as possible toward those who made her what she is at present. She must picture a future different from the present, taking place against a background that she can't visualize, in which she will answer to another name. Possibility opens up in front of her, dazzling her with its prospects, but at the same time she finds herself stripped of the protection she has taken for granted until now. Liberation is always a loss as well as a gain.

How, and when, do women get to know themselves as self-willed sexual beings, distinct from their families? By looking in a mirror, especially during adolescence, which is not at all the way a boy learns to know himself. Teenage girls peer into mirrors all day long to find out how others see them, what impact they're going to have on the world around them, what can be improved or projected better or awaited, and what can only be deplored—critiques in the mirror's voice that change from hour to hour. ("Flat," says the mirror. "Still flat. You'll never get a man, not with those goose bumps you call breasts. Why don't you rethink your hair? Some streaks—that might be good. Or a French braid. And don't stand like a Girl Scout at flag-raising. You want to smolder. . . . That's better. You know what? You've got potential, girl. Your day is coming.")

This isn't the time-wasting obsession that adults think it is. Like it or not, an adolescent girl recognizes that she's an object as well as a subject, a soul encased in a carcass that's the material she was given to work with in order to attract a mate and advance nature's program of making a mother of her.

At any age, can a woman stand in front of a mirror for more than thirty seconds and acknowledge herself simply as an object in space, without correcting her appearance in some way—running her fingers through her hair or wiping the corners of her lips—while making some silent comment about her looks, more often than not unfavorable?

In short, looks matter. We can manage to be more than the body, but there's no way we can be less.

"SNOW WHITE" IS A STORY about looks, looking and being looked at, a glittery tale of a window, a snowfall, a mirror, and a coffin made of glass. The females in it are a good mother who looks out the window at a fresh snowfall, a bad mother who looks only at her own reflection in the mirror, and a daughter who lies still as death and is looked at. But any story that deals with looks and looking is necessarily a story about time, which is a force that defeats beauty.

A girl named Snow White lives with her stepmother, a Queen obsessed with her own appearance, who possesses a magic mirror. But in a palace ruled by this mirror's pronouncements as to who is the most beautiful in the land, how is it that the heroine has no mirror of her own, or, if she has one, lacks the heart to use it? Who has convinced her that her looks aren't worth bothering about, since no one will pay attention to her anyway? While the Queen glories in her superiority, her stepdaughter, who is just coming into her own beauty, has no idea what she looks like, none of the usual self-consciousness of adolescence, which is how we know that she hasn't yet gone through the turmoil that is about to engulf her.

A CHILD'S FIRST MIRROR is her mother's eyes, which determine what reflections she'll see for the rest of her life. If a mother admires her daughter—let's say the girl is eleven or twelve years old and prepubescent—the girl learns to use an actual mirror as a tool for self-study. (I didn't say if the mother "loves her daughter," since we don't know how to recognize love in its many guises. "Admires" is the operative word here.) She does this because of the confidence her mother pours into her.

Snow White, on the other hand, has no picture of her future as a sexual creature when we first meet her. Except for the Queen, she's the only female in the palace; there are no siblings or friends, no other images of womanhood in front of her. Her stepmother is what it means to be female; her stepmother is Queen, but the girl is nothing like her stepmother and, what's more, never will be, which means that there must be something the matter with her. The longer she scrutinizes the older woman, the more of an outcast she feels in a woman's world, scrutiny being the female equivalent of male sparring as a way for two people of the same gender to gauge each other's strength.

But there are sexually mature girls, there are even grown women, who don't acquire their own mirrors because, for one reason or another, their vision has been blinkered by their mothers and they can't bear to come face-to-face with their unaccepted and unacceptable selves.

"I was around fourteen—maybe fifteen—when my mother paid one of her rare visits to the house where I was being brought up by my grandmother," said a friend of mine who is now the mother of three children. "I was coming out of the shower when she walked into the bathroom and saw me naked for the first time in six months. Maybe more. From her look of shock, I understood what she was seeing: my developing breasts, nipples that had grown darker and slightly puffy, pubic hair, rounded hips and belly. She left in a hurry and shut the door. I looked in the bathroom mirror, which had been there all along, of course, but I didn't see beauty reflected back at me. I saw danger. I loathed the body that was causing this separation between us. From that time on, I did my best to make myself disappear: anorexia, hair hanging over my face, baggy T-shirts to hide those breasts. All the sad disguises. Not until I was in the delivery room years later, giving birth to my first child, did I understand the power and beauty of a woman's body."

LIKE MANY OF THE BEST-LOVED TALES, the Grimms' story of Snow White starts with a wish.

On a day in the middle of winter, a Queen sits beside her window, watching a snowstorm while she sews. Suddenly her needle slips, she pricks her finger, and three drops of blood fall upon the snow: always three, the magic number. The red drops look pretty on the snow, and she thinks to herself, "Would that I had a child as white as snow, as red as blood, and as black as the ebony window frame."

White, red, black. Seeing nothing but snow in front of her, the original Queen, who is the Good Mother, has summoned the ancient trinity of colors to compose a wish-child. Together they form a series, putting us on notice in the opening sentences that this will be a magical story in which each color, in turn, will determine a stage in the life of the child created by the wish. The heroine, who will be more luscious than blood on snow—life on top of death—will move through three phases of life to reach a fourth stage her mother has never dreamed of—gold—while, at the same time, her future stepmother, who cannot stage-manage her own colors, will be nudged against her will from red into black.

At the moment when the Queen makes her wish, the earth sleeps beneath the falling snow, pure but barren, and awaits its reawakening the way Snow White will sleep in her glass coffin later on, and so the first color to appear on the scene has to be the heroine's name: Snow White.

White is innocence, virginity, purity, light without heat, a window into the future, but white by itself is sterile. Something more than snow is required to produce life.

The child must also be as red as the drops of blood that flow from her mother's finger. The Queen has felt a prick, just as Sleeping Beauty will be pricked by a spindle. "Prick" is a word we still use for penis; in street language, an upraised middle finger is understood as a sexual act. The Queen's blood is the same as menstrual blood, so common that the loss is scarcely noticed, even though it signals life's capacity to regenerate itself. But it's also the blood that flows from a ruptured hymen when a woman loses her virginity and conceives a child, which is what has happened to the Queen here.

Blood is red, the womb is red, the vulva is red, especially when stimulated. Paleolithic cliff tombs were painted red, to show that the earth, the body of the goddess, is the womb of life as well as its tomb. Above all, sex is red, as in Eve's apple, a virgin's "cherry," Persephone's pomegranate or the Devil's cloak, the red-light district, red shoes, red satin boxes shaped like hearts and filled with candies to be licked on Valentine's Day, or a *Scarlet letter* A for adultery, embroidered in gold on a Puritan gown.

White and red together make a child's story, as in "Snow White and Rose Red," but a crucial element is lacking: the perspective of time. The Queen's child must also be black as the window frame (black as a raven's wing in other versions), a strange condition to insist on before birth, since black is the color of unconsciousness and death. Put together, the three colors paint a picture of time and growth, the phases of the moon as crescent, full, and waning, which correspond to the ancient goddess in her triple phases as Maiden, Matron, Crone.

These colors are on the earthly level, however, leading to the fourth and final color: gold. In "Snow White," the golden element is hidden until the story is nearly over.

But fairy tales are no simpler than real life. The heroine can't move directly from white to red, from childhood to sexuality, without passing through a period of blackness, which in the first three stories in this book—"Snow White," "Cinderella," and "Sleeping Beauty"—takes the form of either work or sleep.

Cinderella works while living among the ashes. Sleeping Beauty sleeps. Snow White does both, as she moves from her mother's palace through the dwarfs' cottage and into a coffin before finding a home of her own. In each case, an interval of darkness shrouds the heroine while she goes through her transformation from one plane of existence to the next.

This may be why we remember certain patches of childhood and adolescence vividly, and others not at all. Or why we remember ourselves at school—a junior-high actress starring in the school play, a girl in the cafeteria gossiping with friends, a success on the hockey field—but not as bodies at home. What we can't remember happened during the dark spells, when we couldn't bear to look at ourselves yet.

SCARCELY IS SNOW WHITE BORN than her good mother, who longed to have a child, dies, leaving a vacancy for a stepmother to fill.

This is the basic mother fantasy for both girls and boys. In the beginning, the child is inside the mother's belly, and then on the mother's breast. But a time comes when Mother witholds her breast, ignores her child's cries of distress, and lavishes her attention on a sibling who must be her own flesh and blood while the hero or heroine is treated like a stepchild. (In modern times, the telephone is the most hated sibling of all.) To the child's dismay, Mother turns out to have moods and priorities of her own.

As child psychologist Bruno Bettelheim pointed out a century and a half after the Grimms' fairy tales were written, it is unbearable for a child to think that Mother can be indifferent to his needs, angry, punitive, threatening—can even want to be rid of him for a while—so he concludes that the heartless female must be an intruder who has taken the place of his good, kind mother while he wasn't looking. She must be a stepmother, witch, ogress, or wolf who will be replaced when his good mother reappears on the scene.

The brothers Grimm, who started their work as scholars bent on unearthing the roots of their Germanic culture, unconsciously colluded in this fantasy of the split mother. When they realized that the first editions of their *Nursery and Household Tales* were being sold not only to their fellow folklore scholars as planned, but primarily to newly prosperous middle-class parents who wanted stories to read to their children at bedtime, they censored their language. In the original edition of this story, printed in 1812, Snow White is persecuted by a woman identified as her mother, but by 1819 the Grimms quailed at suggesting that a biological mother could want her child killed, and so her status was changed to that of stepmother, the jealous Queen who may also be a witch but should never be called "Mother" again.

A truth is hidden here: Every woman knows that her child is miraculously her own, flesh of her flesh, and yet not her own at all, not built to prenatal specifications, a newcomer in the family with perfections and capacities that she would never have dreamed of, but also with quirks of its own along with an inconvenient will, as if it were a foundling. ("How could she possibly behave like that? There was none of that in *my* family.") From hour to hour, the mother changes the face she shows to her family, like those Red Riding Hood dolls, now out of fashion, in which the top half showed kindly Grandmother, but when the doll was turned upside down the skirt fell away to reveal the head of the wolf.

EVERY MORNING, Snow White's stepmother, who is indeed beautiful, inspects herself in her magic mirror and demands to know if she is still the fairest in the land.

"Slave!" is the first word she utters in the Walt Disney movie as she sweeps up the stairs toward her mirror, cloaked in black and crowned, with a hood covering her head so that not a hair can be seen: invisible hair is the sign of repressed sexuality. Burning like dry ice with self-regard and scorn, she commands the genie in the glass to speak:

"Magic Mirror on the wall,
Who is the fairest one of all?"

The mirror tells her what she wants to hear, which means that there's no trouble between stepmother and stepdaughter for the time being.

But a day comes when the mirror delivers the answer that its owner must have been dreading for a long time:

"Thou art fairer than all who are here, Lady Queen.
But more beautiful still is Snow White, as I ween."

At that, the Queen "turned yellow and green with envy . . . her heart heaved in her breast, she hated the girl so much" for this act of domestic treason. Snow White's new beauty implies that there will soon be two menstruating females in the palace, a prospect that the older woman can't tolerate.

"Huntsman!" she calls, preparing for a preemptive strike. She cannot bear to look at this girl who is trying to push her from red toward black before her time. The huntsman must take the child out into the forest among the wildflowers and kill her. "Bring me back her lungs and liver as a token," the Queen commands him. She wants them, but not as a token. She wants to eat them, for this Queen is not only a self-centered stepmother but a cannibal witch as well.

And yet she is more fundamental than that; she is a force darker and more inevitable than any human classification. Beyond the level of a gingerbread-house witch, she is the Terrible Mother herself, the black side of nature kept hidden from our daytime consciousness, who spawns the earth's children and is responsible for keeping them coming, only to swallow them back into her belly again.

Or, looking at nature in a more favorable light, she is the force that pushes the pubertal girl out of her snug childhood home and into the trackless forest, where she will either die or find a mate and reproduce—nature doesn't much care which, so long as the species survives.

How old must a heroine be, then, to arouse the attention of the mother?

According to the brothers Grimm, Snow White is seven years old, but we can disregard this as sexual whitewash. Her stepmother's intuition is right on target. She must be on the verge of puberty, which is the way Walt Disney presents her in the movie *Snow White and the Seven Dwarfs:* She wears a high collar to indicate her royal birth, but puffed sleeves and a hair ribbon to show that she—and her stepmother—have kept her mind as virginal as a field dormant beneath a cover of snow.

In Europe, during the seventeenth and eighteenth centuries, the average age at menarche, the first menstrual period, was sixteen, though it was often eighteen or even twenty among peasant girls in the countryside, whose diet was poorer than that of the middle class, so we must assume that all the fairy-tale heroines in this book, including Snow White, are older than their sexual development suggests. The average age in the United States today, where girls are generally well nourished, is around twelve and a half.

Our stories start sooner in a girl's life and last longer.

OBEYING THE QUEEN'S ORDER, the huntsman takes Snow White into the forest to pick flowers, but he doesn't have the heart to kill her. After telling her to run farther into the woods, where he's sure wild beasts will do the job for him, he kills a young boar instead and brings its lungs and liver back to the palace. The Queen eats the innards for dinner, nicely salted by the cook, and thinks she has eaten Snow White.

Details in fairy tales are never accidental. The liver is an organ filled with blood, which formerly was thought to be the site not only of life but of the soul, in much the same way that we now regard the heart. In ancient forms of prophecy, the liver of a sacrificed animal was read for omens of the future, since it was thought to embody messages from the gods.

Lungs provide the body with air, the breath of life, which the Greeks and the Romans considered to be the substance of our souls.

The boar is a ferocious wild animal, black as midnight, with curved tusks like two crescent moons, representing the death-dealing and castrating god who was the lover of the Terrible Mother. When the Queen in this story eats the boar, she feeds on her own rage.

But what has the girl done wrong that she should be forced out of her stepmother's house and into the forest, where wild beasts lie in wait for her? Nothing. It's her body that has caused this trouble, without any awareness on her part that harm has been done. This is the initiation story that all women experience: innocence forced into consciousness of sex and its consequences.

MUNCHING ON THE BOAR'S LIVER AND LUNGS, the Queen thinks that she has disposed of her competitor, who has been called the fairest in the land. But, as with many fairy-tale characters, we have to think of this Queen on several levels at once: as Nature in the form of the Terrible Mother or a storybook witch, but also as a nightmare projection of a human mother. From a daughter's point of view, is it fantastic to imagine that a woman might want to devour her child, or rather her child's life, emotionally if not physically?

A mother who criticizes all her daughter's boyfriends, or charms them (*The Graduate*), or listens in on her phone calls, or buys herself duplicates of the clothes she buys for her daughter is undoubtedly eating up her daughter's life. If a mother boasts that she's her daughter's best friend, the girl would never keep any secrets from her— why, then, the daughter has already been salted, popped into her mouth, and swallowed, and the mother is wiping her lips. If an unhappily married woman keeps her daughter firmly attached to her side as a consolation prize for the devotion she doesn't get from her husband, the daughter feels plagued by guilt when she reaches for the happiness that her mother never thought possible.

These women don't want to destroy their daughters in the process of eating them. What they want is to absorb their daughters' youth to make up for what they themselves have been deprived of, or once had and lost. And who can blame them, when the ripeness that comes over the daughters is so sudden, so unmerited? In an orderly world, beauty would make itself visible by degrees, endurable like dawn as our eyes adjust to the light, but it does no such thing. Play-

ing the dramatist, it forces itself on our attention in one swoop—
"My God! My daughter. And she's beautiful!"—just as the mirror reported.

One evening the girl, on her way to a prom, walks down the stairs
in a long dress, her braces off at last and a corsage on her wrist, her
fingers grazing the stair railing as if she has always known how to do
exactly this. I have been supplanted, the mother says to herself.
Maybe she isn't violently jealous of her daughter's beauty—that's a
fairy-tale metaphor—but in a deeper sense she is jealous of the op-
portunities that lie ahead of the girl: the beauty of babies and lovers
and homes not yet known, the beauty of energy that hasn't peaked,
of hopes that haven't evaporated, of limits not yet reached. Soon the
daughter will be busier and more in demand than the mother, more
central to a family, fertile for decades after her mother becomes barren, increasing in influence during the years that her mother wanes,
possibly expanding and flourishing in ways her mother never
dreamed of.

A mother who admires as well as loves her daughter may still feel
grief over the waste of her own life. If she herself wanted a college
degree, a career, a lover, a trip to Paris, but got no encouragement,
she may rage because of doors open for this generation that never
opened for her. More galling yet, she may understand in retrospect
that those doors were unlocked but she never pushed hard enough to
shoulder them open. In that case, her darkness takes the form of despair and self-loathing rather than malice, and the Queen's murderous hatred of her stepdaughter is turned inward on the young and
hopeful part of herself that Snow White represents.

On the other hand, Bruno Bettelheim suggests that Snow White
is jealous of her stepmother rather than the other way around, presumably because her stepmother is the one who goes to bed with the
invisible father. "If a child cannot permit himself to feel his jealousy
of a parent (this is very threatening to his security), he projects his
feelings onto this parent," Bettelheim says. "Then 'I am jealous of all

the advantages and prerogatives of Mother' turns into the wishful thought: 'Mother is jealous of me.'"

This may be too contorted and, at the same time, simpleminded an explanation for the feelings that plague certain daughters. Of course, a little girl may be jealous because she isn't allowed to marry her father, but it's equally possible that she knows perfectly well that her father prefers her to her mother, and feels an oddly satisfying guilt on that account.

Or her jealousy may appear in a more benign form as an aspect of admiration. Susan, an acquaintance of mine in her mid-thirties, has a mother who is a defeated-looking woman, the color bleached out of her by a disastrous early marriage and divorce, followed by years of overwork at a job that was beneath her intelligence in order to support her children, which was then followed by illness. And yet Susan is jealous: not of her mother as she is today, but of her mother as the radiant teenager whose picture she has seen in the high-school yearbook from forty years ago, the girl labeled "Best Dancer" and "First to Marry" in the senior-class predictions. Why wasn't she ever as pretty as the girl in the yearbook photo? Susan wonders. Why couldn't she have been invited to the Dartmouth Winter Carnival by a sophomore, premed, when she was still in high school? If Susan feels inadequate, it's in comparison to a teenager who vanished before she was born.

INSTEAD OF ARGUING whether Snow White's stepmother is jealous of the heroine, as the fairy tale says, or the other way around, as Bettelheim insists, we would do better to concede that mother and daughter are endlessly entwined in a way that is quite different from mother and son. The two females watch each other, criticize, reprove, admire, envy, imitate, deplore, all at the same time and in both directions. Even if the daughter vows to be nothing like Mother when she has her own home—nothing at all—or, more poignantly, never to be trapped in Mother's unfortunate situation, that's another form of entanglement. The two females share the same profession, after all: attracting a man and producing children, who will look at them askance when another twenty years or so have passed.

Snow White is struggling to hack her way through adolescence, a stage that requires her to feel coolly superior to her parents, or at least independent of them and resentful of their control. Otherwise, separation would be unbearable. Suddenly Mother, who used to be perfect, can't do anything right in her daughter's eyes. "Oh, *Mother!*" is the war cry heard in the house. At the same time, even the most devoted mother—especially the devoted mother—feels pangs of resentment toward the self-willed and critical young woman she harbors under her roof.

In Orthodox Jewish families, when a girl had her first menstrual period it used to be traditional for her mother to slap her face. Which made the point perfectly clear.

BUT SOMEONE IS MISSING HERE. In this storm of mother-daughter conflict, what has happened to Snow White's father, the King, who hasn't been heard from since he made such a predictably bad choice of a second wife?

Fairy tales deal with only one parent at a time, as if our hearts are too cramped to pay attention to two people at once. If Mother is harsh, then Father, who may have loved his wife and children once upon a time, must be absent, or else he has thrown up his hands in defeat, like the father of poor, abandoned Hansel and Gretel. On the other hand, if it's Father who sets the plot in motion, as in "Beauty and the Beast" or *King Lear,* then Mother isn't mentioned unless the story deals with incest. Even then, she gets only a few lines of text to explain that the incest is all her fault for being so incomparably beautiful that only her daughter can replace her.

One parent at a time, then, either because we can't cope with two or because when one parent is domineering, the other takes a subservient role: perhaps like that of the Queen's huntsman, who may be the person we're looking for, Snow White's father in disguise, and part of his daughter's story after all.

Like many men married to hot-tempered women, the father may pose as a servant subject to orders, a huntsman who puts meat on the table like the good provider he's meant to be, but nonetheless a servant unprepared to argue with the Queen. At the crucial moment when Snow White, like many adolescents, thinks she's about to die, the huntsman/father tells her no, she's not going to die, he's on her side. He refuses to kill her. "Run away," we imagine him urging her. "Lie low until the storm blows over. You and I know your mother when she gets into these states, don't we?"

This interruption of the mother's plans may be the passive father's most valuable function in real life. He's the family member who introduces a new possibility, like the smell of pine woods seeping through an open window. If there are two points of view, then there can be many, and no threat is as dire as it seems.

But he doesn't offer to go through the forest with Snow White and take care of her. He certainly doesn't consider going back to the palace to oust the Queen and make a home for his daughter, who owes him her life. After sending the girl on her way, he vanishes like legions of fathers we know: the Wizard of Oz, for instance, lifting off from his kingdom in his hot-air balloon but accidentally leaving Dorothy behind; or Daddy Warbucks, rescuing Little Orphan Annie when she escapes from his estranged wife, frozen-faced Mrs. Warbucks, by running away in a snowstorm. "So you had a feed last Sunday, eh?" says Daddy Warbucks. "But nothing since? Great Caesar's Aunt! No wonder you were stumbling all over the road when I first saw you!" He feeds her, he saves her, and then leaves her to face the future alone.

Oddly enough, a daughter never reproaches her father for the disappearing act. In fact, she never seems to expect anything else. For many a grown woman, this remains her dream: that Daddy will drive down the road one day and make everything in her life all right.

Her stepmother/mother, on the other hand, is always closer than she thinks, as the Queen will prove later in this story.

SO THIS IS THE HEROINE'S FAMILY, as distinct from the hero's: a loving biological mother who dies during her daughter's childhood, though her spirit may appear in another form later on; a jealous, powerful mother, sometimes accompanied by sisters who lie low until the girl approaches puberty, and whose assaults she must survive; and a well-meaning but passive father. (In Disney's movie *The Little Mermaid,* King Triton is reduced by the sea witch to a trembling shrimp, still wearing his crown.)

Only the females—the mothers—seem to have access to otherworldly magic that is bound to the processes of life, occasionally power for good as wielded by fairy godmothers, but more often a force that seems harsh when viewed from the human perspective. To our surprise, it's the Queen, the Terrible Mother, who turns out to be the agent of growth in the story: not the Good Mother, who would keep her snow-white child by her side forever if she could, and certainly not the Prince, who doesn't show up until the end of the story. It's the Mother Goddess in her dark aspect, devoted to fertility and death but caring nothing about personal happiness, who forces the girl to grow up.

If the wicked stepmother is vain, that proves how sexual she is. If her heart heaves with envy, that's because she embodies growth, and growth leads to withering and old age. Forcing her stepdaughter out of her childhood home and into the wilderness, she oppresses the girl, but at the same time she starts her on the path to consciousness. The example she sets is one of implacable strength, but it's the solitary, furious strength of the procreating mothers, who are capable of murder, not the harnessed and adaptable strength of the wife-mother-homemaker who casts her lot with her husband.

CHAPTER 2

Snow White:
Tempted by the Witch's Wares

The Disney Movie vs. the Grimms' Fairy Tale

Peering under the bushes and catching her clothes on thorns, Snow White runs through the forest, where wild beasts pass her by but do her no harm. If she falls and cries for help, or if she's attacked by beasts, no one in the world will hear her.

This is her first conscious journey from the known into the unknown, the first step in her transformation from childhood to womanhood. She's no longer her parents' daughter. Neither is she anyone's sweetheart, lover, or wife, and may never become one. She has been stripped of her identity, as if she has shed her swanskin or sealskin and hasn't yet grown a new one.

FOR A FEMALE, this headlong flight has different meaning than it does for a male. The girl is homeless, unable to return to the shelter she just left, and yet by nature she *is* the home, the hearth, whatever else she may be. Her house is an external skin that shields her vulnerable parts from the world, as her womb will be a home someday for her unborn child.

This separation from home and mother, which is the prelude to the Maiden's story, takes either of two directions. Rapunzel, Jane Eyre, the Little Mermaid, Cinderella, yearn to break loose from their homes, and do so at the risk of their lives. Snow White, on the other hand, is lured away and threatened with death if she returns. Either way, the shock of fear and separation reminds the girl that she is alive (though she may not be for long). She must find a home that fits her maturing body.

BY CONTRAST, the young hero jubilantly shuts the door of his childhood behind him and goes off to climb the phallic beanstalk, or join the Star Fleet like Luke Skywalker, in order to confront his ogre-father. He sails to Troy or the Labyrinth of Crete or the moon, and after he gets there, what does he want? To set a course for home, even if the trip takes ten years, twenty years, expecting to find his home just as he left it, in the care of his wife, who hasn't aged a day.

AT DUSK, Snow White is so tired, so torn by branches and bruised by stones, that she can no longer run through the forest. Just in time, she finds the shelter she needs: a home that's the right size for her, not a gloomy marble palace like the one she left, cold as her step-mother's heart, but a cottage in which she finds a table covered with a white cloth, seven little plates and seven mugs, with seven beds beside them, all "neater and cleaner than can be told."

HERE WE COME to a fork in the road. We take it for granted that everyone knows "Snow White," but the truth is that almost no one under the age of seventy remembers the old story, or any other fairy tale, nowadays. Mothers don't read them to their children anymore; they rarely know them themselves. Schoolteachers don't know them, either. The truth is that the Grimms and French writers like Charles Perrault have become as dim in our memories as Homer: stories that everyone refers to but few people have actually read.

My little grandnephew goes to senior kindergarten in a well-regarded public school where the teachers pick a theme each month, which is a common pedagogical ploy to integrate reading skills, art, storytelling, and so forth. The first of the chosen themes this year was "Disney." Each child had to bring a book to class, but it had to be a Disney book, and the classroom discussions centered on those books and movies. While authorship was never explicitly stated, the children were left with the impression that Walt Disney wrote "Cinderella," Walt Disney wrote "The Little Mermaid," and so forth.

In the case of "Snow White," what we know is the version that Walt Disney produced as a film in 1937, the first full-length animated movie ever made, which was so overwhelming in its impact that it has wiped out all memory of the earlier text. Hundreds of millions of people around the world have seen *Snow White and the Seven Dwarfs* over the past three generations (no one, even in the Disney corporation, will take a guess at the number). Tens of millions of copies of the videocassette have been distributed; a million copies of the DVD were sold on the first day of release. The book based on the movie has been translated into forty-five languages. Disney has eaten up the old tale with as much relish as the Queen ate the liver and lungs of the boar.

There's no point in complaining that the Disney films pervert the "real" stories like "Snow White," however, since no such thing as an original or authentic version of an old fairy tale exists. Traditional stories were told for hundreds or thousands of years before they were written down, migrating across continents in versions that changed with each tale-teller's country, century, audience, social class, memory, inventiveness, and personal point of view. As the Greek saying goes, "The fairy tale has no landlord."

At the end of the seventeenth century, Charles Perrault and the ladies of the aristocratic salons purged the old peasant tales of their vulgarity and spiced them with enough sophistication to charm the court of a king. (Little Red Riding Hood was eaten by a wolf? How unfortunate. "Children, especially pretty, nicely brought up young ladies, ought never to talk to strangers; if they are foolish enough to do so, they should not be surprised if some greedy wolf consumes them, elegant red riding hoods and all.") During the nineteenth century, the moralistic Grimms got rid of the slightest hint of sexuality—no more incest, no more pregnancies—in order to make their book suitable for children, but stepped up the violence of punishments for the evildoer. Cinderella's jealous sisters have their eyes pecked out by doves when they escort her to her wedding. Snow White's stepmother will have to dance in red-hot iron shoes by the end of this story.

In our own time, Walt Disney, who reflected his era as effectively as Perrault and the Grimms did theirs, became the leading mythographer, along with his studio. This youngest son of a dirt-poor fundamentalist farmer from Missouri was abused throughout his childhood, beaten regularly with a leather belt from the time he was eight years old as "corrective discipline" to make him work harder. The sexual giddiness of the 1920s, followed by the grimness and somberness of the Depression years, must have reinforced his conservative view of life. Females were divided into impossibly innocent maidens and wicked old witches. The malevolence that was his specialty seemed especially threatening when projected in Technicolor, which was brand-new at the time of this film, on screens as big as the side of a house. This he offset with the tunes and antics of his cartoon characters.

His real change, however, was one that audiences rarely notice, because they take it for granted as the way things are, or at least the way they were in the olden days. While showing us dwarfs who march merrily home from work—"Heigh-ho, heigh-ho, it's home from work we go"—and capering squirrels who clean house by sweeping the dust under the rug with their bushy tails, Disney projects a sugary view of a woman's life, radically different from the mystical stories of pain and transcendence found in Grimms' and other traditional works. In place of transformation, Disney puts romance at the core of a woman's life. The tales change from the old accounts of inner development, which is the heroine's natural plot, to musical romances in which a young couple fall in love the instant they meet but must overcome the monster-parent before they can marry.

The responsibility for her fate shifts from the heroine herself to the formerly almost invisible hero, who now becomes the agent of change. In the Disney version of the patriarchal tradition, male is ranged against female for possession of the girl, youth against age, manly valor against shape-shifting cunning or demonic evil. (The patriarchal tilt of the Disney fairy tales is even clearer in *Sleeping Beauty* and *The Little Mermaid* than in *Snow White*.)

During the first few minutes of *Snow White and the Seven Dwarfs*, we see the little Princess dressed in rags, scrubbing the palace courtyard on her hands and knees like Cinderella. While she refills her bucket, she leans over a wishing well surmounted by doves and gazes into the water as she sings "I'm wishing—I'm wishing—for the one I love / To find me—to find me—today." (Virgin and dove, a not unfamiliar combination.) Right on cue, a Prince on horseback with a white plume in his bonnet leans over the garden wall and joins her by caroling his love to her. The Queen peers out from behind the curtains of a palace window, her eyes narrowed by sexual jealousy.

A Prince at the beginning of a heroine's story? Who ever heard of such a thing? In classic fairy tales, the hero appears only at the end, and then not as a flesh-and-blood man but as living proof that the heroine is now mature enough for love and marriage; he's a graduation gift of sorts. In the Disney movie, on the contrary, he declares his love in the first scene. He's on Snow White's mind in the middle of the film, when she sings soulfully, "Some day my Prince will come. . . . And away to his castle we'll go, / To be happy forever, I know." And he's essential at the end, when he rouses her from death. Even when he's not onscreen, he pervades her story, which consists chiefly of waiting to be found and acknowledged as his Queen.

From Disney's point of view, of course, the slow, painful growth of consciousness isn't what multimillion-dollar animated movies are made of. Every medium has messages that it can deliver successfully and others that elude it. In one sense, Disney restored fairy tales to their roots by attracting a mass audience, much of it pre-literate, who share a group experience of terror and delight in the dark—the same appeal as ghost stories told around a campfire at night. We needn't resist Disney's sugary appeal, but if we want our children to absorb stories of the essential transformations that lie ahead in their lives, we must turn back to old-fashioned books, in this case a fairy tale not ten pages long.

TWO FORCES ARE OPPOSED to each other in the Grimms' tale, but, unlike the Disney scenario, both forces are females. We see them at whatever level we are prepared to see them.

We can see them as the still beautiful but aging mother and her pubescent daughter, both of them victims of time. Or we can see them on a mythical scale as the Terrible Mother, who is the ruthless goddess of fertility, eternally pitted against a fertile young woman whose virginity stands in the way of nature's purpose. (The Mother shows up again as Venus in the story of Cupid and Psyche.) Finally, we can see the two of them as forces within the girl herself: her fear of the dangers and burdens that lie ahead, which is overcome, while she sleeps, by the maturing process that makes sexuality appear in the guise of a Prince.

At each of these levels we are given the heroine's story rather than the hero's, her trajectory into adult sexuality as separate from her involvement with a particular man.

"SNOW-DROP" WAS the original English title for the German story we know as "Snow White." Disney expanded this to *Snow White and the Seven Dwarfs,* giving equal billing to the little fellows who occupy more than half the film's running time.

In folklore, there's nothing lovable, much less merry, about these stunted men who can never grow bigger or marry or have children. (Female dwarfs are as scarce as mermen in fairyland.) Even though they are enormously rich and have nothing to spend their money on, the dwarfs never stop working, never think of anything but burrowing into the mountains for ore all day long.

In the Grimms' story, when Snow White reaches the cottage she takes no more than a single bite of vegetable from each little plate, and a single swallow of wine from each mug, so as not to deprive any one of her hosts. (Moderation with food is a prime virtue in fairy tales.) Then she tries the neatly made beds. One proves too short and one too long, but the seventh is just right for her, which emphasizes that she is approximately the same size as the dwarfs, and seven years old in the Grimms' accounting. "And so she remained in it, said a prayer and went to sleep."

For the storybook Snow White, the dwarfs represent a good father split into seven parts, providing food and shelter without threatening her in any way. Had there been only one dwarf, the situation might have been awkward, but these seven try hard to shield her from sexuality, especially since they won't develop into sexual adults themselves and see no reason why their foster child should be exposed to such a risk. Of course the dwarfs love the homeless girl at first sight—"Oh, heavens!" they cry in the Grimms' story when they see her. "What a lovely child!"—but that doesn't mean that they make life easy for her. "If you will take care of our house, cook, make the beds, wash, sew, and knit, and if you will keep everything neat and clean," they propose in the story, "you can stay with us and you shall want for nothing." "Yes," says Snow White, "with all my heart."

This bargain strikes horror into the hearts of modern feminists, but it seemed clear to the Grimms that father figures should instill a sense of responsibility and good work habits while a child is a member of the household.

A hundred years pass between the Grimms and Disney, during which time the scene turns upside down. In the movie version, when the dwarfs return from their day in the mines, they discover, to their horror, that the cottage has been cleaned.

" 'Things look different. Sort of unhealthy!' Sleepy said.

" 'There's dirty work afoot!' growled Grumpy, making a fierce face. 'The whole place is *clean*!' " Disney was the first to individualize his "little men," as he called them, which he did so successfully that millions of adults who can no longer name the nine planets or the seven colors of the rainbow, much less the thirteen original colonies, can still reel off the names of the dwarfs.

" 'Sink's empty! Hey! Someone's stole our dishes!' hissed Sleepy.

" 'Huh! My cup's been washed,' said Happy, running a finger around the rim. 'Sugar's gone!' "

No, the sugar isn't gone. It has been layered on top. The dwarfs have been transformed into adorably messy little boys, so greedy for home cooking that they invite Snow White to stay with them despite their fear of the Queen's vengeance—it's the vision of gooseberry pie that is their undoing. Snow White towers over them like a den mother at a Cub Scout meeting, a tender little parent with impeccable standards.

"Let me see your hands," she demands with her own hands on her hips in mock severity. "Worse than I thought! How shocking! . . . March straight outdoors and wash, or you'll not get a bite to eat!"

What's this? Has Snow White become the dwarfs' mother? In this apparently superficial change between two works a century apart lies a shift in our view of human nature that parallels the shift from the heroine's story of development to the hero's promise of rescue.

If the heroine is instantly transformed into a perfect mother as soon as she leaves home, she has no need for future growth, and motherhood must be a childishly simple task. This means that the visits from her stepmother become senseless persecution, providing nothing more than a motive for the Prince to rescue her. On the other hand, if the dwarfs are father figures, she is still maturing, and will mature further while she lives with them.

In our society, we fail to understand that the growth of consciousness is a long and convoluted process. We don't see that growth is what we require—not happiness but growth, which means the chance to experience or do or make new things, or make old things in a new way, always with a twinge of anxiety because we are doing what we don't quite know how to do. (This is the essence of parenthood, since a child changes every day, and the parent's response can't be mapped out in advance.) Without growth, we have no life story. We shrivel into dwarfs who work all day in the mines without knowing why, and then go home to satisfy our craving for gooseberry pie.

That's on the individual level. But if we don't believe in inner growth we can't believe that parents are capable of teaching their children anything worthwhile, or restraining them from harming themselves or others. We can't rely on either fathers or mothers for protection and guidance, any more than we can rely on the gods, kings, ministers, teachers, politicians, or even doctors and scientists of the past.

THE BEST-KNOWN FANTASY of flight from growth is *Peter Pan,* the play by J. M. Barrie about Never Land that was turned into a Disney movie seven years after *Snow White and the Seven Dwarfs.* Wendy Darling and her two brothers are lured away from a home where their mother is so vaguely benevolent and their father such a spoiled child that the only responsible adult in the household is the nurse, Nana, a Newfoundland dog. ("Of course Nana has been trained by Mrs. Darling, but like all treasures she was born to it.") In a fit of pique one evening, Mr. Darling chains Nana in the backyard, which is unfortunate, because fictional dogs in movies often represent a man's instinctive nature, exactly the part of himself that ought to be trusted to mind the children, while he and Mrs. Darling wander off to a dinner party. Left alone, those Darling children fly to Never

Land with Peter, where seven Lost Boys, like the seven Disney dwarfs, are in need of a mother.

"Wendy, one girl is worth more than twenty boys," Peter says at the beginning of the Barrie play, a view of woman as the angel-in-the-house that distances her from males every bit as effectively as if he had said the reverse.

Peter and the boys keep busy warding off Captain Hook with his iron claw. Like all parental figures, in fact like the Queen in "Snow White," Captain Hook is relentlessly pursued by time, which in his case takes the form of a crocodile with a clock ticking in its belly. Wendy spends her evenings darning the Lost Boys' socks. She suffers no real wounds, she learns no lessons. In the end, she promises to return to Never Land one week each year to do Peter's spring cleaning.

There we have her: the ideal wife and mother as seen in the first six or seven decades of the twentieth century. A pubertal girl, whisked away from home before she discovers her sexuality. (What boy wants to compete with his father for the attention of a full-blown sexual woman?) A girl for whom motherhood is a lark, earning her children's affection but scarcely their respect, since her work is only a step removed from playing with dolls. June Cleaver in *Leave It to Beaver*, pushing a vacuum while dressed in pumps and pearls.

IN FAIRYLAND, by contrast, parents appear as we remember them from childhood, vast and terrible, life-threatening, on occasion life-saving, but always as unpredictable and unassailable as gods. The heroine's task is first to separate from her mother and then to grow enough so that she can supplant her.

In the Grimms' story, the Queen reigns supreme now that she is convinced she has eaten her stepdaughter's lungs and liver—why would she doubt it?—which means that she must be the fairest in the land. All the same, she feels compelled to consult her magic mirror once again. This time, the mirror, which does not know how to lie, has an unexpected message:

"Over the hills, where the seven dwarfs dwell,
Snow White is still alive and well,
And none is so fair as she."

Beside herself with rage, the Queen paints her face to look old. She dresses in the clothes of a peddler, this woman who is so obsessed with her beauty, and travels over seven hills and through seven valleys until she reaches the cottage of the seven dwarfs.

"Pretty things to sell. Very cheap," she croaks outside the window.

Snow White has been left alone while the dwarfs are at work, but she's not the unselfconscious child who used to live in her stepmother's palace, however long ago that may have been. Surrounded by the admiration of seven males, she has undoubtedly learned that her body is as alluring as it is vulnerable.

"Pretty colors to go with your pretty gown," the peddler cries, holding up silken staylaces, which were used in earlier centuries to tighten a woman's corselette.

"I might as well let the worthy woman in," Snow White says to herself as she unbolts the cottage door. In the face of sexual temptation, she reaches out her hand to stroke the staylaces, and in the process she edges from the innocence of white toward sexual red, while the Queen pretends to pass from red to black, turning into a crone who peddles finery to susceptible girls. In her role as Terrible Mother, the Queen, who is too old to give birth herself, must propel Snow White out of her virginal state so that the life cycle can start over.

"Child, said the old woman, what a fright you look. Come, I will lace you properly for once." The Terrible Mother's voice always has a punitive edge to it. "Your time has come," she seems to say. "No more piggyback rides for you. Just wait until a man gets into you. And wait until a baby comes out of you. You won't look so snowy white anymore."

Her choice of the girl's figure as target is venomously accurate. The mother points to the area that should have attracted a man—

would have attracted one if the girl weren't as shapeless as an ironing board—and in this way makes the daughter aware of her sexuality and deeply ashamed of her inadequacy at the same time.

The Queen laces her so that she can scarcely breathe. Snow White feels the constriction of adulthood, she feels her stepmother's control over her body, but before she loses consciousness it's possible that she gets a look at herself in a mirror, laced taut: Her waist is small, her breasts puff up; she's no longer a girl but a desirable young woman. The lacing knocks the breath out of her. She falls to the floor as if dead.

Fortunately, it's nearly evening, and the dwarfs return home in time to cut the laces.

"WOULD YOU BELIEVE she threw the shopping bag across the room?" my mother said to her friends on the phone the next day, in her aggrieved voice. I never heard her refer to me by name. I was always "she."

Inside the bag were two foam-rubber bust pads, as they were called at the time, that I was supposed to slip inside my training bra, as if my flat chest had magically bloomed overnight.

"You know what I told her?" my mother asked her confidantes. She used the tone reserved for her daughter's peculiarities. "I told her the man in the store had them made specially for her. He saw me coming down the street and put them in the store window where I'd see them, because she's the only person in the world who needs them. Made them just for her. *That's* what I said."

I couldn't look at them, because they were everything I wasn't and probably never would be. A foam-rubber reproach. I don't remember throwing them down, but I never picked them up.

The next day, I found the pads tucked into my bureau drawer.

AGAIN THE HAUGHTY QUEEN consults her mirror and learns that Snow White lives, and again she comes to the cottage while the dwarfs are at work, disguised as another peddler armed with a poisoned comb this time. (Disney's movie omits these two visits.) For Snow White, the comb is an irresistible temptation to become what she longs to become. Against orders, she unbolts the door, having learned nothing from experience. "Now I'll comb you properly for once," says the peddler Queen once she's in the house. "Left to yourself, you'll never get a man," her tone implies. We can imagine that she pulls Snow White's hair so tight with the poisoned comb that all thoughts, dreams, plans, comprehension, memories, even grievances stored inside her mind, are yanked out of it, just as her breath, expelling her emotions, was choked by the staylaces. With her hair piled on top of her head, she looks like a woman of marriageable age.

Once again, she falls unconscious until the dwarfs come back in time to remove the comb and restore her life and girlhood.

EVEN IF WE IMAGINE very different conditions—a situation where the mother is too devoted rather than too self-centered, so that the daughter has nothing to rebel against—the girl is still obliged to flee, and the mother is bound to pursue. This isn't a story of maternal violence so much as a story of the first part of a girl's journey to adulthood.

In this reversed script from real life, a childless good woman sits by the window, watching a snowstorm and dreaming of a child white as snow, with lips red as roses, rather than blood. A daughter is born; she grows into a beautiful young woman. She looks into her mother's eyes and sees reflected there the perfect daughter of the perfect mother, and so she flees from that sight in order to save her life. Away from the comforts of her home she runs, away from the place where she was the only young beauty of marriageable age, and on through the forest until she reaches a small, congested house—a college dorm room with three roommates and inadequate plumbing, no doubt.

She knows intuitively that she ought to preserve her separation, but there's Mother, sorrowfully knocking on the door, bringing her a new jacket, a box of cakes, a silver heart on a fine silver chain. How can a girl resist this wordless appeal from the loving parent she has abandoned? She opens the door, and as soon as the silver heart on a silver chain is fastened around her neck, she falls into the swoon of childhood again.

THE QUEEN'S THIRD ASSAULT on Snow White drives the poison home.

"Snow White shall die," she cries as she retreats to a secret room in the palace where she practices witchcraft, "even if it costs me my life." Dressed as a farmer's wife for this last assault (a beak-nosed humpbacked witch in the Disney movie), she returns to the dwarfs' cottage bearing a basketful of apples, holding a particularly pretty sample, with one cheek red as sexuality and the other white as barrenness, cradling the black seeds of fertility and death at its core.

Warned by past encounters, the girl refuses to take the apple. "Are you afraid of poison?" the old woman asks cannily. To show how harmless it is, she cuts the apple in half and eats the white portion herself, saving the red for the girl. But only the red cheek was poisoned.

In the Garden of Eden the snake offered Eve an apple, with seeds as black as death inside. After a single mouthful, Eve was overcome by knowledge and left innocence and the Garden behind.

Snow White sees the old woman eat half the apple and cannot resist reaching for the other half. One bite and she falls lifeless to the ground. The Queen laughs aloud. "White as snow, red as blood, black as ebony-wood! This time the dwarfs cannot wake you again," she predicts correctly.

The poison inside the apple is knowledge of a particular sort: knowledge that sex and death can neither be separated nor refused, especially not by women, since women give birth to children who are bound to die. Snow White sees what lies ahead of her: loss of virginity, which is never called loss when it happens to a man. Lust, which will require satisfaction. Pleasure that's dependent on someone else. Ignorance. Pain of childbirth. Inadequacy to play a sovereign role like her royal stepmother. She foresees even the day when her fertility will come to an end, leaving her as empty and envious as the Queen.

As Snow White bites into the apple, she advances from white toward red, but the dose of carnal knowledge is poured into her too quickly. She can't fight it off or digest it by drops, and so she loses consciousness. Black intervenes. The Queen has every right to suppose that death is the end of Snow White's story.

But, of course, it's not the end. Unwilling to bury someone who still has the flush of life in her cheeks, the dwarfs lay Snow White in a coffin made of glass, so that she can be seen from all sides. They then write her name on it in golden letters, and add that she was a king's daughter. The fourth color, gold, which is always the final stage of transformation, has entered the story.

But the piece of the poisoned apple has stuck in her throat. In her lifeless state, she can neither swallow it nor spit it out.

GLASS IS A MAGICAL SUBSTANCE that lets light in but doesn't let heat, which is life, out. Snow White's glass casket is the opposite of the Queen's mirror: Anyone who passes by can admire her in her showcase, and yet she cannot see her own reflection. Like Sleeping Beauty, she can't move or speak, can't change her status or make decisions, doesn't even know that she is being preserved for now in a sleep-death that is beyond time and outward change, so that her emotions will have a chance to catch up with her body.

While Snow White lies in the coffin, dormant as a field covered with snow, three birds perch overhead: a dove, the bird of love, which is white; a raven, the bird of death and the afterworld, which is black; and an owl, the bird of wisdom—at a guess, a horned screech owl in its reddish phase, a ghostly creature. White, black, and red look down on her from their tree branch like feathered gods.

For a long time, says the tale, she lies there, presumably absorbing knowledge drop by drop, since there was nourishment as well as poison in the apple that her stepmother gave her. At this point, she's no longer a daughter; she isn't even a victim anymore. She's an object displayed like a piece of jewelry in a jeweler's window, which is the way the Grimms' hero first encounters her: as "it."

As with Sleeping Beauty, transformation arrives in the semblance of a man, which doesn't mean that he revives Snow White with "love's first kiss." That touch appears only in the Disney movie. In the Grimms' story, a king's son wanders into the heart of the forest and sees the girl, who is still as white as snow and as red as blood, with hair as black as ebony. "Let me have the coffin," he says to the dwarfs. "I will give you whatever you want for it." Of course they refuse to sell Snow White for gold.

Since this fairy-tale Prince is wiser than he sounds at first, he realizes that nothing of value (life, love, parenthood, laughter) can be bought or even earned; it can be had only as a gift. He proves his worthiness when he says, "Then give her to me as a gift, for I cannot live without seeing Snow White." The dwarfs give him the coffin, and he orders his servants to carry it away.

No kiss to wake her? No kiss. Our understanding of the traditional story depends on this point.

In the Disney movie, Snow White is persuaded to take the fatal bite of apple only because the witch swears that "it's a magic wishing apple . . . one bite and all your dreams will come true. . . . There must be something your little heart desires." Indeed, there is. The magic works, but not as the witch intended. Snow White dies to this life the instant she tastes the fruit and knows nothing more until the Prince rouses her with "love's first kiss," which is the only antidote to this poison brewed from spite.

By contrast, the Grimms' tale invests the heroine's body and emotions with the power of transformation that Disney hands over to the hero. Snow White is dead when the Prince's servants carry her away in the glass coffin. Presumably she would stay dead, except that through the luck of fairy tales, the servants (who are always the unconscious agents of the hero's or heroine's wishes) stumble over a tree stump. With that jolt, the poisonous bite of apple flies out of the girl's throat.

"Oh heavens, where am I?" she asks when she opens her eyes, meaning, "Where am I in my life?," which is what all of us want to know when carried beyond ourselves by a transforming experience.

"You are with me!" the Prince says joyfully. "You shall be my wife."

The Prince may or may not be a real person, but he represents a new possibility in life that throws Snow White off balance and dislodges the chunk of the past that she could neither swallow nor spit out. During the following years (rather than all at once, which is the way fairy tales portray transformation), Snow White, like many women with unhappy childhoods and teenage years, recovers from the effects of the poisoned fruit. She isn't an unwanted child, after all. The Prince wants her as his wife. This gives her the strength to reject her stepmother's toxic view of life, in which women hold on to power only in proportion to their beauty, and mothers and daughters are natural enemies.

At this point, the Maiden's story traditionally ends with a flourish of trumpets, but we are allowed to imagine what is going on in her mind. She'll create a happier home than she had in her youth, she's convinced of that—the way every bride is confident that she can perpetuate her happiness, and run her home much better than her mother did—whether her mother was the oppressor or the oppressed in the household, the profoundly unlucky or merely inefficient. If brides didn't believe that they will fare better than their mothers, the generations would come to a halt.

IN FAIRY-TALE STYLE, the Prince leads Snow White to his father's palace, where a wedding of great splendor is held, with Snow White's stepmother as one of the invited guests. At the moment that the evil woman recognizes the bride, she is paralyzed with fear, but iron shoes have already been hung over the fire to heat, and when they are red-hot they are borne to her with tongs.

She must put them on, those red-hot shoes, and she must dance at the feast, where she is being replaced as the fertile Queen of the land, a red-hot woman who whirls around the floor for the last time in the final blaze of her sexuality. While her stepdaughter moves in the bridal procession in stately fashion from white to red and on to gold, which marks her transformation to a regal self, the old Queen burns to a black crisp.

But the heroine, in turn, has to be on guard. The trick for a woman is to progress from being Snow White without turning into the wicked Queen/stepmother, watching her daughter with jealous eyes.

This is one of the chief functions of fairy tales: to warn the Snow White in all of us that sooner or later we will play the other leading role in the story, and had better be careful what questions we put to our mirrors.

CHAPTER 3

Cinderella:
Surviving Adolescence

"Cinderella," *Pretty Woman, Jane Eyre*

Here we have it: the ultimate transformation, dust to diamonds. The descent of glory. The waif, the outsider transmuted into a Princess and transported to the ball, where the Prince falls in love with her. The humble are exalted. The meek inherit the earth.

If "Cinderella" is the best-known fairy tale in the Western world, and the one women most often name as their favorite, that's because all of us, male and female, have known despair—and will again, several times in a lifetime—seeing ourselves as unwanted, looked down on by others, forced to do work that is beneath us, even as we remain hopeful that sooner or later we will rise above our circumstances. The problem that faces us meanwhile is how to wait and work as

Cinderella waits, keeping warm near the ashes and biding her time until she gathers the strength to step into her glory.

There she is, sitting at the hearth after her long day's toil because there's no other place for her to rest, which is why she's called Cinderbreech or Cinderbottom by the ruder of her two stepsisters in the version we know best (by Charles Perrault), modified to Cinderella by the less rude. Her life seems blighted right up to the moment when her stepsisters climb into the carriage in their finery, assuring her that the guests at the palace would laugh to see a Cinderbottom at a royal ball. But unless she leaves the hearth and goes to the ball, there's no hope that her life will change.

WHAT CAN WE DISCOVER that's new about this story? Chiefly that we don't understand it. Which is so often the case with the most familiar things.

Rags-to-riches is the way we sum up the plot. And yet, if we look more closely, strange inconsistencies appear. Another, subtler pattern emerges, which tells us much about the roles that suffering and transformation play in our lives.

Why, for instance, should Cinderella be forced to get up before daybreak to carry water, light fires, cook and wash for the household, while her two odious stepsisters—girls her own age, who are her competitors in the marriage market—primp in the bedrooms that Cinderella must clean? She wasn't meant to be a scullery maid, in fact just the reverse. She's the only child of a rich widower who remarries a woman with two daughters of her own, girls as malicious and sharp-tongued as their mother. The house where Cinderella scrubs her stepsisters' chambers used to be the house she shared with her father. She's his only blood kin, though he seems to have forgotten that fact, as has she.

As soon as the trio of usurpers move in, they strip Cinderella of her pretty clothes and dress her in an old gray bedgown—shapeless, we may be sure, to hide her budding breasts—along with wooden shoes that hide her delicate feet. "Just look at the proud princess, how decked out she is!" they laugh as they shove her into the kitchen, which is now her place, never suspecting that their words will come true in the end.

Then why doesn't the heroine protest, or else run away into the woods like Snow White? Because Cinderella may sense that her suffering has meaning; it's an essential aspect of growth now that she is an adolescent, just as her protected status was necessary for growth in childhood. She harbors a secret: The lower she falls, the higher she'll rise.

At every stage of our lives, suffering seems to accompany our transformations from one level of existence to the next, like the pain of first intercourse, when what used to be called a girl's "maidenhead" is pierced, and she's no longer a girl; like the labor pains that a woman suffers when she gives birth to her first child. (And who knows what the baby feels as it frog-kicks its way down the birth canal from the womb into the world?) The gaps from housewife to career woman; from wife to widow; from widow to lover; from lover to single woman again: all involve pain and ungainliness and a change of consciousness, which, in the case of our best-known metamorphosis, from child to adult, we call adolescence. From one self to the next, the opening given us in space and time never seems large enough for us to pass through without pain.

THE BASIC PATTERN OF THE STORY, then, isn't rags-to-riches, since the girl was never a pathetic waif to begin with. It's riches-to-rags-to-greater-riches, which coincides with our intuitive sense of human development. Up, down, higher up we move: Garden of Eden, Paradise Lost, Paradise Regained. Childish complacency, adolescent anguish, glory of womanhood. Rich man's daughter, kitchen drudge, princess. The aim is to arrive before the end at what we were meant to be from the beginning. Uncertainties can come later, in adult life, after the fairy tale is over.

But in fairy tales, as in real life, transformation takes time spent alone. A wave of the wand won't do it. There are two distinct ways in which young women survive this period. Snow White and Sleeping Beauty fall asleep, or die a psychic death—in any case, they numb their consciousness—when confronted with sexuality and the burdens of adulthood, and don't wake up until they are ready for their new roles.

Cinderella, on the other hand, works and suffers while she waits—"watchful waiting," the Bible calls it—although in our society we never think about waiting except in terms of eliminating it. In a household where she has been relegated to the chimney corner, her suffering is more obvious than that of Sleeping Beauty or Snow White, but it may be more readily healed in adulthood because she is aware of it.

Far from being the victim that feminist critics think she is, whose sole hope for bettering herself lies in finding a rich husband, Cinderella is an adolescent who develops her strength through the rigorous exercise of learning what she can live without:

She can live without the parental protection or the comforts of home she took for granted in childhood, she discovers early in the story. Her mother dies young, as the Good Mother invariably dies young in fairy tales. Her father keeps his distance, having chosen a new wife and daughters while ignoring her. In fairy-tale terms, this means that she separates psychically, painfully, from her family, as the first step toward establishing a new family of her own.

She can live without believing in her good looks. Every day, her stepsisters tell her (or she tells herself) that she is ragged and dirty. She has no reason to believe that her looks will change.

Like Snow White, she earns her keep, which means that she needn't depend on anyone to support her. If this self-reliance isn't materially necessary in later life, it will still provide emotional strength.

She can live without being accepted by her peers, which is the greatest cause of her suffering, although her desolation translates into a sense of unworthiness and the other way around. (Living without love is a more debatable question.) Friendless and scorned, she learns that it's possible to survive without the rare blessing known as happiness, if need be.

What saves her is the awareness that she's alone in the world and always will be, but so is everyone else, including the stepsisters who make the mistake of equating marriage with happiness. Lacking Cinderella's disadvantages, the sisters never deepen; they learn nothing about the inconstancy and frailty of life or the wounds other people endure. When a blow falls, they disintegrate. Life has betrayed them, they complain to their mother, who assures them that they deserve a better fate.

They are formidable creatures, these Ugly Sisters. They know just what they want: a Prince. But Cinderella knows what she can do without, which is a surer source of strength.

TWO TRANSFORMATIONS take place rather than one. The first is invisible because it takes place before the story begins, when Cinderella's mother dies and her father takes a new wife. We think it's the malice of the stepmother and stepsisters that turns the daughter of the house into the girl in the cinders, the Ash Girl, but in reality it's a spell that life casts over all of us when the time comes to leave childhood behind: a spell experienced as self-doubt and apprehension about sex, without the promise of sexual fulfillment to go with it. We simplify this by calling it self-consciousness.

The second transformation—the one we think of as magic called down from the sky by a godmother in a bouffant dress with a fairy wand—isn't really an enchantment at all, as Iona and Peter Opie point out in their book *The Classic Fairy Tales,* but a disenchantment that undoes the earlier spell, releasing Cinderella from the oppressed and even dirty condition that seems so uncharacteristic of her.

Round the story swings in a spiral, bringing her to a higher level of consciousness of her innate self, showing her to be so splendid that even the King and Queen have never seen the like.

———

KEEP YOUR EYE on the clothes in stories and (less so, nowadays) in real life. In a story six pages long, the heroine changes clothes either seven or nine times, depending on the version—each time signaling a change of state, as if she were continually changing one skin for another.

First she's the prettily dressed child of a wealthy father. Next she's a stepchild clothed in rags who eventually goes to a ball gowned in silver and silk, with glass slippers—"the finest in the world"—that fit no feet but hers. After she runs away from the ball, she takes off her finery and puts on rags again to fool her stepsisters, but transformation is never reversible. From that moment on, she's no longer an Ash Girl who sees no way to raise herself from the ashes but the opposite: a Princess in hiding, who pretends to be a household drudge.

In the movie *Pretty Woman,* the degrading clothes aren't rags or a gray bedgown but the other extreme, a streetwalker's traffic-stopping costume. The heroine (played by Julia Roberts) is a penniless prostitute whose roommate has just squandered their rent money on drugs. She works her nightly beat on Hollywood Boulevard dressed in a Carol Channing blonde pageboy wig, a skirt that barely covers her crotch, and thigh-high boots, one of which is pinned shut with a safety pin. Her room key hangs on a string around her neck. When she picks up a handsome young mergers-and-acquisitions Prince in a Lotus Esprit (which he can't handle properly but she can), he takes her to his penthouse suite in the Regent Beverly Wilshire Hotel—disguising her first by throwing his raincoat over her shoulders—where they have sex, after which he showers. When he comes back to the bedroom, he finds her sleeping naked in his bed. Her streetwalker wig has been discarded, and the naturally auburn curls she has been hiding tumble over the pillow; the crusted mascara has been wiped from her eyes. She has shucked off her rags to reveal her intrinsic self.

Cinderella's sexuality is hidden by her smock. Pretty Woman's is hidden by her outfit of sex-for-hire. We use clothes, like words, to reveal our natures or disguise them, as we choose.

The next morning, Pretty Woman goes into an elegant boutique with money the Prince has given her to buy clothes. "I don't think we have anything for you," says an impeccably groomed saleswoman in the role of stepsister, looking at her tawdry clothes. "You're obviously in the wrong place. Please leave."

On the following day she goes on a major shopping spree, this time with arrangements made in advance by the Prince. Outfitted in an understated white silk dress and a black skimmer hat perched on top of her auburn hair, she returns to the store where she was snubbed the day before.

"Do you remember me?"

"No, I'm sorry."

"I was in here yesterday. You wouldn't wait on me. You work on commission, right?" The saleswoman agrees. Pretty Woman raises her hands full of shopping bags. "Big mistake. *Big. Huge.*" She waves. "Bye. I have to go shopping now."

In real life as well as in stories, any radical change in body weight, dress, shoes, hair style or length, even transportation (that pumpkin coach, that Lotus Esprit) is an outer signal that transformation is under way. If a career woman with short hair lets her hair grow long or dyes it another color, keep a sharp lookout for the romantic development that's sure to follow.

In past centuries, we used to read a woman's life through scheduled changes in her appearance, like a series of magazine illustrations. A bride wore white with a veil that covered her face on the last day when she was an untouchable virgin, belonging to no man. (She still does this the first time around, frankly in costume, with no implication of virginity.) A widow wore black. Even now, in parts of Europe, women wear black for a year or two, in some places for the rest of their lives, as a reminder to the villagers that they have shared their bed with death. Young girls used to wear short dresses and long hair.

Grown women wore long dresses, their hair piled on top of their heads, and shirtwaists to work. Pregnant women never wore bathing suits.

But society today is bravely, brazenly different. Ours is the first in which men and women dress alike in jeans, sweatshirts, and sneakers, as do people of all ages: toddlers padded by diapers underneath, mothers, grandmothers, great-grandmothers. If girls of fourteen bear babies and so do women in their forties, while those in their sixties and seventies play tennis and have love affairs, no one is willing to send out signals of either unripeness or decay. The dress codes for gender and age have been obliterated. So have the divisions between clothes for work and play, between rich and poor. Or rather, for the first time fashion flows upward from the lower levels, so that basketball players from the ghetto and suburbanites walking the dog dress in much the same way: T-shirts with printed messages, tracksuits, cargo pants and messenger bags (work clothes elevated to high fashion), backpacks, baseball caps, jeans and corduroys bleached before sale, lightweight blue ultrasuede shirts tailored at unimaginable expense to look exactly like denim. If a stepmother wanted Cinderella to look completely unacceptable to her peers these days, she would put her in high-heeled pumps and a crepe dress trimmed with sequins.

Ours is not a classless society but one that tries to look classless. What we have gained is social fluidity and a sense of vigor, to the point of toughness, in clothes. What we have lost is the diorama of our progress through life, marked out through costumes. Which may, in fact, be what we don't choose to contemplate every day.

IN THE HOUSE, Cinderella hears the voices of her stepsisters, entirely buoyant as they preen in front of their full-length bedroom mirrors (an incredible luxury in the seventeenth century, when the story was first written down). Nature is still their doting mother rather than stepmother, delighting them with their good looks and encouraging them to think that they are as fine as their appearance.

Nothing and no one else matters, which is true enough for nature's sole purpose of reproducing the species.

If they are superficial, that's because it's easy to follow the unconscious way of life encouraged by both nature and society, skimming the surface like dragonflies while going about their business of catching a man. But they pay a price. Without a time in which they go into the depths alone and struggle with their limits, they fail to develop a substantial self that can survive a winter. In emotional terms, they never leave home and mother.

By contrast, once Cinderella leaves behind the dependence of childhood and realizes that she is separate from the family—in fact, regarded as peculiar—she sees the mother figure as an oppressive stepmother, less violent than Snow White's but hurtful in an especially female way. "What, you go, Cinderella!" her stepmother scoffs. "Covered in dust and dirt as you are, and would go to the festival? You have no clothes and shoes, and yet would dance!"

Once again, though she gets no credit for it, the wicked stepmother is the force for growth, pushing the heroine out of the family circle and on toward transformation.

HERE WE HAVE TO PULL ourselves up short if we think of the wicked stepmother solely as a human being, which she is, rather than as a flesh-and-blood incarnation of the Terrible Mother, which is another way of looking at her. History, which lies behind every story, often brings us up short when we think we are safely hidden from unpleasant facts in fairyland.

In past centuries, women married young, bore many children, and could expect to die in their twenties or early thirties, often in childbirth. The dead mother was replaced by another young wife, perhaps with children of her own who had to be fed from the skimpy resources of a peasant family. Who was likely, then, to get more food and a better bed: her own child or her stepchild? If there were daughters from two or three wives, which would be promised the biggest dowry, and therefore become most marriageable? Who would inherit the house? (Stepmothers in stories are generally much harsher to their husband's daughters than to his sons, in part because a daughter requires a dowry, and in part because a daughter is a rival for the affection of the supreme lover and benefactor, the father.)

A stepmother in the house, or the specter of a stepmother when one's own mother was seriously ill, was as dreaded and deadly as a shortage of firewood or coal in winter. Even today in France, the word *marâtre*, which is the dictionary term for *stepmother*, cannot be spoken in polite society, because it carries the connotation of "old bitch." The acceptable term for your father's second wife is *ma belle-mère*, which means "my mother-in-law."

But what about father's role in this story? As a child, Cinderella was Daddy's girl, but now we hear that he would only scold her if she complained about her troubles, since "his wife governed him entirely," like the Queen and her huntsman in "Snow White." By the end of the Grimms' story, when the Prince comes to Cinderella's house, searching for the maiden whose foot fits the glass slipper, he asks her father if there is no other maiden in the house who might try it on. "No, said the man, there is still a little stunted kitchen-wench which my late wife left behind her, but she cannot possibly be the bride."

Beginning with adolescence, an erotic current runs between father and daughter that wasn't there before, causing the father to move either too far from the girl or dangerously close. Like Cinderella's father, he may turn away completely, refusing to hear her problems, which he now considers to be her mother's business. He may not want to touch her, much less hug and kiss her, as if she's charged with electricity like a third rail. He may become overly suspicious about her dating behavior and clothes, rigid about the streets she travels and the hour she comes home at night, all of this to make sure that neither he nor any other male gets access to her virginity.

Or he may move in the other direction, growing too affectionate, becoming what the Victorians referred to as an "unnatural father." In a large group of stories that are considered a subset of "Cinderella," the plot is a mirror image of the "Cinderella" we know: It's the father, not the stepmother, who drives his daughter away from home, but because of lust rather than spite.

In the story "Thousand-Furs," a Queen on her deathbed makes her husband swear not to marry anyone "who is not quite as beautiful as I am, and who has not just such golden hair as I have; this you must promise me." The King promises; the Queen closes her eyes and dies. Years later, when the widower contemplates remarriage, he cannot find anyone who equals the late Queen, until he looks at his grown daughter one day and discovers her mother's beauty and golden hair, only more lustrous than before. "I will marry my daughter," he declares to his councillors, "for she is the counterpart of my late wife."

Hearing her father's plans, Thousand-Furs blackens her face with soot, like Cinderella, and disguises herself in a cloak made from scraps of fur taken from every animal in the kingdom: rat skin, rabbit skin, weasel skin, a patch from each. In this disguise, nature in its humblest form, the girl runs away from the palace and finds employment in the kitchen of a neighboring King, where the other servants call her "the hairy animal."

In a patriarchal story like this one, the wife, even if she's dead, must bear the guilt for her husband's incestuous demand. How could a father be so beastly as to want to sleep with his own daughter if his wife hadn't forced him to that extreme by her jealous cunning that extended beyond the grave? Stories like this, which used to be common in pre-Freudian times, have nearly vanished from our bookshelves. We can tolerate fantasies about child abandonment, infanticide, even cannibalism, but not incest. That may be too close to home.

"My father was a king. The king can have sex with anyone," wrote the poet Anne Sexton in her private notes.

"THE HAIRY ANIMAL" IS, of course, a description of any adolescent, male or female. The formerly smooth-skinned nymph, lean as any boy, notices a chiffon wrap of hair growing over her genitals. It forms a furry triangle, pointing to the spot between her legs that shows a predator, "Here it is, here's what you're aiming at," while the rest of her functions as a frame to carry it around. A target it remains until she's past menopause, when the hair grows gray and sparse, revealing the genitals again when no one is interested in them any longer.

Adolescence is Nature in her stepmother phase, taking away a daughter's childish prettiness and giving her acne and menstrual cramps instead. At the beginning of the Perrault fairy tale, the heroine is called Cinderbreech, meaning "Cinderbottom," Dirty Pants: the area of her humiliation. In real life, on her long-awaited day, she's at a party, wearing white linen slacks. The slacks are stained with blood. The blood puts her in the same category as Mother.

Inhibited as well as awed by her new status, she becomes addicted to bath gels and papaya soaps, but no matter how diligently she scrubs, she worries that she smells bad. Meanwhile, her breasts may develop too soon and bob in gym class. Or else she's flat-chested and looks like a child while the other girls are clearly, gloriously women, their sweaters swelling and subsiding with each breath.

"Will you look at this pimple?" she exclaims. "How can I go out?" ("Will anyone ever look at me, look beyond the pimple?" she means, and at the same time she means, "God, I hope no one sees me like this. I hope that I can stay hidden until the time comes when I'm transformed.")

But behind the pimples there are rare times when she sees something else: the face, the future, that are going to be hers.

MORE THAN ANYTHING ELSE, an adolescent wants to belong, wants to be admired: not just by her family, which is a biological cell from which she must divide, but by her age group, and by girls as much as boys, establishing a female task force with which to explore the territory of adulthood. (This may be why Cinderella is obsessed with her stepsisters and their low opinion of her, even more than with her stepmother.)

But what woman feels that as a teenager she was part of the "in" group at school, which so often takes the place of stepsisters in our lives? There's an inconsistency here: If so many women insist that at best they were members of an "out" group of friends, there must have been an "in" group that excluded them, and yet later in life we rarely find anyone who belonged to that glamorous clique. Is it possible that we exaggerated our lowly status? Failed to see how many others shared it?

Suppose that a woman was beautiful, let's say as beautiful as Cinderella, who was "a hundred times handsomer" than her stepsisters even though she was dressed in rags. Suppose that this famous beauty was in front of you at this moment, nearly eighty now, being interviewed on television by David Frost:

"You said once, 'I never thought that I was beautiful,'" Frost confronts his guest. In an incredulous tone, he adds, "You must have known you were."

"No," insists the guest, born Betty Perske but known to us as Lauren Bacall. "I don't believe I ever was, am, will be. Never. No, no . . . I never liked my face very much."

When Bacall was seventeen, she became a model for a fashion house on Seventh Avenue in New York—"a lousy model," she claims. "I was very skinny. All the other models were beautiful and round, just what you would have liked. Really dishy." While talking to her co-workers one day, she revealed that she was Jewish. They drew away from her. "But, of course, it may have been that I was so young. I didn't belong in that crowd."

Too lower middle class, too young, too sexless, wrong religion, wrong age. Too smart, too bookish, too new on the scene, too tall, too stiff, too hardworking. Above all, too desperate to be accepted. With a genius for exclusion, the "in" crowd annihilates the solitary victim through contempt—at least until the bloody day when the stepsisters turn their claws against one another, like Goneril and Regan in *King Lear,* or the Reed sisters in *Jane Eyre.*

Then what does the Cinderella figure want from them? Intimacy. Sisterhood. Confidences from another female who's going through the pangs of growing up. Later there will be time enough for romance, marriage, home.

She wants everyone to love her. No. The truth, hidden from herself, is that she wants someone to love her more than anyone else in the world, and she understands that the only person bound to do this will be her child. And so her body drives her along the road toward motherhood. The Prince, whom she will have to conquer (in her own way) and bind to herself (for her own purpose) isn't what he thinks he is. He thinks he's royalty, but in truth he's a means to her end. When they dance at the ball, he discovers her charms but has no idea who she is, while she knows all she needs to know about him: She knows that he is—or isn't—a suitable father for her children.

BUT WHO ARE these siblings who caused such turmoil during our youth and still frighten us, for the simple reason that they're everything we're not? They are our superiors in the worldly arts— specifically, the worldly female arts, which we can't afford to ignore.

The Ugly Sisters, we call them, and yet they aren't necessarily ugly at all, except in disposition—in fact, they're often strikingly good-looking. "Beautiful and fair of face but vile and black of heart" is the way the Grimms describe Cinderella's stepsisters, whose beauty, along with their clothes and their mother's partiality to their cause, is what makes them such formidable competitors. In the past two centuries, female authors have become bolder at creating heroines with unremarkable looks, like Jane Eyre, who begins her story by saying that she is humbled by her sense of physical inferiority to her good-looking cousins, or tall and gawky Jo March in *Little Women,* or Miss Celie in *The Color Purple.* So who played Jane Eyre in the 1944 movie? Joan Fontaine. And Jo March was played by Katharine Hepburn in the 1933 movie, Winona Ryder in 1994. In plays and movies, we understand the visual code that says the good must be beautiful while the wicked are ugly.

Power women, that's what the sisters are, their mother's darlings, ruling the roost while the Cinderella figure is left out in the cold. When we first meet Jane Eyre, she's a ten-year-old orphan being raised in the home of her stonyhearted Aunt Reed. In this story, Cinderella's stepsisters are transformed into Jane Eyre's cousins, two girls and a boy who cluster around their doting mama near the drawing-room fire, while Jane is excluded. Her fourteen-year-old cousin John, stout and bilious from gorging himself at dinner, "bullied and punished me; not two or three times in the week, not once or twice in the day, but continually . . . every morsel of flesh on my bones shrank when he came near." When John throws a book at her and hurts her so badly that she finally retaliates, Jane is the one who is punished.

As her aunt's lady's maid reminds her: "you ought not to think yourself on an equality with the Misses Reed and Master Reed, because missis kindly allows you to be brought up with them. They will have a great deal of money, and you will have none: it is your place to be humble." Some months later, Jane is sent packing, into the fairy-tale woods alone—in this case, Lowood School—where the students' curls are cut off and they are dressed in disfiguring brown uniforms, Cinderella fashion.

This is the essential polarity of the Cinderella story: Cinderella and her stepsisters. Or Sara Crewe (*A Little Princess*) and her schoolmates. Or Harry Potter, another ten-year-old orphan and his cousin, Dudley, who happily uses Harry as a punching bag whenever a crony is available to pin his arms behind his back. The favored child vs. the outcast; the lazy and overfed child vs. the overworked orphan; the worldly part of our personalities that faces outward and cares only for society's good opinion vs. the solitary inner self.

In short, the Ugly Sisters—who are siblings the heroine's own age, living under the same roof, closely related to her by blood or circumstance but inferior in pedigree—are Cinderella's counterparts as well as oppressors. If she feels humble in front of them, that's because they look the way she longs to look, they have mastered the female arts that she has yet to grasp.

"Cinderella, would you not be glad to go to the ball?" her stepsisters ask while she dresses their hair for the occasion. And the answer is yes, of course she wants to go; they have aroused in her an erotic desire to have fine clothes and to go to the ball and attract partners for the waltz, just as they do. She wants to know what it means to be a woman, a desirable woman, rather than a little girl.

In short, it's the stepsisters' function to make the heroine grow up. They rouse her from her self-pitying daydreams and force her to acknowledge that sexuality has its techniques. Watching them, she sees that women use their appearance to declare themselves, not only in terms of fertility but also in terms of social class, education, taste, all the things we pretend to despise but which tell the world who we are, how much influence we can bring to bear, and what we have in mind for this evening. At the end of the story, the Prince may have to acknowledge Cinderella in her rags before he can claim her as his bride, but he wouldn't have pursued her in the first place if he hadn't seen her in her splendor.

Surfaces count, the Ugly Sisters teach Cinderella in a painful but necessary lesson. The sisters are entirely surface, no souls, which makes them uninteresting human beings. Cinderella has soul but no surface at this point in the story, and this layer of disdain for the reality of the world and the way it works is unworthy of her. The responsibility of the haughty siblings and their mother is to prod her away from the hearth and set her in motion, not in imitation of them or in competition with them, but in defiance.

"Ah!" said Cinderella, "you only banter me; it is not for such as I am to go thither." "You are in the right of it," said they, "it would make the people laugh to see a Cinderbreech at a ball."

But deep inside their ambition and self-satisfaction the stepsisters hide a structural flaw. Despising men, they still take it for granted that they must have a man, along with a child, a house, whatever makes them seem enviable in the eyes of others. To get that, they will do almost anything, including hacking off part of their feet in order to fit into the glass slipper, a ploy that isn't even their own idea but their mother's.

Cinderella, on the other hand, so often scorned by feminists as a passive creature who waits for a Prince to rescue her, can be recognized as the independent member of the household, the one who can support herself as a scullery maid if need be, and therefore feels free to accept or reject a man as she chooses. (This is true of all great Cinderella figures: Jane Eyre, Hester Prynne, Miss Celie, Lucy Snowe, Sara Crewe, and Eliza Doolittle, among others. They have all worked for a living.)

When a woman meets her Prince, the most powerful avowal she can make to herself, at the moment when she finds her future so light in her hands that she can toss it into the air like a golden ball, is "This one I will marry, or I will marry no one. I can manage either way."

Because the stepsisters are in such urgent need of a man, there's one thing they won't do, or can't do: fall in love, which involves allowing an intruder—a male member who isn't even a member of the family—to enter them emotionally as well as physically. Refusing to give up their turf, they sever the connection between their beautifully upholstered bodies and their feelings.

"What do you want?" Pretty Woman asks her new client as he sprawls on the couch in his penthouse suite, while she kneels at the ready on the carpet in front of him. "What do you do?" he counters. This Cinderella has been coached by her best friend, who is a more experienced streetwalker, on the best way to protect herself. "Everything," she says. "But I don't kiss on the mouth." "Neither do I," her client replies. At the climax of the story, however, she confesses to her friend that she has sinned. She has kissed her Prince on the mouth. She has rejected the professional sisterhood in favor of the transformation of romantic love, like a brand-new swimmer giving up her footing and braving the risks of deep water for the first time.

We mustn't be so naïve, however, as to think that the Ugly Sisters—those unnervingly self-possessed women—reflect sibling rivalry at home, or exclusion from a clique at school, and nothing more. The sisters are more pervasive than that. They exist as real people who know how to tweak our strings, but on a more amorphous level they exist as aspects of ourselves, voices that resonate inside our heads, as Charlotte Brontë, of all people, discovered in her sleep.

No author distrusted fashion more than this plain-faced, plain-living daughter of a country parson. And none ever loved her sisters more fervently than Charlotte did, especially the two older ones, Maria and Elizabeth, both of whom died of tuberculosis at the terrible boarding school described in *Jane Eyre*, when they were ten and eleven. The two children were kind and gentle to begin with; their deaths turned them into angels.

This didn't keep the beloved pair from returning to their old home in a dream one night, in the guise of the Ugly Sisters.

Charlotte Brontë recounted the dream years later: She was called down to the drawing room, she said, and there they were, Maria and Elizabeth—but they were changed, so sadly changed that she could hardly speak about it. They had forgotten their old selves. Fashionably dressed, they strolled around the room, criticizing the furnishings, finding fault with details they had probably never noticed when they were alive.

So there we have it. The phantoms represent some vague worldwide sisterhood that seems to make insistent demands on us while scrutinizing our performance. Inside our heads we hear their voices, telling us where we fall short, but only in matters that concern us as women, and only the external aspects. (They never complain that we aren't as kind or charitable as other women, or that we don't know as much as we should about art.) Our children scream louder than any others in the playground, their scornful glances seem to say. Our meals are thrown together, our housekeeping slapdash. Above all, our clothes are never right for the occasion. We look in the closet, hoping to find an outfit that will represent our true selves, but the clothes are too dowdy or too showy or they fit badly or they are at the cleaners, and nothing expresses the person we are at this moment; nothing gives a stranger any sense of the juices frothing inside us. We leave the meaningful part of ourselves at home when we go out, for lack of a fairy godmother to put us together.

In this way, the sisters implant a paralyzing sense of our limitations and frighten us away from any undertaking that will separate us from the usual role of women. ("What? After all these years spent changing diapers and doing laundry, you think *you* should apply to graduate school and compete with those girls straight out of college, you cinder-wench you?")

But we must give the stepsisters their due. Cinderella would never have been transformed if she hadn't burst into tears when the two fashion plates swished out of the door and left her alone. Creating divine discontent is an accomplishment all its own. (Psyche's sisters will do the same thing in a later chapter.)

THE ASHY HEROINE'S NAME is Cendrillon in French, which gives us Cinderella, but *cendres* properly refers to ashes, not to cinders. In the German version, it's Aschenputtel. According to the Grimm Brothers' dictionary, *putteln* means "squatting in ashes," the way chickens or doves, when given a chance, squat down in dust and spray it over their feathers. (Doves will play a prominent part in the German story.) In other regions she's Ashpit, Ashy Pet, Askenbasken, or, at best, Hearth Cat. Never is the story called "The Glass Slipper," although Charles Perrault bravely offered this as an alternative title—no, the title has to be the humble condition that fools everyone, as it's meant to, until the time comes for it to be cast aside.

Ashes are found in the hearth, which is the most functional, least ornamental part of the house, the source of both warmth and food, like Mother. Then why do we call her Cinderella, when cinders are dirty like soot, the result of incomplete combustion, while ashes are matter that has been reduced by complete combustion as near to spirit as possible? Ashes float as clean and light as feathers, or else they are bits of bone—what remains after a body has been cremated, as clean and heavy as beads.

Ashes to ashes and dust to dust, we say. Ash Wednesday follows Mardi Gras, which means Fat Tuesday, the last day of rich living before the devout have their faces streaked with ashes (like Cinderella) to signal the beginning of Lent, while the end of Lent will be Easter, which produces an outburst of new clothes. Mardi Gras, Lent, Easter. Up, down, higher up we go. We live amid ashes, which are curls of nothing, before we rise to worldly everything.

Mysteriously, the Ash Girl in the story seems to know that her isolation is holy in some undefined way, and that she will come out of it more beautiful and potent than she was in the beginning, which is the point of adolescence.

"In the depths of winter I finally learned there was in me an invincible summer," said Albert Camus.

CHAPTER 4

Cinderella:
Stepping into the Dance

"Cinderella," *Pygmalion, My Fair Lady*

> "Well, said her godmother, be but a good girl, and I'll contrive
> thou shalt go. Then she . . . said to her, go into the garden, and
> bring me a pumpkin."

Transformation is the text in every version of "Cinderella"—kitchen
maid to princess bride—but two, or even three, patterns of transformation exist. The variable in the plot is the source of magic, which
changes along with our conception of the world.

The first pattern can be found in at least seven hundred versions
from many parts of the globe, dating back a thousand years. Only
one example exists of the second pattern, which has recently marked

its three hundredth birthday, but that's the only version most of us know: a spiritual adventure story that revolves around a fairy god-mother, seeming as unchangeable as the shining glass slipper, and as perfect a fit.

The question is, where does magic come from? At the climactic moment, does Cinderella let loose the energy of her own transformation, which she has been nurturing for years, or is she transformed by an outside agent? Does she work her way up from the soil, or does glory descend from the sky, dressed in a bouffant gown?

Or is it possible, during the past century, that magic has come down to earth, and she bumps into transformation by accident in front of London's opera house at Covent Garden, late on a rainy night, in the form of a human being who may be a bit more than human?

THE "CINDERELLA" STORY familiar to us was written by Charles Perrault, a government official during the reign of Louis XIV at Versailles, who published a collection of eight short tales in 1699 under the title *Stories or Tales of Olden Times, with Their Morals,* more popularly known by its subtitle, *Tales of My Mother Goose.* This small book also gave us "Sleeping Beauty," "Little Red Riding Hood," "Puss in Boots," "Diamonds and Toads," and "Bluebeard," establishing fairyland as an exotic colony that sent its natural wealth of stories back to the civilized mind. But what listeners remember most vividly is a fairy godmother with a wand that turns mice into mouse-colored horses and a pumpkin into a golden coach that carries a girl wearing glass slippers to a royal ball: all of these images supplied by Perrault.

If this government official, during his retirement years, had never written down a single tale that his mother, the goose, told him, we would picture Cinderella today as an earthy folk heroine cruelly abused by her stepmother, who sets about growing her own salvation in the form of a cow, a little red "calfy," a doll, a fish, a tree, a ewe—some creature that represents her loving but lost mother and is frequently a gift from her. ("Well, my grandmother she told me that in them auld days a ewe might be your mother. It is a very lucky thing to have a black ewe," an old Irish tale says.) The heroine nurtures this creature over a long period of years, and in due time it returns the favor by showering her with the finery she needs to go to the ball. In short, she transforms herself into the magical creature's mother as well as its child, playing both ends of the maternal scale.

A THOUSAND YEARS AGO IN CHINA, a cave dweller told the story of a mistreated stepchild named Sheh Hsien, the daughter of a mountain cave chief, who caught a fish about two inches long with red fins and golden eyes. Every day the girl fed the fish scraps of food, caring for it like a little mother. When it grew big enough, she carried it to the pond behind her house, where it pillowed its head on the bank while it ate, until one day, when it was five feet long, her stepmother tricked it into coming to her while Sheh Hsien was away from home, killed it with a sword, and ate it. Never had any fish tasted half so good.

When the girl discovered her loss and wailed in grief, a shaggy man descended from the sky and told her not to weep. She need only collect the bones that her stepmother had buried under the dung hill, he said, and hide them in her room, where they would fulfill her wishes if she prayed to them.

Some time later, when her stepmother and stepsister set off for a cave festival, leaving Sheh Hsien behind, the bones supplied her with a gauzy blue cloak made of kingfisher feathers, along with golden shoes as light as down that would make no noise even if the wearer trod on stone. Providently, while hurrying home from the festival, she lost one of those shoes, which was brought to the King of a neighboring island. He searched for the owner among all the women of his kingdom, but discovered that the shoe was an inch too short to fit the smallest foot—this in a country where a foot as small as a lotus is prized above all other attributes in a woman. At last the royal servants, on a house search, found a matching shoe in the home of Sheh Hsien, who put on her airy blue cloak and the golden shoes when the King came to her house to meet her.

In these old stories, transformation is basically a kind of body magic that a mother spirit transmits to a child, who develops her own ability to nurture so that she will become a woman and mother in her turn. The heroine's story has nothing to do with salvation through a fairy godmother or a man, although a man—or, rather, the power to attract one—is the essential ending.

Body magic vs. soul magic. Or earth magic vs. sky magic. This gulf between the more archaic stories (including the Grimms') and the Perrault version of "Cinderella" reveals the spiritual change that has occurred in Western civilization and in our sense of ourselves.

"WHAT SHOULD I BRING YOU as presents from the fair?" a father asks his three daughters at the beginning of the Grimm brothers' version of the story, known in German as "Aschenputtel." Beautiful dresses, his two stepdaughters answer predictably enough. Jewels and pearls. His own daughter, Cinderella, on the other hand, asks for a gift that will cost him no money but will eventually unseat him from his position of power. "Father," she says, "break off for me the first branch which knocks against your hat on your way home."

Sure enough, as the father rides through the woods, a hazel twig brushes against him and knocks his hat clear off his head. Now, in folklore, hazel is a magical tree: Hazel twigs were woven into wishing caps to grant the owners' wishes, and forked branches of hazel were favored for divining rods, so it's no coincidence that this particular twig divines the fact that the Ash Girl's father is riding over its roots and leans down to knock off his hat, which serves as his crown.

When the father delivers the twig to his daughter, she plants it on her mother's grave and then lies on the ground and weeps so heartily that her tears water it, and it grows into a tree. "Thrice a day Cinderella went and sat beneath it, and wept and prayed, and a little white bird always came on the tree, and if Cinderella expressed a wish, the bird threw down to her what she had wished for." With its roots wrapped around the mother's body and a spirit bird on the top bough, the tree takes care of the girl, who is its daughter and mother at the same time.

This point is not to be overlooked: The German Cinderella, like her Chinese predecessor, already has the power to get whatever she wants without her stepmother's permission, but in fairy tales as in life, nothing comes to us until we are strong enough to ask for it. To know what we want, we have to know what's wanting in our lives, but we also have to know that we are entitled to get it. Transformation rests in our hands.

One day, a new note sounds through the land, an eruption from the world of male power. The King proclaims a ball that will last three days, to which all the young women of suitable station in the country are invited, so that his son can choose a bride. While the stepsisters go off to their rooms in transports of delight to dress for the occasion, Cinderella, whose sexuality has apparently been awakened by this breach in her hitherto female life, pleads for permission to join them, but her stepmother is adamant that no dirty kitchen wench, no Cinderbreech, will go to the ball and disgrace them.

From this moment on, the French and German heroines take widely divergent paths to transformation.

Cendrillon, the French heroine of Perrault's tale, who is so kind-hearted that she has dressed her stepsisters' hair in the best of taste in spite of their taunts, does nothing but dissolve into tears at her stepmother's refusal.

The German Cinderella, on the other hand, Aschenputtel the Ash Girl, is a sturdy farm girl who must face an ordeal to test her womanhood. When she, too, begs to go to the ball, her stepmother empties a dish of lentils into the ashes and contemptuously promises that if she can pick them all out within two hours her wish will be granted. At once the Ash Girl goes into the garden through the back door, which is her humble opening into the natural world, and calls on "you tame pigeons, you turtledoves and all you birds beneath the sky" to help her. Presumably, the birds are relatives of the white bird that roosts on top of her tree.

In fairy tales and myths as in paintings, birds are spirit messengers, apprentice angels, that fly from earth to sky and back at will. The dove, as in the story of "Snow White," is the bird of Venus, the goddess of love. At the same time, doves, which include pigeons, are common birds to find near home, so the Ash Girl is calling on her backyard nature magic to help her pick, pick, pick the seeds out of the ashes—"The good into the pot, The bad into the crop"—within the given time. The birds succeed, of course, but the stepmother reneges. Now the Ash Girl is challenged to pick two dishes of lentils out of the ashes in a single hour.

"That she most certainly cannot do again," the stepmother says to herself, but with the help of the birds the girl succeeds, and again the stepmother reneges. "All this will not help; you cannot go with us, for you have no clothes and cannot dance; we should be ashamed of you!"

At this, the stepmother and her two daughters flounce out of the door, leaving the Ash Girl behind.

SEEDS, WHICH ARE INERT MATTER that has not yet come to life, have to be plucked from ashes, which are the exact opposite: matter that used to be alive but is now dead. But why should this nonsensical task be so meaningful that it shows up here, there, and elsewhere in folklore, always as a test designed to see whether a girl is ready for marriage and motherhood? Psyche, for instance, a mortal beloved by the beautiful god Cupid, had worse troubles with her prospective mother-in-law, who was the goddess Venus herself, than Cinderella ever had with her stepmother. Outraged at the "vile serving-wench" who had the nerve to be pregnant with Cupid's child, the goddess had the girl mercilessly whipped before confronting her with the first of four ordeals: She must sort a great pile of wheat, barley, millet, lentils, chickpeas, and beans into heaps before the goddess returned that evening from a wedding feast. Psyche's allies were a host of ants, those "nimble nurslings of earth," rather than birds, that rushed up to do the task for her, rescuing her for the moment.

The heroine sifts. She sorts. Or, rather, her body, with its mindless intelligence, sifts and sorts in a way that would be closed off to her if she tried to do it consciously, and one that is altogether foreign to a man. In folktales, small animals always represent our instinctive functions, which achieve what look to us like impossible feats because they operate below the level of consciousness. Magic, we say, when Psyche or Cinderella sorts the seeds, but what is magic except the operation of laws on a level that our minds know nothing about?

In this case, the heroine's female instincts mimic the story of creation itself, which seems to require a process of separation at least as much as the miracle of making.

God "divided the light from the darkness," says the Old Testament, after which he established a firmament in the midst of the waters and divided the waters under the firmament from the waters above the firmament, and then gathered the lower waters in one place, so that there was land and there was sea on the third day of division.

In the opening lines of Ovid's *Metamorphoses,* the author tells us that in the beginning nature was nothing but chaos. Land and air and ocean existed, but "Heat fought with cold, wet fought with dry, the hard / Fought with the soft," until some power—God or nature, we can take our pick—settled all quarrels and brought order out of chaos by a process of division and sorting. "So things evolved, and out of blind confusion / Found each its place, bound in eternal order."

On a different scale, this is what a full-grown woman does every day without thinking about it: She divides, discriminates, brings order out of chaos, which must be seen as the initial, essential step in transformation. Within the family, she separates live possibilities and germinal hopes from dead habits, as she separates the useful leftovers for tomorrow's lunch from today's leavings, or desirable behavior for her children from undesirable. She organizes minutes into life: A man's work comes at him piece by piece, and it often seems (as Lyndon Johnson said of Gerald Ford) that he is incapable of walking and chewing gum at the same time, but a woman is faced with a host of details that demand her attention at once. While she's cooking dinner, she hears the baby cry in another room. The pot boils over, the doorbell rings, the toddler pulls out the knife drawer and examines its contents, and she must rank these claims instantly in order of urgency.

At an even more mindless level, which is where miracles take place, her body plays host to the ordering of a new cosmos. (This is what's happening to poor pregnant Psyche even while she sorts the seeds.) A fertilized egg in her womb divides and subdivides into meaningless undifferentiated cells, which then group themselves according to their destinies, still hidden from us, to become the eyeballs, brain, fingernails, or arteries of a new human being.

Later, in the portion of everyone's story that we refuse to think about, the seeds play their role in reverse. For rural funerals in Greece today, women still prepare *kolliva*, which is a mixture of wheat, nuts, sesame, and other seeds, including the blood-red seeds of the pomegranate, the symbol of fertility and rebirth that Persephone ate in the Underworld. Wherever pre-Christian traditions retain their force, it's the women, rather than the male priests, who pour a libation of wine over the corpse while chanting the ancient words "The earth, your mother, who fed you will eat you now." And as they say this they eat some of the seeds of life that have reverted to the original chaos, while they throw a portion into the earth over the grave—the "pregnant earth," Ovid calls it—to await sorting into a new and unique order.

So, WITH THE HELP OF turtledoves and pigeons, the German Ash Girl passes the test of womanhood that her stepmother set for her but is barred from the ball anyway, just like her French counterpart, Cendrillon, who never faces a test. Two quite different scenes follow. The Grimms' heroine goes directly to her mother's grave and calls out to the hazel tree, which has been standing there all along, ready

to give her whatever she wanted, only she has never asked for anything significant until now:

> *"Shiver and quiver, little tree,*
> *Silver and gold throw down over me."*

At that, the bird who embodies her mother's spirit obligingly throws
down a gold-and-silver dress with slippers embroidered with silver
thread (on the third night of the ball, the slippers will be golden),
and the Ash Girl sets off on foot for the palace.

The French Cinderella, on the other hand, watches her fortunate
stepsisters until they disappear from sight down the road, and then
weeps at the hearth until her godmother, who conveniently happens
to be a fairy, materializes from thin air to interrupt her tears. We
know what happens next: The godmother scoops out a pumpkin
and with a stroke of her wand transforms it into a coach covered
with gold, then turns six mice from the mousetrap into dapple-gray
horses and selects a large rat to be employed as a coachman.

Transformation comes out of the blue here. For Perrault, who
wrote for the court circle of Versailles rather than for peasants in
their cottages, transformation is a conjuring trick performed by a
heavenly spirit, a visitation of grace for a favored child rather than a
crop produced by a cache of bones and entrails. It's no longer earth
magic, in short—we like to think that we transform nature these
days, rather than the other way around—it's sky magic, as capricious
as weather.

With a few strokes of her wand, the godmother produces a work
of baroque stagecraft, as dazzling as a masked ball on a summer
night with its confusion of identities. In fact, the wand that equips
Cinderella for her meeting with the Prince is not unlike the scepter
of Louis XIV, which deployed an army of thirty-six thousand men to
divert rivers and drain the surrounding marshes in order to feed the
fountains of Versailles. Charles Perrault himself was controller general of the department of public works, which meant that he played

a considerable part in the construction of the palaces of Versailles and the Louvre. If scruffy undergrowth could turn into groves of orange trees, why couldn't mice turn into horses?

Everything in this story is congruent. Lizards, with their striped backs and noses in the air, are changed into footmen in striped livery, who cling to the coach as adeptly as lizards cling to a wall. The lizards' fondness for lounging in the sun is matched only by the notorious laziness of footmen. ("Lounge lizards" was my mother's term of contempt for lazy people.) If the stoutest rat becomes the coachman, that's because his bushy whiskers and big rump fit him for the part.

Like modern physics, the godmother's magic proves that anything can be transformed into something else, given the application of a high enough power. Forms are temporary and accidental. Coach, horses, ball gown, slippers: all will revert to their lower forms if the newly revealed Princess disobeys her godmother's orders and stays at the ball one minute past midnight, since fairy-tale gifts are always conditional upon good behavior.

FOR EVERY CINDERELLA, the turning point is the moment when she is transformed into an assertively sexual woman. For the first time, she recognizes her glory, just as the Prince will recognize her as the owner of the slipper, and even the stepsisters will recognize that she's the worthiest of them all. In short, this isn't a story of a girl being rescued by a man whom she hasn't even met yet, or a story of virtue rewarded and wickedness punished, but a story of recognition.

At the moment of transformation Cinderella falls in love with herself, which is the necessary prelude before she can be loved by anyone else. Her fairy godmother has filled her with pride, which shines through her body and looks from the outside like a gold-and-silver gown.

But pride is a concept that women tend to distrust, since we confuse it with the stepsisters' vanity when they look at themselves in the mirror, primped for the ball. When pride is real, it has nothing to do with ball gowns or the prettiness of regular features; it's rooted in the body, in a young woman's sense of the pleasure that she's going to give and get in bed, along with her confidence that at this moment she's doing exactly what she ought to be doing.

Tonight, on Cinderella's way to the ball, the joy of life is coursing through her, and this is what the Prince will respond to—not the obviously pretty face but the energy that streams through a woman who knows that she has been touched by magic. The truth is that most men are unsure of their own taste, and so they wait for a young woman (who may not be the most beautiful one at the ball) to give out signals that she's not only desirable and desirous but capable of handling life for both of them. She gives off an odor of invitation like a ripe peach.

And how long does this sense of her attraction last? A season. A few years. Maybe longer. Maybe only until midnight. But, whatever her age when she looks in the mirror and acknowledges her vitality for the first time, that's the way she will always think of herself.

So Cinderella sets off for the ball, where the Prince dances every dance with her, while her stepmother and stepsisters mistake her for a foreign princess, so dazzling is she in her enchanting gown.

Perrault's French Cinderella must be home by midnight, as we know, or else her fine trappings will disappear. In the Grimms' story, the German Ash Girl is a self-disciplined lass who has no curfew but uses her good sense to leave at an appropriate hour before her stepsisters, only to hear the Prince pursuing her down the road in an attempt to find out where she lives. Running as fast as she can, she reaches her garden and jumps into the pigeon house to hide, taking cover among the birds who have been, in effect, her mother. When the Prince arrives, he tells her father that an unknown maiden is hiding among the pigeons, at which "the old man thought, 'Can it be Cinderella?'"

Resolutely enough, the old man chops down the pigeon house, since it's a father's final duty to turn his daughter over to a younger man, even if he cannot believe that any man, much less a Prince, would want his insignificant child. By this time, the Ash Girl is proving his point by sitting in the ashes again, dressed in her old gray bedgown, having left her finery on her mother's grave for the birds to retrieve.

On the second night of the ball, the same thing happens, except that this time the heroine escapes by shinnying up a pear tree to make her escape—pear, since that fruit is a woman in form: a gently sloping curve on top of a big-hipped, round-rumped bottom that's soft to the touch and all too easily bruised. When Cinderella's father chops down the tree on the Prince's order, no one is found in the branches.

Running as fast as she can, Cinderella flees from the Prince her stepsisters are so desperate to catch, which is how we can tell the difference in femininity between them. Biology, rather than coyness, is at work here: The heroine, the uniquely desirable female, mustn't give herself in marriage except to a male so lusty that he will keep struggling in order to win her, which means that he will be able and willing to support her and her children in later life. He must prove his manhood by his pursuit, as she proved her womanhood in the test of seeds.

At the same time, this is a test of Cinderella's strength. She has outgrown her job as a scullery maid and acknowledged the princess in herself, but in spite of the Prince's flattery she cannot feel sure of him before he sees her and accepts her in the old gray bedgown, her dreariest self, which is one of the selves that a husband must live with on a daily basis. Otherwise, despite her legal title, they will always remain Prince and Ash Girl. Rescuer and victim. Tycoon and trophy wife. Worst of all: power and conniving.

So much for our deluded vision of the humble and grateful bride.

AFTER CINDERELLA RUNS AWAY from the ball each night, she hurriedly changes back into rags before her stepsisters return home, but she is no longer the uncomplaining drudge whom they left weeping by the hearth. She has danced all night with the Prince. The French Cinderella, in particular, has turned into as clever a little puss as ever wore a beauty patch on one cheek, quite as deft at skewering her stepsisters as they have been crude at taunting her.

When she answers their knock on the door, she yawns and rubs her eyes as if still half asleep. The sisters rhapsodize about the Princess—no one knows her name—who has captivated the King's son with her beauty, and, what's equally remarkable, honored the sisters by giving them some oranges and lemons the Prince had presented to her, even though they had never met her.

Cinderella smiles at this proof that her transformation has been complete. No one recognized her at the ball, neither her stepsisters, who see only clothes, nor her stepmother, who sees only flaws. "She must then be very handsome indeed," Cinderella says in the first English translation of the story. "Lord how happy have you been, could not I see her? Ah! good Madam Charlotte, lend me your yellow suit of clothes that you wear every day."

What a risk the girl takes. And what a triumph she scores. If by some terrible mischance Madam Charlotte relents at this last chance and lends her the everyday dress, Cinderella will have to wear it to the ball and spend the rest of her life as so many women do, metaphorically dressed in hand-me-downs, following in her stepsisters' wake. Far better to dress in rags than to accept a grudging gift, a castoff that will never fit properly anyway. But Madam Charlotte is reliably odious to the core.

"Undoubtedly," said Madam Charlotte, "lend my clothes to such a Cinderbreech as you are, who is fool then?"

For two days, Cinderella oscillates between her roles as a kitchen maid dressed in rags and a "foreign princess" in a gold-and-silver gown; radiant in public, shabby at home. Like every woman returning from a party and taking off her makeup and good clothes, she realizes that both roles are no more than that—roles—and the exhilaration lies in switching her appearance from one extreme to the next through personal magic, with relief at both ends.

ON THE NIGHT OF THE FINAL BALL, the clock strikes twelve before Cendrillon realizes it, and she leaves behind a scrap of clothing as she dashes away. The German Ash Girl runs down a staircase that the Prince has smeared with pitch to trap her.

Never mind how it happens. By necessity, the heroine loses a shoe: a slipper embroidered with metallic thread, a clog studded with diamonds and emeralds, the sandal of an Egyptian courtesan, a patten as high as a stilt, a solid-gold shoe the weight of a feather—whatever is most dazzling wherever and whenever the story is told, but in every case a foot covering that twinkles like a firefly when a Prince holds it in his hand.

PERRAULT'S WAS THE FIRST CINDERELLA to wear glass slippers, "the prettiest in the world," but for a century and a half certain scholars—including Balzac and the essayists in the *Encyclopaedia Britannica*—argued that this footwear was not an inspired fancy but a mistake. An oral storyteller must have described "une pantoufle de *vair*," meaning a fur slipper, these critics claimed, and Perrault or some scribe wrote down "une pantoufle de *verre*," a glass slipper, which would be impossible to dance in.

If a mistake was made, Perrault's subconscious served him well. The lost slipper sparkles on the Prince's palm because it represents the owner herself, or, to be more exact, it represents her sexuality, roaming the countryside to find the only foot that slides into it. After all, what can a woman's slipper, which is a smooth casing that fits snugly over a projecting part of her body, suggest except a vagina, which is shaped by nature to fit around a penis? "The shoe or slipper is a . . . symbol of the female genitals," Sigmund Freud wrote in a footnote to the first of his *Three Contributions to the Theory of Sex*, which implies that the foot slipping in and out of the shoe (and in and out again, all over the countryside while the Prince searches for his mate) represents the eager penis doing its job. But fur? "Fur," Freud says in the same essay, "is used as a fetich [sic] probably on account of its association with the hairiness of the *mons veneris*." In other words, pubic hair.

A fur-covered foot may be a gross fantasy suitable chiefly for scholars, but it's not to the taste of fairy godmothers and their authors. Fairies prefer a slipper made of glass, since glass is cool, incapable of stretching, fragile, and impossible to repair once shattered, which is why it's the symbol of virginity in general and of the hymen in particular. At traditional Jewish weddings today, the bridegroom still crushes a glass underfoot to symbolize rupturing his bride's hymen, while his relatives and friends let out an exuberant cheer of "Mazel tov! Congratulations!" at the sound of the glass shattering. As a matter of fact, so important is the requirement that the groom break the glass on the first try that prudent families substitute a lightbulb hidden in a napkin for the traditional goblet.

Shoe and vagina. Shoe and sex. We know this without knowing we know it.

There was an old woman who lived in a shoe.
She had so many children she didn't know what to do.

Of course she didn't know what to do. With her whole life focused on her genital area, so that metaphorically she lived in her shoe, she was bound to have so many children that she had no recourse except to "give them some broth, without any bread," whip them all soundly, and put them to bed.

Nowadays we have Christmas tree ornaments shaped like evening shoes; bracelet bangles, refrigerator magnets, enamel earrings—all made like elaborate shoes in our national mania to display our most overt totem of female sexuality. And what was often hung behind newlyweds' cars until a generation ago? Old shoes, which we might not have treated so cavalierly had we realized what they stood for.

In *Sex and the City,* Carrie Bradshaw (Sarah Jessica Parker) has only one enduring passion: shoes. On the verge of being evicted from her apartment because she hasn't the money for a down payment to buy it, she visits a shoe store with her friend Miranda. She picks up a sample and sniffs it adoringly. She picks up more shoes and hands them to a salesman. "Size seven and a half. But whatever you do, don't let me buy them," she orders him. "I'm just trying them on for fun."

"Where did all my money go?" she asks plaintively as she sits down.

"At four hundred bucks a pop, how many of these do you own?" Miranda wants to know. "Fifty?"

"C'mon."

"A hundred?"

"Would that be wrong?" Carrie sounds defensive.

"A hundred times four hundred dollars—there's your down payment."

Carrie recoils. "I spent forty thousand dollars on shoes, and I have no place to live?" she asks in disbelief. "I'll literally be the old woman who lived in her shoes."

A DAY OR TWO AFTER THE BALL, the royal trumpeters proclaim that the owner of the glass slipper will be chosen as the Prince's bride. And so, in a mass gesture of yearning, hundreds of maidenly feet from all over the kingdom are poked out from under their owners' skirts toward the hand that holds the slipper, each maiden playing the male role by trying to thrust her foot into the slipper where it doesn't belong, unless she happens to be the rightful claimant. The sexes seem to be reversed here, but sex is a versatile and ambiguous game: A bride holds out her fourth finger, left hand, like a penis, while the groom slips the ring over it, mimicking the sexual act in reverse, both partners consenting to both roles in this private theater of intimacy.

Princesses and duchesses try on the slipper. Ladies of the court try it on, all without success, until at last the Prince, or his deputy, reaches the home of Cinderella and her stepsisters. In Perrault's version of the story, the stepsisters simply fail to squeeze their feet into the glass slipper (small being equated with feminine here), but the Grimms tell a bloodier tale.

The older sister, who is proud of her pretty feet, goes into her bedroom first to try on the shoe, accompanied by her mother, but finds that the shoe is too short. At that, her mother takes out a knife and instructs her daughter to lop off her big toe. Like Mother Nature herself, she is determined to force her daughters into marriage and motherhood, and never mind what looks like a bit of pain to an inexperienced girl. "When you are Queen, you will have no more need to go on foot," she offers in consolation.

The girl does as she is told, swallows her pain, and rides off behind the Prince on his horse, but when they pass the grave of Cinderella's mother, two guardian doves sitting on top of the hazel tree cry out a warning to the bridegroom:

"Turn and peep, turn and peep.
There's blood within the shoe,
The shoe it is too small for her,
The true bride waits for you."

Looking down, the Prince sees blood trickling from the shoe. Hurrying back with the false bride, he lets the second sister try on the shoe, but this one has too large a heel, which her mother commands her to slice off. Again the Prince returns the impostor.

What can a young woman sacrifice to get herself a husband, after all, except her virginity, which is why blood trickles out of the shoe, which is also the vagina? As the pigeons point out, neither sister can be the true bride, who must be virgin—which, in the classical sense, doesn't mean physically chaste but emotionally intact: "one-in-herself." By listening to their mother, the sisters have surrendered their claims not only to their bodies but to their own intentions.

"Have you no other daughter?" the Prince demands.

Cinderella's weak-willed father, who can say only whatever his wife wants him to say, admits that there is a "stunted kitchen-wench" inside, but she cannot possibly be the maiden the Prince has in mind.

"Oh no, she is much too dirty, she cannot show herself!" the stepmother protests, but the Prince insists, and Cinderella is brought before him. Curtsying first, she sits on a stool to take off her wooden shoe and try on the slipper, which fits perfectly, of course—not because her foot is the smallest in the kingdom but because foot and slipper were meant for one another and no other. "And when she rose up and the King's son looked at her face he recognized the beautiful maiden who had danced with him and cried: 'That is the true bride!'" The Prince has passed his test of worthiness. He has recognized the Maiden who must be his wife, even while she wears her gray bedgown and a wooden shoe.

Now that Cinderella's glory has been established for good, her magical power equals the Prince's temporal power. But one scene remains. The story hasn't come around yet.

In the Grimms' version, when the stepsisters accompany the bride to church on her wedding day, two doves perch on their shoulders and peck out their eyes. With the usual Germanic joy in bloody punishments, the Grimms make it clear that the sisters were blind to the cinder girl's virtues in the first place, and so have no right to have eyes.

Perrault has the subtler French turn of mind. On her wedding day, Cinderella marries off her stepsisters to two great lords of the court, which, the author says, proves that she is as benevolent as she is beautiful. Seen from another perspective, could any revenge be more delicate than marrying her stepsisters to her husband's employees?

BUT WHY PERRAULT? Why has his account of Cinderella eclipsed all others, leading in a straight line of descent to the Disney movie, the Rodgers and Hammerstein musical, the Prokofiev ballet, children's television films, and linear miles of storybooks? If the Ash Girl of the Grimm brothers' version is so clearly in charge of her own life, why don't we, in this age of empowered women, choose her story rather than that of the glass-slipper girl who does nothing to bring about her transformation? What does it say about us that we would rather be saved by a fairy godmother than by a tree, that we need to put a human face on divinity?

Rooted in the farmyard and based on archaic models, the Grimms' "Cinderella" is an earth story, dealing with bodies and growth as transmitted through the Good Mother who lies buried under the hazel tree. Our problem is that we don't trust Mother Nature to give us what we want. We take it as our mission to improve on whatever we are given: reshape our bodies, rejuvenate, train and trim them, boost our sexuality, keep up our fertility as long as possible.

Neither do we depend on the good dead mother of childhood, whose memory has to be kept fresh, the way Cinderella waters the tree with her tears. The Bad Mother lives on in our imagination—in fact, thrives in memoirs and on talk shows—while the Good Mother is forgotten, since our culture convinces us that we are self-made. Who has ever defended a difficult mother by saying "She gave me life"?

Perrault's story, on the other hand, written more than a century earlier than the Grimms', is much closer to our modern taste, working through a fairy godmother who is the extreme makeover artist of all time. This is what we want: a shining creature who appears out of thin air—*poof!*—when we need her, preferably resembling Billie Burke as Glinda the Good floating down to Oz in a bubble to hand Dorothy the wicked witch's shoes: the perfect mother we never had, all loving, all powerful, with excellent taste in clothes.

But both Perrault's fairy godmother and the Grimms' magical tree bring us a subliminal message. The Cinderella story is, in its own way, a religious vision that describes the entrance of grace into our lives, either welling up from the earth or descending from the sky, which is why we accept it so gladly.

Transformation is what we long for—we can't be satisfied with who we are. We want to become more centered, more purposeful, steadier in our sense of what we are meant to do in the world. We want to be loved by a Prince, who is the only man worthy of fathering our children. In plain terms, we want to be richer, sexier, better-looking. And, of course, we want to live forever. The Cinderella story can be taken as a metaphor for all of this—when the heroine dances with the Prince, she dances with life itself—but for most of us grace has moved out of reach. No tree in the garden is going to shiver and quiver and deliver a ball gown on request.

Then where will transformation come from when we need it?

From human beings. But human beings who are different from us. To transform us, they must be superior in their overly cultivated fields (though they may be grossly deficient elsewhere), teachers of minor arts that seem to be just what we need, since we are modest in our goals: Instead of magic, we dream of personal improvement. The heroine's dearest wish, her golden dream, is "make me higher class."

Curiously, the new stories work out in much the same way as the old. A stranger, whom the heroine would never have met in the ordinary turn of events, strips away her outer disguise (those terrible vowel sounds, that beehive hairdo) and reveals her as the shining creature she was meant to be from the beginning, eminently worthy of being loved by a Prince. Namely, him.

"WHAT DID YOU THROW those slippers at me for?" Professor Henry Higgins of *Pygmalion* and its musical version, *My Fair Lady,* roars at Eliza Doolittle as the clock on the mantelpiece in his study strikes twelve, the hour when Cinderellas must return to the ashes. They have just returned from the Embassy ball, where he has won his bet with his crony Colonel Pickering that he can pass off this flower peddler, this "squashed cabbage leaf" he has plucked from the Covent Garden vegetable market, as a duchess after only six months of tutoring her in phonetics. But he has surpassed his bet.

At the ball, while the younger society ladies climbed on their chairs for a better look at her, Eliza was subjected to inspection by another teacher of phonetics, Hungarian by birth, and declared a fraud. This cannot be Miss Eliza Doolittle of England, the expert declared to the assemblage. No Englishwoman would enunciate the language so perfectly. This stranger can only be a foreigner, specifically Hungarian—not only Hungarian but of the blood royal. Illegitimate, perhaps, but undoubtedly royal. A foreign princess. Who should know better than he?

Back in his study, Higgins complains about the boredom of the Embassy party after the first few minutes of suspense in which his bet was still in doubt. He accepts Pickering's congratulations on his triumph before he turns toward Eliza, superb in her evening cloak, her (rented) diamond collar with a coronet of diamonds shimmering in her hair. Her expression is murderous. Telling her to turn out the lights and give the housekeeper the necessary instructions for breakfast the next morning because he's deucedly sleepy, Higgins prepares to go to bed. At that moment, the elaborately gowned and crowned female he is addressing hurls his slippers straight at his head.

Of course the author, that old fox George Bernard Shaw, knew perfectly well that the slippers ought to be hers, not his, and ought to be delicate and sparkling rather than broken-backed and down-at-the-heels, just as the triumph of turning a flower girl into a foreign princess belongs to her, not him. At this moment he should be kneeling in front of her with a slipper in his hand, but Shaw makes it clear that in our modern world Princes are arrogant, lazy, and unwilling to commit to a relationship with a beautiful young woman, as Professor Higgins (who is over forty, while Eliza is only eighteen) freely admits. On the other hand, if Eliza can't stand the intellectual briskness Higgins offers her, she can go back to the gutter and be damned.

Then Eliza, that "presumptuous insect," "that damned impudent slut," turns on him. In a flash of inspiration, she declares that she will fight him on his own ground. She will capitalize on her new knowledge by teaching phonetics, using the methods that he has taught her, to every woman in London who might also choose to be turned into a duchess in six months at a thousand guineas apiece. At that, Higgins snaps to attention.

"By George, Eliza, I said I'd make a woman of you; and I have," he says, rising from his chair. "Five minutes ago you were like a millstone round my neck. Now you're a tower of strength; a consort battleship. You and I and Pickering will be three old bachelors together instead of only two men and a silly girl."

So transformation has taken place. But into what? Not into anything as trivial as a duchess, which merely requires correcting the vowel sounds and dropped *h*'s that separate class from class and soul from soul, but into a real woman, a consort for the redoubtable Professor Higgins, equipped with equal firing power. Which is a miracle of a modern sort, based on the wistful fairy-tale premise that a heroine's true self longs to be released from the outer husk that hides her worth.

Modern Cinderella stories start from the same point as the fairy tale, with a heroine who is a motherless waif: a "draggle-tailed guttersnipe" selling wilted violets like Eliza Doolittle, a "hooker" selling herself like Vivian in *Pretty Woman,* a "dumb broad" like Billy Dawn in *Born Yesterday.* Or she "ain't fresh," like teenage Celie in Alice Walker's book *The Color Purple,* whose father describes her that way to a prospective husband after the father has raped her repeatedly and she has borne him two children.

Defying our myths about democracy, all of these modern versions are based on class distinctions. When we first meet the heroine, she is separated from what we consider to be decent people by differences in speech, manners, education, attitude (Celie never dares call her husband by his first name), and by her taste in clothes: too flashy more often than too dowdy. ("You *might* want to rethink the jewelry," says the elegant boss lady to her new secretary with the towering hairdo and across-the-river accent, in the movie *Working Girl.*

This heroine has just put her stuffed bunny on the desk for her first day at work.)

In past centuries, these problems never plagued the kitchen wench. Cinderella wasn't allowed to go to the ball because she had no dress and therefore couldn't dance, but as soon as proper clothes were supplied she knew how to curtsy to a Prince and dance as elegantly as her sisters, since it was clear to everyone that she was a member of the same class, temporarily reduced in fortune. In Perrault's time, social distinctions were seen as an inborn part of human nature, and therefore incapable of being taught. Princes were not expected to marry scullery maids, only girls of good family disguised as scullery maids.

In our democratic age, on the other hand, the sole boundary between social classes is money—not even money so much as the impression of having money. Experts stand ready to help the upwardly mobile change their manners to fit their aspirations. But where does that leave an Ash Girl who has no shillings to spend? If her life is to change, some new energy must step up the voltage, something on a worldly level, because this is a worldly story, but an intrusion that breaks the laws of probability.

Some enchanted evening, let's say, while taking shelter from the rain in front of the opera house at Covent Garden, or soliciting customers on Hollywood Boulevard, the heroine meets a fairy godparent, an agent of transformation in the form of a human being—specifically a man, which is a clear break with fairy-tale tradition. Grace doesn't descend on her. She bumps into it through what looks like an accident, an unlikely encounter with a stranger in evening clothes who is her superior in social standing, wealth, education, accomplishments, and self-confidence. The last above all.

More specifically still, this stranger is an expert in whatever it is she lacks. The single person best qualified to teach particular arts (how to speak, dress, tip a bellhop, eat a lobster) encounters the single student most adept at receiving them. The overflowing spoon is extended toward the gaping mouth. Overcome by impulses the two of them don't understand, this oddly matched pair reach out toward one another, intending only a short course of elementary education but finding themselves on the road to a dual transformation.

Who but Eliza could have won Higgins's bet for him? As he himself tells his mother, "The most extraordinary quickness of ear . . . with every possible sort of sound that a human being can make . . . Continental dialects, African dialects, Hottentot clicks, things it took me years to get hold of, she picks them up like a shot, right away." Who could be as hungry to give and get love as Miss Celie? The heroine is a person of singular talent imprisoned in her role by society. And the transformer plans to hand her the keys.

Since he is invariably a bachelor (or bisexual, like Shug Avery in *The Color Purple,* who arouses Miss Celie's sexual ardor for the first time), the transformer combines the roles of fairy godmother and Prince, which changes the story—and with it our sense of where salvation comes from—into a romance, which is a fairy tale in modern clothes. Call the encounter luck, serendipity, fate, but always, in real life or movies, there must be a supernormal force that brings together two people who have no business meeting socially, and through their conjunction transforms them.

In this case, the romance has the erotic pressure of the teacher-student relationship behind it. For a teacher, no situation could be more satisfying. He can mold his guttersnipe into a work of art, without realizing that what he's in love with is his own talent, inflamed by her compliance with his demands. Since he's sure that he's in control of the relationship, at the end he's shocked to find himself transformed, as well as the transformer.

As for the woman, nothing is more seductive than knowledge, so long as it goes deeper than books. Her teacher practices a new and subtler form of penetration, changing her only a little at first, letting her see that there's a higher level of existence and that with his expert guidance she can reach it. He watches her, coaches her, criticizes, corrects, fine-tunes, on rare occasions praises, but constantly pays attention to her. Why? Because she deserves it. And all the time she knows that in the end she'll succeed. She'll bring him to his knees.

BUT WITHOUT THE HELP of a fairy godmother, what power can transform the contemporary Cinderella from a perpetual student like Eliza, or a hired companion like Jane Eyre or Pretty Woman, into a living, seething woman? One thing: anger, which is the corollary of the self-respect she has gained through her lessons. The spark of anger sets her in roaring motion, letting loose the force that has been pent up in her for so long. Eliza Doolittle hurls a pair of slippers. Pretty Woman, Jane Eyre, and Gigi (in the book by Colette) refuse to give themselves as mistresses to the men they love, after they realize that they deserve a nobler station. Through anger and grief, the heroine discovers that she is an authentic human being.

When Professor Higgins tells Eliza at the end of the Shaw play that, by George, he has made a woman of her, he's mistaken. He made a lady of her, a duchess as promised. But it's her anger, along with her newly earned pride, that makes her a woman, at the same time that it transforms her transformer. Professor Higgins believes, like most men, that he can exist perfectly well alone, or, better yet, with an obliging female companion, a good house-buddy, but with no commitment between them. (What woman ever spoke of "commitment" to a man, as if he were a mental institution?) The expert, more than most men, lives for his expertise, until one day he discovers to his astonishment that he's attached to another person, who's about to flee from him or strike back in anger. "I've grown accustomed to her face," Professor Higgins moans.

For the Ash Girl, the educational timetable works in the other direction. No matter how unhappy she has been at home, she doesn't dream of striking out on her own until she steps into her glory and discovers that she doesn't need the transformer any longer. But once she doesn't need him, she's free to want him. On her own terms.

———

WE KNOW WHAT TO EXPECT: At the last moment, the transformer is transformed, and Cinderella marries him. Or does she?

George Bernard Shaw, who is far too clever to give us what we might have thought of for ourselves, leaves his play *Pygmalion* open-ended, with no hint whether Henry Higgins and Eliza go on together or not. In the musical *My Fair Lady,* we get the traditional happy ending, but Shaw writes elsewhere that he can't imagine an outcome less fortunate than a confirmed middle-aged bachelor with a mother fixation marrying a flower girl of eighteen.

But we know better. Eliza and the professor like Cinderella and the Prince must oblige us by marrying, and we have to believe that their marriages will turn out well, since their unions are so improbable that they must be touched with magic.

Our idea of a happy marriage is as vague as our idea of Heaven: We have no reason to believe that it exists—in fact, the experience of our senses is against it. If it does exist, we have no idea how we might get from here to there, and yet we need that vision, with its implied promise, the same way we need the vision of Heaven, as an air pocket that lets us breathe under the suffocating weight of the universe.

SO THE CINDERELLA STORY ENDS as it should. At the same time we know that, unlike other fairy tales, it is bound to start all over again; it never ends.

As soon as we feel unloved—more exactly, when we no longer feel central to somebody's life, though "somebody" may be a child rather than a mate—we turn into adolescents again, prone to despair. We never grew up in the first place, it seems; we only clothed ourselves in magic ball gowns that turned to rags at midnight. Transformations may not be reversible, but they need to be constantly renewed.

In the years we call "ever after," the Prince disappears or dies in the blink of an eye while we were looking elsewhere, or, more likely, he turns out not to have been a Prince at all. These bouts of despair are even more devastating for women than men, since women measure themselves by seeing who loves them—a true Prince?—and how much, and whether they love the men in return. Meanwhile, in our jobs our hard work is ignored, our skills are undervalued, and we are passed over in favor of someone less deserving. Our children leave home. Suddenly our lives, which seemed so ordinary that we took them for granted, are shot out from under us, and we have to start from ashes and wooden shoes all over again, at the never-ending task of inner transformation that will give us the strength to go on living.

At that point, we look in the back of the closet and find Cinderella's gray bedgown still hanging there. Strange to say, it's still the right size.

CHAPTER 5

Sleeping Beauty:
Going to Sleep a Girl . . .

"Sleeping Beauty," the Legend of Brunhilde

Two kinds of energy are available to each of us, whether male or female: Effort or openness. Reaching out for what's beyond us. Or awakening something inside ourselves that never existed until now. In fairy-tale terms, we pass through the story of Cinderella or Sleeping Beauty, usually both by turns.

But how can we compare these two figures? Cinderella is the all-American girl who works from dawn to dark, just like us, while she waits for something wonderful to happen in her life: "Watchful waiting," we called it in the previous chapters. Hers is the optimistic story of a girl who is convinced, without proof, that her future is bound to be better than her present.

Sleeping Beauty is the opposite: an overprotected Princess to begin with, for whom transformation carries a sting she has to absorb. Suddenly made aware of the responsibility, grief, danger, joy, helplessness, and passion in a future that can't be resisted, she does nothing for the rest of the story except lie back and keep her eyes shut, the one truly passive heroine in fairy tales, amoral and erotic.

We call her sleep unconsciousness, but that isn't wholly true. Her mind and emotions may be numb, her body may be paralyzed, but some form of intuitive learning, some digestive process, goes on inside her, so that by the time she wakes up she has been transformed every bit as definitively as Cinderella.

To make any sense of the story, we have to assume that Sleeping Beauty's sleep is a reflection of the portion of each of us that retreats from the world in a castle protected by thorns (a walled garden, a glass coffin, the top of a glass mountain) while building up strength to emerge at a higher level of fruitfulness. We all sleep for unnoticed stretches of time throughout our lives—emotionally and intellectually as well as physically—experiencing paralysis of the will without acknowledging it. "Where did the time go?" we say, referring either to the hour that just passed or the last few decades. In other words, "Where was I while my life went by?"

Confronting "Sleeping Beauty," this most spiritual of all fairy tales, we have to ask why sleep overtook the Princess when it did, and what part of her self was so frightened that it lay dormant for what seemed to her family like countless years. Could there be something that we gain in sleep that can't be gained elsewhere?

Leapfrogging to the end of the story, we have to ask why she wakes up when she does, which may not be as simple as the fact that she has been kissed. Has she been transformed because the right time has come, and so the first Prince who shows up has to be the right one for her? Or is it because the right man knows how to pass through the brambles to reach her and rouse her with a kiss?

SOMEWHERE IN THE MIDDLE of a castle a Princess lies sleeping, which is what she has done for the past hundred years. On the day she fell under the magic spell that had been laid on her at birth—it was her fifteenth birthday, some say—a hedge of thorns grew up around the castle to protect her. In only a quarter of an hour, according to the local legend, the hedge grew tall enough to hide the walls, and after that the roof and the weather vane fastened to the roof, and finally the guardian towers with arrow slits for eyes which could be glimpsed only from a distance.

In the countryside round about, most people have forgotten that this castle exists, but enough of the old tradition survives that from time to time an adventurous Prince tries to pass through the hedge in order to reach the tower where a beautiful Princess is rumored to lie fast asleep, looking no older than she did on the day when she found this room. While she sleeps, her dreams tell her that the skeletons of Princes who arrived too early hang in the briars, where they died a pitiful death, but the dreams also tell her not to wake up yet. Her time has not come around. When it does, at the end of this hundredth year, the thorn hedge will burst into flower—red roses, we can be sure, since her name is Briar Rose in one version of the story—and the flowers will rise around her like a circle of flames while the chosen Prince makes his way through the hedge to greet her.

FARTHER NORTH, on top of a hill crowned with a rocky fort, another virgin lies sleeping in a ring of fire that has been burning for twenty years, although no one stokes the flames. This sleeper is no pink-and-white Princess but a female warrior dressed in full armor, or, to be more exact, a war spirit, the favorite daughter of Wotan, the king of the Norse gods. Until the day that her father put her to sleep, Brunhilde was the leader of the Valkyrie, "Choosers of the Slain," virginal spirits who save the lives of warriors whom the father-god wants saved in battle, and carry the bodies of those whom he wants slain aloft to his hall in Valhalla, where they feast with him while awaiting the battle that will end all battles.

As her father's lieutenant, his "wish-maid," Brunhilde obeyed his commands until the day she discovered that she had a will of her own. On that day, she flouted Wotan's orders by putting up her shield to protect a warrior whom he had singled out for death. (In Richard Wagner's opera *The Valkyrie,* which is part of the *Ring* cycle of four operas, the doomed warrior is the god's own son, Siegmund, the mortal he loves above all others.) Wotan was obliged to kill the hero himself, after which he proceeded to his best-loved daughter's punishment: Banishment from Valhalla forever. Loss of divinity. Sleep on a rock surrounded by flames, until a hero arrives who is bold enough to ride through the flames to reach her, at which time she will awaken as a mortal woman, compelled "to wed as women wed."

In a Norse saga compiled in the twelfth century from older material, the father-god puts his maiden daughter to sleep by pricking her with a sleep-thorn, which ensures that she will remain as young and beautiful as ever until a hero hurtles through the fire. The funeral pyres, where Norse heroes were laid out in full armor like Brunhilde, were woven of thorn branches, emblems of death, and kindled with another thorn branch, like those that grew around Sleeping Beauty's castle.

So Sleeping Beauty sleeps in a ring of briars when pricked by a spindle. Brunhilde sleeps in a ring of fire when pricked by her father's sleep-thorn. Snow White sleeps in a glass coffin, laid low by her stepmother, protected by birds. Juliet sleeps in the family tomb, but fails to wake up when her lover leans over her. The poet Elizabeth Barrett is unable to get up from the couch in her father's home until her Prince, Robert Browning, leans over her and gives her the strength to leave London with him for Italy.

"You all die at fifteen," Diderot, the French philosopher, wrote in a letter to the woman he loved.

In each case, the virgin falls unconscious—maybe asleep, maybe dead, who can tell?—on the day that she is no longer her parents' protected child. She has broken their law by favoring the one man she isn't supposed to favor, or reaching out for the single thing she isn't supposed to touch, or taking a bite from the poisoned apple offered by a false mother. On the other side of parental law lies sexuality, which may mean death but, in any case, means that childhood has been left behind, even though she isn't ready yet for the next step. If she wakes, it can only be in the arms of a man of her own, at which point she will have to become a lover, wife, mother. Mortal. Heading for decay. Giving birth to others who will, in turn, decay. This seems like a sad comedown in the eyes of her father, but it will do him no good to banish spindles from his kingdom, as Sleeping Beauty's father is about to find out.

WE CAN'T UNDERSTAND these stories of virgins who fall asleep and ripen into women ready for sex while they seem to be dead to the world unless we understand that we, too, are often half asleep in our daily lives, sometimes because we are in the midst of transformation.

If we watch carefully, we see that our feelings, our intellect, our will, even our bodies, drowse at the most critical times if we are not ready for the adventure that confronts us. Like Sleeping Beauty or Snow White, we black out when life demands too much from us, or forces too much knowledge on us at once (including sexual knowledge, which used to be called "knowing" a man or woman). We also sleep if life demands too little, leaving us with no outlet for our talents, feelings, sexuality, ambition.

In a state of semi-sleep, we hurry to the office, stalk through the supermarket aisles, lie in bed with our lovers. Do I doubt that I sleep the years away? Then let me try to remember what I was doing a month ago, a decade ago. Let me try to remember my children when they were little, not in the form of well-worked anecdotes, as composed as photos, that I tell myself about them, but as they actually were, the touch and smell of them, and myself in my many moods when I was with them; and I find that I'm left with nothing but shadows except for a few brief patches of light.

Our minds sleep, and we don't notice the absence of attention: While we are doing one thing we think of a dozen others, but without purpose. Thoughts tumble around in our minds in no particular order, like clothes tumbling past the window of a washing machine, while we wonder how soon this chore will be over.

Emotional sleep is more obvious to outsiders: Under stress, our emotions grow numb, leaving us limp as a mouse caught in the jaws of a cat. Patients in psychiatrists' offices complain about tiredness, depression. They are bored with the whole psychiatric process, not to mention irritated at the cost, just at the critical time when they are about to reach a new level of awareness. When the change comes, it may be a long-awaited breakthrough, said the analyst Marie-Louise von Franz; or it may be a psychotic episode, a thunderstorm. We don't wake up until we are strong enough to bear the assault of consciousness without being blinded by its glare. But no one can predict what will happen when the trance is broken.

In a third form of sleep, our willpower crumples. We lose track of our purpose. At the most ordinary level, I see myself going to the kitchen to take something out of the freezer for dinner. The phone rings. I answer. I pause for a snack. An hour later, while sitting at my desk, I realize that I never took the food out of the freezer. Nothing to fuss about. Absent-minded, I say. But if my mind is mine and my will is absent, where can it be if not asleep? Is my excuse that I was lost in thought? Then what great thought did I carry out of the kitchen?

Most of the time we don't know that we aren't fully awake, any more than we know that we're dreaming in the midst of a dream. But let a jolt come and we wake up with a start.

While I sit in the radiologist's examining room waiting for the result of a test, pricked by the frailty of life, the quite ordinary vase in the corner filled with artificial flowers grows luminous, like a votive candle—the hands that placed it there must have been blessed. But if the result of the test is good, fifteen minutes later the glow has dimmed to the light of common day and I'm in my car again, ready to run errands in my usual half-conscious state but forgetting where I put the car keys.

Why does consciousness fade so fast, why can't we remain aware of what we are doing? Joy and fear and the massive change we call transformation may prick us awake for a while, but fear more often is the anesthetic that puts us to sleep. For a young woman, sleep is the soul-savior that protects her inner self while her body passes through metamorphosis. For an adult, fear, which is the emotion that underlies our existence, is the sleep-thorn that keeps us from seeing where we are, for the simple reason that while we are alive— right *now, here*—we can't bear to remember that someday we won't be. Time is washing us down to the delta. Those children for whom we're prowling the supermarket aisles in search of breakfast cereal won't be living in our house much longer. For that matter, neither will we.

Despite our resistance to the idea that we aren't fully awake, we have to bear in mind that sleep is a positive force that makes life and creative work, as well as transformation, possible. In the Sleeping Beauty story, it's the period of incubation that the heroine's soul needs in order to absorb what we so blithely call "the facts of life," and gather the strength for new growth in spite of them, but for all of us, the ultimate fact of life is death. We couldn't go about our business if we thought about that all the time.

This is what happens in sleep: One part of us knows a secret that the other parts don't know yet, and tells it in our sleep. If we fail to understand this, if we don't realize that all of us play the Sleeping Beauty role from time to time, we can't understand the story or sympathize with the heroine, who seems as lifeless as a codfish stretched out on a bed of ice in the fish store.

Two myths of sleep and darkness are at odds with each other in our culture. In the old male tradition (which is shared by the masculine portion of women's lives), darkness stands for barrenness, unconsciousness that must be fought with even the smallest light of reason, the way that Pinocchio's father lights a candle and reads a book while living in the belly of a whale. A man sees sleep as a defeat or a lost opportunity for heroism—a time when he is extinguished, and his deeds along with him: "So, could you not watch with me one hour?" Jesus asked Peter in the Garden of Gethsemane, and the answer was no, he couldn't, his eyelids were too heavy. Three times Jesus went off to pray, and three times Peter, along with the other disciples, fell asleep, like a fairy-tale hero's unworthy brothers, faced with a reality they were powerless to change.

Wake up, is the message the Gospels send us. Keep watch, especially during moments of crisis. Watch not only what you do, which is your active, masculine self, but also what happens to you, what you become. And yet we can't keep watch; our attention, if not our flesh, is weak. We nod and miss the moment.

The biblical hero Samson falls asleep on Delilah's knees, and while he sleeps she cuts off his hair, and his strength along with it. Judith, a beautiful Israeli widow, takes off her widow's weeds and puts on her most seductive clothes, what the Bible calls "her garments of gladness," to dine in the tent of the conquering Assyrian general Holofernes. After waiting for him to fall into a drunken stupor, she cuts off his head with his sword, which he has hung above his bed. In our own time, Lorena Bobbitt castrates her abusive husband in his sleep.

This is what a man fears most: While he sleeps, he lies disarmed in a woman's power, especially when drained of his sexual juices. A woman, on the other hand, is more likely to realize that through sleep and waiting she gains what she couldn't gain in any other way, provided she doesn't wait too long (until waiting turns to withering, that is).

When a man sets out on an adventure, his system pumps him full of adrenaline, so that he's wide awake and raring to go, more energetic and aggressive than before.

When a heroine faces her great female adventure, which involves as much pain and danger as a hero's, her hormone reaction is equally strong, especially in the first few months, but opposite in effect. Withdrawing her attention from the outside world, which has become foreign to her, she wants nothing more than to lie down on a couch and sleep, and from her sense that she's drowning in honey, infinitely sweet and sticky, she suspects that the adventure is under way. She's pregnant. Energy seeps out of her arms and legs and brain, and centers in her womb, where she transforms a fertilized egg into a transparent shrimp, a shrimp into a fetus, ultimately a fetus into a child, as if she's dreaming her baby into existence. Sleep (or drowsiness) is the baby-maker.

She incubates. In her career, she may be a high-powered executive, fueled by the same adrenaline as a man, but she realizes that she can't produce a full-term baby in less than nine months any more than she can bake instant bread. She will have to wait and ripen like a pear, from the inside out.

During this time, if her pregnancy is threatened, her impulse is to struggle heroically, the way she would rush into a burning building to save her child, but she soon learns that to carry out her purpose she must do the opposite. No matter how great the strain, her heroic act is to lie down. Maybe she must lie down for months. The greater the urgency, the greater the need to rest.

"I was forty-one at the time," my editor, a woman as smart and hard-driving as they come, told me, "I'd already had a pregnancy that had to be removed by a D and C, and after that I lost a baby through a miscarriage. I say 'a baby,' not 'a fetus,' because that's the way I think of him. My son who died. When I became pregnant again, because of my age I figured this was my last chance.

"Then, in my fifth month, I started to bleed and cramp, and my doctor told me that if I hoped to save the child I had no choice. I would have to go to bed for the remaining four months. There I was in a hospital bed, my feet elevated higher than my head to take pressure off the cervix, not allowed to touch my feet to the floor, not even to go to the bathroom, and not allowed to have any visitors except my husband. It was difficult to hold a book because of my angle of tilt, so I gave up reading except for poetry, which comes in small portions, and William James's *Varieties of Religious Experience* in paperback, which can be read in sections, but mostly I lay there, half asleep, aware of nothing but the calendar.

"Thirty-six weeks. I had to bring my baby through the thirty-sixth week. I could feel a clock ticking inside me. And every minute that it ticked I lay in fear of killing my child. So I lay still, and I brought him to term. And I'd do it all over again if I had the chance. Strange to say, when the four months were over, I'd not only become a mother but I'd solved a number of professional problems that had been bothering me for a long time, which I didn't even know were drifting around in my head."

To be a good vessel is not easy. "Vessel" is a term we deplore these days and apply only to women, as if it implies passivity, but the opposite is true: To be a good vessel requires willfully emptying oneself of everything but a single intention. It requires stillness. And it demands constant vigilance to protect the virgin self—the contained and therefore continent self—against intrusion. Contents, no matter how valuable, are useless without a proper container.

Like a pregnant woman, a nursing mother exists in two time frames at once, each with its claim on her energy, especially if she's also a working woman. This leads to the curious spectacle of a career woman sitting at her desk with her office door locked, listening on a Walkman to her baby's cries in order to produce the stream of breast milk that she'll pump into a nursing bottle. The baby's cries stimulate the flow of the hormone oxytocin, which is a natural tranquilizer that causes her milk to let down, at the same time that it relaxes her tensions. Tranquillity, which means surrendering to the animal part of herself as well as to her baby, brings on the milk—not because of her efforts, but superseding them.

In more natural circumstances at home, she nuzzles the baby. The baby's sucking makes more oxytocin flow, some of which passes through the milk into the baby's bloodstream and quiets him. Mother and child feed each other's sleep.

BOTH GENDERS GO THROUGH periods of sleep and waking, but it's the masculine ideal of action that prevails in the Western world. We abhor seclusion and silence. "Being left out" sounds like a witch's curse. Since childhood, we have been taught to admire and expect only what we have struggled for and mastered. Never what overpowers us by stealth.

Within the family, a man boasts about how few hours of sleep he gets each night, which he takes as a measure of how busy he is, how valuable, and therefore how valuable his time is. "I outlasted my junior associates," says a partner at a major law firm as he gets off the plane after a thirty-six-hour round-trip to Paris, pleased that the young lions haven't caught hold of the old lion's tail yet. At his hourly billing rate, who can afford to sleep?

Or else he complains that he's been deprived of sleep all week, as if everyone else wins a nightly lottery while he's left holding a ticket but no prize. If he values sleep, it's only because it allows him to work harder the next day, not for its own sake. Still, he regards it as a form of income tax, extorted by nature, that forces him to pay back a third of his life.

Given this cultural background ("No pain, no gain"), it isn't easy to have faith in an old story that holds out the possibility that after a time of withdrawal and self-absorption rather than hard work, we may be roused to new life at a higher level, just as we get up in the morning after a good night's sleep feeling more capable than we did when we went to bed. In the words of the old Irish folk saying, "Morning is wiser than evening."

HOW MUCH DO WE KNOW about physical sleep itself, the nightly blacking out of consciousness? Not much, though it has always been obvious that sleep is necessary for sanity and ultimately for life, the way a sense of balance is necessary for walking. But this much scientists are sure of: Whatever sleep is, it's not nothing.

The dreaming stage called rapid eye movement sleep, or REM, was the first to be studied, doubtless because of the influence of psychiatry. In this stage, our inner organs spring to life, the flow of blood to the brain actually increases 40 percent (in cats' brains, it doubles), the heartbeat speeds up and slows without apparent reason, metabolism increases, and the clitoris or penis has erections that then subside, testifying to our absorption in the closet adventures that we call dreams.

And yet we travel deeper than this every night, down to the lightless level known as deep sleep, or slow-wave, which has proved, to the astonishment of researchers, to be the obscure realm where links are forged in our brains. Here, below the level of dreams, cells that carry short-term memories "talk" to long-term memories and associations in order to establish and update connections, so that the Irish folk saying proves to be scientifically exact. We know more in the morning than we did when we went to bed. Our significant memories have been consolidated in a more accessible way, which may be the reason, says Dr. Terence J. Sejnowski of the Salk Institute, that there is such a close connection between sleep and creativity.

Scientists and artists in all fields could have told us this in practice long ago, though not in theory. Despite the male prejudice against sleep, these creators—most of them men—discovered that at a certain stage of exploration hard work is not enough. In fact, it can be counterproductive, like struggling to remember the name of a former neighbor we haven't seen for years. The name doesn't come to mind until hours later, when we've given up and shut our minds to the problem, and then it returns to consciousness unbidden, like a cat coming out from under a bed long after you've stopped calling it.

These creators testify that what we think of as a flash of inspiration from above is, at least in part, the product of images welling up from below, either into dreams or the mists we call daydreams: Friedrich Kekulé, one of the founders of organic chemistry, struggled to define the benzene molecule as a chain of carbon atoms, until in a daydream he saw snakes swallowing their own tails and conceived the idea that the benzene molecule must be a circle rather than a chain.

Wolfgang Mozart said of himself, "When I am, as it were, completely myself, entirely alone and of good cheer—say, traveling in a carriage . . . or during the night when I cannot sleep; it is on such occasions that my ideas flow best and most abundantly. *Whence* and *how* they come, I know not; nor can I force them. . . . All this inventing, this producing, takes place in a pleasing, lively dream." When the time came to put down on paper the music composed in his dream, he was able to do it while chatting with the people around him, "but only of fowls or geese."

For writers who are unable to write the next chapter, which they suspect will be the key to their book, the sleep of blank pages that we call writer's block may last for years. And still we cannot skip that level of deep sleep when memories coalesce, followed by the dream state, or we simply repeat what has already been said, possibly by us.

No work of art was ever created by the conscious mind alone. The period of germination at the deepest level, followed by gestation, still in darkness, is crucial. Women and artists know instinctively that there are times in life when we must be unreachable, times when we must insist that those around us, especially those nearest and dearest, remain at a distance if anything significant is to develop inside us. Whatever is touched too soon cannot grow. This is true of an idea as well as a fetus. It's also true of a love affair.

Feelings and sensations that are talked about too soon, especially to the lover, seem as foolish as dreams when we try to make sense of them. "Lovers should guard their strangeness," said Ralph Waldo Emerson.

Sleeping Beauty's sleep is not nothing, then; not simply repair of the spindle's prick, though that must be accomplished too; certainly not a punishment imposed on her or her father. In some way that we are only beginning to understand, it's a time for growth. While she sleeps, her cells network and form new perceptions; her emotions catch up with her body, even if her mind doesn't understand either of them. This is a time of transformation, after which— if she wakes up—she'll have the strength to face what overwhelmed her, bearing in mind that Beauties have more to be wary of than other females.

"Ah, if only we had a child!" a King and Queen said to one another every day in mournful voices. "But they never had one." So begins the story we call "Sleeping Beauty," which was the first tale in Charles Perrault's celebrated collection ("La Belle au Bois Dormant," "The Sleeping Beauty in the Wood"), later rewritten by the Grimms as "Little Briar Rose." This should have taught the royal couple something about the limits of parental power, but didn't.

As always with the Grimms, in contrast to Perrault, the long-desired miracle comes from nature, up from below. One day, while the Queen is bathing in a pond, a frog pops out of the water, as squashy as a man's genitals and just as apt to puff itself up on a sunny rock before deflating again. Without being asked, the old water-splasher announces, "Your wish shall be fulfilled. Before a year has gone by, you shall have a daughter." By the time the Queen steps out of the pond, she is an expectant mother.

Nine months later, the King, who is delirious with joy, plans a splendid christening feast for his newborn daughter and invites all the fairies in his kingdom to stand as godmothers to the child—all but one, that is, who throws the gathering into turmoil by showing up anyway.

How could a King, of all people, make such a fateful mistake? The oldest of the fairies has been overlooked, Perrault explains, because she hasn't been seen outside her tower in fifty years (not since the King himself was born, no doubt), and so she was thought to be either dead or enchanted. No, say the Grimms, she was excluded because there were thirteen Wise Women in the kingdom, but the King had only twelve golden plates.

Never mind the excuses. We know better than to believe them. What the King lacks isn't an extra place setting but what all parents lack: the imagination to encompass the night side of human existence for their child with its pain and passion, danger and death as well as love and laughter. And so he sees to it that he invites the band of fairies—or Wise Women, or Norns, or whatever name they go by in his kingdom—who will give his infant daughter the gifts that he considers especially desirable for a girl: beauty surpassing everyone else's, of course (that comes first), the grace of a dancer, a nightingale's voice, all the usual trimmings. But he leaves out the most powerful female attribute of all, the one that made him a father and ought to be honored above all others. The oldest fairy, who has been closed in her tower so long, brings the gift of female sexuality, which leads to birth, and therefore death. She pays no attention to minor distractions.

"The King's daughter shall in her fifteenth year prick herself with a spindle, and fall down dead," the uninvited guest cries, her head shaking with spite, as she storms out of the hall and disappears.

At this point we see the source of the King's mistake. What father can look at a daughter in her crib, pink and flawless, and picture her bedding clotted with menstrual blood? What father wants to see his daughter pawed by some strange young Prince with a sword at his side and acne on his chin, who plans to carry her off to a distant kingdom? Preserve her from sex, the father prays secretly as he leans over his daughter's crib. Keep her intact. Keep her a child. Most important, keep her here with me. The only thing as painful for a father as a weakling son is a prematurely sexual daughter (which means sexual before her father is prepared to accept the fact).

Fortunately, the youngest fairy, who is crafty as well as kind, hides behind the curtains and holds back her own gift until she hears what the oldest has to say. When her turn comes, she cannot undo the curse, but she can soften the blow: "The Princess shall indeed pierce her hand with a spindle; but instead of death, she shall fall into a profound sleep which shall last a hundred years. At the end of that time, a King's son shall come and wake her."

Even this amendment doesn't soothe the King, however. He has no intention of letting his daughter be pricked, no matter what a bloody-minded old fairy says, so he gives orders that every spindle in the kingdom must be burned, on pain of death to the criminal who harbors one.

Through all of this, the Queen remains silent. (In the entire Walt Disney movie of *Sleeping Beauty*, she has only one line.) She would never have forgotten to invite the oldest fairy to the feast in the first place, particularly so soon after becoming a mother herself, just as she knows that it's a waste of time to ban spindles. Like all good mothers in fairy tales her role is only to give birth to the long-awaited child and then to vanish before the story grows sexual.

During the years that follow, the Princess grows up in a kingdom rich in everything known on earth, except spindles.

FIFTEEN YEARS GO BY. This brings the Princess to the average age of the first menstrual period in past centuries, when girls remained prepubertal children well into their teens and then moved swiftly into their roles as wives and mothers. One day the King and Queen go out to visit one of their "houses of pleasure," which is a privilege of adulthood, leaving their daughter alone to amuse herself by running up and down the staircases of the palace and exploring the numerous apartments.

As Freud says, "a house is the only regularly occurring symbol of the (whole) human body in dreams," which is particularly true for women, although he doesn't say so. Around the time when a girl matures, the house she dreams about marvelously expands not only in size but also in functions, so that she barely recognizes it. In a mysterious way, it belongs to her, and yet doesn't belong to her, it's not under her control; it contains some untouchable secret that has dark sexual connotations. (Think of Bluebeard's last wife, Jane Eyre, the anonymous heroine of *Rebecca,* and Mary Lennox of *The Secret Garden:* these poor-girl heroines are suddenly promoted to disconcertingly handsome mansions that they are sternly forbidden to explore.)

In the few hours that have passed since Sleeping Beauty was left alone, the palace has branched out into innumerable corridors and apartments, locked cupboards containing who knows what, winding staircases and alcoves that the Princess knew nothing about, although she has lived here all her life. Puberty is at hand, the house tells her, which is why the royal parents have slipped out of their daughter's sight and mind. It's time for the girl to discover the magic power hidden in the house's recesses.

Climbing to the top of the tower, she comes to a little door with a rusty key in the lock.

According to Bruno Bettelheim, a locked room stands for the female genitals, especially if it's a small and humble room tucked out of sight in a grand house. The key that turns in the lock to open the door is a symbol for sexual intercourse (as in the story of "Bluebeard"). If the key is rusty, that can only mean that nobody has entered this out-of-the-way chamber for years, perhaps not since the girl was conceived. Whoever, or whatever, waits inside has been waiting, hiding, while iron rusts and a virgin grows up.

The Princess turns the key. The door springs open. In the room sits an old woman with a spindle, busily spinning flax. "Good day, old mother," the Princess says politely. "What are you doing there?"

No other fairy-tale heroine ever asked such a question. Not to know what spinning is? She might as well not know what breasts are for and which sex has them, or how babies come into the world—probably doesn't know anything about those subjects either, if she doesn't know that in her era, and up until the past two centuries, spinning (with drop spindles, not spinning wheels) was what women did all day when their hands weren't busy doing something else. Yarn flowed from their fingertips the way milk flowed from their nipples. They spun while they rocked the baby or herded the cows on their way to pasture. They spun as they walked home from the village in the evening, even while courting. In fact, spinning defined women so absolutely that we still speak of an unmarried woman as a "spinster" and the female members of the family as the "distaff side."

Spinning is woman's work: The woman of the house not only provides fabric for the family's clothing but clothes an embryo inside herself with flesh, often at the same time. "I am spinning, my pretty child," the old woman answers.

According to Perrault, the spinner is a "good old lady" who never heard the King's edict, but we know perfectly well that she's the thirteenth fairy, biding her time. She isn't a good old soul, as Perrault claims, but on the other hand neither was she wicked to begin with when she uttered what sounded like a curse over the newborn child. (Certainly she does not conform to Walt Disney's image of Maleficent, the insulted witch who materializes at the baby's christening in a gale of thunder, lightning, and green fire, wearing a black headdress with horns to show that she's of the Devil's party.) The old woman in the story is what she is: the physical aspect of human beings, destiny itself; neither good nor evil, but unaffected by our actions.

In former times, this spinner was the first of three divine sisters whom the Greeks called Moirae and the Romans called Fates. One sister spins what we still call the thread of life (her name is Clothos, the clothier), the second measures each person's alloted span, and the third, who is the smallest but most terrible, snips it off with her shears.

The sister who spins the thread of life is clearly the one responsible for fertility. Any King so engrossed with his golden place settings that he thinks he can ban her from the table will have to deal with her revenge later on.

"What is that, that jumps around so merrily?" the Princess wants to know. The object that mesmerizes her can only be a handheld spindle, which dangles from the yarn like a yo-yo by the spinner's side, while she twists the fibers with one hand.

A spindle, which is as central to the story as the slipper is to Cinderella, is a wooden rod about a foot long with a tapered tip, usually with a disk near one end to give it stability, so that it looks remarkably like a man's genitals. Dangling in the air next to the old woman's thigh, it bobs up and down merrily, just as the Princess said.

"How do you do that? Let me try," she demands, stretching out her hand the way Snow White reaches for the apple the witch offers her, or Eve plucks one from the tree.

The moment she touches the spindle, she pricks her finger on the hook near the tip that keeps the yarn in line. We can assume that the prick draws blood, which signals transformation in a woman. Bearing in mind the Princess's age, it implies that she's about to have her first menstrual period, which is still known among teenage girls as "the curse."

Or does the prick of the spindle imply the show of blood when a virgin has intercourse? (No one will penetrate a man's body, except with a knife.) This, too, is likely, since the spindle is also a penis. Adolescent girls are bound to reach out sooner or later to grasp their chance of being pricked, no matter how hard their fathers try to prevent it.

The Princess, who will be known as Sleeping Beauty from now on, may be ripe physically, but she's not ripe emotionally for the transformation from girlhood to womanhood. Her spirit isn't strong enough yet for sexual desire, repulsion, motherhood, risk, ambiguity, guilt. Never to be entirely right in what she does when awake, and never to be entirely forgiven.

Maybe the best part of her life is over, she thinks to herself. Or maybe it's just dawning, and she won't know how to handle it. Choices loom before her: In Sleeping Beauty's era, her father the King will pick a husband for her. In our time, she has to pick for herself, bearing the burden of self-doubt and reproach if she's wrong, but getting no credit if she's right, which is considered her undeserved good luck. Either way, one choice precludes all others. Her future shrinks from four dimensions to three: The comforting area of possibility will be eliminated.

But a new life waits for her. A baby, babies, someone who will love her better than anyone else in the world. She will become Queen in her own household.

Conceiving a child means "Your Death has entered into you," Cotton Mather wrote in 1710, soon after Perrault's story "The Sleeping Beauty in the Wood" was published. He had reason to know, since two of his three wives died in their prime, and nine of his fifteen offspring died in childhood, with only one surviving him.

At the time that the story was written, two mothers died for every hundred childbirths, and it was not unusual for a woman to go through childbirth ten times or more. (George Washington's sister bore eleven children of her own, and was stepmother to three whom her husband fathered by his first wife. The mother of the birth-control advocate Margaret Sanger had eighteen pregnancies, seven of which were miscarriages, and died at the age of forty-nine.) Those mothers who escaped death themselves and survived the pain of lengthy labors without anesthetic and cesarean sections, and without forceps deliveries until the second half of the eighteenth century, still didn't escape grief. In Crulai, Normandy, around the time that "Sleeping Beauty" was written, one child out of four died before reaching its first birthday. Half died before the age of ten. Until the twentieth century in Europe and America, it was a rare woman who did not lose at least one child in its early years.

Physical terrors change from one century to the next. Childbed fever and infant mortality are replaced by syphilis, which is replaced by AIDS and an increased rate of babies who survive with major birth defects. But emotional risks remain constant: Incompatible husbands, brutal husbands, lack of husbands. Money troubles. No chance of escape from sorrow. Responsibility for the lives of others.

The Princess isn't strong enough to face transformation yet. But she can't resist or avoid it, either. She isn't who she was before her finger was pricked. Down she falls, onto the bed that the old spinster keeps so conveniently close at hand, as if expecting her.

And when she falls asleep, every creature in the castle sleeps with her: not only the maids of honor and guards with muskets on their shoulders but the horses in the stable, the flies on the walls, her pet spaniel stretched out on the foot of her bed. The spit in the fireplace no longer turns the fowls for dinner, the fowls stop crackling as the fire dies down, and the cook, who was chasing the kitchen boy to hit him with a ladle a minute ago, snores near the stove with the ladle in her hand.

THIS IS EVERY GIRL'S DREAM: to fall asleep at the beginning of adolescence, when life becomes perplexing, and skip the whole rigmarole of dating and spurning and yearning and guarding herself, which can lead to disaster. When she's ready, she'll wake as a woman, her problems resolved and the perfect man leaning over the bed.

Before the sleeper has drawn a dozen breaths, the bushes and brambles have grown so thick around the castle that not even a rabbit can work his way through them. She dreams; she stirs; perhaps she cries out in her sleep. But no one is awake to hear her and hinder the work going on.

CHAPTER 6

Sleeping Beauty:
. . . Waking as a Woman

**"Sleeping Beauty," "Talia,"
"Daphne and Apollo," *The Kiss,*
the True Story of Florence Nightingale**

Sleep and time pull us along, free us from decisions and consequences, make escape possible when we need one, and provide a vehicle for transformation, not only in adolescence but from that time on. This is true for both sexes, but it's especially significant for women, which is why "Sleeping Beauty" is written about a Princess rather than a Prince.

But sleep can also seduce and seriously harm us if we choose to leave the real and problematic world behind indefinitely, in exchange for a world of our own creation.

DURING PUBERTY, sleep is the refuge in which an adolescent girl can absorb the new sense of herself that she gains from the prick of the spindle, and changes from girl to woman: a transformation more radical than that from boy to man. While a teenage boy grows stronger and more forceful in his demands from adolescence on, he remains basically the same person he always was, only more so. He may have qualms about his sexual performance while he's still inexperienced, but sex in general seems like a splendid new outlet for the energy stored in his revved-up body.

A girl, on the other hand, is transformed into a person-producing-person, which is a profound difference in kind rather than degree. This explains why a middle-aged man can double back in his tracks and act like a boy again while he watches a football game on television and howls instructions to the players, or urinates in the bushes and admires the arc he makes, but a woman never fools herself that she can undo her womanhood to turn back into the girl she used to be. For her, life runs in one direction only.

Younger than a boy when she reaches puberty, her experience is more traumatic. She is confronted by a sight that would shock any male: blood flowing where there is no wound, which teaches her that sexuality is beyond her control and costs her something dear. Suddenly her appearance, clothes, and behavior are the target of other girls' malicious comments (Cinderella and her stepsisters). Her body is the object of male desire and, beyond that, of pursuit and rape (Daphne and Apollo). She is more beautiful than her mother (Snow White), so beautiful that she may at any moment be snatched away from home by a stranger (Persephone). If, at this point, she becomes a stranger to her parents, remote and critical, while her schoolwork plummets, that's because she can no longer see any future that fits her. She does not want to be a mother, and yet, usually without knowing it, she is determined to have a baby. She does not want to be a sex object pinned down in the backseat of a car, but she does not want to be left at home, either. The only thing worse than getting married, she sees all too clearly, is not getting married.

Transformation is her only hope for coherence in a situation tainted by irony. The teenage girl finds herself at the peak of her value in society's eyes long before she develops a sense of self powerful enough to match her body. In this field alone of all fields, youth and inexperience command a premium. A recent college graduate doesn't expect to start out as president of the company in his or her first job; a young man bedding his first woman worries whether his performance is up to par; but a young virgin begins her erotic career at the top, at least in terms of market value, and goes downhill from there. At fourteen, she's interesting; at fifteen, a tempting nymphet with hips not much wider than her waist; at eighteen, wildly desirable. But let another fifteen or twenty years pass and no matter how sophisticated she may have become in bed, she'll be no more than another anxious seller on a market overcrowded with fresh goods.

A peak is an uncomfortable place to rest. Just when the girl is most valued, she's also most vulnerable. She's natural prey to the outside world and to her own feelings, coping with situations for which no school exists, with no time to gain experience (the way she'll go through training programs in her professional life later on); no mentors, no trial runs or room for mistakes, nothing but a sense of potential for either happiness or disaster, which will shape the remainder of her life.

What she needs is time in which to ripen. Sleeping Beauty and Snow White retreat from the world in sleep the way Cinderella hides in rags. In real life, a teenage girl does both, switching modes from one day to the next.

A NEWLY FORCEFUL MALE, a freshly desirable female: This unstable combination is commonplace in the real world, but at the same time it's a narrative about the way in which all women are overcome at times by situations we can neither fight against nor flee. Like animals, our only other choice is to take cover. Freeze in place.

Daphne, the heroine of the best of many myths on this subject, was a virgin huntress in love with woods and wild animals but scornful of men. She begged her father, a minor river god, to let her stay perpetually husbandless, but, as Ovid puts it, her beauty spoke against her prayer. One day, while she was out hunting, she had the bad luck to catch the eye of the god Apollo, who instantly desired her with the passion that only a god can feel, and that even a god feels only for his first love. Daphne ran away, her long hair streaming over her shoulders. (What would that hair look like if properly combed? the god wondered.) Apollo followed, calling out that he was no enemy; nor was he a peasant boy stinking like his cattle. He was the lord of Delphi himself, the son of Jove; he could foresee the future, he was the inventor of the lyre and song. He was a god who longed to be her bridegroom.

Instead of slowing down, she ran faster, but no mortal can outrace a god in heat. With Apollo's breath on her shoulders, Daphne called out to her father with the last of her strength, if there was any power left in slow-moving rivers, to rid her of the body that was causing her so much pain. As she spoke, her legs grew stiff and numb, her breasts felt rough as bark, her hair rustled in the wind like leaves. Her feet, which had moved so swiftly a few minutes ago, dug into the earth and took root.

When the god clasped her, he could feel her heart still pounding beneath the bark of what had been transformed into a laurel tree (still called *Daphne* under its botanical name), which he declared his sacred tree, to be used for the wreaths of victors in their triumphs.

In desperation, a woman can withdraw from life and slide down the scale of consciousness into a creature lower than herself who suffers proportionately less: A laurel tree. A fountain. A sleeper. She doesn't escape as she was, but she survives. At least her essential core survives: the part of her that chooses to say "no." As a tree, Daphne stays rooted in one spot and goes on bearing leaves and flowers year after year (victory wreaths for mortal men), which isn't what she was born for. But she remains intact.

She wasn't the last woman to turn herself into a stick of wood in a man's arms.

A SECOND DAPHNE STORY, this time in modern form: Another beautiful young woman—from real life this time, an author named Kathryn Harrison, who tells her story in her memoir, *The Kiss*—struggled against an overwhelming father-god, or, to be literal, a father who was a minister, a "man of God," as he said.

Her parents married when they were seventeen, with her mother already pregnant, and parted six months after their daughter's birth, leaving Kathryn and her mother to live with her grandparents. All she knew of her father was that he was something missing, like the holes her grandmother snipped out of the family photographs with her manicure scissors to remove his unwanted face. When she was six, her mother moved out of the house, leaving her daughter behind in the same way that she left a closet full of designer dresses hanging bodiless in the closet, along with shoes in fifteen different colors. Although the child had two parents living, she was parentless.

Not until the week of her twentieth birthday did Kathryn—who had developed into a perfect California nymph by that time, with hair that fell below her hips and soulful eyes—finally get to know her banished father, who flew west for a visit. When it was time for him to leave, she drove him to the airport.

In the terminal, her father kissed her goodbye. It was not a father's kiss. Pressing his hand behind her head, he pushed his tongue inside her mouth, oversized like the rest of him. She turned numb, as if stung by an asp.

As soon as she was back at college, his phone calls and letters flooded her every day. "Is it possible for a man to love any woman as much as I do you?" he wrote. Ravenous for love all her life, Kathryn was now gorged with it. Like Apollo in pursuit of Daphne, her father called out his credentials in his letters: "I gave you whatever life you have. My heart pumps in your chest, my blood in your veins. I have as much right to you as any other man, and more than you have to yourself." Lord of Delphi, he pronounced himself, son of Jove, inventor of music and healing. "I will define what it is to be a father, and I will teach you what it means to be a woman," he said.

She took drugs. She thought of killing herself by putting his pistol into her mouth. Like Daphne, she wanted to be rid of the body that was causing her so much pain. When the phone rang in her college room, she knew right away who it was, but she answered anyway. Exhaustion made her eyes burn. She mustn't lie down or even sit down, or she'd fall asleep at the sound of his voice. She bit the skin on the back of her hands to keep herself awake; she tore shreds from her cuticles and poked pencils under her fingernails, but nothing kept her upright. When her housemates came in an hour later, they stepped over her body as she lay asleep on the floor, the phone in her hand still bleating, "If you'd like to make a call, please hang up and try again. If you need help, hang up and dial your operator. If you'd like to make a call . . ."

And yet, obscurely, sleep was on her side, protecting her inner self. While her father had the power to touch her body as he chose, he couldn't penetrate her soul, which withdrew in distress, leaving him enraged by her silence, her stupor.

At last he delivered an ultimatum: either/or. Either choose him or the rest of the world. She chose the world.

AT THEIR CORE, these stories deal with more than the obvious sexuality of a godlike male overpowering a resistant female. The essential element is the sleep that assails all of us—old as well as young, male and female—when we are violated by certain conditions, ultimately by death, and seek transformation at a darker level until we are strong enough to bear it.

We have all had such experiences. In my own case, the pursuing god overtook me while I slept.

When the phone rang a few minutes before seven in the morning, I was in bed in my suburban home, not with my husband in his hospital room in the city. I knew what I would hear before I lifted the receiver. If the call had come in the middle of the night, it would have meant that my husband was still alive and asking for me, but this way I could imagine the doctor—someone—saying hours ago why not let her get a night's rest, what can she do about it anyway? Seven is early enough to catch her before she leaves the house.

No one told me to stay in the hospital with my husband that night in December. No one called me to put down the book I was reading in bed and drive to the city. If he was still awake at half past three in the morning (I read the time on the death certificate later on) and if he woke up, coughed, cried out for me, left a message for me, didn't leave a message because he was drowning from the fluid that had filled his lungs, I knew nothing about it. I blinked and the moment was gone. There is no such thing, no such time, as dying. There is life. And there is death.

While the doctor was telling me what had happened, I did the single thing I would have sworn I'd never do. I fell asleep. I don't mean I fainted. I know the difference perfectly well. I remember an instant in which my left ear ached for the pillow, and I told myself it was all right, no one would ever find out how much time had passed since the doctor called me. What did it matter how long I slept? For three and a half hours already, I hadn't been the wife I thought I was. There was another word for me now.

Two years passed before I woke up, and when I did, I found that I spoke in another voice.

MY HUSBAND'S DEATH was not the only occasion in my life; nor am I the only person who craved the relief of the sleep-thorn from too strong a barrage of reality. If Peter could not stay awake through one night on Gethsemane, how can we expect so much more of ourselves?

Sleep—with eyes open and senses more or less functioning as we go about our daily routines—sleep that lulls the pregnant woman and the nursing mother into the healthy animality necessary to foster new life, is an elemental force that puts body and mind into a proper balance. But like every elemental force, it has negative aspects as well as positive. It's a temptation for those with little willpower who crave escape from the pains of the world. It's also a temptation for those with so much willpower that they think they can create a world that suits them better.

Emotional numbness. Drug addiction. Alcoholism. Depression. If we accept sleep as any means of remaining alive without being present, these must be recognized as a few of its forms.

Narcotics and alcohol, which are more popular among men than they are among women, have been used by every society since civilization began. With depression, on the other hand, the reported incidence is twice as high among women as men—perhaps because women are more apt to acknowledge their painful feelings and seek professional help. Most sufferers sleep for an unreasonable number of hours at night and take naps during the afternoon, while a minority complain about the opposite: They can't sleep when they go to bed at night because of the futility of the day now closed behind them, well aware that their insomnia will leave them exhausted and useless the following day. They are desperate for the oblivion of sleep, the way alcoholics are desperate for liquor.

During the Victorian era there was a tremendous vogue, particularly in England, for hysteria, which encompassed all sorts of mental and physical paralyses or vacancies that removed the patient from the ordinary world: trances, amnesia, sleepwalking, emotional outbursts, a sensation of choking, hysterical blindness or deafness, loss of voice or speech. So common was this syndrome among young women in well-to-do families that it was known as "the daughters' disease," an exaggeration of the frailty considered normal—in fact, desirably feminine—in young women who had been properly brought up. (The word itself derives from the Greek word *hysterikós,* or "womb." Since the condition began at puberty and ended at menopause, it was attributed by the ancients to a "wandering womb.") In the nineteenth century, doctors classified it as a neurological disease, the cutting edge of medicine at the time, which became the testing ground for psychoanalysis under Sigmund Freud and Josef Breuer.

Today we recognize hysteria as a product of Victorian repression. Sufferers were sexually frustrated young women, but in broader terms they were frustrated in their craving for higher education, independence, and work in the outside world, work as significant as what their brothers did. The most energetic and aspiring women, the best and brightest, were apt to be those struck down by the sleep-thorn.

Florence Nightingale, for instance, was an English beauty from a well-to-do family who slept for almost a third of a century and then awakened, but on her own terms. When she was seventeen, this young lady heard the voice of God: "On February 7th, 1837, God spoke to me and called me to His service," she wrote in a private note. The trouble was that He gave no hint as to what sort of service He wanted from her.

After a biblical gap of seven years, Florence discovered for herself that her destiny must be in hospitals, caring for the sick, but first she must be trained for the mission. She dared not even mention the idea to her parents. Her mother was pressing for a brilliant match for this daughter who had plenty of suitors, but of all possible vocations, nursing was the furthest beyond the pale, a profession given over in England at that time almost entirely to drunks and prostitutes. She might as well have said she wanted to find work in the red-light district.

Cooped up at home like a dutiful daughter for another seven years and deprived of any hope of using her talents, Florence turned her fury inward and succumbed to sleep. She fell into trances at dinner parties, she blotted out hours, she moved like a robot and could not remember what had been said or where she had been. "I have no desire but to die," she wrote when she was thirty. "There is not a night that I do not lie down on my bed, wishing that I may leave it no more."

Meanwhile, she was courted for years by Richard Monckton Milnes, a cultured artistocrat who introduced the poetry of Keats to the British public. This future peer was sociable; he liked to entertain, particularly at breakfast parties. ("What would happen if Jesus Christ were to return to earth?" Thomas Carlyle was asked, to which he replied, "Monckton Milnes would invite him to breakfast.") Unable to shrink her ambitions to the scale of a hostess on a lordly estate, Florence turned him down.

And yet she didn't. Not quite. Two years later, when she saw him again at a party, he barely spoke to her, which shocked her. In this case, it was the lack of the kiss from a Prince who she assumed was still longing for her that awakened her to her true nature. A few months later, she found the courage to break with her family at last—they called her heartless—go to the Continent for professional training, and enter her first job at the age of thirty-three.

During the following years, this fainting, melancholy woman single-handedly reformed the barbaric military hospitals in Turkey and the Crimea, often working twenty hours without relief, not simply at nursing, which gratified her, but in battles with the bureaucracy that kept army blankets and food stashed in warehouses while nine thousand of her "boys" died of starvation, exposure, cholera, and dysentery. After the war, she went on working fifteen hours a day or more, reforming hospitals in England and later in India, then moving on to public-health reform, while setting up the first training school for nurses and establishing nursing as a skilled profession.

Does this mean that she found herself healthy and fulfilled after her awakening? Not at all. She was often sick and always filled with fury and self-reproach over problems left unsolved, but she was wide awake to both the triumphs and defeats of her life.

She remained a conscious human being, who died at the age of ninety, still single.

PATHOLOGICAL SLEEP—eyes open or shut—changes its forms, oddly enough, like women's fashions, always mimicking the feminine ideal of the times. Hysteria, which was so common from roughly 1870 until World War I, died out in developed countries after the war, like a dress that had been worn to parties once too often, although in the less sophisticated countries of southern Europe it remained a problem as recently as 1970.

Psychosomatic illness serves its own ends. The paralyses and trances of hysteria made it impossible for the so-called daughter of the house to carry out her "womanly duties" in kitchen, parlor, or sickroom, caring for others with the attitude of cheerful self-sacrifice that was expected of her. It was the ailment of a girl or woman with a body beyond her control. So long as she suffered, she was safe from the prison that people call real life.

In our era, the identical role is played by eating disorders, including anorexia (willful excessive thinness), bulimia (finger-down-the-throat vomiting and strong laxatives to purge the body of food), and binge-eating. Of the three, anorexia, though statistically the least common, gains the most attention and secret admiration. More than nine out of ten anorexics and bulimics are female, almost all of whom develop the symptoms between the ages of twelve and twenty-five, the Sleeping Beauty age.

Like her Victorian predecessor, the anorexic is often the most gifted of her peers, but her ailment reverses the symptoms: Instead of inhabiting a body that is out of control, she turns herself into a tyrant who regiments her body and its cravings, lashing it to the brink of death. As spectacular in her thinness as a Russian wolfhound, self-disciplined as a prime athlete (many female athletes are, in fact, anorexic), prouder of her body than a fashion model, and yet harsher to it than the saints, this child-woman tends to be the superachiever in our overachieving society, the embodiment of willpower. Will is what's required to starve in the midst of plenty.

At the same time, she delights in coming up with recipes and serving elaborate meals for the family that she herself won't touch. The fatter they grow, the thinner and more austere she seems.

"Thin?" a teenager thinks when her mother gives her a size-six dress for her fifteenth birthday with exquisite calculation, at a time when the girl wears size ten. "You want thin? I'll give you thin. But on my terms." She goes from size ten to six, but she doesn't stop there. By starving herself, she goes to four, then two; she becomes so thin that not only her bones but her veins protrude. She no longer menstruates. "When I looked in the mirror and counted my ribs, I thought I was beautiful," the young woman says now. "Those knobs in my skeleton made me feel holy, like counting a rosary. I was pure. In the past I'd been a failure, but now I'd triumphed. I was no longer human."

As long as she fasts, the anorexic has the body of a child who has not experienced the bloody mess of periods yet, a body cleaner than a grown woman ought to have. Her thighs and breasts shrink to nothing; her belly is too flat to hold a baby. She wills herself to stay asleep to bodily needs, like a woman who refuses to wake up when her baby cries, and yet she thinks of nothing else. If she persists long enough, she suffers bone loss and possible brain loss that can never be reversed.

When a girl rejects food to the extent that she stops menstruating, she rejects her mother, since the mother always represents food, but at the same time she stifles the potential mother inside herself, which is precisely her aim. She cannot become pregnant. By force of will, she transforms downward to an earlier level of existence—a child again, whose mind and feelings refuse to hear the messages sent by her body. In the same way, the alcoholic, the drug addict, and the depressive lack the willpower to face the changes inherent in growth, so they insulate themselves by means of sleep that degenerates into stupor. They choose unconsciousness, rather than periods of wakefulness interrupted by the subconscious work of sleep.

FAIRY TALES ARE KIND TO US. They explain the lassitude that overcomes so many of us during part of our lives in terms of a curse laid on a newborn babe, to be brought into effect years later by a Spinning Woman who holds out the promise of a reawakening to come. We no longer believe in spinning women or thirteenth fairies, except as forces inside our heads. But neither do we examine our lives to see whether part of ourselves has lain dormant for years—lulled in a silken bed in a golden room—a part we never knew existed until circumstances changed and roused it to action. The awakening may have nothing to do with a Prince. Or he may be no more than a bit player.

In a seventeenth-century Neapolitan Sleeping Beauty story by Giambattista Basile, written sixty years before the familiar Perrault version, a King summons his wise men to predict the future of his newborn daughter, Talia, and is appalled to learn that her life will be endangered by a splinter in a piece of flax. Naturally enough, he bans flax from the palace. Equally naturally, when Talia has grown into a "beauteous damsel," she looks out her window and sees a woman spinning for the first time and reaches for the yarn. A piece of flax lodges under her fingernail, and she falls to the ground. At that, her father seats her apparently lifeless body on a velvet throne, closes the doors of the palace, and abandons his daughter forever. (Fathers leave the scene once their rules are broken.)

In due time, a King who is hunting in the forest happens upon the mysteriously silent palace, climbs in one of the windows, finds the beautiful sleeper (his blood is running hot in his veins), and does exactly what we would expect him to do: He carries Talia to the nearest bed and rapes her, after which he departs for his own kingdom, "where, in the pressing business of his realm, he for a time thought no more of this incident." Nine months later, Talia, still sleeping, gives birth to a pair of twins. Sex with the King doesn't wake her, much less a kiss. Neither does childbirth. She doesn't open her eyes until one of the infants, in the course of rooting around for her breast, sucks on her finger instead, pulling out the splinter embedded there, just as Snow White is jolted back to life when she coughs up the chunk of apple that was stuck in her throat.

With her eyes open, Talia holds the infants—whom she names Sun and Moon—to her breast and suckles them, "and the babes were dearer to her than her own life." Some time later, the King remembers his former exploit, returns to the palace, and finds Talia taking care of the children. They talk, and in the course of the visit, according to a nineteenth-century translation, the two of them form "a great league and friendship."

We wake when we are needed. We wake when we are sure that we are doing what has to be done. We come to life when we are confronted by a new stage of life and new sensations, stronger than those we have known—fear or anger as well as love, but none stronger than a baby tugging at our nipples, which squeezes the uterus, with greed and love beyond anything we could have imagined.

Talia goes to sleep as a maiden entranced by a spindle, and wakes as a mother. Her mind and emotions have caught up with her body.

Or the transformation may work the other way around. The woman who gives birth when she has not yet grown up may fall asleep from the shock and find herself in a dream world in which she is forever a teenager, disconcerted to hear herself called "Mother." In fairy-tale terms, she has been transformed down the scale of being into a white duck swimming in a river, hoping to find her husband's castle (more about this in Chapter Eleven). For every story there exists a counterstory.

A HUNDRED YEARS PASS while Sleeping Beauty sleeps. After this time, a strange Prince arrives in the kingdom and hears a rumor from a grandfather, who heard it from his grandfather: In the castle whose towers are visible over the treetops lies the most beautiful Princess ever born, sleeping behind a hedge of thorns, and all her court sleeps with her. So great is his desire to see this beauty, and so perfect his courage (of course) that he ignores the warnings that the Princes who preceded him are now skeletons rattling among the branches.

But there are signs that the season has changed. On this last day of the hundredth year, the hedge has burst into bloom. When the final and timely Prince arrives, "the branches part like thighs," as the author Robert Coover puts it. Flower petals brush against his cheeks. A current of springtime apparently runs from the hedge to the bedroom, where the Princess stirs in her bed but doesn't waken.

"What a little surprised him, was, that he saw none of his people could follow him, because the trees closed again, as soon as he had passed through them," Perrault adds. (A curious analogy may have been at the back of the storyteller's mind while he wrote this sentence. With the help of that elegant new tool, the microscope, two Dutch scientists had just discovered multitudes of "animalcules" in semen, all of them racing toward the relatively huge and motionless egg. As soon as one lusty animalcule pierced the egg's membrane, it closed behind him and "did not allow another worm to enter," one of the scientists wrote in an essay published in Paris in 1694, a year before the manuscript of "Sleeping Beauty" was completed.)

The valiant and amorous Prince forges ahead. In the courtyard he finds pigeons sleeping in the gutters and flies motionless on the walls. A kitchen maid lies in the poultry yard with an axe in her hand, felled in the act of chasing a goose for dinner, while the goose lies thirty yards ahead of her, sound asleep, its beak open in alarm.

Through the halls of the palace the Prince strides, past slumbering courtiers and ladies-in-waiting dressed in antique costumes, until he finds a gilded bedroom in which a Princess lies on satin sheets, halfway between sleep and waking.

"Is it you, my Prince?" the Princess says as she opens her eyes. "You have kept me waiting a long time." "My Prince," she calls this man who has kept her waiting, even though she has never set eyes on him before.

This is how we know that two young people are experiencing true love: no astonishment at meeting, quite the reverse, a lucid conviction on the heroine's part that this is the man she has been waiting for without realizing it. They must have known one another for a long time—in another life, perhaps. The only surprise is that it took so many years and such vexing dreams before she reaches the moment that changes everything that preceded it.

The distinguishing mark of a passionate marriage (which isn't always, or necessarily, happy) is that the Prince and Princess could never imagine being married to anyone else. They waited too long for what they got.

WHAT HAPPENS NEXT—THE KISS? Not in the original French version. Perrault was too tactful a courtier to permit such intimacy between two young people newly met. Instead, they chat decorously for four hours (the Princess has more to say than the Prince, since she has had so much time to think), after which the Lord Almoner marries the couple in the castle chapel.

This leaves us with our original question: Which is the agent of transformation—the right man or the right time? If the King's son fails to appear at the end of a hundred years, does that mean that the sleeper, or at least her sexuality, will never be aroused?

In keeping with the cult of the individual in our culture, we believe that a woman's story depends on the arrival of the chosen lover who can slip through her defenses as easily as through the flowering shrubs. But what happens if he shows up too soon, before the heroine is fully awake?

Never in history have women had a longer stretch of unscheduled time to fill between the onset of sexual maturity and the inevitable end of their fertility, a gap they can spend in dreams. In the United States today, breast buds, which are considered the first sign of puberty, appear when white girls are less than ten years old on average, and black girls not quite nine.

For these child-women, the spindle prick is as great a shock as ever. A girl I know (am I supposed to call her a woman?) got her first period recently, a month after her eleventh birthday. When she told her best friend the news, the two of them found a box big enough to crawl into, which they furnished with crib blankets and all the stuffed animals they could lay their hands on. There they spent the afternoon, reading her baby sister's picture books to each other in their improvised crib.

At the other end of the time scale, a woman can wait until she is in her forties to bear her first child, so a quarter of a century may slide by while she dozes, daydreams, spins her way through possibilities, suffers from nightmares, wakes with a start, falls asleep again, always waiting for a clear-cut signal. From her twenties on, she wants to be married, or, more specifically, she wants a wedding. She wants to walk down the aisle on her father's arm in a cloud of white tulle, but that's not the same as wanting a specific man for her husband. (Her best friend has been married for years already.) She wants to escape from her low-paying job and her studio apartment. Beyond that, she doesn't know what she wants, and so the man she's with tonight, who's amiable enough and a good provider, might as well be the one, and when she has a new name she'll be somebody else. She'll start life all over again.

Off she goes into marriage, still half asleep, though she may not be as lucky as Talia; she may not wake up when a baby sucks at her breast. Ten years could pass before she opens her eyes one morning in the kitchen at breakfast to see a man pouring coffee from the coffeemaker, and wonders where he came from (not that there's anything particularly wrong with him) and asks herself whatever made her decide to pick this one. If she decided, that is. She can't remember making a decision, though she remembers buying the coffeemaker. Has she been asleep all these years and only now awakened for a minute of consciousness? Or is it the other way around, and this moment is a dream that she'll shrug off as soon as she finishes her breakfast?

There's another possibility: Suppose Sleeping Beauty opens her eyes, more than rested after her hundred-year nap, but there's no Prince in sight? We know too well what happens next. She looks around the palace, where the courtiers and servants and animals are not only awake but churning away at their business while wondering what on earth is the matter with this girl, why doesn't she set them free by bringing the story to an end? Glumly, she blames herself for the wasted years. She concludes that there are no Princes to be found in the kingdom anymore. There used to be plenty when she was a girl, or so she thought, but now there's a shortage of heterosexual, decent, responsible single men who are mature enough to become Kings in their own right.

Men don't want to be fathers or even husbands these days, she tells herself, they want to be the oldest child in the house (although that's at least better than being the family tyrant). It's possible, she reflects, that in our society women are more mature than men, because by nature they are bound to the spiral of generations: They want to become mothers even more than they want to become wives, and they want homes to cherish that will surround them faithfully after their children have gone—while men are unattached to anything beyond themselves. Men suffer from the auto-intoxication of freedom, which they consider a treasure not to be handed over lightly, with the same fearful determination with which women once hung on to their chastity.

THE FAIRY TALE of Sleeping Beauty leads the stunned maiden as far as marriage and motherhood, which are assumed to be her goals, but we can see the story as a metaphor for whatever vision is needed to rouse us—specifically, to rouse the part of us that has remained untouched and virginal at any age.

Once the heroine outgrows her anxiety about the next stage of her life, she opens her eyes and welcomes the world in terms of somebody or something other than the parents and home that used to be hers. If she falls asleep while threatened by pressure toward marriage and domesticity, or (more likely nowadays) if she becomes paralyzed by the fear that she'll never get that far, she may wake up once she's over thirty and past that shoal. She may choose a Princess as partner instead of a Prince. She may choose the career that she longs for, as Florence Nightingale did.

Or she may have the opposite reaction, like Charlotte Brontë. Living alone in a country parsonage with her irascible father, the thirty-seven-year-old author was startled one day by an explosive declaration of love from her father's curate, a generally dull but dependable man whom she had considered unfeeling. Her father objected vigorously. "Father, I am not a young girl," Charlotte argued, "nor a young woman, even—I never was pretty. I now am ugly." Well aware that her parish duties as a wife would swallow her career as a writer, she married the curate, over her father's repeated objections. Less than nine months later, she died—pregnant—having conceived a child but failed to write another chapter of her new novel, *Emma.* Like Brunhilde, when she woke up she gave up her maiden glory "to wed as women wed."

After her death, her husband faithfully took care of Mr. Brontë until the end of his life, while the old man sat in the parsonage and snipped bits from his famous daughter's letters to send to souvenir hunters.

In fact, during every transformation in a woman's life there's the possibility of feeling the prick of the sleep-thorn and dropping into sleep. But there's also the possibility of going to sleep as one self and waking as another, finding it hard to believe that there's any continuity between the two. When we look back at a former self, we think of a dear, naïve, nearly forgotten friend who thought that her problems, like her pleasures, were fixed in place, but there's no way we can reach her from the side of the hedge that closed behind us after we passed through it.

FOR TWO YEARS AFTER my husband's death, I slept, which wasn't an easy feat. To stay asleep, I had to concoct a dream: My husband wasn't dead; that was a misunderstanding. He was away on a long business trip. (As proof, his bathrobe was hanging untouched in our bedroom closet with Kleenex still in the pocket.) Better yet, I dreamed that he was the captain of a whaling ship in the nineteenth century, circling the globe for two years, maybe three, depending on the hunt. There were plenty of wives in Nantucket and Cape Cod, after all, who had paced the fenced-in widow's walks on the roof of their houses, looking out to sea, at the same time that they raised children and kept house and managed budgets and even earned money, so why couldn't I do the same?

But sleep doesn't last forever. Eventually a voice said to me wake up, get moving, you've had enough rest, and time is finite. I discovered professional work I could do, starting as a beginner all over again, less experienced than my grown-up children and apprehensive about my lack of training, but no longer asleep.

Of all the transformations in a woman's life, the thorniest is the journey from "we" to "I."

THE TRUTH IS THAT we have no idea why we wake when we do. Call it an inner migration from the Underworld to the upperworld, brought about by some seasonal change in the light.

At any age, if we get a taste of who we are, if we fall in love with life in whatever form we find it and choose to embrace it, we can fairly call that moment "the Prince's kiss."

CHAPTER 7

Sleeping Beauty, American Style

How Walt Disney Changed the Meaning

How sure we are that "Sleeping Beauty" has to end the way we want it to end: a royal wedding in the castle chapel, followed by a dance that goes on until morning because, not surprisingly, no one in the palace feels the need for sleep. Nothing need be added except the assurance that the young couple's happiness will last forever after.

But that's not the way things work out in the classic versions of the tale. In Perrault's seventeenth-century account, the Prince ungallantly leaves Sleeping Beauty the morning after the wedding in order to return alone to his own kingdom. There he keeps his visits to his bride secret for two years, during which time she bears two children and he inherits the throne. He has good reason, it seems, for secrecy: His mother is descended from a line of ogres and has ogreish tastes of her own, so when her son finally makes his marriage public she resorts to that standby remedy of jealous fairy-tale Queens: cannibalism. The chief cook is ordered to kill her grandchildren one at a time and serve them to her with an oniony, vinegary sauce Robert, but the cook, like the huntsman in "Snow White," substitutes young animals. The royal husband returns from war just in time to save his wife and children, while the old Queen perishes in a suitably dreadful manner.

The Grimm brothers, usually so fond of grisly crimes and punishments, omit this postscript altogether, and modern adapters have followed their example, with one exception. Walt Disney, relying on his instincts (as far as we know, he read none of the old tale-tellers except the Grimms), puts the wicked female at the center of the story, not as a dispossessed Queen-mother, or as a magical Spinning Woman, ushering the heroine into puberty through her spindle, but as the bad fairy Maleficent, the Mistress of All Evil. By doing that, he changes the fairy tale into a duel between the witch (who turns herself into a dragon) and the hero for possession of the heroine. Solitude and stillness, those ancient retreats of heroines, are regarded as a curse that the fairy laid on an innocent baby. Masculine action is required to interrupt the silence and save the day.

In 1959, when Disney's *Sleeping Beauty* film was released, the Cold War was at its height. The time was right for a dragon-slayer in our midst, but the period also marked the end of the American ancien régime, the final years before the sexual upheaval of the 1960s changed our ideas of gender and virtue. In Disney movies, at least, social change was suspended as effectively as a sleeping Princess. The heroine had to be young, desirable, and ignorant of everyone and everything but the hero.

Like *Snow White and the Seven Dwarfs* a generation earlier, this movie introduces the hero in the first reel, in this case as a little boy at the christening scene, when his father and the Princess's father betroth their children to each other to join their kingdoms through marriage.

But an arranged marriage is out of the question in a twentieth-century American movie. To satisfy our romantic standards, the boy and girl must be reared apart and meet by accident when the Princess is almost sixteen, falling in love contrary to their parents' wishes, or so they think, while really fulfilling the parental plans.

In Disney's *Sleeping Beauty*, the love story is only the background for the major theme, however, which is the conflict of good against evil—evil in monstrous female form, preying on the helpless, as in the stories of Basile and Perrault—but in Disney's world the heroine's survival depends on a royal hero, not on the kindness of a base-born cook.

Three good fairies are present at the christening. Half the size of adults (like Snow White's dwarfs), they are dumpy, chinless little creatures with wings the size of bumblebees', who bustle and bumble their way through the action. Opposed to them stands the uninvited fairy Maleficent, Mistress of All Evil, robed entirely in black, with wings as widespread as those of the raven perched on her shoulder. Bearing a scepter in her hand, she's as stark a figure as Snow White's stepmother: the same black eyes in a bone-white face; the Joan Crawford mouth, as sensuous as it is predatory.

For the young audience, the message is obvious: "Girls, don't listen to your mothers. They may be good-hearted little dears, but they know nothing about sex and power, which are the forces that rule the world. And so they can't protect you from either."

Maleficent lets loose her curse, to take effect by the Princess's sixteenth birthday. As in the fairy tale, the last of the good fairies mitigates the curse, but her words end on a different note:

> *"Not in death, but just in sleep*
> *The fateful prophecy you'll keep,*
> *And from this slumber you shall wake*
> *When true love's kiss the spell shall break."*

"For true love conquers all," an angelic chorus sings offscreen. Not a word is mentioned about a time limit for the heroine's slumber. The timing of "true love's kiss" depends solely on the hero and how long it takes him to break through the obstacles that confront him.

With the permission of the royal parents, the three good fairies steal away with the infant, whom they call Briar Rose, and raise her in a woodcutter's cottage in the forest, where she serves the same domestic apprenticeship as Snow White and Cinderella. Disney was a poor boy who believed in humble beginnings.

This satisfies another romantic requirement of the modern age: A Prince must not marry a girl who has been brought up as a Princess. She will never make a satisfactory wife unless she has endured hardship—and yet at the level of character and blood she must be a Princess in disguise, unknown even to herself.

On the fateful day of her sixteenth birthday, Disney's heroine goes barefoot into the woods to gather berries, and there she meets her Prince. Like a flame, like the pagan sun hero that he is, Prince Phillip canters onto the scene with his red cloak streaming behind him and his pointed red cap tipped by a quivering red feather. The young couple fall in love while the heroine is still awake.

"I'm sorry, child, you must never see that young man again," one of the good fairies tells Briar Rose as she's brought back to her father's castle to celebrate the end of the day by which the curse was scheduled to take effect.

In the castle she's left alone for a moment, during which time Maleficent materializes in a whirlpool of green fire to lead the girl up a spiral staircase to the top of the tower. Briar Rose follows in a trance. Her eyes stare straight ahead, unblinking; her arms stick out at her sides. She is as tall as Maleficent; she has nothing to do with the pint-size good fairies anymore. As she mounts the stairs, her face turns blue, her golden hair turns green. Her step is a funeral march.

"Touch the spindle," Maleficent commands when they reach the hidden chamber. The ghost girl hesitates. "Touch it, I say!"

But no spindle is present. There is only a phantom spinning wheel conjured by Maleficent's hypnotic spell. In other words, sex exists only in a girl's head. The spindle prick is no longer the generative energy of life that a teenage girl cannot resist reaching out for, as it was in the fairy tale. It has dwindled into a figment of her imagination, not sex but the fantasy of sex, which saps her will. She touches it and sinks down onto the bed that is also her bier.

Just before the guns of the sexual revolution begin to fire, Walt Disney's vision of the feminine ideal climaxes in the images of Sleeping Beauty and Snow White lying motionless, blanched, incapable of feeling sexual desire or even curiosity until a man comes along to rouse them. This prolongs the Victorian ideal that a woman is physically passionless unless stimulated. Unaware of time, the heroine is dead until the hero chooses to say, "Live and be mine."

Sure enough, the drama shifts to the Prince, who is imprisoned in Maleficent's dungeon until the good fairies, who were unable to protect their foster daughter, cut off his shackles with their wands and arm him with the enchanted Shield of Virtue and the mighty Sword of Truth. (Good Mothers know how to empower their sons.) Off he goes to do battle with the witch, who transforms herself into a fire-spouting dragon as tall as a castle.

"Now shall you deal with *me,* O Prince, and all the Powers of *Evil!*" Maleficent cries in Disney fashion. The Prince loses his shield. Desperate, he hurls the sword at the dragon. Evil tumbles to the bottom of the cliff. The girl belongs to the wielder of the sword.

As Phillip enters the castle, which is wrapped in twilight, his scarlet cloak floats upstairs like a torch. He reaches the room where the heroine lies. We know what he does that brings the color back to her face even before she opens her eyes.

THE HERO AND THE DRAGON: the male story in brief. The hero slays the dragon, who usually represents the father holding onto his treasure—except in the oldest texts and the newest, like Disney's inverted world, where the dragon or sea monster is female. (She will appear again as Ursula, the sea witch, in *The Little Mermaid.*) The maiden is freed by the conquering hero. Saint George, Siegfried, Jason, Crocodile Dundee, King Kong (who slays a dinosaur to save the heroine): dragon killers all.

There's nothing wrong with this, except that we have been deprived of the heroine's story, which is obscured by the glare of the hero's victory. For Disney, sleep is death. The chamber at the top of the stairs is a tomb, the young woman a hapless victim, the insulted fairy a fiend. Only a hero can bring the Princess back to life, and life back to her world, but when he does she will be on no higher level than when she fell asleep.

In our culture, we have relinquished the idea of a mysterious energy at work inside us, for which we have to wait. (Disney's Sleeping Beauty apparently sleeps for no more than a day.) We have no notion of a part of ourselves that withdraws when withdrawal is beneficial, like the sap of a tree, and emerges when growth becomes possible. This is particularly a loss for women, whose life moves through biological transformations.

The part of ourselves that we call masculine longs for victory, the other part for transformation. Victory is the easier of the two stories to understand: "Look! There's a dead dragon lying on the ground!" But transformation is what we're after. "Make me someone else," a beauty murmurs in her sleep, meaning make me a wife, make me a maker of other human beings and the human beings they will make in their turn, make me understand the thrust of my life.

What Sleeping Beauty experiences in the Disney version is rescue, not transformation.

CHAPTER 8

Beauties and Beasts:
Borne on the Back of Desire

**"Beauty and the Beast," "East of the
Sun and West of the Moon,"**
Phantom of the Opera, King Kong

When I was a child, I had a fairy-tale book with an illustration in it that sent a flame from the page right through my pelvis and up my spine. It was a picture of a great lumbering white bear with his head lowered, moving slowly, even humbly, as he trudges away from the farms in the background and into the forest with a half-naked girl on his back. I could feel his haunches ripple back and forth beneath the girl's legs in a movement she has never felt before. Her thighs are pressed together on his back. His fur warms her crotch. Everything she owns in the world is tied in a kerchief slung on her hip, and she knows that if she ever returns to this spot, she'll no longer be a girl.

The story that accompanied this picture, "East of the Sun and

West of the Moon," is a Norwegian Beauty-and-Beast tale that begins with a poor husbandman who had so many children that there
wasn't enough food to go around. They were all pretty, but according
to the law of fairy tales the prettiest was the youngest daughter, who
was prettier than anyone could imagine. On a Thursday evening in
autumn, when rain fell in sheets and the wind was so wild that the
walls of the cottage shivered in its blasts, three taps were heard on
the windowpane.

The man went outside to see what could be the matter, and when
he got there, he saw a great White Bear.

"Good evening to you," said the White Bear.

"Good evening," said the man.

"Will you give me your youngest daughter?" said the White Bear.
"If you will, you shall be as rich as you now are poor."

"I must ask my daughter about this," the husbandman replied.

At first the unhappy lass said no, but her father talked her into it,
telling her how well off she would be and her family with her, so that
finally she washed and mended her few rags and made herself ready
for a journey. When the Bear returned to the house a week later, she
climbed up onto his back with her bundle, and off they went.

"Are you afraid?" the White Bear asked.

"No!" she said. Though of course she was.

"Well, hold tight to my shaggy coat, and then there's nothing to
fear," said the Bear as he gathered speed, galloping a long way until
he reached a steep hill with a doorway set into the slope. Behind the
door lay rooms shining with silver and gold, all of them brilliantly lit
in the girl's honor, and a table set with more foods than she knew
names for. There the Bear gave her a silver bell that she need only
ring to have anything she wanted placed at her disposal.

When she finished supper, she was transported to a bedroom,
where a bed was made up with silk pillows edged with golden fringe.
After she blew out the light, a man came in and lay down beside
her. Only he wasn't a man, she discovered later, but the White Bear,

who threw off his beast shape every night to join her and left every morning before daybreak.

IN A MEADOW NEAR THE SEA in Asia Minor, the animal-lover is not a white bear but a bull the color of sea foam, with small horns polished like jewels, and an expression on his muzzle so calm and loving that the Princess Europa stops sporting with her friends to gaze at the creature without suspecting that he may be the god Zeus in disguise. Little by little, she gets over her fear. She holds out her hands. The bull kisses them. His breath smells as sweet as the meadow behind her. She twines flowers around his horns while he hollows the sand with his snowy body. After a while, she dares to climb on his back. She hikes her tunic above her knees. His dewlaps wrinkle as he turns to look at her. He kneels. He rises to his feet and ambles to the water and begins swimming from Asia to Europe, which takes her name, and never turns back.

AMONG BEASTS WHO LUST for a human virgin, the most familiar to us is the one who appears in the classic fairy tale "Beauty and the Beast," written by Madame Leprince de Beaumont, a French governess in the time of Louis XVI, and published in a magazine for teenage girls. In other words, it was aimed at girls who would soon face the prospect of themselves being married off to unknown "beasts," possibly twenty years older than they were, quite possibly sexually demanding or impotent, in matches arranged by their parents.

In this tale, a merchant riding home from town trespasses into the garden of a ferocious Beast, where he plucks a rose as a gift for his youngest (and prettiest) daughter, Beauty. The owner of the castle is about to kill the intruder, but he refrains when the trembling man says the rose was intended for one of his daughters. Instead, the Beast offers to spare the merchant's life if one of the daughters will come in his stead.

Of all the merchant's children, only Beauty volunteers to take her father's place. She sets out for the castle, where she is gently treated and sumptuously entertained by the owner, who loves Beauty from the beginning but doesn't love himself. Beauty learns to value the Beast's kindness, but she cannot consider him as a suitor.

Then Beauty unwittingly endangers the Beast's life. Only when she sees that he is in her power as much as she is in his, and that she may have killed the "monster" who has shown her nothing but devotion, does she realize that she loves him in return and is willing to be his wife. As soon as the Beast feels the warmth of her love, he rejoins human society in the form of a Prince. Two reciprocal transformations take place, his and hers.

The Beauty-and-Beast story surfaces often in modern science fiction and movies, and in romantic fiction almost as often as "Cinderella," which is a simpler story because it doesn't involve choice, only being chosen.

SEX IS WHAT THE Beauty-and-Beast story deals with: sex and bodies that span three levels of creation—gods, animals, and humans, with a human virgin as the Beast's goal. This means that the stories concern fear, desire, disgust, and transformation, as well as the jolt we get whenever another creature penetrates our consciousness.

Oddly enough, in this sex-obsessed society of ours, we have forgotten how to value it. So superficial and promiscuous are we, so determined to drag into the light of day what might thrive better under the bushes, that sex has lost much of its savor. We work out and diet vigorously, in order to stay in good health, and also to attract sex, which we equate with youth and popularity and the evasion of mortality. But what we see in the beautiful bodies paraded in front of our eyes isn't sex but the shadow play of sexiness. This leaves most of us morosely suspecting that we're not getting as much, or as good quality, as we're entitled to, or giving as expertly as others give, especially our younger competitors. Poverty-stricken in a land where everyone else seems to be rich, we dread the further depletion to come.

In its fullest meaning, sex is rarer and rawer than that, more shattering. To be intense, it requires privacy. Intimacy. Seclusion. The opposite of lap-dancing or those reality-television shows set in a rented castle, where the winning female contestant gets a husband as her prize along with a million dollars, while the nation looks on.

In its purest form, sex is the highest energy we know: divine energy, low as the animals and high as the gods, energy that expresses itself only in the language of bodies, since we live in and through our bodies. But we aren't accustomed to energy that cannot stop or be stopped before it has taken its fill. Only while we are being born, pushed from darkness into "the terrible novelty of light," or while we are giving birth to others, or in moments of fullest orgasm, free from the distraction of thought, do we get a sense of how much force comes from a level higher than any we ordinarily deal with, moving through us but not because of our efforts.

In these stories, the heroine is chosen by the Beast at the beginning, before the tale is fully under way. The plot requires her to accept or refuse, to discriminate and waver and thaw, or not. This raises questions that are especially pertinent for our time, when women select mates without guidance, from a pool of acquaintances and then lovers, with no assurance of how they will measure up as husbands, fathers, providers—more than that, companions of the soul.

In modern terms, which male does a woman want as a lover: the hero, who is society's champion, moving from triumph to triumph, or the misfit, the recluse, the seductive and thrilling Beast? She will have to choose between them, because in the contemporary world the two are opposites. Then again, which will she want—or need— as a provider for her children?

While the young woman is making her choice, what makes her so sure that she can distinguish between a surly, misunderstood Beast, whose soul longs for her, and a brute who is determined to extinguish his own cravings in the suffering of others? To complicate the question, it's not unusual for a male to be a brute one day and a repentant Beast the next, who swears that he will reform if she will only stand by him. Or he may be a devoted Beast to one woman but a brute to another. In *Wuthering Heights,* for instance, Heathcliff, an abused orphan of unknown origin, pours his ardor into his love for Catherine; but after Catherine marries their wealthy neighbor he proves a brute to his own wife, Isabella, vowing to turn "her blue eyes black every day or two."

Another issue: Why should a woman suppose that she can find a way to tame the Beast for her own domestic purposes without destroying his solitary grandeur, his kinship to the wilderness—the beasthood that lured her in the first place?

THE BEAUTY-AND-BEAST STORY, which is our chronicle of sex in its hundreds of versions, always follows a simple plot. The Beast-god, or the human who considers himself a Beast, comes out of his hiding place lusting for a female virgin, not any virgin but the particular one he has his eye on. All-powerful in his own realm, he is needy and suffering in ours, locked in a grim picture of himself that isolates him from humanity. His life cannot take on meaning except through the body of a human female.

In myths, the god in the form of a beast sleeps with a virgin in order to perpetuate her race through his outpouring of energy. He may be disguised, like Zeus in the shape of a bull when he carries off Europa. Or he may be dispossessed, like the White Bear, who must be the ghost of the great northern bear-god whose shrines reach back at least seventy-five thousand years to Neanderthal times.

He could be the Master Buffalo who hears a Blackfoot Indian maiden cry out in desperation that she will do anything, even marry a buffalo, if he will lead his herd over the edge of a cliff to their deaths, so that her people need not starve for lack of meat.

He's the Minotaur of Crete, half man and half bull. Or he's a woman-eating serpent.

In modern times, he's often less than a god but more than human: an alien from outer space like Starman, who takes refuge in the body of a young widow's recently dead husband. "I gave you a baby tonight," Starman tells her when it's time for him to leave the planet. That's impossible, she assures him to her sorrow. She's infertile. Starman ignores her protest. "He will be human. He will be the baby of your husband. He will also be my baby. And when he is grown, he will be a Teacher." Together they look for the alien's star in the sky. "Look. *There.*"

He's the Phantom of the Opera, rising from the waters of a lake beneath the Paris Opera House as the Angel of Music, who has been sent to a young singer by her dead father. Born disfigured, the Phantom was locked in his mask by his mother when he was a child.

He's a human being who feels truly at home in the wilderness, like Tarzan of the Apes or the gamekeeper who becomes Lady Chatterley's lover.

Always he's an outsider beyond our laws, half masked or disguised (if only by a scowl), a mysterious dynamo of sex energy. But one thing he's not is a monster. Only to a hero whose dearest wish is to be a monster-slayer does he look like one—even when he's King Kong in the 1933 movie, holding Fay Wray in his fist fifty feet above the ground and delicately flicking off the layers of her dress, as if stripping the petals off a rose. He sniffs the fabric off her skirt, then puts his fingers to his nose. The expression on his face is bemused. What is he supposed to do with such a marvel?

No, he's more familiar to us than that. He's the raw, red, engorged penis sticking straight out of a man's body, pointing at his mate (the man's genital is a spear, the woman's a rose), frightening, compelling, and never quite big enough to suit her, which is the secret she never tells. At the peak of fullest arousal, what she wants isn't pleasure or even conception but an invasion of energy that clamps her tight and wipes out the world around her—demon energy or god energy, whatever it seems to her at the moment, that makes the energy of everyday life seem dim and distractible by comparison.

ON AN EVENING THAT BEGINS like any other, claws rap on a windowpane three times, or a flower is plucked in a garden, and a Beast appears as if summoned. The youngest daughter, more than half in love with her father, need not respond but does. As a result, she leaves home, giving up security and a child's immunity from responsibility in exchange for freedom, risk, adulthood. Until now, the walls of her father's home have served as an exterior hymen of sorts, sealing her off from her future.

Europa doesn't have to climb on the white bull's back just because he lies at her feet on the golden sand.

The heroine of "Beauty and the Beast" could stay home with her scornful sisters rather than take her father's place in the castle. Instead, she heads out the door in the only direction possible for her, which is toward the Beast—toward sex and motherhood, and away from her life as her father's daughter.

The lonely and difficult Beast has the power to crush the heroine whenever he chooses ("devour" is the word she and her sisters will use, the Beast devouring the heroine, which is the female nightmare image of marriage), and no one except her family will notice the loss. But he chooses not to do so. Instead, he keeps the motherless virgin imprisoned, or perhaps sheltered, in some enchanted region of his own beyond the law.

She must be a virgin emotionally, though not necessarily physically, like Lady Constance Chatterley, whose excessively clever husband, confined to a wheelchair, is the lord of a great manor and a well-known author besides, but who has never satisfied her body's capacities. Constance wanders into her husband's forest, where she discovers a gamekeeper's hut, and in the hut a gamekeeper with beautiful thighs.

Not only is the heroine the active partner in these stories, she's the stronger one, as women usually are in fairy tales. If Beauty doesn't go and live in the Beast's castle, her father's life will be forfeit. Further on in the story, after she visits her family, if she doesn't return to the Beast's castle as promised, he will die of grief—she's not in the least surprised when he tells her this—but she's perfectly capable of living in the outside world without him.

If Jane Eyre does not work her way back to blind and maimed Mr. Rochester, stumbling through the rooms of his dismal manor house, he might as well be dead. In fact, he probably will be dead soon.

As the rescuer, it's Beauty's job to tame the Beast, unlike the male hero, who only knows how to kill or capture him. She teaches the Beast not to snarl or pursue raw meat, she reassures him that his appearance isn't as repulsive as he thinks, and she frees him from self-loathing. In short, she puts an end to his beasthood.

THROUGH THESE BEAUTY-AND-BEAST STORIES runs a dark and bracing current of fear mingled with curiosity and desire—fear that in past centuries was intensified by the constraints of arranged marriages, mingled with the longing for adulthood.

"Beast surely has a mind to fatten me before he eats me, since he provides such plentiful entertainment," says Beauty to herself as she lifts the silver covers from the dishes set in front of her at her first meal in the Beast's castle.

But what bodily pleasure, what new level of consciousness—beginning with the shock of birth—doesn't come to us first under the cover of fear? Not only in bed but in our more extreme sports (ski jumping, hang gliding, rock climbing), or social initiation rites (learning to drive a car), we need a spurt of fear mixed with triumph to rouse our flesh to full consciousness of the body's existence.

Especially during first intercourse, fear, or at least anxiety, spices the experience, since the male can so easily hurt the female, whether he means to or not. She worries whether she has picked the wrong partner. She worries whether she will lose him. Or whether she's obliged to commit to him now. She worries that she may not be sexy enough, lubricated enough, moaning enough to suit him. She wonders if she is capable of being aroused. (Drunk on risk, she often forgets to fear pregnancy, AIDS, and other STDs.) Her partner worries about not getting hard enough, coming too soon, not coming at all, violating what he has been taught to regard as a secret, sealed-off chamber. He must be a Beast to think of pushing his way in there with such a nice girl.

Even today, when sexual activity begins so early (almost one third of high-school students have had intercourse by the age of fifteen, according to the *Journal of Family Planning Perspectives*), there's queasiness when confronting genitals for the first time. In the Grimms' fairy tale "The Frog King," a Princess is forced by her royal father to let a clammy, rubbery frog climb into her bed (puff himself up and deflate again), because she has promised to do this if he returns her favorite toy, her golden ball. ("Take off they pants, I say, and men look like frogs to me," says Miss Celie in *The Color Purple*. "No matter how you kiss 'em, as far as I'm concern, frogs is what they stay.")

In other traditions, virgins must throw back their bedclothes and accept into their beds a pig who has rolled in filth, or lie with a goat who has snot running out of his nose and slobber dripping down his chin. Apparently the aversion is innate, although parents aggravate the situation by forcing a daughter into marriage. The Bantus of Africa, who might be thought to be less sexually inhibited than we are, have a story in which a bride must lick the nose of a crocodile in order to transform him into a desirable bridegroom. The gist is that the sexual act seems abhorrent to an inexperienced girl (stories scarcely ever deal with male virgins), especially if she faces marriage to a man she would never have chosen.

There are two ways of looking at this message: Either the girl's marriage is a trap set by the parents for their financial or social advantage, and the Beast is a repulsive, sex-hungry bridegroom foisted on her, but with forbearance she'll get used to him. Or, else, in the Freudian view, the Beast was never a beast to begin with. That was only the way he looked to an overwrought virgin who was still fixated on her family. Given enough time—an important requirement—once she outgrows her attachment to her father and accepts the idea of a more suitable partner, the Beast will magically turn into a Prince in her eyes. (In an old version of "The Frog King," the heroine has to share her bed with the frog for three weeks before he's transformed into a Prince "with kind and beautiful eyes.") As long as one partner views sex as animal-like, the mate remains partially animal, says Bruno Bettelheim.

THROUGH THE CENTURIES, the Beast travels under many names and titles that express our changing views of sexuality. The heroine, on the other hand, bears a generic name, since all women find themselves in the company of a Beast or brute sooner or later.

She is known as Beauty, Belle, Psyche (soul, looking for body). Is-a-bella, Is-a-Beauty, deluded enough to marry Heathcliff even after he pauses on the way to their elopement long enough to hang her pet spaniel from a bridle hook in the garden. Plain Jane, as in Tarzan's mate, or the Jane who is as pure and spritelike as Eyre. "Kid" in *Casablanca*, as in "Here's looking at you, kid." Or "Miss," which is what grizzled Humphrey Bogart insists on calling Katharine Hepburn, the straight-backed virgin missionary in *The African Queen*, even though her real name is Rose, like Beauty's rose, the flower of both Venus and Mary. Most anonymous of all is the heroine of that elegantly pornographic fairy tale *The Story of O*, who does not have a first name but a letter that is as round as the three openings through which her body will be penetrated. O, oh, oh-oh.

IN THE CLASSIC STORY "Beauty and the Beast," as told by Madame de Beaumont, her name is Beauty, and she is the loveliest as well as the youngest of a merchant's three daughters. While his children were growing up, the merchant was wealthy and gave them the best of everything, but not long before the story begins he loses his entire fortune except for a small farm, to the dismay of his older daughters, who are horrified at living and laboring so far from the pleasures and courtships of town.

The prologue is essential. Father has lost his money, which means that he has lost power, status, the ability to bestow benefits as he pleases. Translated from fairy-tale terms, this means that the father's image necessarily shrinks in the daughter's mind as she reaches adolescence. He is no longer King, as he was in her childhood; his throne sits vacant, waiting for a younger, more potent male to claim it. Her erotic life is about to change.

Then, about a year after moving to the country, the merchant receives news that one of the ships carrying his cargo has returned to port and may bring him a substantial profit. Beside themselves with joy, the older sisters ask him to bring presents from town: gowns, headdresses, the usual frippery. And Beauty, what does she want? Nothing, really. But if she must add something to the list so as not to seem superior to her sisters, let it be a rose.

(Fathers, beware of the youngest daughter, the unassuming one, who wants nothing but a hazel twig, like Cinderella, or a rose, like Beauty, something alive that will tear a piece out of her father's world when he snips it off and hands it to her, instead of a gift that can be paid for with money. Beware of girls like Cordelia in *King Lear,* another youngest and kindest daughter, who when asked what she can say about her love for her father answers, "Nothing." Nothing indeed. Nothing is a sinkhole that drains away the masculine world of striving and power and leaves a man howling naked in a storm, powerless in the face of nothing.)

So the merchant goes to town, where he is faced with a lawsuit that results in the loss of his fortune forever. Not a gold piece richer, he sets out for home, but it seems that the world has turned against him. In the midst of a blinding snowstorm, he loses his way in a forest where the wind howls in the trees and wolves run in packs looking for prey. Twice, gusts of wind are so strong that he is toppled from his high horse. Night is falling. Without shelter he will freeze to death, if he doesn't become a meal for the wolves first.

Suddenly he sees a light in the distance that proves to be a castle lit from top to bottom. The door of a stable stands open to receive his famished horse, with hay and oats in the manger. Entering the hall, the merchant finds a fire crackling in the fireplace near a table on which dinner and wine are laid out for one person. Hungry as he is, he doesn't dare sit down to eat, but by eleven o'clock at night he works up enough courage to gulp a roast chicken in a dozen bites and wash it down with wine before wandering the corridors in search of a bedroom, where he finds a bed already made up and waiting.

The lord of the castle still has not made an appearance by the next morning, but the merchant wakes up to find a fine set of clothes and a cup of hot chocolate laid out for him. Apparently the climate has changed overnight. As he heads for the stable to reclaim his horse, instead of snow he sees lush gardens filled with flowers—of all things, a rosebush in full bloom—right in his path. Joyfully, he breaks off a spray for Beauty.

At that instant, a heart-stopping roar is heard as a terrible Beast issues from the castle. The trespasser must die for this transgression, growls the Beast. His life has been saved from the storm, even his horse has been fed and bedded, and what does the insolent fellow do in return? He despoils the garden of roses, which the Beast values more highly than anything on earth. Falling to his knees, the merchant explains that he meant no harm. He picked the rose to give to his youngest daughter, Beauty, who desired no other gift, while her worldly sisters demanded dresses, ornaments, and jewels. Hearing the word "daughter," the Beast stops his tirade short. He will spare the merchant's life, he offers, if one of those daughters will come to the castle to suffer in her father's stead—but she must come willingly, of her own accord. In that case, not only will the merchant's life be spared but a chest full of gold will be delivered to his house in exchange.

When the merchant returns home and tells his story, Beauty will hear of only one solution to the crisis. She will go in her father's place as reparation for the trouble she has caused with her request. Not a tear does she shed, so happy is she that she can prove her love for her father by saving his life.

This is more than fairy-tale insistence on the heroine's superhuman goodness in contrast to the rest of her family. Her father's willingness to accept the loss of her, mingled with his sorrow, expresses a simple truth: A man can be certain of living beyond his personal death only through his daughter. His son's children may be illegitimate—"Mother's baby, father's maybe," as the saying goes—but his daughter's children are bound to be blood of his blood (assuming that his daughter is truly his, of course). Only through her can he live on.

The next day, Beauty mounts the horse behind her father and heads for the castle, while her brothers threaten to hunt down and kill the monster, and her sisters rub their eyes with onions to force a few tears to hide their delight at being rid of this paragon. Beauty is the only one who does not weep, although she is sure that her life has come to an end, which is something she will be convinced of many times in years to come (when her children leave home, when her mate dies or vanishes, when she loses her looks), since a woman's life, built around relationships, is discontinuous in a way that a man's is not.

This time, when Beauty and her father reach the castle, the splendidly set table is laid with two covers. Beauty pretends to eat in order to console her father. After supper, a great noise marks the approach of the castle's owner. "Has she come of her own accord?" the Beast demands to know when he sees her, as if that is the determining point that will change her taste in his mouth. Yes, she says, not without a tremor as she looks at his "horrid form." "I am greatly obliged to you," the monster replies.

The next evening, when she sits down alone to dinner for the first time, with music to entertain her although there are no musicians to be seen, she hears footsteps behind her. "Beauty, said the monster, will you give me leave to see you sup? That is as you please, answered Beauty, trembling. No, replied the Beast, you alone are mistress here, you need only bid me gone, if my presence is troublesome, and I will immediately withdraw. Beauty ate a hearty supper, and had almost conquered her dread of the monster; but she had like to have fainted away, when he said to her, Beauty, will you be my wife?"

———

SO THE STORY BEGINS: not with "Beauty and the Beast" but with "The Beast and Father," the erotic triangle of father, Beast, and daughter, in which mother plays no part.

The wretched merchant has dared to pick a rose that stands for his virgin daughter, while the Beast reserves the right to deflower his roses himself. (In some versions of the story, the rose bleeds when plucked.) Castle, gardens, servants, silver dishes—all of these embellishments are demonstrations of the Beast's power, while Beauty's father, who was so recently the master of the family, is revealed as past his prime, more humble than his daughter could have imagined. Brought to his knees by the Beast, the old King's day is over.

Up to the moment when Beauty enters the castle, her father has been the only man in her life—"the prehistoric, unforgettable other person," Freud calls him, who must be challenged and outclassed if his daughter is ever to move away from him and into a new life with a mate of her own. Always there is an erotic edge to the father-daughter relationship, especially if she happens to be the youngest daughter, the sweet and unworldly one (and all daughters are the youngest for some period in their lives), the one he calls Beauty.

Mother and father teach a daughter different lessons. From her mother a girl acquires the female strength to bear and raise children, deal with the gritty realities of daily life, keep going no matter what. She also picks up the habit of complaining.

But from early childhood on—particularly as a girl approaches puberty—if she is lucky her father teaches her that she is desirable as a female; many men are bound to desire her, a lesson that makes it possible in later life for some women to get a man whenever they want one, while others, just as attractive but with less seductive fathers, grow into middle age wearing shapeless gray coats, bad haircuts, and no makeup, still suffering the wound of failing to attract the first man they wanted.

At the same time, father is the one who introduces play into the home. For a son, play is linked to competition and strength. For a daughter, it's linked to sex. The girl who plays games with her father, rough-and-tumble physical games, will enjoy playing in bed later on, which is why mother is nowhere to be seen in the early part of Beauty-and-Beast tales. Since these games foreshadow the daughter's introduction to sex, the mother, with her possibly negative attitudes of suspicion and jealousy, must be eliminated from the scene.

And what does father want in return from his little Beauty? Total love. Exaggerated respect for his power as a male. If she is his sweetheart, then he is his younger self as long as he is with her. She belongs to him, he can choose to give her away to some man or god in the future, if anyone deserves her—or, better yet, he can keep her for himself. At least so he thinks. (If these feelings, with their tinge of incest, terrify him so that he keeps too much distance between the two of them, she may become filled with anger, either fire or ice, and neither father nor daughter will know why.)

THE MISTAKE MADE BY Freudian psychiatrists is their conviction that all daughters dote on their "unforgettable" fathers the way that Anna Freud worshiped her father, Sigmund. The truth is that they can dislike him just as unforgettably. A daughter may despise her father because he insists on telling dirty jokes in front of her friends. She may resent his caustic treatment of her mother and brothers, even if he pampers her; his tyrannical rages; his infidelities; his stinginess or his inability to make a decent living; his stern rules when she's of dating age; his insistence on regarding her as a child. On the other hand, if her father disappeared from the family long ago, his ghost may haunt her dreams, where he is transformed into whatever she needs him to be.

Doting on a father or detesting him: The past is always present, but for a daughter the future lies in finding a younger male who can outface her father and make up for his deficiencies, or else equal his virtues. When asked why an attractive young woman like Anna Freud didn't marry, one of her father's patients answered, "Well, look at her father. This is an ideal that very few men could live up to, and it would surely be a comedown for her to attach herself to a lesser man."

In the struggle that goes on within a woman's soul between the images of father and lover, two males who may never meet, the woman is both the judge and the prize. Anything can be a show of strength: height, income, bowling scores, adeptness at fixing a car. As a woman I know said to me when she was single, "Why should I marry anyone my father can beat at chess?"

The daughter of a successful doctor may pick a lawyer rather than a doctor for a husband, or pick a medical student who has the talent to become as notable in the profession in the future, or she may marry a rock musician because he introduces her to another world that is beyond her father's reach. But she had better not choose a pharmacist as a husband—that marriage will be a disaster—not because pharmacists make less money but because they are subject to a doctor's orders.

MY FATHER WAS A LAWYER by profession but a Prince by his own making (not a King, that was too weighty a burden for him to choose). Tall and handsome, he had a gift for flattery and also for holding grudges.

During the years when I was too young for school, I used to sit on his lap every morning while he ate breakfast and steal spoonful after spoonful of cornflakes from his bowl. He pretended to be chagrined at the loss. He would be starving by lunchtime, he moaned dramatically. That was the only nourishment I took willingly all day, he said to me pridefully in later years.

His shirts had French cuffs; his lisle socks had embroidered clocks. His mustache was trimmed like Clark Gable's. When he finished eating, he took a cigar from the humidor, removed the cellophane wrapper, and bit off the end, which he deposited in an ashtray. He then slipped off the cigar's scarlet-and-gold paper band, embossed with the seal of Anthony & Cleopatra, and slid it on the fourth finger of my left hand. I bent the knuckle to admire my paper wedding ring.

After that he blew smoke rings through pursed lips, with a little popping sound for each puff, circles that wavered and grew vaguer as they floated toward the ceiling. Keeping my eye on each circle as it rose, I reached up my index finger and poked it through the center with satisfaction.

The best part, the part that made this a nuptial rite rather than a game, was the fact that *she* wasn't with us; my mother was still asleep in the bedroom and would be for another hour. The room, the ceremony, belonged to the two of us.

Any other man in my life would be my second.

Twenty years passed. I was out of college and working, but still lived with my parents, who were out for dinner on the night that my blind date, a much younger lawyer, called for me. Looking back, I could swear that he came through the door already talking. He was in a bearish mood, soaked by the February rain, with a full box of Kleenex tucked under his arm because he had a cold, which was always much worse than anybody else's cold, he wanted me to know.

He had had a terrible day in court, he told me as we headed downtown in a taxi, the entire afternoon wasted sitting in the back of the room during a contested-will case—hardly a way for a young associate to further his career. The trouble was caused by a lawyer who had been appointed by the court to be Special Guardian, who was keeping at least two dozen other lawyers sitting idle while he made a good thing out of this case, fattening his fee with every passing hour. A crony of the judge, no doubt. On and on my date went, as if I were his wife already, required to listen with sympathy to his account of the day. The spine of the narrative carried me through the evening traffic, leaving me silent, transported. His profile could have been engraved on a Greek coin.

The trouble was with the court system in general, he said, the system of Special Guardians in particular, and this Special Guardian above all others. When he paused to pay the taxi driver in front of the concert hall, I interrupted, one foot stretching its way out of the cab already. "I know," I said. "I've heard something about that case. You see, the Special Guardian happens to be my father." I pointed my toe and waited for my date to be destroyed.

"Is he really?" he said, and went on talking with no change in tone, as I watched my foot in its ankle-strap sandal arch its way between the cab and curb. That was it. The ball of my foot touched the curb. In a young woman's life, a moment comes when her fear of the future is done with forever, vanquished because here is one man who isn't wary of hurt feelings, doesn't apologize or pretend that he meant something else, and doesn't sidle around an obstacle blocking his way but flies over it, as he'll fly over anything life may put in his path.

My father wasn't overcome in my mind so much as surpassed. Flown over like a dearly remembered part of the landscape. As for me, I was changed forever by the assurance that I, too, could fly above my qualms. This was the man I would marry, this one or no one, now that I was someone else. If only he would ask me.

Chapter 9

Beauties and Beasts:
Descending into the Body

"Cupid and Psyche," *The African Queen,*
the Legend of the Minotaur,
Jane Eyre, Casablanca

In every Beauty-and-Beast story, the heroine encounters sexual passion for the first time, inside herself as well as outside in the form of a Beast. Her consciousness changes. Mind meets body, if we want to look at it that way; the soul (called the *psyche*) experiences itself through flesh, especially her own. While tracking the stages of love in a woman's life, this story raises the possibility of learning to love what we fear, which is always more erotic than learning how to get what we want. The first approach is "Beauty and the Beast," the second "Cinderella."

In our society, the transformation to adulthood takes place over a period of years. Girls reach sexual maturity early here and expect freedom in their choices, so we let our children dawdle at each stage of ripening, perhaps because we are afraid to make their mistakes for them.

When a daughter finishes high school, her parents hire a U-Haul and drive her to college, where she moves into a freshman dorm with roommates assigned at random, sharing her sleeping space and bathroom for the first time with unfamiliar bodies. The following years, she picks her own roommates, before taking an apartment with friends of the same sex. She loses her virginity, if she hasn't done so already. She moves in with a lover. Step by sanctioned and expected step, she closes doors behind her and opens new ones, heading for the goal, which is a home of her own.

Before 1950, our society was closer to the fairy-tale world than it is today. A virgin knew little about Beasts before she chose one for a husband (or was given to him in marriage), any more than she knew about paying electricity bills or figuring out her food budget. At last she came into contact with a male Beast. She touched him. Nothing more than that at first, but her senses were alerted to new messages. She married and moved, not only out of her family home and into her own but down into her body, lapped in the pleasure of the present moment, until one day she woke up, suspecting that time was passing at another rate outside the realm of enchantment. There seemed to be something else she wanted, something more demanding that was essential for her future, though she wasn't sure how to get it.

IN ANCIENT TIMES (in a classical myth that is another version of the Beauty-and-Beast story), a princess named Psyche had the misfortune to be more beautiful than any human had a right to be—so beautiful, in fact, that her father's subjects deserted the temples of Venus, the great goddess of love and fertility, known as "the Universal Mother," and worshiped the fresh young girl instead.

The two female spirits could not have been more different. Venus, sprung from the sea foam, represented mindless, boundless sex energy that wants fertility and nothing else, paying no attention to individual personalities, which only get in the way. ("Get married, get married," our grandmothers still tell us, not specifying to whom.) Psyche was the opposite: a human virgin, which made her a mortal affront to the sex goddess—a creature of the earth rather than of the sea. Unmarried and humble in her suffering, she never dreamed that she might embody a new ideal of love.

Wild with jealousy, the goddess Venus called her winged son, Cupid, to her side (he was always bent on mischief, anyway), kissed him long and tenderly in a way that mothers aren't supposed to kiss their sons, and begged him to avenge her by using his arrows to make the blasphemously beautiful girl fall in love with "some perfect outcast" of a man, the most degraded creature he could find, the vilest of the vile. "That wicked boy" is the way Venus thought of her son, who flies over the rooftops at night, stirring up trouble in respectable homes. But in truth he was no boy, and certainly not the cherub with dimpled knees that we see on valentines. He was the youthful god of love at the peak of masculine beauty, susceptible himself to the passion he spread so casually with his random arrows.

As a result, when Psyche's father, the King, went to the oracle of Apollo to ask why his youngest daughter was so exceptional that no man, not even a prince or king, dared to court her, he was told in fancy Latin verse that she was about to get a husband: She must be sacrificed from the top of a mountain, dressed as a bride. Her wedding ceremony would also serve as her funeral, since her bridegroom would not be a mortal but a flying demon, "fierce and wild and of the dragon breed," who would swoop through the air with fire and sword to collect her.

And so the wedding party set out with smoky torches and mournful music, interrupted by howls of grief from the heartbroken parents and their sympathizers as they followed poor Psyche to the crest of a hill. There they left her alone to weep. Suddenly a friendly west wind swirled around her ankles and billowed out her cloak, which it used as a sail to carry her down to a valley and lay her on a flowery bank, so softly cushioned that she fell asleep. When she woke up, feeling calmer, she followed a stream that led her to a palace so marvelous that she knew no human being could have built it. Passing through the gates, she saw ceilings supported by golden columns and walls faced with massive gold blocks that streamed with light of their own, even when no sun was shining. The floor was a series of mosaic pictures made from jewels. How could anyone fail to be happy who walked on a pavement like that?

A demon was what the oracle had predicted her husband would be, a winged pestilence that even Jupiter was afraid of, but this palace had to be the creation of a god, she told herself. What's more, the god must be in residence at this minute.

Wealth is the first sign of the Beast that the heroine encounters, wealth and luxury in contrast to the bleakness of her former life. This she understands in spiritual as well as material terms. The Beast who owns this castle is no starveling wolf lying in wait for Little Red Riding Hood to satisfy both of his appetites, one for gobbling up little girls and the other for getting them into bed. The proprietor here has to be a great lord—"my master" is the way Jane Eyre refers to Mr. Rochester, an erotic phrase for a woman to use if ever there was one—lord of the beasts, king of the forest, a demigod or even a god, as Psyche claims.

Because of his wealth, he needn't do what would be impossible for him to do: call any man master. This is an essential piece of information for a woman during courtship, since nothing dampens romantic ardor so quickly as to hear a lover mention "my boss." A woman may choose to be dominated in bed, often chooses just that, but it means nothing to be dominated by a man, or to dominate him, unless he's the strongest in her world. Otherwise, when she hears the words "my boss," her mind strays from the familiar arms and legs wound around her, and in their place she visualizes—who else?—her mate's boss. A Beast capable of holding her down.

Of course, the Beast's wealth does not come to him in the ordinary way, by working for it, or in the hero's way of fighting for it. He's magically rich (in his palace, tears turn into diamonds as they fall) for the same reason a mermaid is rich: because below the surface level on which we lead our everyday lives, all of us can lay claim to unimaginable treasures, of which the greatest, as Beauty's Beast claimed, is a rose. As a result, the Beast is as rich as the hero is poor.

By nature, a hero's whole life is centered on what he wants and doesn't have, even if it is as unattainable as the Holy Grail, and so he is the poorest of the poor, constantly thinking of what he must do next to get what he lacks, even while he's in bed with the heroine. The Beast, on the other hand, wants nothing except to stay locked up in his lair and wait for Beauty to arrive, and so his home looks like a castle in his eyes and hers. To her surprise, once she is cut off from home and family (a prisoner liberated by her imprisonment) she finds that she has come up in the world, not down, in terms of pleasure and power.

In real life, this is the development that scandalizes parents, when a young woman moves in with a lover, or into a college apartment shared only with age-mates: bunk beds; clothes strewn over the floor for lack of closet space; no place to hang wet towels; no reading lamp; clutter and mess in territory that is her own, where the walls radiate light even in bad weather because here, one day, she expects to be kissed.

"Do these treasures astonish your Royal Highness? They are all yours," the spirit voices inform Psyche. As long as the heroine stays home she is propertyless, no matter how rich her family may be, because nothing belongs to her, but the first time that she picks out a comforter for her bed—even if she then leaves the bed unmade for two weeks—her body expands in space and power. Every object in the stores is potentially hers. Floating above her previous life, she says, like a magic incantation, "No one in the world knows where I am at this moment. Not even my boyfriend. No one knows what I'm going to have for supper."

Mess in the modern world equals splendor for a fairy-tale heroine: wealth that her parents can't provide, or control.

THE HABITAT CHANGES from palace to rain forest, the heroine's
background changes, the medium in which the story is told shifts
from a myth to a movie, but the theme of a woman forced out of her
home who ripens sexually in a lusher setting remains the same.

This time the heroine (Katharine Hepburn) is an overaged spinster who plays the organ with quivering intensity for her missionary
brother in an African village on the bank of a river, until German
troops invade their compound during World War I. On the day when
Rose's brother dies, the skipper of the *African Queen* (Humphrey
Bogart) steams up to the dock in his cranky teakettle of a boat. This
Beast who rises from the river is unshaven, unwashed, with a rag tied
around his neck, a cigar clamped in his teeth, and bursts of intestinal
gas erupting from his insides. Up to now, his only mate has been his
gin bottle, but he is lord of the Congo all the same, the only person
who can navigate the river and save her from the Germans.

Wearing a collar buttoned up to her chin and a wide-brimmed
hat, Rose steps aboard the boat, and learns almost at once that ahead
of them lie "a hundred miles of water like it's coming out of a fire
hose." The *African Queen* enters the first stretch of rapids. Water
boils around the rocks. The skipper wrestles with the tiller as the
boat dives over waterfalls and fishtails from side to side. Despite his
wish to stay uninvolved in the war, the virgin is about to transform
him from a Beast into a hero.

"Well, miss? . . . How d'ya like it?" he asks when they have passed
safely through the rapids. He chuckles benignly and takes a cigarette
from behind his ear, while she wipes the spray off her cheeks with
the back of her hand.

"Like it?"

"White water. Rapids."

"I never dreamed . . ."

"I don't blame you for being scared, Miss. Not one little bit. Ain't no person in their right mind ain't scared of white water."

She has stars in her eyes. "I never *dreamed* that any mere physical experience could be so stimulating . . . I've only known such excitement a few times before. A few times in my dear brother's sermons when the spirit was really upon him!"

"You mean—you want to go on?"

"Naturally."

Isolated in the world except for the Beast, in danger of being killed at any minute, the heroine transcends downward into her body. This is a rare experience, she discovers, every bit as illuminating as transcending upward beyond her physical state, and equally difficult to sustain without interruption from the mind.

Since puberty, she has been aware of her body, but only of how it looks to others when seen from the outside and what effect her appearance will have on her future. Now, in a combination of exhilaration and terror, she sits rooted to her seat in the wildly careening riverboat, the small space allotted her on earth, existing inside a body that feels excruciatingly mortal but vividly alive in a particle of time.

Fear stimulates us to full consciousness as effectively as sensual pleasure does. Only through the body, which is our gateway to knowledge, can we understand abstractions like time, space, and willpower that we mistakenly think come from our minds. (Contrary to what we expect, time slows down for us, rather than speeding up, when we are in danger.) Through fear and sex and a brush with death, we experience mortality intertwined with its opposite—a love of life so overwhelming that we weep at the thought that some day we must leave it.

In our civilization, it's not easy to put the mind to sleep and live solely in the present like an animal, with an animal's singleness of purpose—which is what we mean by transcending downward—yet every woman must do just that at times if she is to become fully female. From here on, the heroine will experience the delights offered by the Beast as another path of descent into her body, coming at a period when she's still available. Right now, unmarried, she doesn't sense her life through the bodies of her mate, children, home. Her body is all she has, but it's her own.

"Why not go to your bedroom now, and rest your tired limbs," a bodiless voice suggests to Psyche after she wanders through rooms loaded with treasures. "When you feel inclined to bathe, we will be there to help you—this is one of your maids speaking—and afterwards you will find your wedding banquet ready for you."

Following the airborne suggestions, Psyche sits down to eat, alone like Beauty, and instantly the finest dishes float in front of her of their own accord, while an invisible singer entertains her, accompanied by an invisible player on an equally invisible lyre. (Modern women approximate these stimuli through CDs, scented candles, rings of perfumed oil to hang around lightbulbs, loofahs, aromatic bath gels, Jacuzzis. Alcohol. Drugs. Anything that arouses the senses and swathes her in pleasure, leaving the body open, without discrimination. Especially open to him.)

Even if Psyche wants to, she can't escape these luxuries by running away. She can only submit—that's the exquisitely erotic element— while her senses are massaged by the bath, followed by dinner and off to bed on silken sheets.

And then something better. Around midnight, she hears gentle whispers beside her. "Now he was climbing into bed with her. Now he was making her his wife." She learns his body (which doesn't feel the way she supposes a demon's body feels) by touching and being touched, the way a baby learns a mother, which means she knows him more intimately than anyone else. While she has been desirable for years, at last she is desired. In fact, demanded. She is the cause of the passion that carries her along in its wake.

Before daybreak, her bedmate departs.

In this fantasy of erotic pleasure without commitment, Psyche's husband makes his presence known only in the dark, just as the brave lass who rode off with the White Bear is joined in bed every night by a man she never sees by daylight, and Jane Eyre is summoned to the library by Mr. Rochester only in the evenings. All day the heroine is free to go her own way as if she's still a single woman, while she waits eagerly, but modestly, for evening to come.

On the dot of nine every evening, Beauty's Beast comes into the dining room to talk to Beauty—with good common sense, though no cleverness—while she eats her supper. He could force himself on her, but he doesn't. Time passes agreeably until she stands up to go to bed, when the Beast turns to her and asks her to be his wife. "I shall always esteem you as a friend," she answers in the time-honored female evasion. "You must try to be satisfied with that."

The Beast moans. "Promise you will never leave me" is all he can say.

For three months the honeymoon is resumed every evening, flirtatious but not sexual in Beauty's case. Nothing is so compelling to a woman as power held on a leash by consideration for her.

PSYCHE'S HUSBAND WILL BE a creature "fierce and wild and of the dragon breed," the oracle predicted, but what else could be of the dragon breed except a serpent? Even though the body wound around Psyche feels like a man's, in older versions of the myth he was undoubtedly just what the oracle said, the Snake God as the consort of the Mother Goddess, twining himself around the tree of life. Like the White Bear, he is master of immortality: lord of death with his poisonous tongue, but, at the same time, lord of rebirth, who periodically coils himself into a spiral and casts off his old scarred skin, to emerge a few days later as bright as a painted belt.

Bear, serpent, bull, the beast-god takes on whatever shape he pleases, and always for the same reason: to gain access to the body of a woman whom he claims as his mate—not any woman, but the Beauty he has his eye on. He is divine, and he is a Beast, but a layer in between is missing that can be filled only by a woman. As a conduit linking three levels of being—animal, human, and divine—she alone can produce children who will be as fleshly as animals but will also inherit the spiritual power of their father.

For him, she represents earth as opposed to heaven, body as opposed to spirit—daily life, which is what gives substance to transcendent ideas. In fact, she is matter. *Mater.* Mother.

FOR CENTURIES, the animal is a god, or the god slips in and out of an animal body at will. Until one day he can't do it any longer; he's stuck halfway. The last of the bull gods, known as the Minotaur (the *taurus,* or bull, of his father, Minos) bears the head and hooves of a bull on the body of a human. Earlier in his existence he was the holy bull, the sex energy that fertilized his island of Crete, but as soon as this energy no longer seemed divine he was regarded as a monster to be penned in a maze called the Labyrinth. To the Athenians, he was never a god in the first place but a devil who devoured seven Athenian youths and seven maidens in the tribute Athens paid to Crete once every nine years.

Baffled and terrifying, the Minotaur waits for the sun hero Theseus to come down from Athens with his patriarchal ideals of discipline and combat, to put an end to this monstrous energy with the help of the king's daughter, Ariadne. Both of them know that if the Minotaur is killed the civilization of Crete will crumble.

This struggle marks a breaking point in the consciousness of Western civilization: The hero, who is wholly human, conquers the male who is half beast. Mind dominates body. Law takes precedence over energy. Chastity, rather than fertility, becomes the startling new ideal for women. But first the Beast has to die, in order to guarantee that the hero will be the one to mate with Beauty and reproduce his kind.

(The struggle between Theseus and the Minotaur is still being fought out in the bullrings of Spain and Mexico, where the matador, the sun hero in his glittering *traje de luces,* or "suit of lights," confronts the power of the moon bull.)

After Theseus kills the Minotaur, he does what heroes always do:

He disappears. He sails back to Athens for his next adventure, abandoning Ariadne on an island, even though he promised to make her his bride if she would help him kill her half brother, the Minotaur. The last that the heroine sees of the hero is always his back as he sails or rides into the sunset.

From this point on, for thousands of years in Europe, the wild beast is seen as the enemy, the marauder in the forests, like the wolf or boar, or at best the object of royal hunts, like the stag. Or perhaps he's a slavering fool, like a bear who dances at the end of a chain. For a man to wear the head of an animal is no longer a sign of divine power uniting two orders of being but a curse, a sign of inferiority. The hero is the ideal.

THE PENDULUM SWINGS the other way. Ever since the start of the Industrial Revolution, nature has slipped away from us: "The world is too much with us," sighed Wordsworth. Wilderness is what we long for, with its sense of authenticity, its emphasis on uninhibited growth, its reliance on body assurance.

Instead of inspiring terror, the Beast has turned into a romantic character who makes our ordinary lives look pallid. Tousled, irritable, difficult to deal with; often scarred; isolated in self-hatred, and contemptuous of worldly success, he lives in his own world. (In real life these days, we find our Beast-men on boats, in fishing and hunting camps, in workshops or garages, always in touch with bodies of one sort or another, literally in touch, since their fingertips are another kind of brain.)

Heroes are supposed to be handsome, but Beasts are ugly, or at least think they are ugly. "You examine me, Miss Eyre," says Mr. Rochester a short time after he meets the new governess he has hired. "Do you think me handsome?" Jane says that if she had stopped to think she would have given a conventionally polite reply, "but the answer somehow slipped from my tongue before I was aware: 'No, sir.' " And yet she admits to herself that if the stranger she met on the highway had been good-looking and gallant, if he had acted grateful for her help in getting up after a fall from his horse (another fall from a high horse, like that of Beauty's father in the fairy tale, when he was about to encounter sexuality), she would have known instinctively that there could be no sympathy between them.

A handsome man has had his gold plating rubbed thin by contact with the world. His life has been too easy; he knows nothing about suffering. Well aware that he can get any woman he wants whenever he wants one, he never commits to a single woman with the channeled intensity of a Beast.

A hint of ugliness, in fact, is spice for an erotic banquet. Too much ruins everything, but none at all is bland.

The hero is equal and opposite to the Beast, which is not surprising in view of the fact that they are alter egos. In stories, the hero is agreeable, polished, well mannered, dedicated to some noble undertaking larger than himself. The heroine cannot help but lean toward him, irresistibly drawn to a man so influential in world affairs that he doesn't need her.

In our terms, he's Victor Laszlo, the heroic leader of the French Resistance forces in the movie *Casablanca* (Paul Henreid). Without him, the Resistance will collapse. It's possible that no one will sing "The Marseillaise" in Morocco ever again. Meanwhile, the Beast named Rick (Bogart again) stays out of the fray, a drink in front of him and a cigarette dangling from his lips, licking his erotic wounds in his lair known as Rick's Cafe.

The heroine of *Casablanca* (Ingrid Bergman) makes no choice between them—the choice is made for her by the two men involved, which is fortunate, since she admires the sterling virtues of the hero, who happens to be her husband, but realizes the sad truth that heroes don't have much time to devote to women, not even their wives. Heroes don't wholeheartedly care for women, or for happiness either, not the way they care about their quests.

Lord Byron, Heathcliff, Edward Rochester, Rhett Butler. The intimidating Beast who isn't housebroken yet has ousted Prince Charming as the sex object of choice, even with his hands still smoking from crime (incest, wife-battering, bigamy, smuggling, in that order), though the heroine may not know her own heart at first.

Cathy Earnshaw of *Wuthering Heights* marries upper-class Edgar Linton, the master of Thrushcross Grange, but in life and death she remains the counterpart of Heathcliff, with the smells of the stables and moors about him.

Scarlett O'Hara, that Scarlett woman in *Gone with the Wind*, is madly in love with Ashley Wilkes, the hero with a classic profile who will soon ride off to fight for the Confederate cause, even though he knows it is doomed. But we understand at once that her soul mate is the mustachioed stranger with a quizzical half smile who shows up at a barbecue that is the last fling of Southern gentility before the Civil War begins.

"Who is that man? The one looking at us with a smile, the nasty dark one?" Scarlett asks another belle.

"My dear, don't you know?" her friend whispers. "Why, that's Rhett Butler. He has the most *terrible* reputation."

Scarlett peers at him over her shoulder. "He looks as if—as if he knows what I look like without my shimmy."

"My dear, he isn't received," her confidante continues. "He has to spend most of his time up North because his relatives in Charleston won't speak to him. . . . And then there's that business about the girl he wouldn't marry."

"Tell, tell!"

"*Well*, he took a girl out buggy-riding after dark without a chaperone, and then . . ." (the girls put their heads together and whisper) ". . . and then he refused to marry her."

For a moment, Scarlett forgets that she's in love with Ashley, not with the Beast who has loped down from the North.

It's in this gap between the male hero and the Beast that the heroine finds the work of transformation laid out for her, which we accept without question as her task, not his. Women are biologically engineered for transformation. Lacking a man's strength to resist the unknown, a woman tries to enfold it when she meets it, change it if she can, or adapt to it if she can't. She takes a man's penis, which is strange to her, inside her body. She gives birth to a baby, and says to herself, "This isn't me. This is someone perfect, and I could never make anything perfect." (The fetus and placenta are the only foreign proteins that are not attacked and rejected by the human immune system.)

For a Beauty, this is the ultimate seduction, this sense that only she has the power to transform her Beast. If she accepts a man the way he is, because his faults are part of him, the two of them stay friends. But the moment she thinks that she can change the way he dresses, clean up his manners, persuade him to put his talents to use by getting a steady job, she admits to herself that she loves him. Her friends she can put up with the way they are, but her lovers and children must be popped into her cauldron and transformed by the heat into paragons of high achievement.

So long as the Beast remains a misfit, he attracts her, but he is of no use to her as a potential mate or to society as a whole, and so she goes out and serves society's ends without meaning to. She transforms him into a productive member of the group, which is harder than his job of transforming a virgin into a bedmate, even if she is still half in love with her father. A double transformation takes place: While he grows milder through her increasing acceptance of him and the love he feels, she becomes receptive to sex. He grows tender as she grows stronger.

In the end, she gets herself a Prince, whom she turns into a husband, co-signer of a mortgage, the future father of her children. She'd better hope that's what she wants instead of the sexually avid, socially marginal Beast he was in the first place.

In fiction, the heroine decides once and for all whether she chooses the hero or the Beast, but in real life every man embodies both, although one aspect or the other predominates, and only one appears at a time. Because of her ambivalence, a woman's split expectations may be too much for her mate. She wants to be loved by a Beast, vehemently, violently:

Oh, violate me in violet time
In the vilest way you know

as an old music-hall song implores. She wants Stanley Kowalski, in his sweaty wife-beater shirt (*A Streetcar Named Desire*), to carry her into the bedroom and throw her on the bed. But she also wants to stay a virginal Beauty. She wants every move she makes to be scrutinized by a Beast focused on her, but she also wants the liberty of being ignored at times by a hero. She wants to be a hero herself, but biology keeps nudging her toward motherhood, which means an end to the time of courtship when she and an enchanted Beast lived only for the moment and for one another.

In a sense, she outgrows her Beast. She still wants him. In bed, she will always want him—if denied, she may go out looking for him—but by daylight she wants a father for her children, along with protection for herself in her role as a parent. Biology tells her to find a hero, armored with health insurance and a portable pension plan, who will work fifty, sixty hours a week at his job, whipped on by personal ambition to climb the career ladder. The price is that he'll come home too late to have supper with the children, also too exhausted to pay attention to her in bed—there's always a choice to be made between security and sex—but the family will own a house, and the children will have karate lessons, summer camp, and college tuition. If this doesn't work out according to plan, she may have to become a hero herself.

Torn between the Beast and the hero, what's a woman to do? She might listen to the anthropologist Margaret Mead (married three times herself), who said that every woman needs three mates: the first when she's young, for sex; the second for parenthood; and the third, presumably when her children are grown—when she's released at last from the dire imperatives of sex, fertility, and money—for companionship.

CENTURIES PASS. The wilderness shrinks. The predatory animals that used to be hunted (lions, tigers, crocodiles) have to be protected from extinction in wilderness sanctuaries. Sex, or at least our view of it, changes at the same time.

Nowadays, in this country a young woman more or less has to do what in the past she was forbidden to do: sleep around, or indulge in oral sex with the mistaken notion that this will protect her from the danger of AIDS. The girl may find herself freer than she wants to be, but conflicted. Once she gives up her virginity, she has to make a fresh decision at every encounter.

For a visual history of our shifting attitudes toward sex and the wilderness, we need only look at various artists' pictures of the Beast, who is never specifically described in fairy tales. In the early nineteenth century, illustrations in children's books showed Beauty's Beast as a huge black mole, or an imbecilic giant, or a wolf with the tusks and snout of a boar—whichever would be most loathsome to a virgin, in or out of marriage. By the end of the century, however, when arranged marriages were uncommon in Western countries, and when sex was not so fearsome a prospect for a virgin, the Beast's appearance undergoes a radical change. For the first time, he is shown wearing clothes and walking on two legs, revealing himself as the exiled aristocrat he is.

Suddenly, we see him as a man who carries an insupportable burden on his shoulders that cuts him off from his kind: the head of an animal, like Beauty's Beast; or a mask like the one worn by the Phantom of the Opera, to hide something worse that lies underneath; or if not a mask, then a perpetual scowl like Heathcliff or Mr. Rochester, meant to keep the world at a distance. His head is the remnant of his wild nature, the emblem of his suffering. Poised on top of the male's wide shoulders, it lets the heroine know that this creature is whatever he thinks he is, and he thinks himself a monster.

In Jean Cocteau's movie *Beauty and the Beast,* made in 1946, the Beast (as played by Cocteau's male lover, Jean Marais), is overwhelming, magnificent, noble as well as terrifying, like sex itself, a deserted god with glowing eyes and hands that gesture helplessly in jeweled gauntlets. A lace ruff supports his lionlike head, as if display-ing it on a tray.

Beauty faints at her first glimpse of him. He lifts her off the ground and carries her to her room, the panels of his robe flowing up the stairs behind him. Tenderly, he lays her on the bed. His muzzle hovers over her face, the brow furrowed with lines that might have been made with a branding iron. She wakes and gasps. "You mustn't look into my eyes!" he exclaims, cringing as he raises his hands to screen his head. "Have no fear. You will see me only at seven each evening. But you must never look into my eyes." No horror, no pity—those he cannot endure. He wants a mate, not a mother. Hunched in shame, he backs out of the room and shuts the door.

In the Disney studio's version of the story, the inspiration for the Beast came from the head of a buffalo, a massive creature with crescent-shaped horns like that of the Minotaur, the ancient moon bull that is now a reminder of our former Wild West. Why a buffalo? the Disney artist was asked. Because the eyes are so sad, he replied. There is a profound seriousness in the expression of all wild crea-tures, but the buffalo in particular is the animal that white settlers al-most exterminated in the American West, the native of the plains that once thundered in herds but must now be reestablished and fos-tered, primarily for the sake of their milk, which makes superior mozzarella, and their meat, which is uncontaminated by the hor-mones and antibiotics we pour into domestic cattle feed.

As we know the modern Beast, he lives in the wilderness we have destroyed, suffers from the erotic passion we have diluted, sur-vives as an outcast who used to be a god. "Don't look into my eyes," he says to the heroine. Don't see my face, my suffering. Who are you to know what lies behind a mask? Something better or much worse perhaps, but not to be revealed.

And who has the right to strip away his shield?

CHAPTER 10

Beauties and Beasts:
Looking Love in the Face

"Cupid and Psyche," "Beauty and the Beast,"
"East of the Sun and West of the Moon,"
the Jean Cocteau Movie *Beauty and the Beast*

Too much isn't good enough. Too much splendor, devotion, bedtime ecstasy, attention to her wishes, rich wine, ripe fruit—this surfeit doesn't satisfy Beauty or Psyche after a few months have gone by. Feeling smothered in an erotic dream, the heroine tires of what comes to seem a prolonged adolescence. She opens herself to contact with time and reality, which will ultimately lead her to motherhood. Fresh air is what she needs. A chance to see the light.

But why would a girl who is the most exquisitely caressed of mortals, favored by Love himself, choose anything but darkness?

"WHEN I WAS SEVENTEEN, I decided that I wasn't going to hang on to this jewel, my virginity, until I was married," says a woman who left home at that age and moved to New York alone. "I was going to enjoy sex for its own sake. In the beginning, while I was experimenting with sex, it was curiosity that drove me. And exhilaration, like a really good game of tennis. I thought of what my partner was feeling. The attention he gave me, the flattery—that was deeply satisfying. There was no connection between sex and pregnancy in my mind— I shudder now at the risks I ran, sex with no protection. But later on, when I began to wonder what all this might mean to me, I felt hunger for intimacy rather than sensation." And intimacy is predicated on knowledge.

FOR A LONG TIME Psyche's invisible lover speaks to her only with endearments, and she answers with more of the same, but a night comes when he issues a grim warning: "Lovely Psyche, darling wife, beware," he says. "Roused by the report of your death, your sisters are about to hunt for traces of you on the rock where they left you. If you happen to hear them crying for you, pay no attention. Don't answer, don't even look up toward them, or you will cause grief to me and your own destruction."

The poor girl weeps all the next day and refuses to eat, undone by the thought that she is living in a prison radiant with golden light, without a lock on a door but also without a single human being to talk to. When her lover slips into her bed that night, she swears to him that she will die if she is not allowed to see her sisters and put their minds to rest about her safety.

The same longing to see her family overcomes Beauty when she sees in her magic mirror that her father has made himself ill over the loss of her, despite the chest full of gold the Beast has given him. "I have so great a desire to see my father, that I shall fret to death if you refuse me that satisfaction," she says to the Beast. But when he permits her to return home, it's her sisters rather than her father who engage her attention.

At this point, the heroine wakes up from her trance with a start, wondering if it's right to enjoy herself in this palace with a male so shockingly different. Suddenly her blood family, particularly the circle of women, has a renewed hold on her. Only through them will she find out if she's leading the life she ought to be leading in this obscure paradise, if she's as happy as she thinks she is. Can wonders be wonderful if they bind her to a man, or in the fairy tales to an animal, when she knows next to nothing about him?

Separation and return. The shift from blood family to lover and back again. The schism illuminates what is lacking in each of them.

WHEN THE BEAST YIELDS to the heroine's pleas, he puts her on notice that she's about to jeopardize their happiness by visiting the enemy camp. All that he can do is lay an injunction on her: If Beauty doesn't return to the castle at the end of a week, her "poor Beast will die with grief."

If the girl who rode off with the White Bear is lonely and sorrowful because she misses her parents, the Bear will carry her back to their fine new home for a visit, but she must promise one thing: not to let her mother get her into a room alone to talk, or else the talk is bound to bring bad fortune to both of them.

Cupid's warning to Psyche is the most dire. He will have her two sisters transported to the palace if she insists, but she must remember that she's in deadly danger and guard herself accordingly. Those evil-minded women will try to make her discover what he looks like, against his orders, and if she listens to them her curiosity will mean the end of her happiness. "I warn you solemnly that when you begin to wish you had listened to me, the harm will have been done." "No, no," she protests. "I'd rather die a hundred times over than lose you. I wouldn't exchange your kisses for the kisses of the god Cupid himself." Winding her arms around him, she whispers in his ear, "My honey, my own husband, soul of my soul!"

The heroine's two lives intersect. When Psyche hears her sisters wailing with supposed grief on the rock where she was abandoned, she sends her lover's servant, the West Wind, to fetch them down to the valley. With joy she shows them her palace, her jewel chests, her closets stacked with dresses embroidered with gold and gems. She feasts them at her magic table, waited on by invisible hands, before loading them down with costly gifts. In short, she makes them venomously jealous as well as miserable.

Who is the godlike husband who has given her these wonders? they demand to know. ("Husband" is what she calls him, although no wedding ceremony has taken place.) Bearing in mind Cupid's warning, Psyche concocts a story about a handsome young man who spends all day hunting in the hills, so unfortunately they won't be able to meet him. Then she claps her hands for the West Wind to carry them away at once before she commits some dreadful blunder.

IN EVERY BEAUTY AND THE BEAST STORY, the jealous sisters are wretched with their own husbands—how could it be otherwise, since they are by nature man-haters or, more precisely, man-despisers?

Psyche's sisters have married rich old men, one of whom is "older than Father, balder than a pumpkin and puny as a little boy," while the other has such bad sciatica that he can have sex with her only once in a blue moon.

Jane Eyre's cousin, Georgiana of the golden curls, snares a "wealthy worn-out man of fashion" as a husband, while the older cousin, sallow and severe, locks herself up in a French convent for life.

In each case, the sisters have chosen husbands (or fates) exactly as the world advised them and are suffering the consequences. But who are these disillusioned, conniving, critical, sex-hating or sex-deprived furies who never speak except in bitterness? Far from being the heroine's natural enemies (though they are certainly enemies of the most hopeful part of herself), they are her shadow selves, the part she is unable to relinquish but does not want her lover to meet.

Before she makes her final commitment to a male, she feels the need to hear their female voices once again and test them against her lover's.

They are no puny force, these charter members of the matriarchy, who are always seen together because they represent the society of women as a group rather than woman as an individual. In fact, they are nothing less than woman's instinctive allegiance to her gender and, in particular, to her blood family. If she must marry outside the family, the sisters say, let her at least pick someone of her own class and marry sensibly, not for anything as beguiling and temporary as love. Lady Chatterley's sister, who is in the middle of a divorce herself and is relieved to be rid of all that nasty commotion about sex, is particularly scornful of the fact that her sibling is carrying on an affair with her husband's gamekeeper.

If, on the other hand, the heroine shuts her eyes and gives herself away in the throes of sexual pleasure, when she wakes up she's bound to find herself in bed with a serpent, a monster, a troll, even a servant in her own household.

Her group of intimates, which often includes her mother as well as her sisters and female friends, represents female ambition for power and concern about appearances, which is why they are invariably older than the heroine, since only the feeling, sensing part of ourselves remains perpetually young and tender, still capable of growth. Having sold themselves to men for one price or another, naturally enough they scorn their husbands, which partly explains their dislike of sex and their resentment of the power that a man wields over a woman simply because he has a penis.

"Perhaps you are fascinated by living alone with your voices all day, and at night having secret and disgusting relations with a poisonous snake," say Psyche's sisters, which is a true sisterly picture of what goes on in bed.

On the other hand, this consciousness-raising group of supposedly "evil-minded women" forces the heroine to grow up, in much the same way that Cinderella's sisters prod her toward the ball. Their suspicions teach Psyche to be self-protective. Their protest declares their independence from male domination. "Don't forget that you belonged to the world of mothers and sisters before you ever laid eyes on this man," their voices remind a young woman, borne to her on the West Wind. "Don't expect any man, especially a rich one, to further your welfare. He's out for what he can get from you. Don't give up your life, your friends, the job that you worked so hard to get (you never know when you may need it again), your own checking account. And don't forget to look through his pockets once in a while. You never can tell what you'll find there."

Looking, in fact, is their strong suit. In this story, the sisters' mission is always the same: to persuade their unreasonably beautiful youngest member that she must take a dispassionate look at her lover, which is the one thing he can't bear. She must look at him precisely because he doesn't want to be looked at. Find out what he's hiding. They intend nothing good, of course, and yet through their carping they prompt her to break loose from the injunction laid on her, if only to prove that she doesn't belong to any male, particularly one who tries to separate her from her family.

By this time Cupid has informed Psyche that although still a child herself, she will soon bear a child of her own. (It's a sign of her naïveté that she hasn't discovered this fact for herself.) The stakes have gone up. If she resists the temptation to look at him, her baby will be born a god, he says, but if she yields to those she-wolves she calls sisters, her child will be nothing more than mortal. "Have pity on yourself, me and our unborn child," he urges. "Keep my secret."

On their next visit, the sisters can scarcely wait to rush to Psyche's side and tell her, like the true and caring sisters they pretend to be, that they have discovered she's in imminent danger: "It's this. The husband who comes secretly gliding into your bed at night is an enormous snake with gaping jaws and a body that could coil around you a dozen times.... Farmers have met him coming home at nightfall from his feeding ground. They say that he won't pamper you much longer, but when your nine months are nearly up he'll eat you alive. Apparently his favorite food is a woman far gone in pregnancy."

While "poor silly Psyche" trembles, and admits that she has never seen her lover's face, nor does she have any idea where he comes from, the sisters propose the only way that she can save herself. She must get hold of a sharp carving knife and a lamp filled with oil, hide them in the bedroom, and wait for the serpent to stretch out beside her and fall asleep. Then she must slip out of bed and by the light of her lamp plunge the knife into the serpent's neck and cut off his head.

"We promise to stand close by and keep careful watch," the sisters reassure Psyche just before they run off to their ships and sail away to escape the coming catastrophe.

How can she mistrust her own experience—those arms, kisses, amorous whispers? Do serpents whisper? No, but the sisters must mean that he will turn into a monster when the honeymoon period is over. Or when she's fat and blue-veined in pregnancy.

The White Bear's bedmate hears the same instructions when she admits to her mother that she has never set eyes on her bedmate. "Oh my, he may well be a Troll you slept with," her mother says, "but I'll teach you how to set eyes on him. I'll give you a bit of candle to carry home in your bosom and light while he's asleep, but mind not to drop any wax on him."

Beauty's sisters have a more subtle plan. The Beast has given Beauty a ring that she need only lay on her table before going to bed in order to return to him, but if they can detain her longer than her scheduled week "perhaps the silly monster will be so enraged at her for breaking her word that he will devour her." When her week's leave is over, they shower the unsuspecting girl with such trumped-up affection that she agrees to stay with them for another week.

In an uncomfortable way, the sisters tell the truth, which is why the Beast is right to regard them as deadly enemies. Of course he's prepared to devour his mate's life in order to nourish himself, particularly if he's beautiful and single. He wants his woman kept in the dark about his life; he doesn't even give her his name. He wants her consciousness limited to her body, which he's so adept at satisfying, but she mustn't have a single thought or friend or family member that might deflect her attention for a minute, particularly in the nighttime hours that belong to him.

Nature invariably opposes higher consciousness, which interrupts the business of fertility with other concerns. And Nature, named Venus in this story, is the mother of Cupid, who gave him his arrows tipped with lust.

Looking at the story from a modern point of view, we see a lover who wants the male paradise: pleasure in the present moment, sex in the dark with no entanglement, no commitment. He wants a bed-mate, a mistress, in ordinary life a housekeeper, a mother for his children, but not a woman who will be his partner in anything but bed, and there he doesn't care for instructions.

At first, a young woman is content to stay in Eden, but sooner or later questions arise: What sort of lover is this who won't let her share his daytime life? Where is she headed from here? Open your eyes, the modern matriarchs say, not just your legs. You won't always be what you are today. What happens when you become sick, wrinkled, old (assuming that you remain mortal, that is)? What happens when your lover finds a younger Psyche, as he will, since he's so sure that he's the god of love?

The problem that is being raised, more urgently than ever in these days of choice, is how much of her self-interest a woman should stifle in her pursuit of love. Most women, in marriages more than affairs, and in second marriages more than first, tend to define love as comfort combined with safety. Comfort, safety, and a wedding ring. How much more should a woman want?

True enough, if a woman devotes herself to a man without seeing who he is, she runs the risk of being devoured. What the story doesn't mention is that this is what most women want. Decades may go by—a wife and mother may be on her deathbed—before she realizes that her life was eaten up long ago, and maybe that was fine with her, to be indispensable to somebody's existence, so long as that somebody thinks she is wonderful.

"How could you let my father get away with it all these years?" I demanded of my stepmother as she lay dying in the second bedroom of their Florida condominium.

She was the opposite of a fairy-tale stepmother: a beautifully groomed lady with silver-gray pageboy hair and pearls, ceaselessly attentive to her husband's well-being. As a young woman brought up in the South, she had been taught that her primary role in life, whatever else she might do, was to find a good man and take care of him.

When she met my father at a dinner party in New York, he was recently divorced and she was a fifty-six-year-old widow, which meant that she was eleven years younger than he was, exactly the same age as my mother. He was the perfect cavalier. The morning after the dinner, he had roses delivered to her hotel room, and when she flew back South, she found telephone servicemen in her bedroom, installing a private line that connected his home directly to hers. She hid the instrument under her bed so that her teenage sons wouldn't see it, she told me afterward.

A few months later the two of them married, and her sons were packed off to boarding school, since my father declared himself too old to cope with teenagers. She rarely saw them after that. I was entertained often, not because of my charms but because I was my father's only child.

After a few years, the newlyweds moved to the west coast of Florida and began life afresh with hibiscus colors, all-white carpeting, and a new circle of friends. My stepmother was the social queen of the condominium. My father was the host who put the martini glasses in the freezer to chill before their dinner parties.

Through the long stretch of her husband's seventies and eighties and well into his nineties, my stepmother spent her days catering to him. She made his doctor's appointments and drove him there, she counted out his pills and washed his socks, she clipped his toenails. In return, he assured everyone that his bride, as he always called her, was not human but an angel.

Some time after their silver wedding anniversary, my father, who was ninety-five by then, gave my stepmother conclusive proof of his need for her. When she was handed a diagnosis of inoperable cancer, he suffered his first major stroke. She moved into the second bedroom in order not to disturb him. He stayed in his own bed, cared for by a blonde nurse who was a happily married woman with two children.

"Don't go into that room, whatever you do," my father whispered when I came to visit, jutting his chin toward the room where his wife lay. He was as good-looking as ever, though thinner. "There's a skeleton lying in there. I saw when the door was open."

He was never one to stay under the same roof with suffering. That wasn't his style. Befriended by the stroke, his mind broke loose from the present and floated back to his days as a free-flying bachelor, which suited his temperament so well, the youthful god of love all over again. There he lay, in bed, stroked and tended by a blonde with the bluest eyes he had ever seen. "Did I tell you we're engaged to be married?" he asked me, looking at his happily married nurse possessively. "Soon. But don't let the Old One know."

I went into the other room. "Why didn't you demand more from him?" I asked my stepmother, taking on the tone of Psyche's sisters. "You gave up your home, your friends for him. You gave up your sons." She didn't answer, but I had heard her on this subject before. Children grow up and leave you; hers were teenagers when she married. But a husband stays with you, if you're lucky and clever, until death. Yours or his.

I couldn't bear to let this woman die without realizing the extent of her sacrifices. "What about your mother? Ten years ago, when she was dying, you didn't go visit her—you, her oldest child." She had numerous siblings, I knew, but none had kept in touch.

"Your father never wanted me to leave him. Not even for a night," she said.

"But I said I'd come down here and stay with him whenever you wanted me. He was perfectly well at the time."

She opened her eyes and looked at me with pity for my naïveté. I was a widow by then, living alone. She was the wife of the handsomest man on that strip of the coast, the man who had given me his cigar band as my first wedding ring when I sat on his lap as a child.

Maybe I had missed the point, and she was as great a devourer as he was, devouring everything else in her life in order to mince it up and feed it to him. "What could I do?" she said. "You know how your father is."

She died without disturbing him. After the cremation, my father told the friends, gathered on his balcony at sunset for a private service, about the honeymoon in Ireland he planned—he'd already bought the plane tickets, he said—with the nurse of the bewitching blue eyes.

Five weeks later, he died. In the end, the devourer was devoured.

PSYCHE HAS CHANGED since her sisters warned her about the woman-eating snake. At the beginning of the story, she was a simpleminded virgin, lonely because no one courted her, while her less beautiful sisters were already married. In bed with the Beast-god, she transcended downward into her senses, blocking out the rest of the world, but now something wider and bolder is required of her. She must see and know what she is dealing with. By the light she sheds—no matter what she sees—she will become the real *psyche,* the soul, conscious of itself.

In the middle of the night, Psyche creeps out of bed where her lover lies sexually sated. At this moment she's wide awake, standing above him not as his captive but as his potential killer. This time he's the one who sees nothing. It's female curiosity that's about to be unleashed. Seizing the carving knife with a fierce suspicion that she may have acted like a beast herself and given way to beastly pleasures during these past few months, she reaches for the covered lamp. She's prepared to cut off her lover's head (which symbolizes cutting off his penis, putting an end to his godhood), but it's the lamp, not the knife, that's the critical weapon poised above him.

Like Bluebeard's wife opening the forbidden door, she breaks the taboo by shining her light on what she's not permitted to see, and her curiosity isn't weakness, as men think, but strength. How can she understand what she doesn't see, and how can she transform what she doesn't understand? In particular, she casts light on sex, which is a form of activity that does not like the light. Her love affair may end because of this defiance, but that doesn't stop her, since she has discovered that happiness, which is what she thought she wanted, is not as powerful as consciousness, even though consciousness brings suffering in its wake, for which men will blame her.

So Psyche lifts up the knife in one hand and the lamp in the other, but she uses the lamp first.

On the bed lies the most beautiful of all wild creatures, Cupid, whose other name is Love, with a tangle of golden curls she has never seen, although she has inhaled their fragrance every night, and wings whose tips flutter as if begging to be stroked. At his feet lie his bow and arrows. She touches the point of an arrow to test it, but her hand is shaking and she pierces her finger. The arrow does its work. Psyche falls in love with Love himself.

Instead of a serpent, that phallic creature which represented her childish fear of sex as well as her sisters' view of it, she discovers a god (though not an entirely adult god yet), invisible to humans until now. As a god, his role is to fly above the earth looking down at mortals to pick targets for his marksmanship. The last thing he expected was for a mortal to look down on him, least of all a female who scrutinizes him while he sleeps, which must remind him uncomfortably of his mother. Once seen, a god is limited. He must be this and not that, here and not there, no longer inscrutable.

Most unsettling of all, Cupid never expected to be the object of passion. As Psyche flings herself on top of him to cover him with kisses, a drop of oil from her lamp scalds his shoulder. The god leaps out of bed in pain, sees the lamp and knife, and flies out the window, but not before the girl grabs his leg and clings to it until her hands grow weak and she tumbles to earth.

Consciousness has just intruded on free-flying sexual pleasure, struggling to transform it into what we humans call love.

Like any male, Cupid refuses to be pinned down by her ardor, which has already injured one of his wings. Unfurling them as best he can, he flies to the top of a tree, where he perches long enough to reproach her for her crime. "As for your sisters who turned you against me . . . I'll soon be avenged on them," he says. "But your punishment will simply be that I'll fly away from you." He does just that and disappears.

"MIND," SAYS THE WHITE BEAR, when he carries his chosen sweetheart back from her visit to her family. "If you have listened to your mother's advice, then all that has passed between us will be as nothing." No, she says, she hasn't listened, she wouldn't do such a thing. But that night she stands over their bed, strikes a match, and lights the forbidden candle. On the bed she sees the loveliest Prince in the world sound asleep, so lovely that it would take a heart much colder than hers not to bend over and kiss him. Three drops of hot candle wax fall on his shirt.

"What have you done?" he cries. If only she had held firm for a year, he would have been free from a curse laid on him by his stepmother. But now he must be whirled away to a castle that lies East of the Sun and West of the Moon, inhabited by a troll princess with a nose three ells long, who is the bride he must wed. There he doubts that the heroine will ever find him.

But the girl appeals to the four winds for help. Three lack the strength to blow that far, but they recommend her to their brother, the oldest and strongest. Borne on the back of the North Wind, which has blown East of the Sun and West of the Moon only once, and then while carrying nothing heavier than an aspen leaf, the girl is deposited on the shore beneath the castle by the wind's last puff. There, on the top floor, her bear-Prince, who has been drugged by the troll Princess, lies in a sleep from which only she can rouse him.

———

IN EACH OF THESE STORIES, the heroine finds herself pursuing her lover, just when she thought she was set for the rest of her life. She has mistrusted her Beast. Defied him. Maybe killed him. When she stands over him in the glaring light of consciousness, she can't help but see herself as well, and learn that she can be deceitful, self-protective, naïve, unreliable, possibly murderous—as well as just plain wrong—like the rest of humanity, rather than the cosseted Beauty she thought she was. This moment marks her true loss of innocence, after which her spirit is no longer sealed off from the world—a change greater than the piercing of her hymen. "I am the monster," Beauty confesses to her Beast as he lies dying.

The moment of insight is the moment of transformation, during which the two protagonists switch roles. Once the Beast has been seen for what he is, he never appears as the lord of the forest again. Stunned by his new condition, he lies indoors in a trance, waiting to be roused like a male Sleeping Beauty, while the heroine, burning with her new consciousness, displays an energy as purposeful as any mythic hero's in order to save him.

Without strength, love is trivial—a nuisance, in fact. To complete her education, the heroine must pass alone through a series of ordeals that transform her from a love-struck girl into a woman capable of rescuing her man, as she does in these stories—living without him, if that's what lies in the cards, or with him, which may be more strenuous. A woman needs physical courage—she's the one who's going to bear the babies, after all—but she also needs the moral stamina to hold on to her awareness that love is bound to be contaminated sooner or later by imbalance, guilt, and the hovering possibility of loss.

In each story, the heroine is flogged along by a raging older female who is infuriated by the idea of male-female love, since she represents and insists on the power of the matriarchy to control relationships.

AFTER CUPID FLIES OUT THE WINDOW, Psyche tries to drown herself, but the river refuses to accept her. Whipped and battered by her mother-in-law, Venus, who is unwilling to relinquish her dear son to a mere mortal, the pregnant girl must climb a precipice where a stream of icy black water, guarded by dragons, plunges into the River of Wailing. There she must fetch a drink for the goddess. After she survives that ordeal, she must descend to the depths of the Underworld to ask Persephone for a casket full of beauty for Venus. Meanwhile, Cupid languishes in bed in his mother's palace like the momma's boy he still is, nursing his sore shoulder. Not until Psyche falls to the ground unconscious—possibly dead—after completing her last trial, does he discover the power of his love for her. At that moment, he also discovers that his wing has healed and he can fly to her aid. (More will be heard about Psyche's plight in the chapter on the "Fitcher's Bird.")

Besotted by love himself, now that he knows he could lose her, Cupid flies to the topmost heaven and throws himself at the feet of Jupiter, king of the gods (the Roman equivalent of Zeus), to ask for help. Jupiter is more than willing to oblige. Hasn't this rascal caused no end of trouble with his arrows that have pierced Jupiter himself time after time, causing the god to commit naughty deeds with the tempting females who walk the earth? This behavior must stop. Cupid must be fettered by the strongest of all fetters, which means he must be married to that pretty girl, Psyche, whom he has seduced. From now on, he won't be an idle troublemaker but a law-abiding husband and father.

At the wedding breakfast that follows, the bridegroom reclines with the bride's head nestled on his chest. Bacchus serves the wine, and Apollo sings such catchy songs, accompanying himself on the lyre, that mother Venus cannot resist getting up to perform a lively step dance.

Which may have been the prototype for the dance Snow White's jealous stepmother dances at a wedding in her red-hot iron shoes.

BEAUTY'S ORDEAL IS SIMPLE, as fits her story. On the tenth night of her visit to her family home, she awakens in horror from a dream in which she sees the Beast stretched out on the grass near a ditch, close to death because she has broken her promise.

"Is it his fault he is so ugly?" she asks herself. "Why did I refuse to marry him? I should be happier with the monster than my sisters are with their husbands." Laying her magic ring on the night table to work its wonder, she falls asleep again. The next morning she awakens in the Beast's palace, where she runs frantically through the garden in search of him. She finds him stretched on the ground near the ditch, senseless, evidently dead because of her neglect.

In despair, she throws herself on top of him. For the first time, her body touches his. On the brink of loss and by the light of death, her disgust and dread disappear. So do friendship and gratitude. "I resolved to starve myself," says the Beast, "but now I die satisfied." "No, dear Beast," says Beauty. "You must not die. Live to be my husband. . . . The grief I now feel convinces me that I cannot live without you."

A paean of music bursts forth from the palace, which sparkles with light from cellar to turret. Fireworks crackle in the sky. Beauty turns to see if her Beast is all right, but where she left him there stands a gallant Prince, who bows to her in thanks.

To her astonishment, the Prince offers an explanation for his transformation: "A wicked fairy had condemned me to remain under that shape till a beautiful virgin should consent to marry me. There was only you in the world generous enough to be won by the goodness of my temper." Readers can interpret this miraculous change in two ways: From the male viewpoint, the story implies that at some point in a boy's youth, his mother or nurse may have caught him in what she considered disgusting acts. He then remains bestial in his own eyes until a younger incarnation of female goodness undoes the sexual curse of the "bad fairy" by welcoming him into her bed. In fairy tales, old females cripple or destroy life. Beautiful virgins restore it.

Or we can accept the usual psychiatric explanation that when a girl matures enough to transfer her affection from her childish fixation on her father to a younger male, she no longer sees sex as a bestial act.

Both explanations can be valid. Beauty and her Beast are transformed at the same time and magically transported to the Prince's domain, where Beauty's sisters are turned into statues who stand in front of the palace gate. Their perpetual punishment is to witness her happiness.

A WOMAN'S LOVE SOCIALIZES A MALE, turning a Beast into a "charming Prince," an outcast into a husband and father, who will have to accept the harness of domestic life from now on.

The gamekeeper on the Chatterley estate leaves his job under fire because of his affair with Lady Chatterley, who is pregnant with his child. Instead of nurturing wild animals in the woods, he takes a job on a farm, alongside other men, no longer able to maintain the life of a recluse—milking a herd of cows, the dullest and most docile of all animals.

When Jane finds Edward Rochester again, he is no longer the master of Thornfield Hall, which has burned down in her absence, but a deserted wretch, blind and mutilated, holed up in a hunting lodge that he owns. Life pulls him along like a bear at the end of a chain. Jane runs her hand through his shaggy mane, which she claims to find alarming. "It is time some one undertook to rehumanize you," she says, setting to work with a pocket comb. He holds up the stump of his arm where his hand used to be. "A ghastly sight!" he says. "Don't you think so, Jane?"

"It is a pity to see it," she replies. "And a pity to see your eyes—and the scar of fire on your forehead; and the worst of it is, one is in danger of loving you too well for all this."

One way or the other, this is what Beauties want—to domesticate the Beast—and what nature programs them to want. (Psyche and Constance Chatterley are already pregnant; Jane Eyre soon will be.) But from now on, the lover's body will not be fully available to the woman, nor hers to him. When they are in bed together, each of them will keep an ear cocked for the children's cries, and each will worry about being too tired to get up and go to work the next morning. In the enchanted garden of youth, sex was sex and nothing else, single-minded as animals, with no thought of money or clocks or babies or employers, or jealous sisters, for that matter.

At the end of Jean Cocteau's film *Beauty and the Beast,* the Beast, who was near death a minute ago, springs up from the ground, transformed into a gorgeous exemplar of royalty: curled, ruffed, jeweled, sashed, bonneted, and plumed. He bows to Beauty like a ballet master. She can scarcely believe the miracle, and yet for a moment her eyes are downcast. "What's the matter, Beauty?" the Prince asks. "Do you miss my ugliness?"

It was the Beast she fell in love with in the first place. Each night, when the Beast asked Beauty to be his wife, his eyes seethed with passion. She was given only one chance to touch the steaming fur on his forehead before he disappeared.

"You loved the Beast!" he exclaims.

"Yes!" Her eyes shine.

"You're a strange little girl, Beauty. A strange girl."

The beginning of the story is the answer to a maiden's prayer. The end belongs to the woman. She isn't a girl any longer, or even primarily a lover. She's about to become a wife, perhaps the mother of a girl who will leave home one night, when three raps are heard on the windowpane, and ride into the woods to find an enchanted castle of her own.

Beauty looks up at the Prince, who in no way resembles her vanished Beast, and lays her head on his chest. With his arm around her waist and her skirt billowing above her in the air, they soar off to his kingdom, where she will rule as Queen.

"Give me back my Beast!" wailed Greta Garbo after seeing this scene in the movie theater.

We ask ourselves if what we have gained is equal to what we have lost.

PART 2

Matron

The Age of Attachment

"The White Bride and the Black Bride"
"Rapunzel" and Jane Eyre
"The Seal Wife"
"Fitcher's Bird"

At the end of the Maiden's trials, we are told that the Beast "married Beauty, and lived with her many years, and their happiness as it was founded on virtue was complete." But fairy tales don't always stop at that point, as we suppose. Other stories continue the heroine's challenges, with the wedding as a problematic beginning rather than a romantic end.

Unlike puberty and sexuality, which were the themes of the Maiden's stories, marriage is a social rather than a biological transformation. We don't decide when to be born, when to become fertile, when to take the baby out of the womb (though we may try to regulate the time of conception), but marriage, with all its questions of choice and timing, is left to human guesswork. This means that transformation in the Matron stage of life is just as significant as in the Maiden stage, but less predictable and generic. Our later lives often laugh at our earlier ones.

ON THE DAY WHEN *a White Bride leaps eagerly into the royal coach the King has sent to collect her for the wedding, she knows nothing about the man she is about to marry except that he is called King, and not much more about herself. In particular, she has no idea what sort of person marriage will evoke in her. All she knows for sure is that she's no longer willing to stay single.*

A moment after she sits down in the coach, her greedy stepsister, the Black Bride, who is her shadow self, climbs in beside her, strips off the White Bride's wedding gown, and throws her into the river, where she turns into a hapless white duck ("The White Bride and the Black Bride," by the brothers Grimm). She must endure a time of exile before she is ready to assume her proper shape and role as Queen.

This is the essence of the Matron's story: The Maiden, who used to consider herself single in every sense, finds herself doubled, split, fragmented when she weds (or acquires a partner), exiled from her native home, subject to fits of temper and exhaustion, followed by spasms of guilt or regret. She was a Maiden for scarcely more than a dozen years. She may be a Matron for four decades or more, the major part of her life, when her power and responsibilities are at their peak.

The part of herself known as the White Bride in the next two chapters sees marriage and motherhood as her fulfillment, but the Black Bride bristles at the confinement that lies ahead while she must serve the needs of others (Jane Eyre and Bertha Mason, Melanie Hamilton and Scarlett O'Hara). In real life, this switching of selves, White to Black and back again, does not happen only on the way to the wedding, as it does in the fairy tale, but every day, almost every hour, in one direction or the other.

In other stories, instead of dividing into Black and White, the heroine's life fractures into Before and After.

After a number of years as a housewife, a woman may admit to herself that marriage was not what she wanted in the first place, or if she did, she doesn't want it anymore. The animal skin of the Seal Wife is stolen one night by a fisherman, who keeps her onshore to be his wife and the mother of his children. Years later, when she finds her original skin, she has to choose between her children and freedom in her native element.

If the Maiden marries impulsively from love or greed (including greed for happiness), she may discover that she doesn't know as much as she should about the man who shares her bed. At the center of the house is a chamber that he forbids her to enter. She goes in anyway. In a pool of blood she finds the hacked-up bodies of her younger selves, who fell to pieces in front of knowledge that was more than they could bear ("Bluebeard," "Fitcher's Bird," in real life the story of Eleanor Roosevelt).

Now she splits in a different way: Her toughened self looks back in grief at the self-protective ignorance she has lost. She wonders at her past innocence, but wonders more at her present strength. The Matron's story becomes an account of progress from youthful, sex-dazzled unconsciousness to growing confidence in her ability to survive in a state of consciousness. Eventually, she grows strong enough to demand forbidden knowledge and face down the consequences, like Psyche or Jane Eyre.

But why do the White and Black Brides hurry so unthinkingly to take their places in the wedding coach? Why do seal maidens swim to shore and slip out of their skins, when they know that there are fishermen in the neighborhood who may capture them? In modern life, if we poll senior citizens between the ages of sixty-five and seventy-four in this country, why do we find that 96 percent of them married at some time in their lives?

The reasons for marriage are obvious: We marry for parenthood, sex, companionship, and consolation, and we lump these attractions together and call them love. We marry for enough money and helpful hands (or so we hope) to raise a family. We marry to be part of a self-contained unit independent of the rest of the world, including, or especially, our parents.

But we may be less aware of what we marry against, which is

the fear of calamity. We fear those masked intruders bound to break into our homes: we fear pain, illness, accident, debility, death that will choose to strike at night while we are alone in the house. Among many other things, marriage is a sort of bet in which each partner gambles that the other will be longer-lived and willing to reach out a hand when needed to the other side of the bed. In old age, the fear of dying alone is every bit as convincing an argument to stay in an imperfect marriage as the urge to reproduce was in youth. Death is the last child that a husband and wife breed between them.

In the period after the destruction of the World Trade Center towers, single New Yorkers who had been plunged into a new sort of wilderness were transformed in their view of their lives. "I was the most commitment-phobic person on earth . . . a serial dater, I'd go out on maybe three dates a week," a twenty-five-year-old waitress told a newspaper reporter a few weeks later. But after September 11, she understood the value of belonging to someone else. "Feeling your own despair was just too much to bear."

BEHIND THE STORIES *in this section lies a broader view of the woman's dilemma during this central portion of her life. The fragmented Matron discovers that she cannot be wholeheartedly the wife her husband wants and at the same time a good mother to her children, a daughter to her parents, a confidante to her friends, a working woman climbing the ladder in her career. Neither can she be wholly herself. True marriage, as envisioned by the Maiden, is impossible. But so is remaining single.*

A woman is never entirely one thing or another; the second half of her life is often discontinuous with the first. She survives intact only because she is mutable.

CHAPTER 11

The White Bride and the Black Bride:
The Discovery of Two Selves

"The White Bride and the Black Bride,"
Gone with the Wind, the Legend of
the Demon Lilith

On the day when the courtship romance ends—when Beauty says to the Beast, "Live to be my husband," and the palace sparkles with light—a different and more disturbing story begins. Not one person in a hundred knows this story, despite the fact that there are four versions in Grimms' alone ("The White Bride and the Black Bride" is the example used here, although "The Goose Girl" is more familiar), for the simple reason that its message isn't pleasant to acknowledge.

Just when a woman thinks that she is about to enter into a permanent union with a man, when there seems to be nothing to do but live happily conjoined ever after, this fairy tale tells us that she splits in two. At the last moment, when the coach dispatched by the King is about to set out for the wedding, a (morally) dark sister or servant steps in and seats herself beside the trusting White Bride. (Women, whose lives are shaped in good part by their relations with others, split in two when ripe more readily than men do, which is why we tell this story in terms of double brides rather than double grooms.)

Two spirits compete for space in the coach that represents the woman's body: two spirits found in all of us, in proportions that vary from one person to another, from one stage of life to another, not only on the wedding day (though the division seems most obtrusive then) but from hour to hour.

The intruding Black Bride is aggressive, dynamic, mercenary (often for necessary reasons), on fire with jealousy, self-centered, and self-reliant. In a more general view, she is the determination that enables a woman to get what she wants and empowers her to protect herself and her family; she is the subversive force that has been repressed in maidenhood until it explodes on the way to the wedding.

As a maiden, she always had to be pleasing. But once she is seated in the coach, her impulses toward control are fully liberated for the first time by the social and financial security she expects to find in marriage. The Black Bride gets into the coach last but reaches the destination first.

If the Black Bride represents individual willpower, the White Bride is the caring side of a woman, defining her as daughter, sister, stepsister, stepdaughter, friend, with the roles of wife and mother soon to come. Hurrying to marry a man she does not know, the White Bride is sure that in the years ahead she will never experience betrayal, rage, boredom, much less divorce or despair. She is the one who is thrown out of the coach in the middle of the journey.

The bridegroom fails to notice that there has been a substitution and the White Bride has been left behind. Ignorance is the theme of his story, growth the theme of hers.

AT THE BEGINNING OF THE TALE, a King, who is a widower still grieving for his incomparable Queen, has vowed never to marry again unless he finds a bride who matches his late wife's beauty. By chance, he discovers that his coachman, who lives in the palace, stands in front of a portrait every day that hangs on the wall of his room and talks to it in terms of endearment. The King demands to see the painting, which turns out to be a portrait of a young woman exactly like the lost Queen, only—by some miracle—much younger and more beautiful. So dearly does he love his sister, the coachman explains (perhaps too dearly for a brother), that he has painted this picture in order to keep her likeness constantly in front of his eyes.

One look at the portrait sets the plot in motion: The King determines to make this girl, and no other, his Queen. At once he sends the coachman off with the royal coach and four horses, along with splendid garments made of cloth of gold, to fetch his intended bride.

Dressed in these royal clothes, the girl we know as the White Bride sits down in the back of the coach at her brother's invitation, rejoicing in her good fortune. She doesn't remain alone for long. Her stepsister, known as the Black Bride, climbs in and sits down beside her, and right behind the Black Bride comes the stepmother, the old mother-witch, pushing her child forward toward mating and reproduction like Mother Nature herself.

TWO BRIDES RIDE TO THE WEDDING, when the King has sent for one. Two brides, of whom the lawful one will be expelled by treachery, while the other, whom the King knows nothing about and who isn't nearly so well suited to marriage, stays on for the end of the ride.

"Of what use are your arts to me now?" the Black stepsister demands furiously of her mother as she looks at the White Bride's golden garments. The stepsister lusts for these clothes, not only because of their value but because the wearer is recognized by the public as bride and Queen, while in her shabby dress the Black Bride is taken for a servant at her side. "Such luck should have been mine," she mutters.

"Keep quiet!" the mother-witch hisses. Luck can be shunted from one to another by those who know what they are doing. The old woman has already used witchcraft to trouble the eyes of the coachman-brother so that he is half blind, and to muffle the hearing of the White Bride so that she is half deaf.

> *"Cover thee well, my sister dear,*
> *That the rain may not wet thee,*
> *That the wind may not load thee with dust,*
> *That thou may'st be fair and beautiful*
> *When thou appearest before the king,"*

the coachman sings, but being hard of hearing, the White Bride turns to her stepmother, who relays the message that her brother wants her to take off the golden dress and hand it over to her stepsister. She slides out of the dress, which is too grand for her anyway, and puts on the Black maiden's shabby gray gown in exchange. The golden clothes belong to the King, and so does the woman who wears them.

A little farther down the road, the coachman sings again, and this time the White Bride is told that her brother wants her to give her stepsister the golden hood and travel with her head bare. In old clothes she becomes a child again or a servant, ignored by the principal players, too unimportant to do anything wrong.

By now the White Bride scarcely knows who she is, and in her deafness she cannot hear the voice that tells her to guard herself well. The Black Bride sees only the golden clothes. The coachman-brother is so dazzled by love for his sister that he is pulled down the road by the steaming horses oblivious to what goes on behind his back. Only the mother-witch knows precisely what she's after: a marriage that can be kept under female control, with the King serving as the woman's tool. Toward that end, she decides that her own daughter, the Black Bride, must take the place of the bewildered White Bride, who could never match wits with a King.

And so, when the coachman sings out a third time, the witch relays the order that "your brother says you must look out of the carriage," which she does just as the coach rolls across a bridge. As she leans out of the window, the stepmother and stepsister push her into the river, where the water closes over her head. The next moment, a snow-white duck bobs to the surface and swims away.

METAMORPHOSIS, MORPHING—which means changing from one body to another to match the level of consciousness—can move downward as well as up, in this case down to a simple level, which is all the heroine can handle at the moment. Growing up is never easy, the fairy tales and myths warn us. Consciousness is increasingly painful the more of it we get. What we think of as a cruel enchantment imposed from outside may be the way in which the heroine bides her time.

As we have seen, Daphne turns into a tree when pursued by a god bent on rape, becoming a block of wood in the pursuer's arms. Sleeping Beauty falls into a trance when pricked by a spindle. The White Bride, faced with the prospect of becoming a Queen before she is ready for the role, turns into an innocent duck, bobbing her head into the water as if she might find new insights down there.

It is conceivable that many of our emotional problems—apathy, depression, compulsion, feelings of inadequacy, rootlessness, all of which are unconscious attempts to deal with life's circumstances before we are ready—can be expressed in terms of morphing downward.

WHEN THE COACH REACHES the palace and the Black Bride dismounts with her mother, the King is so dismayed by her ugliness, which is so different from what he expected, that he orders the coachman-brother to be thrown into a pit full of snakes, but the resourceful witch muddles his eyesight. This is fairy-tale language for an observable truth. In real-life terms, men see what they expect to see. Or they see what they are told they see. For their purpose, one youthful body in bed isn't so different from another. Women have sharper, more critical eyes in order to see what is going to need transforming.

All the King knows for sure is that he wanted a bride in a golden dress, and got one. The wearer of the dress must be his Queen. Blinded by lack of faith in his own instincts, he marries the Black maiden a few days later.

Meanwhile, the duck paddles in the river. "I'm too young for this adventure," we imagine her telling herself. "I'm only a little duck. Still, I might as well swim upstream a bit and see if this river leads to the King's palace."

THIS PARTICULAR FAIRY TALE may be relatively unknown, but duality has become an obsessive subject, especially during recent centuries, when women have been able to imagine alternative ways to construct their lives.

Two by two, the females come in our double-bride stories: a man-woman, devoted to independent achievements; and a woman-woman, devoted to relationships, in each pair. In each case, the White Bride, who is full of self-doubt, is opposed by the more aggressive Black Bride, who was on the scene earlier, a predecessor she never reckoned on: Jane Eyre and Bertha Mason. Melanie Hamilton and Scarlett O'Hara. Isabel Archer and the conniving Black Bride, Madame Merle, in *The Portrait of a Lady*. (A merle is a European blackbird.) In the novel and movie of *Rebecca,* the nameless second wife and the first Mrs. Maxim de Winter she replaces.

The shock of these stories isn't that a sly, opportunistic woman pretends to be a dear, sweet girl until she is married, and then throws off the disguise. The shock is that the bride and groom accept one another so casually, knowing little about their own desires, and even less about their partner's. To us this seems too far-fetched for anything but a fairy tale. We consider ourselves rational beings who make deliberate choices—in fact, contemporary couples cohabit for years without any commitment—and yet, looked at with hindsight, our choices seem no more perceptive than the fairy tale implies.

The King sends a messenger to fetch his picture bride. The maiden, who has decided that she's ripe for marriage (better to be a bit green than overripe) hurries to answer the summons. Without questioning their impulses, both sexes follow nature's directives for selecting a mate, with different qualities preferred by each gender.

When David Buss, a pioneer in the field of evolutionary psychology, asked people in thirty-seven widely different cultures to rate the characteristics they would consider in choosing a spouse, both sexes put affection, dependability, intelligence, and kindness at the top of their lists, but farther down the line their tastes diverged. Men, whose basic urge is to father as many children as possible, stress a woman's youth and good looks, which are indicators of health and fertility as well as incentives to sexual activity. In addition, the wife's good looks are taken as a sign of the husband's success in the world. In another study, scientists from Saint Edward's University in Austin, Texas, placed ads in personal columns posing as two fictitious women, one listed as fifty pounds overweight and the other as a recovering narcotic addict. The addict received 80 percent of the replies. When choosing from schematic drawings of women's figures, most men picked a woman whose hips were wider than her waist in a ratio of roughly ten to six or seven; wide hips indicate that she is ready to bear children.

So the bridegroom sees what nature has programmed him to see: a female in a golden dress, which in real life usually translates as full breasts, long hair, a "cute" appearance that suggests youth, a symmetrical face (favored by both genders) that implies healthy genes but, above all, confidence in her own desirability, enough to assure him that she is the golden one he is waiting for.

For her part, a woman of marriageable age puts power and status near the top of her list. Cinderella wants to be loved by the Prince, not by the good-looking but lazy kitchen boy. Sleeping Beauty will wake up only for the man who can hack his way through the briars. Prodded by biology at least as much as by social conditioning, a young woman reacts to a powerful man by giving him what he wants: herself.

While a girl is young, she sees power lined up on the football field in terms of height, strength, and aggression, along with athletic skill (the cheerleader mates with the football captain). But when a woman is ready to marry, power translates less romantically as money, or rather the prospect of earning money, which is more valuable in our society. In contrast to a man, she is able to produce relatively few children, so her deepest instinct is to raise them safely to maturity. For that she needs a strong and focused mate beside her, someone who can pay for her children's dental bills and college education, even if she holds a job herself. She's not the weaker sex; she's the burdened one, already responsive to the needs of offspring not yet born. Beyond that, she realizes that by the time her children are grown she may find herself worn out and vulnerable if she doesn't have enough money to care for herself in her old age, which is apt to last five or six years beyond her widowhood, even if she and her husband were the same age when they married.

So all marriages are arranged—the only question is by whom—and all women marry for money, the question being how much. The answer is, or should be, enough so that she can sleep comfortably at night.

But there's more to it than that. In fairy tales, Kings may occasionally marry penniless maidens, but beggar maidens never marry beggar lads. When the White Bride rides off to wed the King, she wants him as more than a provider and protector. She wants his genes to pass along to her children. Only a King can father future Kings.

"Power is the great aphrodisiac," said Henry Kissinger, condensing into five words numerous sociological studies proving that single men with high-status jobs and a superior education have more active sex lives than their fellows.

Among Zulus, the author Robert Wright points out, a chief may have a hundred wives, permitting him to spread his genes wider in the next generation than any of his subjects. Today, in the lands of the former Mongol Empire, 8 percent of the males carry the Y chromosome of Genghis Khan and his royal family.

In our own society, the great chiefs of industry substitute serial monogyny (one wife at a time) for polygyny, divorcing their aging wives, whom they maintain in separate establishments while they acquire progressively younger and sexier bedfellows. "A lasting relationship with a woman is only possible if you are a business failure," said the billionaire J. Paul Getty while he was in his eighties, after marrying and divorcing five times.

According to a common truism, men marry down, toward youth, which means fertility; women marry up, toward age, power, and money, but these trends are less clear today than in the past. For the time being, the fiery male who can sweep obstacles out of his way still heats a woman's imagination, but fire can scorch as well as warm. The maiden, who so impetuously chose the King, may complain that he is domineering and unfeeling, married to his work rather than to her, and at the same time unfaithful.

Instead of the high-intensity male who will breed strong children and strong passions, the contemporary heroine may choose a type who does not exist in fairy tales: a softer, more sympathetic partner, more considerate in bed, generous with his time as well as his money, who will help raise the children and run the house since she also goes to work every day—in other words, a husband who will be a lot like her in age and background.

At the end of the nineteenth century, the median age difference between a bride and a groom was four years. In first marriages now, the age gap is scarcely more than two years, and this may not be the end. The newest fantasy, still seen as predatory in the United States but on its way toward becoming an erotic turn-on, is the older woman with a younger man, which is the prerogative of a Queen: *Sunset Boulevard* and *The Graduate* in the movies; the two novellas of *Chéri* by Colette (who lived out her own fantasies by marrying, for the third and last time at the age of sixty-two, a man sixteen years her junior). Other examples from real life: Empress Catherine the Great of Russia, ten years older than her lover, Potemkin. Susan Sarandon, twelve years older than her longtime partner, Tim Robbins. Mary Tyler Moore, married for more than twenty years to a doctor eighteen years her junior.

Bedding youth is one way to hold on to it.

MOST WOMEN VACILLATE between the two types of men, changing their bias from one day to the next. The White Bride part of a woman wants to be dominated but also cherished and praised by her King-father. She can tolerate only a man she can't beat down. The Black Bride wants to be Queen in her own right, not merely the King's wife. She wants a male who will take over half her burdens, leaving her free to concentrate on her own ambitions.

"A man who'll do what I tell him," says a married woman at a dinner table when Freud's famous question is raised of what it is that women want. The next moment her voice changes, as if the Black Bride has vanished from the table and the White Bride has slipped into her seat. "But I'll say this for my Bert. If ever there's another terrorist attack like September 11 and I'm lost downtown, I have absolute faith that he'll find me—I don't know how, but he will. And get me out of there."

This alternation of desire for two sorts of men has been studied by a scientist who showed women slightly varied computer images of the same male face and asked them to choose the one they liked best. On days when the women were ovulating, they picked a macho, sexualized look with a square jaw and a prominent brow, promising powerful genes. The rest of the month they gave priority to a gentler, slightly more feminine face, a nurturer rather than an impregnator.

But is it realistic to expect the mate who was right for us at twenty-five to be right for us at forty-five or sixty-five, much less till death do us part? We come back to Margaret Mead's prescription for women.

Three heterosexual relationships in a lifetime: The first for sex. The second for parenthood. The third, after the hormone tumult dies down, for companionship.

But this prescription doesn't satisfy our deepest yearning, which is to find a partner who will grow with us from one stage into the next and next. Marriage involves not one transformation but a stream of transformations over time, reinforcing or opposing one another, and the fact we overlook is that time itself is a magical element. Married couples share two bonds that are deeper than sex: children and memories, either of which may be troublesome, and yet indisputably, indissolubly their own.

CURIOUS GAMES WERE PLAYED in the French countryside as late as the twentieth century on the evening before a wedding. In Bresse, the bride-to-be and her girlfriends gathered in a room where they exchanged clothes. (Presumably they also put on masks, although the chronicler, who wrote his account in 1823, does not mention this.) The groom and his men arrived at the bride's house and found it locked, but gained entry by claiming that they had to search for an ewe they had lost. After some delay, while the men were told there was no ewe on the property that belonged to them, the girls' room was discovered and the girls were obliged to come out one at a time and dance in front of the groom. If he failed to recognize the woman he would marry the next day, "he becomes the object of banter for the rest of the evening," the observer said.

In other parts of Europe, the bride sat in full view of the assemblage variously disguised as an old man smoking a pipe by the fire, a beggar, a grandmother crocheting lace, who waited to see if the groom could recognize her as the person hidden beneath the borrowed clothes. (In *Jane Eyre*, Mr. Rochester disguises himself as a gypsy fortune-teller, and fools all his unmarried female guests except Jane.) Ethnologists account for these games by saying that in past ages a marriageable woman could be valuable property, and so her community might try to palm off a less desirable female, a child or crone perhaps, in exchange for the agreed upon bride-price.

Something more basic than the fear of fraud must underlie these charades, however, or they would not have survived as late as the nineteenth century. The message runs deeper. The true bride is not who you think she is, the games warn us. She takes on many guises. An undeserving groom may fail to find her. The bride hides for the same reason Cinderella hides from her Prince: Not until he picks her out among all the women of his kingdom will she have anything to do with him, because only then can she be sure that the acuteness of his vision of her is equal to the force of his desire.

These games of the hidden or substitute bride remained common in rural Europe until the more modern wedding outfit became fashionable in the 1870s, with a veil that covered the bride's face. Until recently, it was considered bad luck for a groom to see the bride on the wedding day before they reached the altar.

During the years when a young woman is single, she longs to be admired for her beauty, without recognizing beauty as a veil of another sort—a golden gown that dazzles a suitor's eyes and prevents him from establishing contact with the self hidden underneath. But no woman regards her appearance as intrinsic to her self. She knows perfectly well that it has been worked over by outsiders as well as by herself (Marilyn Monroe wasn't blonde to begin with; that was a photographer's inspiration), so that it fluctuates wildly in value from day to day but also from breakfast to supper. A bad-hair day is emphatically a bad day. Not a day when she will be loved. In time, she may be left with nothing but bad-hair days, wrinkled-face days, drooping-body days.

For this reason, when a lover praises his sweetheart's beauty, she grows nervous as well as gratified. She wants to be perfect in his eyes—never mind the fact that she's feeling irritable today and is suffering from cramps—but at the same time she wants him to penetrate her veil. More than anything, she wants to be known for who she is, to have her disguises seen through and to be wanted nonetheless, but only by one person while remaining veiled to everyone else. In particular, she wants her chosen man to appreciate the willfulness, contempt, and appetites of the Black Bride inside her, whom she recognizes as her secret treasure, and love her because of her strength. This is why modern women so often find it thrilling to fall in love with psychiatrists, doctors, artists, teachers, people to whom we attribute insights greater than the norm. By contrast, the woman who wants her lover to think she is always kind and caring is apt to wind up in the divorce courts.

At the gala barbecue near the beginning of *Gone with the Wind*, after Scarlett O'Hara has seen Rhett Butler but not yet spoken to him, her beloved Ashley Wilkes devastates her with the announcement that he plans to marry his cousin Melanie Hamilton. Scarlett has already described Melanie as "a pale-faced mealy-mouth ninny"—in other words, a gentle soul, a flawless White Bride chosen by the King. In a state of shock, Scarlett draws Ashley into the library, away from the other guests, and declares her passionate love for him.

"Isn't it enough that you have the heart of every other man here?" Ashley replies tenderly. "You've always had mine. You cut your teeth on it."

"Have I your heart, my darling?" Scarlett asks in rapture. "Don't you want to marry me?"

"I'm going to marry Melanie," he insists. "Oh my dear . . . how could I help loving you? You have all the passion for life I lack. But that kind of passion isn't enough to make a marriage."

"But you're going to marry Melanie."

"She's like me. She's part of my blood. We understand each other."

Scarlett slaps his face. The Black Bride is determined to usurp the role of the White. Ashley, the perfect gentleman, withdraws in silence and closes the door. A moment later, Scarlett hurls a porcelain vase across the room, smashing it against the fireplace. From behind the sofa appears Rhett Butler, who has apparently been napping there. "Phew!" he exclaims. "Has the war started?"

Scarlett is aghast. "Sir! You should have made your presence known."

"In the middle of that beautiful love scene?"

"Sir! You are no gentleman."

"And you, miss, are no lady." His tone is one of amused admiration. Sparks of passion fly through the air. "But don't think I hold that against you."

With the perverse hunger of all Black Brides, Scarlett wants to capture milky Ashley Wilkes, the quintessential White Groom, while Ashley wants Melanie, the White Bride. Meanwhile the Black Groom sees through the Black Bride, right down to her shimmy, and knows instantly that she is the partner for him.

Recognizing the blackness of the Black Bride is seductively easy in our culture, but the White Bride wants to be recognized for her strength as the protective mother, who will almost certainly put her child's interests ahead of her husband's if they conflict, and also for her peculiar form of dominance: She may insist on lying back and having the man possess her, even if he prefers to be enticed.

"Know us both," the bride says to the groom when she raises her veil.

IN FORMER TIMES, the Black Bride was a hideous stepsister with one eye ("Brother and Sister"), or a treacherous servant who steals her mistress's clothes on the way to the wedding ("The Goose Girl"), but in recent centuries blackness has reveled in its function as the emblem of female power, beloved in the form of the "little black dress." Instead of being a sign of evil or grief, darkness now seems impressive, self-sufficient, richer, and more bewitching than light, which reveals everything at a single glance. The Black Bride, with her "bristly black lashes" under "her thick black brows slanted upward," like Scarlett O'Hara in the novel (as distinct from the film)

Gone with the Wind, captivates us so completely that the challenge is to see if anything exists behind the lowered eyelids and pallid complexion of Melanie Hamilton, the White Bride.

Black intimidates us with its glamour. Rebecca, the first Mrs. Maxim de Winter, with her convent-embroidered silk underwear, used to have her dark hair brushed a hundred strokes every night by her faithful housekeeper, Mrs. Danvers, in contrast to the plain-vanilla heroine of the story, a paid companion, who wears schoolgirl sweater sets and tucks her colorless hair behind her ears.

Even Bertha Mason, the beast-bride of Mr. Rochester, whose face has turned purple with rage during her years of confinement, was originally "the boast of Spanish Town" in Jamaica for her dark Creole beauty. These days, we no longer recoil from beast-Bertha. A century after *Jane Eyre* was written, Bertha (renamed Antoinette Cosway) becomes the heroine of a novel in her own right, *Wide Sargasso Sea*, in which the author, Jean Rhys, identifies her with her own youth in Dominica.

Nothing can be added to black or change it, since it contains all colors. In our own time, the Black Bride is rampant, not only permitted but pressured to develop her talents, earn graduate degrees, launch herself into a career, rent an apartment, take a lover, climb up the letterhead, change jobs, change lovers and hairdos (one presages the other), ring all the possible variations on singleness, until one day (quite possibly in her late thirties) she decides that achievement is not enough. She'll keep her job but also become a wife, maybe a mother—in which case she'll be the perfect mother, so much more companionable and athletic than her own mother was, and at the same time a force in the outer world.

White, on the other hand, is possibility, an expanse waiting for something to be written on it. White defines herself by the relationships she enters into. She, too, is overburdened in our time, when marriages are no longer arranged by families, and bachelors stay warily on the sidelines, so that she has to play the matchmaker, the parent of her own welfare, as well as the available maiden, and after that a compulsory wage earner, helping to pay off the mortgage for a two-career family.

But there is one thing the Black Bride cannot do, at least not satisfactorily: mother a child. For her, that's the ultimate fall from the individual role to the generic, from her own path to the needs of others. Only the White Bride can give birth and rear a child properly, which is why she is the essential complement of the Black Bride.

"Why, a cat's a better mother than you are!" Rhett Butler says contemptuously to Scarlett. He's right. Melanie is the Madonna, natural as milk. And yet neither Melanie nor her baby (more to the point, Ashley Wilkes's baby) would have survived had it not been for Scarlett, the man-woman, who delivers the baby, literally under cannon fire from Yankee guns, while resenting childbirth as an implacable force that won't bend to her will. "Oh Melanie, Melanie, I hate you. I hate your baby," Scarlett cries, and yet she stays by Melanie's bedside while Atlanta burns and the other civilians flee. Caught in a bond stronger than like or dislike, and beyond their reach, she delivers the baby alone, and gets mother and child out of the city in a farm wagon, while the remnants of the Southern army straggle out of the city.

This is the compelling attraction of the Black Bride. She is more female than other females, but at the same time she is male, a woman who wears a skirt with a pistol tucked in the waistband. And this is what an older woman senses when she meets her prospective daughter-in-law for the first time: Here stands a woman who can (or, woefully, cannot) get my grandchild safely out of a burning city.

Apparently every baby requires two mothers: a White one for conception and tenderness, a Black one for strength. Seen from that standpoint, the Black Bride is the instinct within us for self-preservation, the White Bride the instinct to continue the species—two wildly different but interdependent urges that serve the same end.

But it's the Black Bride whom all of us have to reckon with first. If she climbs into the King's bed before the White Bride shows up on the scene, that's because she's the part of ourselves we recognize from infancy, before we discover that other people exist apart from their duties in caring for us. We are hungry. We scream. We never forget hunger and the risk that it may not be filled. All our lives, as Saul Bellow says, our hearts thump with the beat "I want—I want—I want," though we try to keep others from hearing it. Later on, with puberty, the dominant goal is to please and attract others, especially boys and men. The Black Bride goes into hiding behind the smiles of the White Bride, not to appear in public again until she's settled in the wedding coach, on her way to capture the King.

Black is power. White is goodness. One is as real and worthy as the other. We tell ourselves that we integrate the two in our lives, but of course we don't. We alternate. In bursts so swift that we don't notice them, we move toward one end of the scale or the other, from appreciation to irritation and back, never reaching either extreme, never remaining in place so long as we are with other people.

ADAM'S FIRST WIFE, according to an ancient Jewish legend, was not Eve but Lilith (whose name means "night spirit"), a creature formed from dust, as Adam was, at the same time he was. Peace did not last long between these two, however, because every time they had intercourse Adam expected his wife to lie flat on her back underneath him.

"Why should I lie with your weight on top of me?" Lilith complained. "I was made by the same hand from the same dust you were. Are we not equal?" When Adam tried to force her to submit, Lilith uttered the unspeakable name of God in rage, rose straight into the air, and flew off to the Red Sea, where she slept with demons in a cave and gave birth to more than a hundred diabolical children every day.

Adam complained to God, who sent three angels to order her return, but Lilith, the furious Black Bride, refused, saying that no woman who spent her nights consorting with demons beside the sea could ever be a docile housewife afterwards. She would follow her own bent, even though God killed a hundred of her children every day. In her scorn for women who lie on their backs and surrender to the thrust of a penis, she vowed to strangle their newborn children, which is what she does to this day unless she's prevented.

Her sole concession to the angels was that she would spare any newborn child protected by an inscription bearing their three magic names, a custom still followed among some Orthodox Jewish families today. But every time that she is prevented from murdering a human child, in frustration she eats one of her own.

Lilith, the child killer—"a demoness with long black hair," the Talmud calls her—became Lilith, the succubus, who appears naked in the night to lie on top of innocent men sleeping alone and force them to have sex with her. To get what she craves, she rubs against them with her belly, which is as smooth as a lima bean because she has no navel, not having been born from a mother. The ungovernable Black Bride, who always comes onto the scene first, turns into the male nightmare of the sexually demanding female come true.

God didn't make the same mistake twice. Adam's second wife, Eve, was shaped from his rib, which made it clear that this White Bride was not of the same primal substance as her husband but simply a chip off the original block, bound to obey her husband as he obeyed God. In time Adam died. Eve died. Lilith, who wasn't present at the Fall, was not condemned to death. To this day, she howls in her loneliness like the night spirit she is, eating her children according to the custom of witches, but she survives.

WHEN THE COACHMAN LATCHES the door of the royal coach with two brides seated inside it, each of the spirits realizes that, without thinking, she has locked herself into the situation. So has the man, of course, but the woman's fear is more acute. She can walk out on her husband, she can divorce him, but she can't divorce her children, whether or not she is a seal wife (Chapter Thirteen). Often she can't divorce her husband, either; she has children to feed.

"We never quarreled until we took the idea of getting married seriously," says a man who has been married for thirty years. In the next breath, in front of his wife, he relates the story of a flirtation he carried on with his private nurse in his home while recovering from heart surgery.

Outside the coach window, the landscape is growing surprisingly flat, as if the peaks and valleys have been ironed out of it. Can the heroine's story be drawing toward an end? Wanting, being wanted, being discarded or discarding, losing hope, losing the glass slipper, proving that her foot fits the slipper without wondering whether she wants to wear it, marrying the King who sends her a dress, or else stealing the dress from her stepsister—how does the story go on from here?

At this point the bride is only a third, or maybe a quarter, of the way through her life span, but already she suspects that she's much closer to middle age than she was when she left home a few hours ago.

"LOOK WHAT I'M GIVING UP," the Black Bride mutters, if we can imagine a dialogue between the two spirits after the coach door closes on them. "Even my name. All these years it's been good enough for me, but now I'm supposed to take his. As if I'm a towel he's monogrammed."

"Right," says the White Bride, smoothing the skirt of her golden gown. "A new name and title. For the first time in my life, I feel secure. When I think of the fellow I almost married, only because he was better than no one . . . I escaped by the skin of my teeth."

"Does he think I'm going to be his servant when we're married? Is that why you're wearing that outrageous getup like a Christmas tree angel while I'm still dressed in this filthy rag?" her Black sister demands. "Lord and master, my eye."

"I couldn't be happy with a man who isn't the King. Though I never thought I could get one," the White Bride says proudly.

"At least I'll have a house I could never afford on my own." Without stirring, the Black Bride has taken possession of the golden gown, while her sister, who has noticed nothing, is now dressed in rags. "But I'm supposed to give up everything in return. Novelty. Sexual adventure—I was pretty good at that, you know. And you, my little pussy willow, you think you'll be crazy about getting into bed with the same man for thirty or forty years? Or do you suppose the only way to be faithful is not to risk knowing anything else?"

Age is her enemy. The Black sister knows all too well that she won't be anything nearly as desirable at forty as she is at twenty-four.

"I'll have a child," the White Bride answers. "That's the only adventure that matters." Age is her enemy, too. She'll no longer be fertile at forty-five, while her husband will continue to be fertile—so unfairly—for decades to come.

"My career will dry up," says the Black Bride. "But not my job. I'll have to go on working whether I want to or not, because every family needs two incomes these days. But a job is the opposite of a career. I expected to be someone special (I don't mind saying so myself), with my education and talents. I thought I might do something no one in the world had done before me. Which requires a kind of chastity you know nothing about—hard work and no time for fooling around."

"Give me the touch of bodies," the White Bride counters imperturbably. "Not only in bed but also in the kitchen and garden. Vegetable as well as human. Marriage needs physical work to keep it real."

The Black Bride smooths her hair under the golden hood, which she has transferred to her own head. "Motherhood!" she interrupts. "Sitting on the floor and playing with blocks by the hour. And then what am I? Sleep-deprived, that's what. I turn into a demon when I'm sleep-deprived. Tell me, why should one particular baby, who doesn't exist yet, love me—just because he depends on me for food? The idea is worse than slavery. At least slaves don't have to kiss the people who own them."

"I want a baby at least as much as a husband," the White Bride admits. "But I don't know if I'm strong enough to be responsible twenty-four hours a day for another human being's life. The only way I'm sure of not doing harm is to stay single and childless. Which I don't want."

"How interesting—we're on a bridge!" her Black sister cries out. "Will you look at the big river we're crossing? If you kick off those golden shoes you'll be able to lean farther out the window and see both shores."

The painful fact, for women, is that raising a child, or children, is simultaneously too much for one woman to do and not enough by itself.

"I SEE THAT MY Black stepsister has taken over the wedding coach," the little duck may say to herself as she paddles in the water. "My golden clothes are gone, too. But these feathers are a lot more comfortable. As soon as I learn to manage my webs and wings, I'll travel a bit. After all, I never had the chance to be alone and think before— and afterward I'll decide what I want to do. These feathers are as good a disguise as any. How lucky for me that my stepsister showed up."

The Black Bride is trapped inside the palace, dependent on her husband, the King, whom she fondles expertly. The witch-mother is by her side, egging her on. Meanwhile, the White Bride, in duck form, relies on herself, lives on her own in the wilderness and grows in strength each day, which is what every White Bride has to do. She is the one who will ultimately bear a child, which is why she must muster enough energy to expel the Black Bride from the palace.

One evening, the white duck swims up the gutter to the palace kitchen, climbs out, and orders the kitchen boy to light a fire so that she can warm her feathers. "What is my stepsister doing?" she inquires.

"She is loved by the King and sitting on his knee," the boy answers.

"May God have mercy on him," says the duck, and disappears. She returns the next night, and the next, with the same question. Hearing about this, on the fourth night the King shows up in the kitchen, and when the duck thrusts her head through the gutter he pulls out his sword and cuts through her neck. In fairy-tale language, when her head falls off, her duck consciousness falls off with it. She no longer sees herself as a hapless creature, less than a woman, but as the rightful Queen restored to her proper place, beautiful as the picture that her brother had painted of her.

With the grisly glee of Grimms' fairy tales, when the whole story is known, the Black Bride and her mother are stripped naked, put into a barrel studded with nails, and dragged by a horse all over the world, while the White Bride reigns as Queen, and her faithful brother, who was released from the snake pit at once, becomes a wealthy and distinguished man.

Virtue and beauty, the old tales tell us, are no guarantee of happiness. They are only preconditions. Strength is what's called for. With luck, eventually we turn into the women whom our husbands should have married in the first place.

CHAPTER 12

Rapunzel and Jane Eyre:
Confronting the Madwoman in the Attic

"Rapunzel," *Jane Eyre, Rebecca*

Two stories. Two Black Brides peering out of top-floor rooms. Two White Brides awaiting their turn. At the scent of male ardor, the Black Bride ousts the White, who may be less innocent than she seems.

IN REAL LIFE, a woman with these two spirits contending inside her is surprised on the morning of her wedding to find herself triumphant but also fearful at the prospect of transformation, an emotion she hadn't expected.

The Black Bride part of herself sees a trap lying in her path. She'll be locked up—not like the first Mrs. Rochester, in a room with a keeper, and not like an unmarried Victorian girl, forbidden to do anything but read a little, paint a little, pay visits a little—but locked into a schedule of married life and motherhood that can't be wrenched open. When she leaves work each day, she'll rush to pick up her youngest child at day care, do the grocery shopping, fix supper, deal with baths and cleanup, remember to ask her husband about his day, wash the children's clothes. Her evening will be spent before she opens the door. Another day snatched from her grasp. And another.

That's what confinement means: No choice over what to do with one's time. No room for impulse. Worse yet, no chance for advancement, which is particularly galling, since she is as competitive as any man. When her children are grown and gone from the house, no one will consider her accomplished. Only old.

The White Bride has an opposite but equally oppressive fear: abandonment. Marriage is forever; so is motherhood, but who on earth is worthy of being loved forever and all the time? If she doesn't preserve her marriage, she'll be a waif left alone to cry in the storm, pounding on a bedroom window with ice-cold fists like the child ghost of Cathy Earnshaw at Wuthering Heights, begging to be let in after being lost on the moors for twenty years.

There's only one way for the White Bride to be sure of getting indoors and staying warm: Marry the right man and wrap a house around herself.

The reaction to confinement is rage, or a more or less continuous state of irritation, although the woman may have no idea what she's irritable about. The fear of abandonment is depression, which is more common among married women than among the unmarried, and twice as common among women between the ages of fifteen and twenty-four as among men of similar age. Confinement and abandonment: Two aspects of the same condition, depression being anger kept under wraps. Fire and snow.

Bertha Mason and Jane Eyre are two faces of Mrs. Rochester familiar to many women, one the mirror image of the other. Sooner or later, the two Mrs. Rochesters are bound to meet in a mirror.

Rapunzel and her foster mother are White Bride and Black mother. Rapunzel is first confined and then abandoned. The mother-witch's fury is what pushes the girl from one condition to the other.

THE FIRST STORY, "Rapunzel," starts with a crime, which is the way that the old order breaks up and makes room for a new one to begin.

A young woman, pregnant with her first child, looks out her window and sees a splendid garden next door enclosed by a wall, a garden that belongs to a powerful sorceress. While the winter earth lies bare everywhere else, in this garden she sees all kinds of plants, in particular a bed full of those hardy greens known in English as rampion, in German called *rapunzel.* So intensely does the expectant mother long for a salad made with rampion that she can practically taste it coursing through her winter-starved body. "Unless you get me what I crave, I shall pine and die," she tells her husband. Appetite has become her master.

And so the frightened husband does what he has to do. Shortly before dark, he climbs over the wall and pulls up a handful of greens, but the moment that he does so the enchantress appears with terrible threats of punishment. Have mercy, the poor man pleads; he stole only in order to save his pregnant wife's life. The enchantress's anger abates a bit. Like the Beast who caught Beauty's father stealing a rose from his garden, she curbs her fury in order to drive a sterner bargain: She will give him as much rampion as he wants for his wife. All he need do in return is give her the child that his wife will soon bring into the world. "I will care for it like a mother," she adds solicitously.

On the day that the child is born, the enchantress appears in the couple's bedroom, takes the infant girl from her mother's side, and names her Rapunzel, for rampion.

Rapunzel grows up in her foster mother's house to be a beautiful girl with golden hair that streams behind her back like a queen's golden train. When she is twelve years old, the sorceress takes her into the forest and shuts her up in a tower that has neither door nor staircase, only a single window winking at the top. (Like a penis, we exclaim in our Freudian loss of innocence, a penis rising above the treetops to guard the sorceress's property.) There Rapunzel's hair continues to grow and grow, two braids like rivulets of spun gold, so that when the old woman wants to visit her foster daughter she need only cry, "Rapunzel, Rapunzel, let down your hair," and the girl untwists the braids from her head, winds them around a hook in the wall, and lowers them to the ground, twenty-five yards below. In this way, the nimble sorceress climbs up to the girl's chamber.

Years pass. The virgin, who has no idea that there is any other way to live, lets down her braids on command for the mother-witch's visits. The rest of the time she spends combing her hair and singing to relieve her loneliness. Nothing can be seen of her except her face and hair, no glimpse of her lower half, which doesn't exist yet in her consciousness but remains sheathed in the tower.

One day Rapunzel's song is overheard by a King's son while he's hunting in the forest. Charmed by the song, he tries to enter the tower but to his amazement he cannot find a door. Every day he returns to his post in the woods, until at last he sees the sorceress approach, hears her demand that Rapunzel let down her hair, and watches her climb up the braids. "If that's the ladder, I too can mount," he says to himself. At dusk the following day, he calls to Rapunzel in the sorceress's words and climbs to her chamber the same way.

Now we understand the purpose for which the hair has been growing. The silky locks streaming down the side of the tower are a banner flaunting Rapunzel's sex appeal to the world, even while no one is there to see it. At the same time, her hair is a ladder of years. If it were shorter, no one would be able to reach her; she would be unavailable for transformation. If it were longer, it would drag in the forest soil. But, coming from her own body, it's exactly the length that's needed. Her hair isn't simply hair; it's her daydreams, night dreams, and sexual desires sprouting in her brain and cascading around her in the form of braided tresses, capable of bringing a Prince to her side.

In our time, the same image holds true. When a girl's hair is so long that it caresses her shoulders, her body is overflowing its bounds and pouring itself out to the world. When she's married with children, a house and career, and her time is short, she cuts her hair equally short to change the message.

Up the stones of the tower and over the windowsill the Prince climbs, terrifying Rapunzel, who has never seen a man. But this one describes in such moving tones how his heart has given him no rest since he heard her sing (he is young and handsome, his legs are as sturdy as tree trunks) that she soon overcomes her fear and allows him to visit every day.

When at last the Prince asks Rapunzel to marry him, she tells herself, "He'll love me more than old Mother Gothel does."

HAIR IS THE TALISMAN by which we know her. If Cinderella is the slipper girl and Sleeping Beauty the dreamer, then Rapunzel is the girl with the longest hair in the world. This makes her the most attractive of all heroines, or rather the most attracting, since hair supposedly radiates energy—in particular, sexual energy—the way the sun radiates heat. The mother-witch must believe this, which is why she keeps the girl locked up in a tower.

Orthodox Jews fear hair as stringently as Rapunzel's witch does, and for the same reason. While a woman is single, the rabbis say, her hair attracts potential husbands, which serves God's purpose of fruitfulness, but once she's married her head must be kept covered by a kerchief or wig in the presence of any man other than her husband. The best wigs are made of human hair, which reveals the bias of the law. Apparently a woman doesn't sin by spending a lot of money and time on her looks, since a fine *sheitel,* or wig, can cost five to seven thousand dollars, with five or six hundred more for styling when it's washed. The sin lies in attracting a man who is not her husband through the power that streams from her hair. Another woman's hair on top of her head can do her no harm. Saint Paul felt the same way, which is why Christian women were commanded to cover their heads in church.

As the only part of the body that can be cut, dyed, changed in style, and then grow back, hair invites the owner to change the signals she sends to the world. Through hair or lack of it, we identify certain females at first sight: Mother Teresa with her kerchief; or the black-hooded Queen in *Snow White,* without a lock visible to betray their sexuality. Childish Goldilocks with yellow curls, or Alice in Wonderland with her hair shoulder length, almost ready for sex but restrained by a girlish ribbon. Cruella de Vil, whose hair is half black and half white, a wickedly unnatural combination. Barbie, the Rapunzel of dolls. A short-haired Barbie would be an oxymoron. And unsalable.

At the same time, hair displays a woman's moral as well as sexual worth. After World War II, French women who had slept with Nazi soldiers were dragged to public squares and tied to chairs while their hair was shaved off. In the fifteenth century, Joan of Arc was condemned to death in part because she had cropped her hair like a boy's and cross-dressed in a warrior's armor, but in illustrations of her story from then on, she is shown with long golden locks like an angel's (as author Marina Warner points out in her book *From the Beast to the Blonde*).

Thelma and Louise set out on their deadly escapade with their hair bound up in rollers and scarves, but early in the film named for them their hair becomes loose, curly—in fact, snaky—but far more beautiful, so that they attract men even as they are prepared to kill them.

BUT HOW IS RAPUNZEL to escape? "Bring me a skein of silk every time you come to visit," she tells the Prince. "I will weave a ladder, and when it's long enough you may come for me on your horse and I will climb down to meet you."

The deed is as good as done. All she has to do now is keep quiet.

She speaks. "Tell me, Mother Gothel," she says in the sanitized later editions of the Grimms' tales, "how is it that you are so much heavier for me to pull up than the Prince? When I pull him up, he's here in a moment." In the original 1812 version of the story, she is less discreet: "Tell me, Mother Gothel, why do you think my clothes have become too tight for me and no longer fit?"

It scarcely matters which she says. The point is that at the last minute the White Bride lets out a cry for help. Stop this wedding, get me out of this situation, I don't know what I'm doing, she cries without realizing it, racked by the terror of getting what she supposes she wants. The cry is directed toward the only person capable of jamming a wrench in the plans, the female fury known as the Black Bride—in this case, the mother-witch.

At the same time, the girl reminds herself that "he will love me more than old Mother Gothel does." Marriage as escape, marriage as spitting in the face of parents: Every girl from an unhappy home longs to throw herself into the arms of a man who will make up to her for everything she has missed, swaddle her with attention so that nothing can bruise her again. If the wedding were to go through now without hindrance, the White Bride part of the heroine would remain a child locked up in a tower, only it would be the Prince's tower rather than the mother-witch's.

The hunger for love is as sharp as the hunger for rampion.

"You wicked child!" cries the sorceress. "I thought I had separated you from the world, and yet you deceived me." Grasping Rapunzel's braids, she wraps them around her left hand, while with her right she seizes a pair of scissors, which have undoubtedly been kept on the spot for just this purpose. Snip, snap. The braids lie on the floor. Afterward, she leads the shorn girl into the wilderness, "where she had to live in great grief and misery."

Without her hair, Rapunzel is thrust beyond the usual marriage plot. Like other women who have lost their looks through illness, old age, or accident, she has to rely on herself and the power stored within her, rather than on her power to attract a man.

DESERT, FOREST, MOORS, OR SNOWSCAPE, the interior landscape is the same—a place of hardship and isolation where transformation to adult independence can take place for those who are ready for it. According to the Bible, the Jews spent forty years in the desert with Moses until everyone who remembered being a slave under Pharaoh in Egypt had died, along with their slavish habits of mind, and the new generation had grown strong enough to handle freedom. Without time spent in the wilderness alone, no real change is possible.

An hour earlier, Rapunzel was the rampion girl rampant, born of her mother's appetite and her father's imprudence. Now she starts life over again in the desert, no longer anybody's protected darling. Although she doesn't know it yet, she will soon become a mother.

WHEN THE PRINCE ARRIVES at the tower that evening and eagerly sings, "Rapunzel, Rapunzel, let down your hair," the braids are lowered as usual. But when he climbs as high as the window the face that bobs out to meet his own is not that of his promised bride but that of the sorceress, with malice gleaming in her eyes. "Aha!" she cries in mockery. "The beautiful bird is no longer singing in the nest. The cat has got it, and will scratch your eyes out as well. You will never see your Rapunzel again." The Black Bride has taken the White Bride's place, appropriating her hair like a golden hood. But the Prince scarcely has a chance to look at her. Stunned, he jumps from the window, escaping alive but landing in a patch of thorns that pierce his eyes and blind him. Blindness or dazzlement is the fate of grooms in these double-bride stories; exile is the fate of brides.

But how can the Prince act like a Prince and save Rapunzel if he is blind? Luckily for her, he can't. Instead, she must wander in the desert, where she gives birth to twins, a boy and a girl, while the Prince stumbles through a forest, surviving on roots and berries.

ANOTHER STORY OF TWO BRIDES, Black and White again, but not a fairy tale this time: These two brides appear in a nineteenth-century gothic setting, where the White one is not the prisoner.

For the White Bride, we have plain Jane, tiny Jane, the governess hired by Edward Rochester for thirty pounds a year and imported to his manor house in his absence to tutor his child ward.

Jane Eyre. Air, airy, aerial. Ariel, the ghostly sprite who materializes on a deserted road under a rising moon, just before her employer's horse slips on a sheet of ice, confining the master to the house with a sprained ankle. But every Ariel must have its Caliban, beast-woman, in this case Bertha the beast—woman, purple with fury. Jane and Bertha. Eyre and ire. A displacement of the vowel: One Mrs. Rochester changes to the other.

Eyre. Eyrie, the eagle's nest, the top floor and rooftop where White Bride and Black Bride confront one another in the place of confinement, and first one, then the other, is undone.

Eyre produces heir. In the end.

WHEN JANE IS TEN, Aunt Reed, the mother-witch, sends the girl out of the house to Lowood School, possibly to die of hunger and disease like many of her schoolmates. There she stays until she is eighteen, when she is old enough to take a job as governess.

Like so many fairy-tale virgins—like Psyche entering the palace of the god of love, or Beauty in the home of the Beast, or any of us in our dreams—when the heroine reaches sexual maturity she leaves behind the cramped quarters of childhood and moves into a mansion that symbolizes her new position, equipped with every luxury but harboring a dark erotic secret.

On her first day as governess, Jane is taken on a tour by the kindly housekeeper. The drawing rooms on the ground floor are furnished with white carpets and crimson couches, white marble fireplaces and ruby Bohemian glass, a showcase of fire and ice, nothing shadowy here, only colors that burn like the passions of the house. The second-floor rooms are furnished for family use, but it's the third floor that interests Jane. (Every story another story.) Here the rooms are low and dark, filled with tapestries whose pictures are as threadbare as old memories.

With its row of small black doors all shut, the top floor looks "like a corridor in some Bluebeard's castle." In Bluebeard's forbidden room, evidence of his previous wives' suffering is locked out of sight. In Mr. Rochester's house, behind one of the doors Jane hears a flat, humorless laugh, a sound unmoderated by reason, growing and echoing through every room on the floor, then dying away. She has heard the voice of "the madwoman in the attic," to use the title of the book by Sandra Gilbert and Susan Gubar that so ably describes one Mrs. Rochester as the alter ego of the other.

A moan or cry would be upsetting and yet human, but a laugh— a toneless laugh and then a "low, slow ha!," which Jane hears often in the days that follow—can only come from a creature with passions that mock our assumption of a rational world.

A few months later, there is a house party attended by elegant ladies, including one particularly haughty beauty whom Mr. Rochester is supposed to marry. Jane has learned to love him, as she admits to herself; she cannot now learn to unlove. A mysterious stranger from abroad, a Mr. Mason, appears at the party. That night—full moon, when lunatics prowl—Jane is awakened by savage screams overhead. The stranger has been slashed by a knife, but also gnawed by a set of teeth. "She worried me like a tigress," he says.

And where does the attack take place? In the room directly above Jane's head.

In a house so large, this rooming arrangement seems improbable, but it expresses the metaphor of the story: mad, embittered beast-Bertha is the shadow soul of the reserved little virgin, pure as Eyre. The Black Bride lodges on top of the White Bride in the tower, just as the Minotaur wore the head of a bull on top of the body of a man, since she embodies the anger that the daytime Jane so steadily represses. Here are two females, two brides, in fact two Mrs.

Rochesters—one actual and hidden in the attic, the other heading toward marriage and cloaked by insignificance: Every time Jane's feelings are violated, or a current of sexual desire runs through the house, Bertha erupts with knife or teeth or fire.

When Mr. Rochester finally proposes marriage to Jane, he sees himself, like Rapunzel's Prince, rescuing an innocent maiden and carrying her off to a distant land, far from the witch in the attic. "You—poor and obscure and small and plain as you are—I entreat to accept me as a husband," he says.

Like Rapunzel, Jane has never known another man, and yet she is too proud not to feel degraded by her lover's determination to deck her in diamonds and cover her head with "a priceless veil" for the wedding, as if she were a peer's daughter. If the marriage goes through as scheduled, she understands that she will still be her husband's employee, though unpaid, his child, his protégée, his concubine, but not his equal.

In this state of desire counterbalanced by dismay, Jane does what Rapunzel does: She speaks—or rather, writes—where she had better stay silent. She sends a letter to her unknown uncle in Madeira, who has said that he wants to make her his heir, letting him know about her wedding plans. In effect, like Rapunzel, she lets out a call for help to stop the marriage, even while she longs for it.

Thirty-six hours before the wedding, Jane is alone in the mansion, her emotions at fever pitch. With everything ready for the ceremony, she goes to bed and dreams terrible dreams of the hall in ruins, "the retreat of bats and owls." Apparently the nightmares rise above her head and seep through the ceiling to the chamber of the Black Bride.

During the night, Jane is awakened by a gleam of light. A silent female, holding a candle, surveys the wedding dress and veil that Jane has hung in readiness for the morning. The intruder is the size of a man, with matted black hair hanging down her back, dressed in a straight white gown that could be a nightgown or sheet or shroud. Holding up the "priceless veil" that Jane never wanted to wear because it was too grand for her, like the golden gown in the fairy tale, the apparition stares at it—does she remember wearing it herself?—throws it over her head and turns toward the mirror. White gown, bridal veil, the outfit is complete. Black Bride has taken over the costume of White Bride.

The horror in the mirror is not because the reflection is strange but because it's not entirely strange.

All of us are crazy ladies at times, especially during the blood years between puberty and menopause (though we try to rein ourselves in and pass for sane), driven mad by anger, lust, or tedium, or simply the passage of days. Locked in the room from which she has briefly escaped, Bertha knows a kind of freedom that Jane, for all her elfin grace, has never dreamed of: the freedom to be outrageous, to be ugly, which is thrust on all of us when we are old or sick and no longer care what anyone thinks of us, because we know we are beneath approval and can do nothing about it.

Forget the smoothly combed hair pinned in a bun, Bertha would say to Jane if she could. Forget your black stuff dress and ladylike behavior while you seethe inside. Come out in your nightgown, ready to slash, bite, burn. Or, if you insist that you love your deceiver, virtuous little governess, then live with him in bigamy, live in adultery in the south of France. Which is what he's going to propose to you anyway. Live on top of him and the law.

The next moment, the Black Bride tears the veil off her head, rips it in two (a sexual metaphor) and tramples on it, before blowing out the candle and leaving the room.

During the ceremony the following morning, when the clergyman asks the routine question whether anyone present knows of any impediment why this man and woman may not lawfully be joined in matrimony, a man speaks up from the back of the church. He turns out to be the lawyer for Mr. Mason. There is indeed an impediment, the lawyer asserts: the existence of a living wife, Mr. Mason's sister, Bertha Mason Rochester, the madwoman who has been imprisoned in the attic. How did he find out about the prospective bigamy? Mr.

Mason was alerted by the letter that Jane sent to her uncle in Madeira, where Mason happened to be a houseguest.

Like Rapunzel's Prince, when Edward Rochester thinks he is about to collect his chosen bride he finds himself face-to-face with the Black Bride, the witch-wife in the tower. Leading the thwarted wedding party from the church to his house, he opens the door to the room "she has now for ten years made a wild beast's den—a goblin's cell." The first Mrs. Rochester crawls on all fours. She growls like an animal as she attacks her husband with the androgynous strength of the Black Bride. Madness and malignancy have fed her flames.

There will be no wedding until the fires burn themselves out.

WITHIN AN HOUR Jane has changed from a ripe, expectant bride into an abandoned child. "A Christmas frost had come at midsummer." The next morning, she uses the few shillings in her purse to take a coach to a village chosen at random, with no money, no food or lover to rely on. Her life is over, she tells herself. She is not yet twenty.

For two days and nights, Jane tramps through pelting rain and sleeps on the open moor. When nearly dead from exposure, she sees a light from a cottage in the distance (much like the cottage that Snow White finds), humbler than the house she has left but safer. As she learns later, the owners of the house are cousins she never knew she had.

Jane Eyre is, at bottom, a fairy tale.

THE MOOR FOR JANE, the river for the white duck, the desert for Rapunzel. Just when she thought she had done with loneliness forever, the heroine finds herself struggling to survive alone in the wilderness.

Loneliness is the alchemy that turns an adolescent into an adult. Adolescents are profoundly lonely, but believe that their pangs will be solved by finding a lover, while the adult recognizes loneliness as the defining term of the human condition. This is what can bring tears to a woman's eyes after sex: For a short while she has known union, she has been complete, but the interval is over, and she must return to the chilly sheets on the other side of the bed.

Sooner or later, every woman is schooled in solitude, whether she is a jilted lover, discarded wife, outgrown parent, or widow. The new widow does not miss her late husband, with all his quirks and particularities, so much as she dreads the silence in her house. "I am alone," she says to herself, and her answer must be, "Of course. I always was. I just didn't know it." Journeys end in partners parting.

On the moor, Jane Eyre learns her lessons: She existed before she met Edward Rochester, and can go on existing without him, if she must. She didn't really know him in the first place; she was marrying her "dear master." Now she sees him with different eyes, loving him none the less but seeing him with a twinge of pity mixed with horror. Like Cinderella (Chapter Three), she learns what she can live without, though her list is different: Without a husband. Without motherhood. Without love, if she can substitute work that has a compelling purpose. Even without happiness, so long as she has a chance for growth.

DURING THE FOLLOWING MONTHS, Jane finds work as the mistress of the village school, a post that provides her with a two-room cottage of her own. Her uncle dies, making her the heir of his fortune. Her male cousin, handsome as a Greek statue and just as cold, proposes marriage. She turns him down.

One night, Jane hears a disembodied voice issuing not from the house or garden or ground, and not from overhead: the voice of Edward Rochester calling, "Jane! Jane! Jane!" She leaves her cottage the next morning in search of him.

Since last hearing that voice, Jane has acquired everything she lacked as a White Bride: a home, a job, blood relatives, money of her own, a choice between two men. All these are essential. Marriage must not come to a woman in the form of a life raft. It must come as a choice, if she is not to remain a little white duck forever.

She has also acquired something more formidable that isn't described in fairy tales: she has acquired a vision of a quiet, consistent central self, alone in the universe. This is the bedrock on which a woman's decision to marry must stand. Her marriage can't be successful until she no longer needs it—which doesn't mean that she doesn't want it, but the difference between want and need is critical.

ANOTHER GAME WAS PLAYED in the French countryside in past centuries, besides the masquerades of hidden or substitute brides described in the last chapter: Friends of the family threw a dummy called "the first bride," or "the ghost," off the roof of the house to the young men gathered in the courtyard, who then set fire to the figure.

Mrs. Danvers, the implacable housekeeper and mother-witch for her beloved dead Rebecca, the first wife of Maxim de Winter, burns down the superb mansion of Manderley rather than see control pass to the timid second wife who has taken Rebecca's place. Framed by fire, the housekeeper stands in a top-floor window, looking down on the hated successor, the White Bride and her groom, until the building collapses beneath her.

Bertha Mason, the imprisoned wife of Mr. Rochester, will erupt in fury during Jane Eyre's absence and appear on the roof of her husband's mansion, after first setting fire to the bed of the hated little governess.

Black Brides have a penchant for rooftops, attics, upper balconies, top-floor windows, as if their feelings smolder in the brains of the houses they inhabit. When the White Bride, small as she may be, finds her strength, the Black Bride knows herself doomed. Her only revenge is to bring the house down with her.

Late one night, two months after Jane leaves the Rochester house, Bertha steals the keys to her room from her keeper's pocket. By the time Edward Rochester climbs to the roof and catches up with her, the house is blazing. As she stands on the battlements, her long black hair streams in the flames; her shouts fly out over the countryside. Rochester climbs through the skylight to rescue her, but as he does so she springs backward and falls to her death on the pavement below.

After saving his servants, Mr. Rochester is crushed by the burning timbers of the house, one eye knocked out of his head and the other injured, his arm maimed. He is left as "stone blind" as Rapunzel's Prince, who fell from the sorceress's tower onto the thorn bushes that pierced his eyes. And what is the name of the house that blinds Mr. Rochester? Thornfield Hall.

Rapunzel's Prince wanders in the wilderness for years, until one day he hears a familiar voice. Rapunzel recognizes him and falls weeping on his neck. Two of her tears wet his eyes, which grow clear again.

After Jane and Edward Rochester are reunited, she serves as his eyes and guide as well as comforter without upsetting either of them by the shift of power, because of their mutual love, "bone of his bone and flesh of his flesh." Two years after their marriage, the sight in his single eye is restored, not by Jane's tears but, presumably, by her love.

As in so many stories, the heroine heals and redeems the man, rather than the man rescuing the woman. By the time that Rochester's firstborn child is placed in his arms, "he could see that the boy had inherited his own eyes, as they once were."

IN EVERY STORY, the White Bride emerges from the wilderness as the man's equal, in some ways his superior. The Black Bride is heard from no more.

But we know that the Black Bride hasn't disappeared. She waits in the bottom of every woman's soul, ready to storm onto the scene on those days when domestic life seems "a goblin's cell," or she waits for another story to begin. In this other story—in a different guise—she is as determined as ever not to surrender her independence to anyone, not even her children, but she no longer wants a golden robe and the title of Queen. Instead, she wants what seems to be the opposite: her freedom. A return to her earlier existence. This implies her transformation, at least temporarily, into the Seal Wife who appears in the next chapter.

Meanwhile, the White Bride achieves her own transformation with the christening of her first child.

CHAPTER 13

The Seal Wife:

Hungry for Intimacy, Thirsty for Silence

"The Seal Wife," *The Awakening, Kramer vs. Kramer,* the Early Life of Doris Lessing

Every woman spends much of her life wavering on the borderline between independence and intimacy. In terms of her story, if she thinks about the matter at all she supposes that she'll cross the border a few times in her life in the direction of intimacy (when she becomes a lover, when she marries, most particularly when she bears children) and cross it a few times in the opposite direction (when her parents die, when her children leave home, or when her marriage comes to an end one way or the other).

The less dramatic truth is that she crosses it many times a day in each direction, never without a stab of impatience or guilt. Is she most herself when her emotions are tumbled by children, laundry, the dirt on the kitchen floor, grocery shopping, the logistics of getting the car serviced and taking the dog to the vet, or when she is alone? Which does she really want: intimacy or isolation, to use Erik Erikson's terms? To be herself or to belong to others? Depth or breadth of experience? Every morning when her feet touch the floor she dedicates herself, willy-nilly, to the demands of a family; she is fractured into a multitude of shards. But every night, when she falls asleep, she floats alone and ageless in the slippery world of dreams.

These questions are valid for a man as well but seem less urgent, since a woman is more apt to split down the middle, as we saw in the chapters on the "White Bride and the Black Bride." She's a person, but after puberty she's potentially a person-producing-person, as Rapunzel found out. She's a daughter even after her parents are gone; if she's a mother, then she's a mother until she dies.

Meditation and solitude are what a woman needs in order to replenish herself, especially during her child-rearing years. Amid the distractions of daily life, her most transformative experience next to giving birth or nursing a baby isn't sex, not even adulterous sex, but a moment of fully experienced solitude, when the soul copulates with the body. Such a moment may terrify her. Everything falls away, as at the moment of death. A small death, in fact, is what it is, a descent to the bottom of the sea. For the time being, she feels herself deep, deep and narrow as an abyss, rather than broad.

Later, as the children grow up and the house is quiet and her time, she says, is her own, as if she can hold on to it forever, she cannot stand up to such moments very long. Solitude sucks her down like an undertow. Afraid of being carried away, she switches on the television set as soon as she comes into a room, to be numbed by the sound of voices that demand nothing from her.

Inside every married woman the Black Bride and the White Bride coexist, though it's the Black Bride who takes center stage in the story of "The Seal Wife," no longer seen as a female greedy for her sister's golden cloak but as the one who yearns for the original skin she lost. I can remember a time before I had a husband or partner, she says, before I had children, when I lived in a one-room studio and supported myself, and managed just fine. And I can imagine a time to come when they'll no longer be with me, and I'll be solitary again. In fact, I'm a solitary self right now, holed up behind my little picket fence of irritabilities that protect me from at least some of the intrusions.

I'm my past self, still virgin, and I'm potential. Above all, I'm the part that has to be preserved, though well hidden.

THE HEROINE OF THIS STORY in its hundreds of variations is a female who changes her skin. She sheds her childhood along with her tail, revealing, at least for a night, her beautiful long legs and the valuable packet that lies between them, which until now have been hidden in her unconscious. Half wild and half human, marriageable but unmarried, she is an adolescent who moves from one element to another, from formless, sexless sky or water to dry land, where men live in houses and want mates.

She thinks that she does this only for a night, but she is caught, and her young, lean self is mysteriously swaddled with a husband, house, lamps, hearth, larder, washtub, and several sons, all of them hungry—all of which she may shuck off like an overcoat when the tide turns. Transformation seems impossible an hour before it happens, inevitable later on.

Depending on the area where the story is told, the heroine is most commonly captured in the form of a seal or swan. She shows up as a porpoise in Oceania, a mermaid or undine in Europe, a wild duck or goose, a magical serpent, in modern Greece a tortoise, occasionally a fox that lopes off into the darkness of the forest, but generally a creature of two elements, if not three. Water and land. Sea and sky. Movement, shape-shifting bodies changing speed as they move from one element to another. A swan stretching out its neck and taking off from the water with a thunderous crack of wings, unexpected as an angel, while on dry land it waddles like a goose.

Not quite ready for transformation to our coarse world of domestic expectations, but no longer content to stay below the waves, this folktale heroine leaves one element for another but never relinquishes the memories of her youth.

In this version, she takes the form of a seal.

EARLY ONE MORNING, a fisherman from one of the islands in the North Sea was walking along the shore of a small bay. His oilskin was wet from the mist that shrouded the rising sun and hung in folds over the hills and trees. Every morning this fisherman was the first out to his boat, for no better reason, perhaps, than that he had no wife to keep him in the featherbed.

As he picked his way among the rocks that lay humped like sleeping seals alongside the water, he heard a musical tone coming from a cave in the rocks that sounded as high as wind in the rigging, only there was no rigging nearby, and then another tone as low as the song of whales, which he heard sometimes through the wooden hull of his boat.

The tones grew into a song that became gayer and faster, and he heard laughter and clapping, while a little way ahead of him he saw a heap of what might have been seaweed but turned out to be sealskins. He picked one up and held it against his chest to warm himself. Tune flowed into tune. The clapping grew faster, and the mist lifted high enough that he could see nine or ten sea people, not a piece of clothing among them, troop out of the cave, stretching out their hands to help the others with their delicate feet cross over the boulders.

The instant they saw him, an alarm ran through them like a rock thrown into a school of fish. They hurried to the pile of skins, seized them, and slid into them, after which they dropped onto their bellies on the rocks and plunged into the sea in the form of seals.

One dancer was left, a young woman, still naked. She hunted for her skin, she called for her companions to wait for her. She saw the fisherman standing with the skin held against his chest and wordlessly pleaded with him to return it, but he did no such thing. Some yards offshore, the seal people wrinkled their necks to look back at her while they churned the shallow water in distress. The fisherman held fast. The seals spied him and moved farther offshore. Then, one by one, they turned to face the horizon and swam to deep water with only the tips of their noses showing above the water and an occasional cry to express their pain.

When they could no longer be seen, the fisherman tried to put his arm around the girl to comfort her, but when she tugged at the sealskin he held it more firmly and made it clear that the skin, and along with it the former owner, was now his. She could no more return to the frigid seawater and her old selkie life than he could.

By this time the girl was shivering, though she hadn't seemed cold a few minutes ago when she ran out of the cave. The fisherman took off his oilskin slicker, buttoned it around her, and tied the sleeves together so that she could hardly move. Then he led her into his cottage, where he dressed her in clothes.

In the years that followed the wedding of the fisherman and the selkie, she gave birth to three sons who were like every other woman's sons except for a short web between their fingers, which didn't hinder them at all, and an upward tilt where the fingers joined the palms, so that their hands looked a bit like the forepaws of seals. The Seal Wife learned to bake good bread and tended the hearth with the fascination that all sea folk feel for fire. She learned to wash herself in fresh water, which had no tang to it, no bite of home. In time, she grew fond of the fisherman, who was good to her. She was a loving mother to her sons (in legends, the children always seem to be sons), but when her husband tried to show his love for her there was a faint chill in her response. Sometimes when he took her in bed, he felt a not unpleasant shiver run through his body, as if a school of fish had swum between his legs.

As the years passed, she made no further fuss about her sealskin, which was locked away in a trunk bound with iron hoops, but from time to time she would go down to the water's edge alone, particularly in the evening when supper was done, and look out to sea with the mournful brown eyes of a seal.

At this point the storytellers give different accounts of what she saw. Some say that she went down to the water's edge to meet a large male seal who patrolled the coast, with whom she conversed in an unknown language until it was time to put her sons to bed. Others mention no such rendezvous, but agree that she sat on the rocks and looked out to sea, keeping her back turned to the land.

One Sunday her husband went to church as usual, accompanied by his boys. The Seal Wife never went with them. She feared the church and its plot of land, where she had seen a dead man put into a box and lowered into a hole in the ground where not even the highest tide could reach him. The church was the place where, soon after she came to shore, a man in a white smock had made it clear that she belonged to the fisherman from that time on, and what was more, the fisherman belonged to her. In fear and scorn she stayed home when the church bells rang, and generally used the time to go to the shore and gaze out to sea.

On this particular day, the fisherman was in such a hurry that when he put on his Sunday clothes he forgot to transfer the key of the trunk from the pocket of his work pants. The selkie kept her eye on his back until he and their sons were safely down the path, and then she picked up the pants, found the key in the pocket, and unlocked the trunk, forcing open the rusty lock and hinges. There was her sealskin, but not as she remembered it. During the years on land, it had dried out; it had cracked like a mud flat long deprived of water. She would no longer be the beautiful, moist animal she had been on the night when she came ashore.

The Seal Wife sat down and got to work chewing the pelt, mouthing it one stiff mouthful at a time to soften it. The church service had never been long enough to suit her wish to be alone, but today it seemed especially short as she moistened bite after bite. Only a little while before her husband and sons returned, the sealskin was supple enough for her to run down to the sea, clasping it under her arm, and slip it on.

Without waiting to say goodbye, she plunged into the water and swam away. And here some versions say that she swam offshore to where the great gray male was waiting, as if the storytellers in their masculine pride cannot conceive of any other reason for a wife to abandon her husband and children.

Of course, adultery is a common enough motive, a twist on the original marriage plot: think of Anna Karenina abandoning the little son she adored and a husband twenty years her senior in order to set off for Italy with the dashing Count Vronski. But the last thing the true Seal Wife/swan wife wants is another house and husband. She seeks the supple self she lost when she left her own realm and settled on dry land and learned to bathe in fresh water.

Other storytellers say that the selkie swam alone, missing her sons even while she rejoiced in her freedom. When they were grown, she swam around their fishing boats, watching with moist brown eyes those she loved and had left, and saw to it that they always had excellent luck with their fishing.

"It is given to them that their sea-longing shall be land-longing, and their land-longing shall be sea-longing," the Scottish storytellers used to say about such wives and mothers.

LONGING IS THE KEYNOTE HERE—not a single longing, as in romances, but two or more, overlapping and undercutting each other, never to be satisfied at the same time. The woman is hungry for intimacy but thirsty for silence, which is her original self gliding through the sea. How can she give up one or the other? Life is too full of potential for a single choice—she needs more than one existence to explore who she might become.

After all, why would seal maidens risk their freedom by swimming to shore and dancing in a cave if they were entirely content with their virginal existence in the sea? Transformation is a tug as irresistible as the tide, carrying us where we had no idea that we wanted to go. If the seal sisters swim to shore, it must be for the specific purpose of shedding their skins and flippers and exercising their long legs, which have been kept hidden until now (just as the Little Mermaid sheds her tail), so it can't be much of a shock if one of their number is captured by a fisherman and turned into a wife before she knows what has happened. What else did she expect?

In and out the tides go, carrying us even while we swim. From the time of her first menstrual period a girl knows that no matter what else she may be, she is a lifetime member of her gender and age group, caught up in what both her body and society tell her must be done, as subject to monthly spring tides and neap tides as the sea. A boy knows no such thing. He thinks his mission is to overcome nature, not be swept along by it. He regards himself as a self-made man, while no female ever called herself a self-made woman, not even if she has climbed to the top rung of her profession. To be self-made implies starting from scratch, erasing parents, family, and teachers, while a career woman still thinks of herself as a daughter and mother, or possibly a mother-to-be, if not in biological terms, then as a mentor and protector, but always as part of a chain.

Raising their heads from the water and looking toward shore in the few hours of summer darkness, the seal maidens see lights shining through the windows of houses. Firelight entices sea people, the stories tell us. It's the jewel they don't find at the bottom of the sea. Fire means cooked food and a man waiting in a featherbed, thick walls to keep out the wind and dampness, everything that is foreign to the sea. Fire also means an enclosed hearth of another kind, the oven of the womb that will produce children.

These preferences are not limited to humans and sea people. Out in the wild, fur-bearing seals climb up on boulders, or at least ice floes, to give birth to their young in early summer, and land is where they mate some weeks later. Their young must be taught to swim.

YEARS PASS FOR THE landlocked Seal Wife in every story. One version says fourteen, although most don't say how many, but this much we know: The heroine stays in the home until her children are no longer babies, unless there are servants in the house. Meanwhile, she has no cause to complain about her husband. He's a good man by the world's standards. He doesn't beat or insult his wife or chase other women; he isn't overly demanding; he's a good father and provider. In fact, he dotes on her youth and beauty, possibly because there is always something elusive in the response of this Seal Wife who has never opened fully to her captor or his land life.

Doting may be one of his faults. "My squirrel," "my sweet little songbird," Torvald Helmer calls his wife, Nora, in Ibsen's play *A Doll's House.* "My most precious possession. Mine—all mine." In Kate Chopin's turn-of-the-century novel *The Awakening,* the heroine's husband is alarmed when his wife chooses to bathe in the sea in the midday sun. "'You are burnt beyond recognition,'" he cries, "looking at his wife as one looks at a valuable piece of personal property which has suffered some damage." The wife may recognize that her spouse is trying to be kind, or that he thinks his tone is appropriate when he treats her as a child, a pet, a trophy, a superior servant, even a beneficent fairy, but his denseness stems from his inability to take his wife as seriously as he takes himself. He cannot believe that she is made of the same self-willed and aspiring stuff that he is.

For years she has worn the role he gives her like the fussy, constricting garment it is. But the Seal Wife story isn't a tract on woman's liberation—it digs down to the mortal predicament of having only one life to live, and moving deeper than that, to the questions of who we think we were created to be, or might have been had chance or circumstance affected us differently.

Of course, this theme of an alternative existence inspires a number of male plots as well. In contemporary terms, it seems most meaningful when two transformations take place at the same time, male and female, not only confronting but causing one another.

In the movie *Kramer vs. Kramer,* the hero is a revved-up advertising executive who is transformed by necessity into his son's mother, resistant and inept at first (the scene in which he folds up bread in a cup to make French toast while his little son sits on the kitchen counter in his underwear), but later fully engrossed. Men may not even remark the simultaneous transformation of Ted's pent-up wife, Joanna, who flees from the apartment, leaving behind her keys, her American Express card, her Bloomingdale's charge card, and the slip from the dry cleaner's for Ted's suit, as well as the suitcase that he wrests from her grasp as the elevator door closes on her. The last thing she laid in the suitcase was her son's T-shirt, for the smell of it. She returns to the wilderness (called California, in this case) as stripped of her housewife garb as the original Seal Wife.

SOONER OR LATER, something wakes up the confined Seal Wife. A romantic brush with a stranger that sets her sexual juices flowing. A tune she remembers from her past. The discovery of her old skin. A moment comes, and if we look at any moment intently enough, a hole opens up, stretches wider and wider until it blocks out the horizon, and we drop right through it.

How did she get here? she wonders. Not that there's anything the matter with here as opposed to anywhere else, but she's sure there were other possibilities in her life, maybe past or potential love affairs, that seemed perfectly real and justified at the time, and now she hardly remembers them. How did she get this particular husband, who wouldn't have been hers if she and her seal sisters had danced on another stretch of beach, in which case her children would have been other children? For the first time, she realizes that she was not only captured—or captivated—by a lonely fisherman in need of a mate; she was captured by life itself, which was lying in wait for her.

THERE IS A PART OF EVERY WIFE, human as well as selkie, that is never married, no matter how long she bears her husband's name, and never belongs to anyone else, not even her children. This shadow self—which may become more prominent after many years of marriage, when her children are old enough to fend for themselves—glides down to invisible depths whenever she chooses to evade her husband's voice or touch.

Needing to keep supple, this elusive self is represented in women's dreams and stories by water: a lake for swan maidens, or better yet the sea, site of wind, waves, sky, birds, spume, seals, and seal maidens, all things uncontrollable by man.

"The voice of the sea is seductive; never ceasing," says Kate Chopin at the beginning and the end of *The Awakening*, "whispering, clamoring, murmuring, inviting the soul to wander for a spell in abysses of solitude. . . . The voice of the sea speaks to the soul."

The sea is consolation. Thinking back to "the suck and drag of bad times" in her life, Doris Lessing remembers, "I dreamed every night about the sea, washing in and out of my sleep in sad slow tides of nostalgia, of longing."

"As everyone knows, water and meditation are wedded forever," says Herman Melville in *Moby-Dick*.

IN THE WARM SUMMER WATER of the Gulf of Mexico one moonlit night, Edna Pontellier, the heroine of *The Awakening*, learns to swim. This is an astonishing development for a twenty-eight-year-old woman, the mother of two little boys, who has spent a number of summers at this island resort of Grand Isle without conquering her dread of the water. But this night is enchanted. She has been moved by passionate piano music she has just heard, moved by moonlight, perhaps more moved than she ought to be by the attentions of Robert Lebrun, the twenty-six-year-old son of the resort proprietor, all of which fill her with a new sense of her existence.

Abruptly, ecstatically, she launches herself on the surface of the water, wanting to swim far out where no woman has swum before her.

Swimming in water over her head involves a return to a time before she was born, relying on instincts she didn't know she had.

Through her skin she is aware of her flesh. (This was especially notable a century ago, when, even on the beach, a lady was protected from the atmosphere by a hat, a face veil, and doeskin gauntlets, along with draperies that reached to her toes.) Edna lifts her feet off the sandy bottom and kicks, she stretches herself and strokes toward the horizon, where the sky is not quite as dark as the sea—nearly exceeding her strength, which she doesn't know how to gauge yet. She leaves the protection of her forty-year-old husband, along with his shore life, so far behind, it seems to her, that for a moment she doubts whether she has enough strength to swim back to him. She has found her sealskin. "How easy it is," she thinks to herself. "Think of the time I have wasted splashing about like a baby."

Ostensibly, her story deals with her unconsummated romance with young Robert Lebrun and the awakening of her sexual desire, but once she learns to swim, once she feels the surge of power that responds to her need, it doesn't matter whether she has an affair with him or not, or an affair with anyone else, or even whether she leaves home for a four-room "pigeon house" of her own. From this point on, she can belong only to herself. (So shocking was this point of view in 1899 that *The Awakening* was taken off the shelves of the library in Kate Chopin's native city of St. Louis, and the author was expelled from the local Fine Arts Club.)

ON THE SURFACE, old folktales like "The Seal Wife" are male fantasies of a shape-shifting bride who comes from a magical world and the lengths to which a man will go in order to tame her and keep her in his grasp. In the late nineteenth and twentieth centuries, however, borne along by a wave of feminism and spurred by Henrik Ibsen, the old legends change. They are absorbed into a worldly female fantasy that is not only nonromantic in essence but antiromantic, even though it may include sexual interludes where the heroine has not yet managed to become a fully developed individual. At the beginning of the plot, the heroine exists solely through her roles as wife, mother, and daughter, inhabiting only a fraction of her consciousness, until finally she breaks loose from her dependence on relationships as the sole source of identity.

Nora in *A Doll's House,* the little squirrel who hides her cache of forbidden macaroons from her banker-husband and delights in trimming the Christmas tree for her children, the "twittering lark," as he calls her, discovers that in a crisis this self-righteous man is more devoted to his reputation than he is to her. She commits a crime in order to save his life after a critical illness, but when the crime is discovered he will do nothing unworthy of his position to shield her. ("There's no one who gives up honor for love," he says defensively in response to her pleas. "Millions of women have done just that," she replies.) She has been no more to him, after all, than a toy. "I've lived by doing tricks for you, Torvald. But that's the way you wanted it. It's a great sin what you and Papa did to me. You're to blame that nothing's become of me." She hasn't been happy, she assures him, even if she thought she was all this time. "Only lighthearted." Also light-minded, though she is just discovering that. "Our home's been nothing but a playpen. I've been your doll-wife here."

Nora leaves her three small children asleep in their beds, hugging their new Christmas presents no doubt, and walks out on her husband in the middle of the night, slamming the front door behind her, with a bang that echoes through the social history of the Western world.

Nora Helmer. Edna Pontellier in *The Awakening.* Joanna Kramer, the brooding wife in the movie *Kramer vs. Kramer,* sitting with her suitcase on her lap while she waits for her husband to come home: One way or another, all of them find the key to the fisherman's trunk and flee, taking little or nothing with them. But in their flight they don't so much run away as run back to where they came from, picking up their lives from the stage where they were lost, to see what else might be made of them.

The heroine of Anne Tyler's novel *Ladder of Years* walks away from her husband and their three grown children on a beach holiday, wearing nothing but a bathing suit and espadrilles and carrying a tote that contains her husband's beach robe and vacation cash. Without any idea what she's doing, she keeps on walking until she has a chance to hitch a ride to a strange town where she can start life over again. Until now she has worn pink dresses with ruffled necks and slippers with bunny ears, but in her first hour of freedom she buys one white bra, one package of white cotton underpants, and an ankle-length gray knit dress, sleek as a fish, her transformation marked (as usual) by a change of clothes.

A self-supporting spinster now, her virginity magically restored, she rents a room with a metal cot, a single lightbulb, and wallpaper that smells like a hornet's nest. This is what she wants. From here on, she'll live self-contained and silent. She longs for less comfort, not more; less responsibility, either domestic or emotional. A smaller house—like the pigeon house Edna Pontellier rents right near her husband's mansion—with less housekeeping attached, and little or no male affection, which she now recognizes as a trap, although sex itself is acceptable.

Unlike a man, the heroine of these stories isn't young and optimistic when she escapes from home. She has been a wife and mother for some years now. Her flesh is wrinkling like the sealskin in the trunk, and her soul has dried out with it, lost its confidence that it can survive in deep water, so that she must chew the skin and re-chew it in her mind while she wonders if she can regain her suppleness.

At the last moment, with no thought except that she has no choice—she insists that she will go mad, if she doesn't kill herself first—she slips into her original skin and makes a break for freedom. In fact, she acts as if a woman is a person who has a right to disappear into the distance alone, as men have done for thousands of years. Unique among women's plots—or fantasies, since this is often the fantasy of an exhausted wife and mother—in this one the heroine shucks off relationships instead of adding them.

"Don't you make me go in there," Joanna Kramer cries as she stands in front of the elevator, pointing at the apartment she has just left. "If you do, I swear someday, next week, maybe next year, I'll go right out the window."

"What about Billy?" her husband demands.

"I'm not taking him with me. I'm no good for him, I have no patience. He's better off without me." The self-protective wail of the Seal Wife is heard in those words.

"I won't look in on the children," says Nora Helmer before she walks out the door. "I know they're in better hands than mine. The way I am now, I'm no use to them."

The Seal Wife isn't nearly as incompetent as she thinks she is, but she finds it difficult to believe in her own capacities. She has never learned how to husband (in the literal sense of the word) her attention, giving some to herself as a wife and mother and keeping some for herself as self. Isolation vs. intimacy, Erickson said. During all the years of her marriage she has surrendered her soul to intimacy. Now the time has come to give up the need to be needed, which has tied her to her life so far.

So the Seal Wife leaves her children, who are invariably sons, or include sons, because part of her problem is that she hasn't reproduced herself but reproduced the masculine spirit that feeds on her. She can love them without believing that she can do anything for them, at least anything right, so what does it matter if she disappears? In this house, which is choking her, she can barely stay alive.

"Mrs. Pontellier was not a mother-woman," says the narrator of *The Awakening*. If one of the little Pontellier boys fell down while playing, he didn't come crying to his mother for comfort but would pick himself up, wipe the sand out of his mouth, and go on with his game. "The mother-women seemed to prevail that summer at Grand Isle. It was easy to know them, fluttering about with extended, protecting wings when any harm, real or imaginary, threatened their precious brood. They were women who idolized their children, worshiped their husbands, and esteemed it a holy privilege to efface themselves as individuals and grow wings as ministering angels. Many of them were delicious in the role."

Mother-women have gone out of fashion in our day, partly because of the need for women to hold jobs outside the home, but also because of our different sense of what constitutes a mature individual. Edna Pontellier, in advance of her time but not far enough ahead for safety, was desperate to preserve the self whose existence had not disturbed her until recently.

She returns to Grand Isle and to the beach, empty in midwinter, wanting no one near her, aware that a time will come when even Robert Lebrun will disappear from her thoughts. "The children appeared before her like antagonists who had overcome her, who had overpowered and sought to drag her into the soul's slavery for the rest of her days. But she knew a way to elude them."

Usually, children are their mother's sea anchor. In a gale, they slow her down and keep her from broaching under the forces of madness or despair. But Edna defeats them. She puts on her swimming clothes as she used to do in summer, but then takes them off, those "unpleasant, pricking garments," and for the first time that she can remember stands naked as a newborn in the light of day. Then she plunges into the cold water, swimming farther and farther toward the horizon until the shore is beyond her reach and her strength is gone.

THIS SOUNDS LIKE romantic exaggeration. Narcissism. Whatever we choose to call it. But the sense of oppression and urgency in a woman's life is present in the autobiography of one of our most intellectual authors, a woman who became the literary mentor for a generation of feminists in England and America in the second half of the twentieth century.

"I will not, I simply will not," Doris Lessing used to repeat to herself like a mantra, while growing up in Southern Rhodesia (now Zimbabwe) in the 1920s and '30s, meaning that she would never turn into a nag and scold like her bitterly disappointed mother, tied to a husband who had lost a leg in the trenches in World War I. She would never wear herself to the bone (sexless bone) like her mother, on a farm at the edge of the bush. She could not possibly put up with the blatantly racist attitudes and boring lifestyle of a British colony where the only recreation consisted of drinking too many "sundowners" every evening. Over and over, she swore that she had no intention of getting married and having children, not for a long time, maybe never. She would escape to Paris or London, to the Gobi Desert, to a hut in the Kalahari.

At the age of fifteen she quit school, prodigiously educated already by the hundreds of books she had read on her own. She took jobs as a live-in nanny, a typist, a telephone switchboard operator in the town of Salisbury (currently Harare). When she was nineteen—drinking too much every night on the veranda of the Sports Club, dancing to the tunes of a society wildly drunk on the expectation of war—she married a civil servant ten years older than she was. She didn't love him, though it was easy to make herself think she did. He didn't love her. In fact, he was engaged to a girl in Britain, but Doris pursued him with what she later called her ruthless female sense of entitlement. *This is my right.*

When she told her father the news, he assumed that she was pregnant. She was, but didn't know it. By the time she recognized the fact and found a reputable doctor, the fetus was too far along to abort.

But how had her life so swiftly reversed course, carrying her into the situation she had always said she abhorred? "Now it seems to me obvious I knew all the time I was pregnant, was in alliance with Nature against myself," she says. Her body hungered to reproduce—not to stop at having sex—which is the case with most women, but the secret was kept from her mind. If this split down the middle happened so easily to one of the most introspective women of our time, then all of us must suspect that our decisions are nowhere near as voluntary and rational as we, in our arrogance, suppose.

"I simply will not," she declared, even while she was being swept into a new life as a marriageable girl, then as a wife and mother, in a single year.

Nature, she said—*Gaia*—was responsible for what happened, the Life Force preparing to replace the multitudes who would be killed in the second Great War that was about to begin. The Zeitgeist had her in its grip, the spirit of the age. "No point in saying, I will *not*—when the Fates are playing war music, dance music." In folktales, the force is taken for granted. When the tide is right and the sea calm, the seal people troop to shore, where they dance in the sand while waiting for one of their number to be caught and to breed.

Doris Lessing gave birth to a boy who was exuberant (hyperactive, we would say nowadays), the sort who refuses to nap or sit on a lap or be cuddled. He exhausted her, but what matter? When her son was nine months old, almost ready to stand up, she became pregnant again, as casually as before. (Can it have been conception and pregnancy that piqued her imagination rather than motherhood, while other women admired her swelling belly?) Might as well get the baby-breeding over and done with while we're still young, the new mothers said to one another on the porch of the country club. She agreed, but already her mind had strayed.

"I was not going to stay in this life . . . desperate, trapped, but behaving beautifully." She was living in only a quarter of her self, with the other three-quarters (writer, thinker, political radical) stirring restively inside her, awaiting their chance.

There she was, with two babies in diapers (the second was a girl), and the tide had changed under her feet, strong enough to sweep her back to the colder depths. She joined a proto-Communist group, like so many utopian liberals of the 1930s and '40s. She devoted her time to political lectures and study groups, but, meanwhile, she talked constantly to her family and fellow radicals about leaving her children and a marriage that she admitted was no worse than most.

Unlike most unhappy women, she did what she said she would do. She abandoned her children and yet continued to live in the same town with them. Like all seal wives, she insisted that if she had not walked out she would have had a nervous breakdown; she would have become an alcoholic and in time a bitter, dried-up woman like those she saw decades later when she revisited Rhodesia.

Not long afterward, to her own surprise, she married again—"an unhappy but kindly marriage," she termed this one—never expecting the relationship to last long but going through the procedure anyway, because it was impossible to live together in that society, at that time, without a marriage license. Her new husband was a German alien and fellow member of her Communist group. While they waited for permission to leave the country after the end of World War II, they decided to "fit in" a baby because they had nothing better to do with their time. Her father thought it odd that she should choose to bear a third child when she had abandoned the first two.

This last child she took with her when she sailed for England in 1949, with the manuscript of her first novel that would be published under her arm. Doris Lessing's life score as a woman and as a writer consists of twenty-four novels, including *The Golden Notebook*, which was seminal in shaping the intellectual female consciousness of the 1960s and '70s, seven volumes of short stories, the libretto for an opera (music by Philip Glass), four plays, one book of poems, nine volumes of nonfiction including two parts of her autobiography, and three children: two abandoned and one retained.

But how can she do it? How can any woman live in the same town with two children after she has deserted them?

How can Sylvia Plath manage to live alone with two small children, getting herself up at four every morning to write her blood-poems—"terrific stuff," she reports in a letter to her mother— and then put her head in the gas oven one night, but not before leaving a cup of milk and a plate of bread next to each child's crib, to tide him over until a strange nanny arrives in the morning?

She can't. But she does. Abandonment is the most terrible act a woman can perform, because it wounds those she ought to shelter, and yet she does it. Every woman does it—not permanently, as a rule, and not with a slam of the door like Nora Helmer, but in snatches of time filched from her children, absentee minutes, lapses of consciousness every single day.

Children are a woman's self in its most promising form, but at the same time they are everything that keeps her from being an independent self. The mistake is to suppose that all women are equally maternal, or that any woman burns with maternal feeling twenty-four hours a day. The would-be artist or passionate gardener or yoga practitioner may be desperate to engage in her craft at eleven in the morning but feel overwhelmed by mother love when she bathes her children in the evening.

During the 1950s and '60s it was taken for granted that women would marry young, produce babies almost at once, and devote themselves to the business of raising them. "I remember a cycle," poet Adrienne Rich says of the period in her life when she had three sons under the age of seven.

> It began when I had picked up a book or began trying to write a letter, or even found myself on the telephone with someone toward whom my voice betrayed eagerness. . . . The child (or children) might be absorbed in busyness, in his own dreamworld, but as soon as he felt me gliding into a world which did not include him, he would come to pull at my hand, ask for help, punch at the typewriter keys. And I would feel his wants . . . as an attempt to defraud me of living even for fifteen minutes as myself. My anger would rise; I would feel . . . the inequality between us: my needs always balanced against those of a child, and always losing. I could love so much better, I told myself, after even a quarter-hour of selfishness, of peace, of detachment from my children.

From the 1980s on, most mothers have been forced or competitively encouraged by our culture to hold jobs outside the home (while still doing four fifths of the housework), which relieves their claustrophobia but none of the guilt of diverting attention from their children.

> *The intellect of man is forced to choose*
> *Perfection of the life or of the work,*

wrote W. B. Yeats, but the trouble is just what he says. It's the man who is forced to choose. A woman has no such option, and none of her decisions are made solely through her intellect in any case, without the partnership of her body. She's tied to life, not solely her life but the lives of her husband and children, so that if she also wants achievement that's truly her own—never mind perfection, she'll settle for much less—she has to steal attention from her children. She has to steal it anyway if she's to remain sane, a whole human being rather than just hands, womb, breast.

It's impossible to give our children as much attention as they need, never mind half as much as they want, for the simple reason that there isn't enough to go around, and every mother is in competition with her children for the available supply. No matter how much she tries to do each day, she's aware of scanting something else, something vital and timebound that won't wait for her to catch up. Her children will be grown up and gone from home before she finds the clarity of soul she wants to devote to them. Her house will crumble, or she'll have moved out before she ever gets it in order. Or she'll give herself to her house and children, and her poems will never be written. More likely, both. Each part of her is inadequately served, no matter how strenuously she neglects the other.

In the end, she doesn't solve the problem. No life problem ever has a solution. She's carried along by time, as if riding in a stranger's car to an undeclared destination where the view is different, the altitude is different, and the old problem has been forgotten in contemplation of new ones.

———

"HOW MUCH TIME did you have for yourself when your son was a baby?" I ask my next-door neighbor, whose only child is now a junior in high school.

"None," she says. "Not a free minute. I was an assistant professor when he was born, teaching a full load, writing articles for scholarly journals because I was looking toward tenure, nursing the baby, keeping house, and serving on the board of the state university, all at the same time. Even while I was doing my exercises with a videotape, the baby was right next to me in his high chair. He was over four and in nursery school before I got a break, and what I did was hire a flute teacher—that was my present to myself—and try to practice a little every day. Do you know, that was the first thing I'd ever done where I didn't have to excel? My husband and I didn't have another child. But I often thought that if we'd had two or three others after him, as we had originally planned, I'd have gone under."

The flute. Breath passes from the woman's lungs to her throat and lips. What might otherwise have come out of her as self-reproach or complaints or just plain anger moves across the mouthpiece, and the flute transforms those passing breaths into melody.

DURING THE YEARS that the selkie spends onshore with the fisherman and her sons, she probably thinks that her former skin is gone forever, locked up or destroyed by her husband to keep her away from the sea. But she's wrong; it isn't destroyed. It's hidden, maybe badly preserved so that it stiffens and cracks, but preserved until the day comes when she finds the key to the trunk. Or maybe, in another version, the sealskin was never put into a trunk in the first place, and it isn't the Seal Wife who finds it. It's her children, half grown now, who find it under last year's hay while playing hide-and-seek, and run to show it to their mother before returning to their game.

Does she understand that it wasn't the fisherman who hid it? It was life, disguising itself as a husband and children, that kept it away from her all these years. So time gives back her freedom. The seal woman puts on her original skin and dives to depths where her children can't follow. But that doesn't mean that she forgets them.

Not so many years after she leaves them—or they leave her, which was bound to happen if she had only waited a bit—she swims around their fishing boat, hoping for a glimpse of them, but finds full-grown men in oilskin jackets instead, with a good catch of fish in their boat, who have nothing in common with her sons except their names and the webs between their fingers. In fact, they look nothing like her boys. They are as big as the lonely fisherman who captured her that first night when she swam to shore with the seal folk and peeled off her skin and danced in the cave. For some reason, she thought these brawny creatures she spawned would remain her children forever.

The assistant professor who kept a grip on her sanity by playing the flute became not only a tenured professor but also the author of notable academic books in her field of law. But she did not become a college president, which is the path that would undoubtedly have opened up for her if she had been free to move from one city to another and another, without a husband and son to tether her.

Women rarely achieve perfection of either life or work. As creatures of two elements, they are never sure which to leave and where to linger.

"It is given to them that their sea-longing shall be land-longing, and their land-longing shall be sea-longing."

CHAPTER 14

Bluebeard's Wife and the Fitcher's Bird: Taking Her Life in Her Hands

"Bluebeard," "Fitcher's Bird," "Cupid and Psyche," an Event in the Life of Eleanor Roosevelt

"Here," said Bluebeard to his last wife, "are the keys of the two great rooms that hold my best and richest furniture . . . and this is the master-key that opens all my apartments. But for this little one here, it is the key of the closet at the end of the great gallery on the ground floor. Open them all, go into all . . . except that little closet, which I forbid you in such a manner, that if you happen to open it, there is nothing but what you may expect from my just anger and resentment."

At the heart of every marriage, this story tells us, lies a secret—a bloody and often dangerous secret overlaid by the details of daily life.

We marry without knowing who we are, like the White Bride and the Black Bride, and without knowing who our partner is. From the wedding day on, we walk past closed doors to which we carry the key. This is why marriage is so much riskier as well as richer than friendship or romance.

But what can be hidden in the little closet that must on no account be opened? Whatever we don't want known. More to the point, whatever we don't want to know. Whatever tears a hole in the intimacy of man and woman. Needless to say, a wife may have secrets of her own, but a woman has more at stake in marriage than a man does, and so she is generally more willing to bend and more skillful at concealing than he is.

In traditional stories, the secret is brought into the open through forbidden female curiosity, operating against male orders, as if curiosity is sinful, and only women are curious. In modern life, on the other hand, where "sharing" and "openness" are magic words in every relationship, and a partner's demand for privacy is the clue to pick up the phone and hire a private investigator, the husband wouldn't dare put his wife on notice that there is a barely visible crack in the golden bowl of their marriage.

But revealed it is, sooner or later, often through some accident that the wife would have given a great deal to avoid. The phone rings on the day before Christmas, and the unsuspecting wife (in this real-life case Katharine Graham, who later became the publisher of the *Washington Post*) innocently picks up an extension in another room in time to hear her husband talking to his lover "in words that made the situation plain." In another family, a bill is erroneously mailed to the home address from an unknown jewelry store where the husband has made purchases, or the husband's car is spotted by his mother-in-law parked outside his secretary's home during the lunch hour. Adultery is the common scenario, the bones of past lovers strewn on the floor of the Bloody Chamber, because adultery is emblematic of all other betrayals, and yet it's more often a result than a cause of domestic trouble.

These days the secret of the little closet is often homosexuality, when a husband doesn't understand his own sexual orientation until well into the marriage, or suspects it but keeps quiet. (Which is more devastating for a wife? To have her husband and the father of her children leave her for another woman, which means that he has found someone who beats her at her own game, or to have him leave her for a man, which means that she never made him happy in the first place, whether he realized what the trouble was or not? Right from the beginning, she never had an inkling of what he was suffering or thinking during the nights they spent in the same bed.)

If not adultery or sexuality, the taboo subject may be gambling, alcoholism, drugs, anxiety, depression, brutality, impotence, irresponsibility. Nay-saying to life: A longtime bachelor tells the woman he's involved with that he wants to marry her but he doesn't want to have children, because he's Catholic and she's not. But later, when she brings up the subject of family again, he doesn't object. She takes his silence as a signal that he has changed.

Maybe the secret isn't revealed until the husband is dead, when death focuses a harsh spotlight on a life, rather than the darkness we expect, and in the glare the widow sees traces she would rather not have seen. ("It won't matter once I'm dead," she can imagine him saying.) Can a widow be wounded by a dead husband? If she is honest, eventually she recognizes that at some subconscious level she suspected there was a flaw all along, and in fact may have married him to be paired with just this flaw that made her comfortable.

In whatever fashion the revelation comes about, the wife cannot understand how she could have been so naïve. There were signs. Plain as day. There was every reason to ask questions. (While Bluebeard's last wife waits for the knife blade to fall on her neck, does she marvel that she never asked what happened to those previous wives who vanished without a trace?) She was blindfolded by nature during the years while she was busy setting up a home, bearing children, and raising them: carrying out nature's imperatives.

The pity would be if later on, after she discovers her ignorance, she rejects those years of early happiness, thinking they must have been delusory. Happiness that comes from delusion is every bit as real and nourishing as happiness from a sounder source.

Seeing what she sees, the wife may go to pieces emotionally and physically, and never recover. Or she may come out of the Bloody Chamber transformed, if she has the potential for transformation, gristly as a weathered bone, in which case a reversal of power takes place between husband and wife. She is the stronger one now, toughened by experience, as happened with Eleanor Roosevelt.

In any case, a human being, male or female, is too complex to enter into anything wholeheartedly, marriage least of all.

THE "BLUEBEARD" STORY by Charles Perrault deals with a fabulously wealthy widower, married several times before, whose courtship is rejected by two sisters because of the frightful blue beard that grows on his chin. Undiscouraged, he invites them to his country home, where he entertains them so lavishly that the younger one decides "the master of the house had not a *Beard* so very *Blue*" after all.

A month after the wedding, Bluebeard announces to his bride that he is obliged to go on a business trip that will last at least six weeks. During his absence, she is welcome to invite all her friends to visit, and she may help herself to the contents of every room in the house except one (here he hands over his bunch of keys), an insignificant closet opened by this particular key.

Of course, she can scarcely wait for him to leave before she runs through the house, unlocking rooms and admiring the jewels and chests full of gold that she finds there, but above all others she is determined to see the "insignificant closet" she is forbidden to enter. What can be so much more precious than the treasures she has already seen that her husband reserves it for himself?

She finds the room. Her hand quivers as she turns the key. When her eyes grow accustomed to the gloom, she sees the corpses of young women propped against the walls, around a floor clotted with blood. In terror, she drops the key, but picks it up and, with a hand shaking far more than before, locks the room again and hurries upstairs to wipe off the blood-spattered key.

The blood won't come off. The key is indelibly stained, revealing to the master of the house what she has done when he returns that evening—much sooner than expected, which she realizes too late was a trap.

"You were resolv'd to go into the closet, were you not?" he asks ominously. "Very well, Madam, you shall go in, and take your place amongst the ladies you saw there."

Only the timely arrival of the wife's brothers, who gallop through the gate just as the brother-in-law is about to cut off her head, prevents Bluebeard from carrying out his usual punishment. Afterward, the relieved widow uses the fortune she inherits to buy amiable husbands for her sister and herself.

BLUEBEARD'S WIFE. The Fitcher's Bird. Eve. Psyche. Pandora.

Curled inside the taboo in each story, like the spring of a loaded trap, is the lord and master's expectation that it's bound to be broken. He requires the woman to disobey him. He needs her to shatter the taboo, destroy the old law and set a new one in its place, while he pretends to be far away. Two forces coexist: The static masculine force of law and order provides earthly comfort and security, the way that a parent cares for a child's needs, but imposes death as the penalty for disobedience. The female force intrudes wherever she is told not to intrude, bringing suffering in her wake but also birth, sexuality, change, possibility, knowledge. In human terms, if a woman sees what she isn't supposed to see, and survives the shock, she steps out of the old domestic plot and forges a new, unprotected life for herself and perhaps for her children.

"Now the serpent . . . said unto the woman, Yea, hath God said, Ye shall not eat of every tree of the garden? And the woman said unto the serpent, We may eat of the fruit of the trees of the garden: But of the fruit of the tree which is in the midst of the garden, God hath said, Ye shall not eat of it, neither shall ye touch it, lest ye die."

Then what is that tree doing in plain sight, the tree of knowledge with its blood-red fruit hanging within easy reach, if the woman is not to touch it?

Whatever is forbidden is bound to come about. If Sleeping Beauty grows up in a kingdom where spindles have been banned by her father's order, she is sure to find one in the least accessible room of the palace, and with it find sexuality.

If the ravishing Pandora (whose name means All-Gifts), the Greek version of Eve, is sent to earth by the father-god Zeus for his own malicious purpose, where she encounters a box that she's forbidden to open, we know (as Zeus knows) that she's certain to open it, letting loose sickness, suffering, vice, hunger, old age, and all other plagues on mankind. At the bottom of the box, which the faithless Pandora hesitates to open a second time, lies hope, which has been put there to keep men from killing themselves.

CHARLES PERRAULT'S "BLUEBEARD," written in 1697, is one of the few fairy tales in which the heroine, who is far from admirable, has to be rescued from disaster by her male relatives.

There's another version of the story, however—more archaic, although written down more than a century later—told by the Grimms under the title "Fitcher's Bird." In this one, the heroine isn't a fortune hunter like Bluebeard's last wife. Just the opposite, she's giving away bread when we meet her. At the end, she not only rescues her sisters and herself and kills the villain but does something even more astonishing: She steps out of the marriage plot altogether. In archaic stories, as was said in the Introduction to this book, peasant heroines are much bolder and more resourceful than their upper-class descendants, while they are a world apart from the twentieth-century Disney beauties, who can only sigh and sing until their Prince comes along to save them.

At the beginning of the "Fitcher's Bird" story, a beggar with a basket on his back approaches the house of a man who has three pretty daughters and begs for food. The oldest daughter, who is as kindhearted as she is beautiful, comes out of the cottage and hands him a loaf of bread, as if offering herself fresh from the oven. The beggar touches her—just once, but that's enough. She's touched. Into the basket she must jump, for this is no beggar but a wizard who could have chosen any disguise he wanted for his game of catching pretty girls and carrying them off to his lair, after which they are never seen again.

With the basket slung over his shoulder, he lopes off into the forest, which grows darker with every step, as dark as the unconsciousness in which many a girl jumps into an implausible match simply because it's offered at the right time. (I ACCIDENTALLY GOT MARRIED SATURDAY, the author M.F.K. Fisher telegraphed a friend when she became the sixth wife of a book editor whom she had known for two weeks. Not long afterward, he had a mental collapse. He lost his head instead of the bride losing hers, and the marriage came to an end.)

The sorcerer's house turns out to be a mansion, which isn't surprising, given the identification in so many fairy tales between the luscious and complex body of the marriageable young woman and the lavish new home to which her future husband brings her—but the sorcerer's is also a house of locks and keys.

Once the girl disappears, her father and sisters never inquire about her. Marriage is an impenetrable country, where another language is spoken.

After a short time, as expected, the wizard announces that he must go away and leave his companion for a while. But here the Grimms' story diverges from "Bluebeard." "You may open every door in the house with the keys I am giving you," he tells the captive, his voice like a sharpened blade, "so long as you do not open the single room I have forbidden you to enter. And so long as you carry this egg continually about with you. If the egg drops, your fortunes drop with it." Taking the keys in one hand and the egg in the other, she promises to obey.

———

EGG AND KEY. The female sex symbol, the male sex symbol. A key is an iron rod that dangles from a man's belt like a penis. An egg is an oval container snug as a womb with a baby inside it. In this story, the woman walks with one symbol in each hand, as if her body were the conductor through which energy flows from one set of genes to the other.

Stories change, but symbols stay the same for thousands of years. Eggs still represent birth or rebirth on the Jewish Passover plate, or in a child's Easter basket, just as they did when painted on a funeral urn in Neolithic times. Before the Great Goddess made herself known to men in human form, she reigned as bird goddess, sometimes shown as a waterfowl—a goose? a swan?—with a red egg filling her belly, the Cosmic Egg from which the universe and everything in it is about to hatch. Egg, blood, bird. The images will come together later in this story.

But what does the egg mean to the bride-to-be trapped in the sorcerer's mansion, balancing it on the palm of her hand? Fertility, of course, but also chastity, which is the opposite: a woman's sense of herself and her sexuality as entirely private, enclosed in a shell so fragile that a man can crack it with one hand if he chooses but never repair it, any more than he can repair a shattered glass slipper.

Fertility and chastity, those old bugaboos of married life, no longer terrify us as they once did, however. For us, the fairy tale is meaningful only if it rises above blood and terror and turns into an account of the wife's transformation during the course of her marriage. All we know about the heroine in the beginning is that she comes running out of her cottage, a nymph for a little while in the way that all young girls are awarded a brief period of mythological identity, during which their fertility operates at full blast but is still impersonal, capable of bearing any man's child. She runs toward a man or away from him, lies down and spreads her legs or leaps up in horror, always in motion until the moment something inside her is touched, when she tumbles into the basket.

As soon as she is brought to the castle, she comes down to the human plane. Her hand balances the egg that she must carry wherever she goes (except to bed, we have to believe). She has been given to the egg as much as the egg has been given to her. It must be more valuable than anything else in the castle, or her life wouldn't depend on its survival.

By this simple trick, the girl has been tamed. She has become careful. More than that, she has become caring, full of cares—a caregiver, as we say today—which makes her vulnerable. While she was single, she cared about getting married and not much else, and thought she would feel safe as soon as that was over and done with, but now she sees that she has traded possibility, which is the power of a goddess, for the human weight of responsibility.

Responsibility steadies her palm, which she notices isn't flat, as she supposed, but cupped to form a nest, so that she can move around as long as she doesn't try to do anything else with that hand. In a while, she no longer sees herself as a person but as a support system sustaining the egg.

Fairy tales and their images are never outdated. In Life Skills class, or whatever it's called in certain experimental middle schools today, all students, boys and girls alike, are required to carry an egg around with them for a number of hours without breaking it, to learn the meaning of responsibility for a dependent creature.

IN ORDER TO KEEP his wife to himself, the wizard in "Fitcher's Bird," like Bluebeard, resorts to locks and dire punishment. His pride won't let him admit that her body has a hidden chamber of its own, apparently filled with an endless supply of blood, that produces babies from time to time who may or may not be his. Every month, blood drips from her chamber. Does it come from babies she has killed inside her belly? Is her blood hunting for his? Plagued by envy, the male imitates the female's creation: He builds a chamber in the depths of his castle that has a pool of blood in the middle and dead bodies the age of his wife ranged around it.

His myth reverses hers. The chamber that he guards with such violence is death to enter. Her chamber was given to her by nature. And hers is life to leave. This is one way to think about the story.

FAIRY-TALE TIME TAKES OVER. In the Grimms' story, we are told that the heroine explores the mansion as soon as the wizard leaves on a trip. In real life, decades may pass before she unlocks the forbidden door.

But sooner or later the day comes around, as the sorcerer knew it would. His captive bristles at being excluded from this single room as if she were a servant who can't be trusted. Left alone, she inspects the chamber door, which looks no more sinister than any other. She turns the key in the lock. The hinge swings open. In the dim light, she sees what seems to be a pool—no, a basin—full of blood, and in the blood lie the arms, legs, torsos, and staring heads of young women, their mouths still open in their final screams. Behind the basin she sees a bloody chopping block with an axe embedded in it.

In shock, the girl throws up her hands, and the egg falls into the basin of blood. She fishes it out, unbroken but stained, and wipes it off with her handkerchief, but the bloodstain returns at once. She carries the egg to her room and scrubs it. No use, the stain keeps coming back.

There's nothing to do but wait for the wizard to return, which he does the same day. "So," he exhales when he sees the egg, like a puff of wind snuffing out a candle. "Since you have gone into the forbidden chamber against my will, you shall return to it against your own." Dragging her back to the room, he chops off her head with the axe, hacks her body into pieces, and throws them into the basin of blood with the others.

After that, he takes on the form of a beggar again and returns to the cottage to fetch the second sister. He has no more trouble getting her into the basket than the first, and she meets the same end.

If either sister had obeyed him to the letter and stayed away from the forbidden room, she would have survived, though only as a mindless puppet whom he would have abandoned sooner or later out of disgust. On the other hand, if she had disobeyed completely, covered her tracks and beat him at his own game, she would have survived on her own terms. Transformation either upward or downward was required. The moral of the story isn't "Wives, don't pry" but "Don't get caught prying."

DISGUISED AS A BEGGAR ONCE MORE, the sorcerer returns to the cottage, touches the third sister, and pops her into his basket.

But why must there always be three sisters or brothers in this sort of tale, with three wishes or gifts to ask for, three jewel caskets laid in a row, or three trials to face in the castle, always three before it becomes possible for the hero or heroine to do what the adventure requires?

In psychological terms, this implies that at first a new problem is too much for us to cope with. Our spirits quail. The second time, our spirits still quail. The older siblings are our preliminary selves, easily unstrung as in this story, or else they are lazy and jealous, like Cinderella's or Psyche's sisters, or power-mad like Cordelia's. Magic eludes them. They have no idea what gift to ask Father to bring back from his business trip, or which path to take at the crossroad. Before we can act heroically, the stories tell us, the spirit needs to get revved up, allowing the right amount of time to summon its resources.

On your mark, get set, go. Ready, aim, fire. Going, going, gone. Alley, alley, hoop-la. The third time is the charm.

BUT THIS THIRD SISTER is as wily as the wizard, who hands her the keys and egg with the usual injunction before he leaves on a trip, giving her the chance to bring about her destruction.

In her eyes, wifely obedience (which is all that's physically possible for women in large parts of the world today) is a bloodless form of suicide, killing the marriage as well as the woman's soul, leaving no room for deceit and betrayal, or love and companionship, for that matter. And so this heroine does what few women manage to do. As soon as she hears the door close behind the sorcerer, she puts the egg down—in a safe spot—and walks away. Simple as that. Freeing herself from relationships for the time being, she sets out to explore the castle that's apparently going to be her home. Like Psyche, she wants to know and love in the same place, which is a powerful combination.

Laying down the egg is the hardest thing a woman can do. Through both nature and culture, she's brought up to form links with other people: dependent on parents and friends, but also depended on by them; sympathetic and loving, but also despising and fearing, because these, too, are forms of relationship. She must be receptive, responsive, available. Especially available. Every part of her is available to others for feeding on demand, emotionally as well as physically, no matter what else she may be doing. She can't let a phone ring without picking up the receiver; she can't go to bed and leave the dishes unwashed; she can't turn down an invitation any more than she can walk away and let a baby cry. In short, from childhood on she's conditioned to be a mother. But she also needs the opposite response: the fierce refusal to be interrupted, like a tiger nursing her young. A hero of either sex has to be single-minded on occasion, which means single in concentration but also single in the sense of unattached, with no obligations to other people for the duration of the story.

PSYCHE, THAT OTHER GREAT TRESPASSER who demanded forbidden knowledge, had to learn what the third sister in the fairy tale knows instinctively on the day that she is brought to the castle.

Breaking the taboo against a woman (worse yet, a wife) intruding on male consciousness, as we saw in Chapter Ten, Psyche shines the light from her lamp on her bedmate and sees the god Cupid lying beside her, Love himself with perfumed curls, who flies away as he swore he would, leaving her to the vengeance of his mother, Venus. The jealous goddess beats and torments her future daughter-in-law, who is already pregnant, and then gives her four ordeals designed to destroy her. So terrible is the last that the girl climbs a tower, planning to throw herself headlong from the top in order to die quickly rather than through slow torment. Venus has ordered her to go down to the Underworld to fetch a gift from Persephone, ruler of that realm, who is Venus's opposite number, the Queen of the Dead in league with the Queen of Love.

As Psyche is about to leap, the tower, who is the stony phallic symbol of masculine strength, speaks. It's easy enough to get down to the Underworld by killing herself, the tower reminds her. In fact, she's bound to get there sooner or later whether she wants to or not, but once she dies she can never return to the living. Listen to me, the tower insists: He'll tell her how to find the gate of Hell. She must bring three cakes with her to throw into the jaws of the three-headed dog that guards the threshold (that magical number three again), so that the dog will snap them up in his jaws instead of eating her. But then he gives advice that no voyager has ever heard before or since: When she has traveled a fair way on her ghostly route, she'll meet a lame ass with a lame driver who'll ask her to hand him a few twigs that have fallen from his load—no more than that, just twigs. She must walk past without stopping. Next, she'll come to a river where a ferryman waits to pole her to the shore of the dead. While crossing the water, the boat will pass a floating corpse that will raise his hands and beg her to take him into the boat. She must keep going without answering. A little farther on, she'll see a group of old women weaving a web who will beg for her help, but she must not give any.

These are traps of Venus, the tower warns Psyche, designed to make her drop one of the cakes so that the guardian dog will eat her.

No pity is allowed on a quest, no helpfulness, no fellow feeling for old women whose ranks she will join one day, not even respect for the dead: traps of Venus, every one of them, meant to make her forget her purpose and lose herself in unthinking responses to need, which in turn establish relationships on which the world's fertility (which is Venus's profession) depends. If she offers help for a minute, she'll be trapped in her feminine nature and lose sight of her own intention. What's more, help "for just a minute" is impossible.

Helpfulness drags intimacy and expectation in its wake. Those bonds of intimacy, those networks we praise so highly, are also chains.

Be careful whose life you save, the ancient Chinese used to warn their heroes. You will be responsible for that person forever after.

The tower continues his advice: When Psyche reaches the house of Persephone at the center of the Underworld, the Queen of the Dead will offer her a chair and serve a fine dinner, but Psyche must sit on the ground and refuse to eat anything but a piece of coarse bread. Hospitality is the opposite, but more alluring, snare of Venus. Whenever a woman becomes a guest or takes a gift, she finds herself bound by obligation, her attention diverted from her proper work.

At the entrance of a hero path, both male and female heroes are warned: No distractions allowed here. No pause once you've begun. Deaf ears, blind eyes except for the goal. This is contrary to everything a girl learns, which doesn't mean that it goes against female nature. On the contrary, it's what a woman deeply involved with her own work dreams of but achieves only in fits and starts before being called back to the daylight world of human entanglement. This world cannot exist without the feminine, generic part of her nature, the White Bride, except for a short time or in a few women, or else humankind will die out. A fertile young woman is the servant of the species, which is why Venus refers to Psyche as her slave girl. But a woman must be able to put that role behind her when called for a higher service.

In particular, it's almost impossible for a mother to lay down the egg. Psyche is far along in pregnancy, but she isn't a wife or mother yet when she undertakes the fourth labor. Had she already given birth, the path through the Underworld would have been closed to her. Once a woman bears a child, she becomes powerful in a limited sphere, but at the same time she becomes vulnerable, and therefore cautious, in a new way for the rest of her life, barred from the adventures that are open only to childless, essentially virginal heroines, or to women in circumstances so disastrous that they have passed beyond life and death, like Sethe in Toni Morrison's *Beloved.*

After Psyche completes the fourth ordeal, she is transformed into a goddess by Jupiter and marries Cupid. In short order, a daughter is born—not a son, as Cupid so confidently predicted, because this is a story about female nature triumphant rather than male priorities. The daughter is named Pleasure, which is something women don't often expect as their reward.

WHEN THE THIRD MAIDEN opens the door of the forbidden room, the sight is cumulatively more terrible than it was for her older sisters, whose hacked-up bodies she sees floating in the basin of blood, but she's the prepared one. She does not drop the egg, because she had the presence of mind to put it aside.

As soon as she can move, she gathers up her sisters' arms, legs, and heads from the welter of body parts and lays them in order, remembering what was dismembered. The limbs begin to stir. Little by little, the sisters pull themselves together. Their eyes open and blink. They collect their wits. Drawing close, they kiss one another, after which the youngest hides them in a closet until she can devise a way to save them. When the wizard returns home, he is astonished to find the egg with no trace of blood on it. "You have stood the test, you shall be my bride," he says to the girl, taking it for granted that marriage to him is the greatest prize a woman can win.

At this moment a reversal of power takes place, which is what happens in every marriage when a woman uncovers what has been hidden from her and survives the discovery without falling apart. She's no longer ignorant. Her husband knows no more than she does. In fact, he knows less, since he can't be sure how much she knows, or how she found out, and how long she has hidden her knowledge.

Stripped of his magic power, the wizard withers. In the past, marriages often rested on the husband's conviction that there was some essential knowledge or masculine experience that belonged exclusively to him, where the wife mustn't tread. He knew how to tame a mustang, take out a bank loan, balance a checkbook, build a house.

But once the wife knows whatever he doesn't want her to know, and knows it without his consent, the fate of the marriage is in her hands. The bridegroom must do what she wants.

"I will prepare for the wedding," the third sister tells the wizard. "But you must first take a basketful of gold to my father and mother, and carry it yourself on your back." Under the gold she hides her sisters. Gasping for breath under his burden, the wizard delivers it to the cottage.

The youngest sister can escape in the same way as those earlier manifestations of herself, but this particular heroine wants to bundle her earlier selves back to the past where they belong, without escaping that way herself. If she returns to her childhood home, full of self-pity and grievance, she will become the youngest daughter again, waiting for another beggar to come down the road.

Rage and horror transform her into someone—something—else, archaic as an idol, basic as bone. While the former wizard carries his load to the cottage, she prepares a marriage feast and sends invitations to his family and friends, after which she concocts a dummy bride. Taking a skull with two rows of grinning teeth and eye sockets as hollow as half an eggshell (a skull couldn't have been hard to find in that house), she puts a lace ruff where the neck should be, hangs earrings where the ears ought to be, and crowns the head with a wreath of flowers. Then she sets it in the garret window, another Black Bride glaring down from the top-floor window at a bridal procession below, getting the last, lipless laugh as skulls always do.

When that's done, she bathes in a barrel of honey, then cuts open a featherbed and rolls in the goose feathers, turning herself into a monstrous bird that stalks down the path to meet the arriving guests. In short, she splits in two. There she is: Skull and waterbird. Death and fertility. Death and Goddess. Or whatever we choose to call the original bird who is the bearer of the egg. Egg, bird, woman. The ingredients come together.

The heroine is no longer young and vulnerable, no longer pretty. She has no use for that game anymore. She isn't ugly either, but

something beyond pretty or ugly, further down the road than the traditional marriage plot. She has moved into the realm of power. This
is the opposite of the Cinderella transformation, in which the fairy
godmother, who is Mother Nature in her most winsome disguise,
beautifies and tenderizes the teenager to make her ripe for marriage
and motherhood, after which her usefulness comes to an end as far
as the godmother is concerned.

The Fitcher's Bird changes the other way around, reconditioning
herself for singlehood, turning herself into a monstrous fowl that's
prehistoric and yet recognizably, rabidly modern, female rather than
feminine, capable of bizarre deeds. This is what happens to women
as they grow old, which they see as the final outrage against them.
They undo the Cinderella transformation, working without nature's
connivance, since they no longer serve the interest of the species.
They grow beaks and claws but also wings, they stop serving other
people and learn to nest alone, fluttering at first but soon transformed, like the fairy-tale heroine, into Tough Old Birds serving
their own ends and cackling with surprise at their ability to endure
freedom.

"O, Fitcher's bird, how com'st thou here?" the wedding guests ask
as they walk up the path to the house accompanied by the bridegroom, who fails to recognize the bird-woman in her feathers.

> *"I come from Fitcher's house quite near."*
> *"And what may the young bride be doing?"*
> *"From cellar to garret she's swept all clean,*
> *And now from the window she's peeping, I ween."*

The bridegroom, formerly reputed to be a wizard, looks up and
sees a head at the top-floor window, which he assumes is his bride
because she's crowned by a bridal wreath. He nods to the death's
head and greets her kindly, seeing what he expects to see. The
death's head grins back.

Once he and his guests are inside the house, the bride's brothers and kinsmen show up, lock the doors, and set the house on fire. Or so the story says. If we choose, we can believe that the tale-tellers are bowing to the patriarchal tradition, and it was the Fitcher's Bird herself who did the deed.

The story says nothing more, but we can imagine the Fitcher's Bird borne aloft on a red-hot updraft of fury like the outraged Medea, flying over the rooftops of Corinth, carrying her children's corpses in a chariot drawn by dragons. Or like Thelma and Louise, soaring in their convertible over the edge of the Grand Canyon into the sky.

WHENEVER THE DOOR to the forbidden chamber is opened, in fact as well as fiction, someone or something dies. Usually it's the heroine's former selves who lie strewn on the floor—trustful, romantic, basing their sense of themselves on the marriage-plot clichés. The painful difference between fairy tales and real life, however, is that in actual cases the heroine need not unlock the door herself. To her dismay, the door has been left ajar, or it flies open of its own devilish accord as she passes by, so that she sees what she cannot help seeing.

"I knew a child once who adored her father. She was an ugly little thing, keenly conscious of her deficiencies." This is the way the author of a twentieth-century story, Eleanor Roosevelt, saw herself: shy, awkward, a solemn little girl without a trace of her mother's or aunts' celebrated beauty, as her mother made clear to her.

Her father, Elliott, a great sportsman, cut a gallant figure in her life as a little girl's irresistible beau. He was also an alcoholic who mixed drugs with his drinks, a notorious adulterer and unstable personality, but this the child did not know. When her mother died of diphtheria, eight-year-old Eleanor thought of only one thing: The death would bring her father home from one of his many unexplained absences.

She was right. He came to visit, folded her in his arms, and promised that they would mean the world to one another from now on, but in short order he was confined to sanatoriums and died less than two years later in a state of delirium. Eleanor was left to the guardianship of her grandmother, who did not believe in spoiling children. This prologue is essential to understanding the rest of her story.

When a girl unloved by her mother and abandoned by her father, who is convinced that she is ugly, falls in love and finds her love reciprocated, the experience is as if a god had descended through the roof in a shower of gold. At the age of nineteen, Eleanor fell in love, not surprisingly, with her distant cousin Franklin Roosevelt, who was her father come back to life, but younger and sounder. One of the most popular bachelors in her social set, the Harvard senior in his straw boater and flannels was as cocky and jovial as she was earnest. Mutual friends thought she had the better brain of the two.

A woman like Eleanor devotes herself passionately to her role as a wife. In this case, the marriage was a triangle, with Franklin's widowed mother, Sara Delano Roosevelt, playing the third angle as the woman who could not bear to loosen her bond to her only child. While the newlyweds were on their honeymoon, Sara not only rented a house for them and furnished it from chandeliers to dish towels, according to the custom of the day in well-to-do families, but staffed it with servants.

Nothing belonged to Eleanor: not her house; not the children she bore later, who were brought up by tyrannical governesses; not the staff, who owed their loyalty to Sara; not even her political loyalties and her choice of friends. Longing to be loved by the only mother figure she had, Eleanor gave up her own liberal opinions and accepted the bigotry and racism of her mother-in-law. She was against women's suffrage, she said, because women did not know enough about politics to vote and should defer to the judgment of their husbands, but when her own husband supported suffrage she switched sides.

By the time World War I broke out, Franklin had risen politically to the post of assistant secretary of the Navy, which meant that Eleanor, though pregnant, had heavy social duties. To help with her schedule, she hired a part-time social secretary, twenty-two-year-old Lucy Mercer.

During the scorching summer of 1918, Franklin went to Europe on Navy business but was shipped home in September with double pneumonia during the influenza epidemic that was raging world-wide. Eleanor met him at the dock with an ambulance and a doctor in attendance, took him home, and prepared to unpack his luggage while he lay in bed.

She lifted the lid of his suitcase. A packet of letters lay there. But why would he bring home letters, handwritten, not even on official stationery? The next moment she recognized the handwriting as that of her social secretary, Lucy Mercer.

Eleanor, who had never been a beauty, was thirty-four years old by this time, the mother of five children, in addition to a sixth who had died in infancy. For an entire decade, as she said, she had either been pregnant or just getting over a pregnancy. Lucy was eight years younger, lovely, cultured, and charming, the daughter of a distin-guished family that had fallen on hard times. In fact, Lucy's charm was a good deal like Franklin's, the Roosevelt children remarked later.

"I did not believe in knowing things which your husband did not wish you to know," Eleanor had said to her cousin Alice Roosevelt a year earlier, when Alice maliciously inquired if Franklin ever told her any secrets. It was a response that Bluebeard would have approved of. But how could anyone with Eleanor's intelligence have been so naïve as to hire a beautiful single girl in the first place? And how could she have failed to know what everyone else in Washington so-ciety had been gossiping about—no doubt, laughing about—for years?

As Eleanor said, she did not choose to know what her husband did not want known. The truth was that she couldn't afford to know, any more than Sleeping Beauty could afford to wake up ahead of schedule, and so it was Eleanor, not her husband, who kept the door to the Bloody Chamber shut tight. A wife is proverbially the last to know what is going on. After all, who else has so much to lose?

As for Franklin, why did he bring those letters home? Did he do it to reassure himself that he could still win the love of a younger woman? Or is it possible that he enjoyed skating blithely on the brink of discovery, just as Bluebeard gave detailed instructions to his wives for finding the chamber he forbade them to enter?

The contest is not between husband and wife here but between not-wanting-to-know and knowing on the part of one spouse, and wanting-to-be-known or not-wanting-to-be-known on the part of the other.

ANY BLOW WE SUFFER, in our careers as well as in our relationships, brings us back to square one, to the self-loathing of adolescence, the fear of not being acceptable, which for a woman revives the never-extinguished fear of abandonment.

Not only the future is wiped out for a wife who has been deceived. That much is bearable, though painful. A new future is always possible, but the past is scooped out from under her as well. She would have sworn she was loved. (What conceit, she sees now, or was it protective blindness?) What's more, she deserved to be loved. She was faithful with her whole heart, all the while that someone else was waiting in the wings. *They* must have talked about her in her absence.

She was a fool. No, worse than a fool, her very innocence must have been an obstacle to what her husband longed for in his life. For years, he must have been thinking thoughts she never dreamed of, which made her end of their conversations sound like the nattering of a child.

But if he had thoughts she never dreamed of, then she and her husband were never one. Even after fourteen years of marriage, she had seen herself as a bride brought home on approval, living in somebody else's house, always fearful of causing displeasure or failing in her duty. After the discovery of her husband's faithlessness—when the wizard had ceased to be a wizard—she discarded the old assumptions, romantic and social, which had been the basis of her life since her schooldays.

In the phrase of the day, Eleanor offered Franklin his freedom—she would divorce him so that he could marry Lucy—but Sara rushed to her daughter-in-law's support. If Franklin disgraced the family by deserting his wife and five children, he wouldn't see another cent of her money, which would not only cancel the prospect of inheriting his beloved Hyde Park but also put an end to his political dreams.

Franklin's choice was clear. The two Roosevelts agreed to stay together (in separate bedrooms, according to their children) and cause each other as little pain as possible. Franklin swore that he would never see Lucy again, but she was with him at his first inaugural as president and she was with him at the time of his death in Warm Springs, twenty-seven years later.

THE FITCHER'S BIRD took a skull and decorated it with a wreath of flowers, so that it was a bride's head staring out the window of the house and, at the same time, in another reflection on marriage, a death's head.

A skull for the Fitcher's Bird. Snow White's glass coffin. Sleeping Beauty's bed. The death of the old self makes possible the birth of something new.

Eleanor stripped herself of everything she could afford to lose, until she reached the point where clarity begins. For many months, she couldn't eat normally, couldn't even take Communion. On the occasions when she managed to eat a normal meal she vomited afterward, as if she found it impossible to stomach what had happened to her. The repeated vomiting may have loosened her already protruding teeth, making them stick out even further, so that, more and more, she resembled the death's head. For hours on end she sat in the cemetery at Rock Creek Park, contemplating Saint-Gaudens's statue popularly known as *Grief.* "I faced myself, my surroundings, my world, honestly for the first time," she wrote a quarter of a century later.

The Fitcher's Bird eventually coaxed the former wizard and his kin into the house, where she locked the doors and burned them to death. This is the way transformation begins: with the destruction of what has been outgrown.

One of Eleanor's first actions on her own behalf was to fire the staff of servants that her mother-in-law had installed in her house, some of whom must have acted as spies for Sara or betrayed Eleanor in favor of Lucy. What was more astonishing, she replaced them with blacks, which was unheard of in Washington in a period of race riots and lynchings when each group dreaded the other. The time had come to take control of her life, beginning with fundamentals: She went to business school to study shorthand and typing; she took cooking lessons from her housekeeper; she learned to drive, which Franklin had discouraged. While she was at it, she drove too fast. But what she required most urgently was work, her own kind of work, aimed at improving the lot of others. After the disastrous election of 1920, in which Franklin's party was roundly defeated, she began her political apprenticeship by joining the League of Women Voters to battle for such causes as unemployment insurance, the abolition of child labor, wages-and-hours legislation, and, above all, the League of Nations.

Her new career was soon interrupted. While vacationing at their isolated summer home on the island of Campobello off the coast of Maine, Franklin came down with violent pains and fever one day, eventually diagnosed as polio, which left him paralyzed from the waist down for the rest of his life. Eleanor nursed him day and night with a degree of intimacy Lucy Mercer knew nothing about, massaging his massive but powerless legs, rolling his heavy torso over in bed, administering enemas and catheters. The jaunty sportsman found himself humiliated in ways he could never have imagined.

Suffering broadened Franklin by teaching him that he was as vulnerable as the rest of humanity, while it taught Eleanor—the daughter who had never managed to please her mother, the wife who had been bypassed as a companion and bedmate by her husband—that she wasn't submissive after all, not even toward her mother-in-law. When Sara returned from Europe to find her son crippled, she was adamant that he must retire to the existence of a country squire among the soothing orchards and woods of Hyde Park, which was what his father had done for the last ten years of his life, following a heart attack. Franklin was in a wheelchair. He was in pain. He must not be weakened further by the bustle of political visitors with which Eleanor surrounded him as if he were his old self.

Eleanor was equally adamant that Franklin must not give up his ambition for a political career, or his life would effectively be over before he turned forty. The history books record her triumph. Had she given in, Eleanor said later, Franklin would have been an invalid for life. She would have become "a completely colorless echo of my husband and mother-in-law and torn between them, I might have stayed a weak character forever if I had not found that out."

The Fitcher's Bird burned the fairy-tale sorcerer and his kin to death along with the house. Eleanor's triumph was more complete: She handed the sorcerer's life back to him, so that he was indebted to her forever after.

FOR THE REST OF FRANKLIN'S LIFE, he and Eleanor worked together as teammates rather than as man and wife, respectful of each other's talents but rarely in the same place at the same time: the prototype of the modern power couple (the Kennedys and Clintons, for instance) whose romance gives way to a more intoxicating joint venture. At her husband's urging, Eleanor overcame her shyness and jumped into New York State politics to keep the Roosevelt name in front of the public while he recovered his strength. Traveling around the country during his presidency, she served as his eyes, ears, and legs, issuing reports and recommendations that were often years in advance of his views, while writing a nationally syndicated newspaper column at the same time. After Franklin's death, instead of retiring from the scene she became this country's delegate to the United Nations. The U.N. Declaration of Human Rights was largely her handiwork.

THAT WAS THE OUTER SHELL. Still married but freed from her expected roles as wife, daughter-in-law, and society matron, Eleanor walked out of the domestic plot and transformed herself into a real-life Tough Old Bird like the fairy-tale heroine, gaunt and beaky, using the terrible knowledge she had gained in the Bloody Chamber to focus on a future that would be individual and intentional rather than generic.

"In conventional terms, ER lived an outrageous life," says her eminent biographer Blanche Wiesen Cook. While Eleanor's husband stayed in Albany as governor of New York State, she spent two and a half days in New York City each week, teaching English and history at a school she had helped found. While he was president, she maintained her own hideaway in Greenwich Village. Most of her friends would never have been invited to sit at her mother-in-law's dinner table. They included not only lesbians (her four closest friends were two lesbian couples) but Jews, blacks, labor-union organizers, political liberals, and radicals of all sorts: birds of her own flock. With three other women, and with her husband's blessing, she built a small house at Hyde Park that Franklin referred to as "the Honeymoon Cottage," and his mother called "that hovel."

In the end, the wife who had considered herself on probation after fourteen years of marriage and five children changed the world.

IN THE MAIDEN SECTION OF THIS BOOK, whether the heroine knows it or not, what she wants is to marry a Prince and bear children. In the Matron section, the White Bride wavers in her attitude toward marriage. The Seal Wife escapes marriage after trying it for years. The "Fitcher's Bird," a tale little known or admired, is the only one in which the heroine transcends marriage—or has it pulled out from under her—surviving in one piece where her earlier selves fell apart, which makes this story particularly relevant to our era of long lives and short marriages.

Sooner or later, what wife doesn't find herself inside the Bloody Chamber? On the day when a woman learns that the cloud on her husband's X-ray is not nothing, not a fair-weather cumulus but a portent of disaster to come, she may not feel shame or resentment, as Eleanor Roosevelt did, but her shock is no less when she finds out that she isn't the person she thought she was. The word "wife" won't fit her much longer.

Forty years may lie ahead after that transformative day during which there is no prescribed role for her to play, especially if her children are grown and gone. She is no longer beautiful, if she ever was, no longer fertile. She has outgrown the marriage plot. Apart from raising her children, what has she done, she asks herself, that was worthy of the quantity of life she gave it?

"Can you learn to live?" asks Colette, an author who discovered bloody chambers of her own. "Yes, if you are not happy. There is no virtue in felicity. To endure without happiness and not to droop, not to pine, is a pursuit in itself, you might almost say a profession." Giving up the youthful ideal of happiness, which has been obliterated by knowledge, the heroine of the fairy tale gains strength, independence, endurance, in exchange, which most women regard as the consolation prizes reserved for those who have lost the golden apples.

"No virtue in felicity," says Colette. But nothing wrong with it, either. Bluebeard's widow used his estate to marry herself "to a very honest gentleman" who made her forget the ill time she had suffered. Eleanor Roosevelt never divorced or remarried, but she had a secret relationship for years while her husband was in the White House— ardent, sensual (perhaps sexual, perhaps not, the question is endlessly debated), tumultuous, and emphatically risky—with a nationally known woman reporter named Lorena Hickok, while retaining her emotional independence.

But how shall an ordinary woman endure, once she has passed through the Bloody Chamber? By finding a challenge worthy of her talents. A niche of her own. Strength grows from pruning away old assumptions, and its final flower is self-respect.

Nothing wrong with felicity, the Fitcher's Bird would agree. But only so long as one doesn't make it a career.

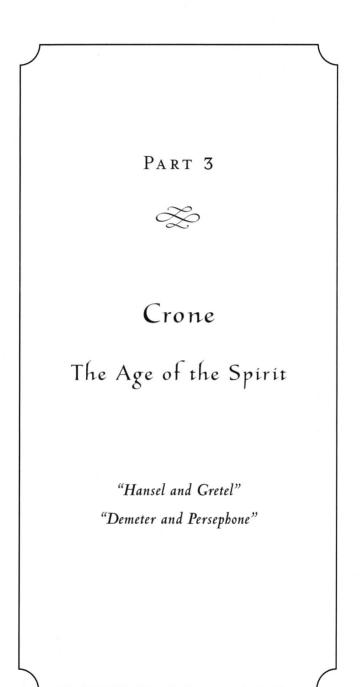

PART 3

Crone

The Age of the Spirit

"Hansel and Gretel"
"Demeter and Persephone"

The end-all is also the be-all, the waning moon almost finished with its cycle reflecting the light of the sun. The stage at which I find myself now.

More aware of my body than at any time since my first pregnancy (these aches and restrictions, this awkwardness in movement even though I'm shrinking these days rather than swelling), I feel myself burning with love for life. My own life rather than my children's. It's time to care for my self.

My spirit peels away from my body, not without pain and loss, but as it separates and grows stronger in proportion to the body's weakness my ardor for the worldly spectacle increases. I have become peripheral to my family rather than central. I am no longer useful to the world in any obvious way—not attractive, either, since I'm no longer meant to attract—which means that I am free to ask the single question worth asking: How can I go on living once I realize I am going to die?

IN FAIRY TALES *there are no old women. Witches we have aplenty, old housewives who live at the bottom of a well turn out to be gift-giving fairies, occasional fairy godmothers, along with spinning women who are Fates in disguise, but no wrinkled human women to counterbalance the incoming stream of innocent maidens.*

Maybe this stems from the fact that in past centuries, when fairy tales were told, few women lived beyond their child-rearing years, and those who did seemed possessed of magic, whether for good or evil. Or maybe it's because we don't know how to face old age, which is a new phase in female history. "I'm getting old," we say to our grown-up children, waiting for them to contradict us—which they do, not only for our sakes but in part for their own: Our death will remove the last buffer between them and mortality. And so we quail at the task of facing death, the most challenging transformation since birth.

In autumn, when each day holds less light than the one before, trees turn incandescent in blazes of scarlet or purple or yellow, sharply distinguished from one another. By this season they have passed through the veiled and timid greens of spring, penetrated by light from the sky, and the more or less uniform green of summer. But green is not their true color. Green is the costume of younger seasons, the chlorophyll that courses through their veins to feed them. When days shorten and tree trunks no longer require nourishment, the chlorophyll ebbs and the leaves are revealed at last, just before they drop, in the colors that were always theirs, hidden beneath that greenery.

I have found this out, and maybe it's the lesson that has been given me to learn: Only in old age, and only for moments in old age, are we free enough in spirit to see the world as God must see it—as a passing fancy that captures us for a while and then lets us go.

THE TWO STORIES IN THIS SECTION, *"Hansel and Gretel" and the myth of Demeter and her daughter, Persephone, represent two opposite views of old age and death.*

In "Hansel and Gretel," the main character looks like a crone, but in a deeper sense she is the death-witch who feeds on children—meaning all of us, since we are all children lost in the woods in comparison to her.

In the Demeter and Persephone story, the crone is the mother goddess Demeter, who turns into a death-witch for a while, prepared to wipe out life on earth when she is robbed of her daughter, but learns to rise above her suffering. She then bestows her blessing by introducing the mystery rites that teach human beings how to greet the approach of death without fear.

CHAPTER 15

Hansel and Gretel:
Life in the Light of Death

In the Christmas season we bring it out of storage and place it in the center of the holiday table: the gingerbread house with its roof of white frosting with colored sprinkles, its mini-marshmallow windows and gumdrop cobblestones—the witch's house in the woods, designed to be as deliciously destructible as the death-witch herself.

But why an image from this particular fairy tale, and why at holiday time? Because we have come to the dark of the year, the winter solstice, and it's possible that the days that shrank so rapidly will never grow longer again; the sun may go on declining into perpetual night, carrying us with it into darkness. Death is the centerpiece of the feast, but it's not to be thought about during this jovial passing and heaping of plates, not to be thought about by anyone except perhaps the grandparents, who may wonder how many Christmases are left to them, and how the family members will rearrange themselves around the table once these seats are vacant.

VIRGIN, MOTHER, CRONE. Female figures all of them, reflections of the ancient goddess in her three aspects, since females are the vehicles of transformation in this world. Of these phases, the last is the uncharted one—the phase, new in history, that enlarges the spirit while it lays waste the body.

(The word *crone* for an elderly woman repels us, but what synonym do we have? *Hag* is even worse. "Wise woman" is false labeling, since foolish young women more often turn into foolish old women than into sages. We need no special term for men, who not only hang on to their sexual and financial power almost to the end but usually have a woman to take care of them. "Old woman" may be accurate, but it implies continuance at best, or more likely withering, rather than the inner growth of the spirit that properly belongs to this stage.)

For the first time since childhood, a woman is free to make choices without being constrained by either biology or ambition (assuming that she has enough money to live on): not only free but forced to make independent choices. Ever since puberty, her life pattern has been cut out for her. Now that she is middle-aged, she must decide what she wants to do, which means that she must discover who she is—not in terms of relationships or job categories but in and of herself, in spirit as well as body, and what she is capable of.

This is a new development in world history. According to nature's program, female mammals of all species go through menopause when their most viable eggs have been exhausted, and then survive long enough for their youngest offspring to manage without them, but not much longer. These days, a woman in our society can expect to outlive her youngest child's coming-of-age by several decades. In 1900, the average American woman died at the age of forty-eight. In

2000, the average age was almost eighty, and rising at the rate of two to three years each decade. This raises the question of what a woman is supposed to do with that bonus life span piled on top of her former life span of service to the species. Or is it arrogant to pretend that we can ever justify the gift of time?

Nearly as full of energy as ever, the postmenopausal, postmaternal woman, no longer responsible for tending her grown children, may also be postmarital if her partner has died or defected, though this needn't mean that she's postsexual. She may be burdened with the care of an ailing mate or motherless grandchildren, but often she exists in the proverbial empty nest, which seems at first to be a void. Actually, it's a God-given opportunity to examine her life and decide which aspects were chosen and which simply happened; who she might become if granted enough time; what her work meant to her, or if that work was ever really hers. Equally important, she faces what she fears. She grows in spirit.

On the verge of becoming a crone, the matron discovers that she requires something new in her life, an altering jolt: New meaning in her job, giving it a new quality of attention now that it's the focus of her life or, at the other extreme, retirement if she can afford it and wants it. A new romance. If she's a nurturer, she goes out into society to help others—maybe as a volunteer tutor in an elementary school, or a teacher of English as a second language to immigrants, or a visitor to those dying alone in a hospice. On the other hand, if she chooses to nurture aspects of herself that haven't had a chance to sprout yet, she may take the college course in psychology that she always wanted to take, or join a writer's group or sculpture class—something radically new, which proves to be not new at all but a notion that has been germinating inside her since childhood. Age has its advantages: An old woman has not much to lose, and no one to fault her if she fails.

In unpredictable ways, the domestic romance, or lack of it, changes its tone. "My grandmother and grandfather fought all the time," a friend told me. "Grandma was sharp-tongued, hostile. She'd been that way at least since she was ten, when the two of them met for the first time in a one-room schoolhouse in rural New Jersey and she kicked him in the shin during recess. Grandpa was softhearted but good at business. When he was in his sixties he retired, which freed my grandmother from her need to compete with him and from her sense of living in his shadow. She allowed herself to soften. Later, as she aged and suffered from the usual ailments, she learned to appreciate the tenderness she had deplored in him. In old age, I suspect that they came closer to the traditional image of sweethearts than at any time earlier."

We grow and diminish at different, uncontrollable rates in different parts of ourselves: physical, intellectual, emotional, spiritual. An older woman may find her social sense branching out in surprising ways, leading her to seek out new friends, preferably younger ones to whom she comes as an exotic visitor from another era. Cross-pollinating the generations, she learns what she missed out on as a young matron (a husband who shared child care). What she missed through ignorance and good luck (fetal alcohol syndrome). What she missed because no one told her she ought to try it (living with a man before marriage; breast-feeding). What she missed because the emotional climate she lived in was more austere than the present: She never offered her children the permissive enthusiasm she envies in young parents these days—those glad cries of "Good job!" they aim at their little ones, who seem to manage their own lives with imperious certainty. In short, she discovers that she was a creature of her time. In that thought, she finds much forgiveness for her shortcomings.

And what does an old woman—a crone like me—offer a young woman in return? Only the realization that problems tend to pass without being solved. The world turns, the problem darkening the sky overhead moves toward the horizon and disappears, while an unexpected one shows up in the east. We try again.

———

ALL OF THIS IS WELL KNOWN and useful. But it's not enough. In the shadows as the moon wanes, a woman must go deeper into the recesses of her soul and spirit to examine what used to be called "final things." She must come to terms with the past: The work she intended to do and might have done well, but didn't. The parent with whom she was never reconciled. The triumphs, as well as failures, that seemed so important in their turn that they paralyzed her. The time wasted—that above all—time in which she had no sense of existing right here, this moment, blood pulsing through her veins, which may not be true much longer.

On a certain morning, the woman, who has been a matron for a good many years now, looks in the mirror and says to herself, "God, I look old." At such a moment, she acknowledges the lines of mortality that she sees carved on her face. The angel of the Annunciation has flown into her bedroom once again, carrying news of the advent of death this time rather than of childbirth, equal in shock to seeing the first blood of menstruation but opposite in its message.

Life is not a gift, it's a loan repayable on demand, the woman reads in those lines on her face. For the first time since childhood, she feels the urgencies that lie behind her days like a horizon behind a seascape. She fears death—specifically, she fears dying as a lonely old woman, the fall down the cellar stairs and no one to hear her call for help. But fear is the essential part of the angel's gift, the goad and root of consciousness. In response to fear, she's overcome by love for life and for her body, still wonderfully intact, which so cleverly poises one foot at a time in midair and bends the other knee while she descends a step. That requires faith in the knees.

A divine duty has been laid on her without her consent, a duty she couldn't face earlier in life. As a Maiden, she had no interest in abstractions like age and death. She was busy grooming herself, separating from her parents, obeying nature's mandate to attract a mate. Her idea of the future was strictly short-term, beckoning brightly.

By the time she became a Matron, she hadn't an ounce of energy to spare from the work of starting a career, or bearing and raising a family, or both. A young mother rushing down the street behind a stroller is terrible in her beauty: Beautiful whenever she bends over her child to fill a need, because all mothers are beautiful in their concern. Terrible because she doesn't see that the moment of need and fulfillment, effort and exhaustion is evaporating already, the apex of her life, but she won't recognize that until it's over, by which time she will have forgotten what it felt like and who she was, so young and distracted and sleep-deprived to be in charge of another life. All that matters at the moment is getting the grocery shopping done and the little one changed and fed in time to pick up her older child from nursery school. "No time to think" is the anesthetic life gives both men and women in the middle years, to make sure that we stay focused on our assigned task of keeping the species going.

Only in the final stage, when the woman has been discharged from the domestic field with the "honors of war," as Isak Dinesen puts it, does she confront death as a reality, and by its light see this world she inhabits. The foreknowledge of death, at whatever age we achieve it, is what transforms us from higher animals into conscious human beings.

At last she faces the question worth asking: How can I go on living a meaningful life when I know that I'm going to die? How can I apprehend a world when I know it will go on without me?

Could the answer (could my answer) be this? "With passion. For this world, not the next. I don't care about the stars, any more than they care about me. What I crave is the human scale—nothing grander than a window seen from the street at night, yellow with light, a golden rectangle framed in the darkness, with a stranger's life beating inside it. That wrings my heart. I say that I can't bear to leave the world—and yet I've been granted ten thousand nights as clear as this one, with thousands of windows lighting the dark, framing thousands of strangers busy with their own lives, but how many of them have I actually looked at? Am I only now learning how to see? Becoming a seer? Only when I live with the knowledge that I am powerless to change what I see, or to hang on to it, am I ready for a transformation of the spirit.

Consciousness is too much to bear for more than a few minutes. The woman in front of the mirror breaks the angel's spell, looks in the mirror again, puts on her makeup with the hand of an art restorer, and goes out into the street as a middle-aged matron with highlights in her hair.

All the same, she has caught a whiff of mortality in the air, like the smell of salt before reaching the sea.

"AT FIFTY (MORE OR LESS) one is either reborn or moribund," Carolyn Heilbrun said about women when she was fifty-five herself.

Eleanor Roosevelt and Florence Nightingale were in their thirties when they left behind their purely domestic concerns and assumed roles on the public stage. Isak Dinesen, the Danish author of *Out of Africa* and "Babette's Feast," among other works, was considerably older when she began her life over again as a writer.

Before she brought herself to that point, she had to see the coffee plantation in Africa, which was so dear to her heart, sold out from under her because of years of debt; lose her husband to divorce; lose two fetuses to miscarriages (she remained childless); lose her foothold in Africa itself. She had to lose her glamorous "white hunter" lover twice, first to quarrels and immediately afterward to death, when his small private plane crashed. She had to lose everything she cared for before she returned to Denmark penniless, emaciated by syphilis, without a clear vision for what she thought of as an afterlife rather than a future. "Only when she had lost what had constituted her life . . . did she become the artist and the 'success' she never would have become otherwise," the historian Hannah Arendt said of her.

Change was the key. "God cannot stand continuance," Dinesen wrote in one of her stories. "No sooner has he created a season of a year, or a time of the day, than he wishes for something quite different, and sweeps it all away. No sooner was one a young man, and happy at that, than the nature of things would rush one into marriage, martyrdom or old age. . . . It is all wrong to imagine paradise as a never-changing state of bliss. It will probably, on the contrary, turn out to be, in the true spirit of God, an incessant up and down, a whirlpool of change. Only you may yourself, by that time . . . have taken to liking it."

She was nearly fifty when this story was published in her first book, which inaugurated her career. The first part of the pen name she adopted, "Isak," means "he who laughs."

ALL FAIRY TALES, in fact all stories, begin with change—transformation—as Dinesen would wish, and often end with it as well. Children are evicted from their homes and childhoods, and deserted in the woods, where they grow up to become Queens and Kings if they do not die. Mother figures turn into crones, who turn into witches.

The fairy tale "Hansel and Gretel" revolves around females and food, two topics of prime importance to the very young and old: Who eats and who is eaten; who cooks, who is fed, who escapes from the oven or cauldron, and for how long? But anything that deals with hunger and food necessarily deals with death and transformation in one form or another. Whenever a meal is eaten, something grows while something else dies.

HANSEL AND GRETEL, two dear little children, live with their parents, who are poor woodcutters, in a house at the edge of a forest. The clearing around the house is sunlit and safe. The forest is dark and patrolled by wolves. A famine holds this part of the country in its grip right now, and in the woodcutters' house there is "little to bite and to break."

One night, when the brother and sister are unable to sleep because of hunger, they overhear their father and stepmother plotting to be rid of them.

"How are we to feed our poor children, when we no longer have anything even for ourselves?" the woodcutter demands of his wife when they are in their bed.

"I'll tell you what, husband," replies the wife, who has obviously been thinking about the question for some time before her hapless husband gets around to it. "Early tomorrow morning we'll take them out where the forest grows thickest. We'll light a fire to keep them warm, and give them each one last piece of bread, and then we'll go to work and leave them alone. They won't find their way home again, and we'll be rid of them."

What no one knows is that at the heart of the forest stands a cottage made of gingerbread, so tempting with its sugar frosting that it will look like a dream house to two starving children. At the core of the house a red-eyed witch sits waiting for them. She can barely see, but she may be able to smell young flesh on its way.

The husband groans, as men do when they realize that their wives are way ahead of them and they will have to give in. "But how can I bear to leave my children alone in the forest?" he wants to know. "Wild animals will tear them to pieces."

"Oh, you fool!" cries the exasperated wife. "Then plane the planks for four coffins." With that, she locks the bread cupboard and pockets the key. Four deaths don't strike her as nobler than two.

Fortunately, Hansel is a resourceful lad. Creeping out of the house late that night, he loads the pockets of his coat with white pebbles that glitter in the moonlight. The next day, the woodcutter and his wife lead the children into the forest, where they build a fire for the children and give each of them a piece of bread. When afternoon comes, Hansel and Gretel fall asleep. By the time they wake up, the woods are as black as a bear's snout, but when the full moon rises the trail home sparkles like a string of pearls in front of them.

Weeks pass, and again only half a loaf of bread is left in the cupboard. The stepmother plans the same desperate remedy, but this time she is more prudent; she locks the cottage door at night. When the children are led into the forest the next day, Hansel has nothing in his pocket but a piece of bread. "Hansel, why do you keep stopping and looking round?" his father asks angrily. "I'm looking back at my shining pigeon sitting on the roof who wants to say goodbye," Hansel answers, as he crumbles the bread to mark the trail, while he and his sister are led deeper into the forest than they have ever been before.

Late that night, when the fire has burned itself out, the brother and sister awaken (these children seem to function only in dream-time) and wait for the moon to rise and show them the way home. But of course the woodland birds—which so often serve in fairy tales as guardian spirits or heavenly messengers—have eaten up the crumbs. In this case, the birds are meddlers that won't allow the children to leave the forest until the adventure has been faced, the work of transformation complete.

"At last," the witch says to herself, biding her time in the cottage. "I have them now. They won't escape me again." If she eats children, it's not because she's hungry. Her house is made of gingerbread, after all. Her purpose is darker and more transformative than ordinary nourishment.

ABANDONMENT IS OUR FIRST experience of the world, prompting our first cry when we find ourselves thrust from the sheltering womb into thin, cold air, while the sustenance that has streamed into us until this moment is cut off with a knife. From everything, we are pushed into nothing. As Genesis tells us, it's our birthright to be dispossessed.

Listening to this story in past centuries, children must have been aware that throughout history multitudes of babies have been disposed of one way or another by parents who were unable to take care of them. Newborns were routinely abandoned because they were deformed, spindly, or illegitimate, but most often because each was one more mouth to feed in a household that already lacked enough to go around. In the 1690s, famine was so severe in northern France that corpses lay in ditches with grass stuffed into their mouths. Mothers, dying of starvation themselves, would deposit their baby by the side of a busy road and delude themselves into believing for a while that he might be picked up by a childless passerby who would raise the infant as his own. Or they might drop him off at a foundling home, where he would at least be baptized and his death hidden from view. In some places, two thirds of all foundlings died before they were a year old. As late as 1850, while the brothers Grimm were still alive, half of the babies born in Vienna were abandoned.

In every story of abandonment, one parent voices qualms about the monstrous solution proposed by the other, but mother is more often allotted the blame. No, not mother, the brothers Grimm decided—that would be an unbearable possibility for children to take to bed after the family story hour. By the fourth edition of their book, the hard-hearted parent had been replaced by a stepmother, just as the Queen mother in "Snow White" tactfully changed into a stepmother for later audiences.

When Hansel and Gretel find themselves abandoned in the woods, their plight resonates with children in all centuries, including our own, since children are vulnerable in a way that adults are not. According to the standard reading of the story, the witch in the forest is an evil demon, a bogeywoman, who exists only in order to be overpowered by a gallant hero (or heroes) at the end. If she differs from child-eating ogres or the wolf that eats Red Riding Hood, it's because she can be seen as a caricature of a human crone, or—worse—a nightmare projection of female fears: an old woman living alone, pushed out of the village, humpbacked, hideous, full of spite toward children.

But if we probe deeper, and think of the plot in spiritual rather than historical terms, we see that all of us, no matter what our age, know ourselves to be children in the face of death. In this reading, Hansel and Gretel represent all human beings, including old people, and the witch is not a make-believe puppet, or a real-life crone, but death itself, lurking in the forest, hiding inside life's sweetness.

Both interpretations are valid. Images from the subconscious are never this thing or that, but this and that combined: the witch as witch, and the witch as death goddess. The task for adults is to absorb what they already know on two levels at once.

We are much too young to die, we protest like Hansel and Gretel. We are too vehemently in love with this world. Our best work lies ahead of us. Somewhere along the way, a mistake must have been made—a misdiagnosis by a doctor, a test or precaution we failed to take—and as a result the birds have eaten up the crumbs. Never mind, we assure one another, holding hands in a show of courage. We will destroy the witch, push Death into the oven, and find our way home.

FOR TWO DAYS MORE, Hansel and Gretel stumble farther into the dark wood with nothing to eat but a few dry berries and Gretel's single slice of bread. On the third morning they begin walking again, their legs growing weaker by the hour, but at midday, sure enough, they hear a song coming from a snow-white bird perched on a bough overhead. When the bird has finished singing, it flies in front of them, guiding them to a little cottage, where it alights on the roof.

Who doesn't know this cottage? In the forest, the berries and nuts are out of season. In the woodcutters' cottage, the supply of food is almost exhausted; and yet the gingerbread house stands in the forest, its windows of sugar icing gleaming moistly in the sun. The owner must be a grain goddess (like Demeter) as well as a death-witch.

"I'll start on the roof," says Hansel, "and you can eat some of the window, Gretel, it will taste sweet."

To the starving children, the cottage, which is also the witch's body (the way the house represents the woman's body in so many other stories), appears as food. Hansel breaks off a piece of the white-frosting roof. The witch, hiding behind the door, hears a thump and sees a patch of light where he has torn off a tile. This is what children do to her, she grumbles to herself. What they used to do to her in her human form, she means. Eat her up. Grow big inside her belly on the food she eats until the day they are born. Drain her breasts of milk.

> *"Nibble, nibble, gnaw,*
> *Who is nibbling at my front door?"*

she inquires in her softest witch voice from inside the house.

Children have not only gnawed her breasts but nibbled her life away, licked off her beauty, sucked up her energy, devoured her days in numberless bites, and broken what they couldn't swallow into crumbs that they drop on the ground. Now they find her dried up, caved in.

Gretel pushes out a windowpane and sits down to enjoy it, while Hansel tears off another piece of the roof. Not only are these two eating the witch out of house and home, as their stepmother complained, they are eating the house itself from over her head. Everything that belonged to her is falling to them.

This is how we know when we are old: when we want nothing except to hold on to what we already have.

Jerking the door open, the witch creeps out on crutches, squinting in the sunlight. The children shrink back at the sight of her.

"Come in, you poor dear children," she entices them. "How hungry you must be."

With Hansel on one side and Gretel on the other, she hobbles into the house, where she heaps a little table with pancakes and sugar, apples and nuts, and sets a pitcher of milk in front of them. After they have eaten all they can hold, she shows them two child-size beds, already made up with clean linen and feather pillows, as if she has been expecting them. The children fall asleep thinking themselves in Heaven. This must be the good, kind mother they lost some time ago, who treats them so bountifully.

Early the next morning, the witch stands over the bed and looks for a moment at the sleeping children with their rosy cheeks and the hair that clings to their foreheads from perspiration. Their helpless-ness and beauty enflame her. Gripping Hansel with her root-like hand, she pulls him into the stable and locks him in a pen behind a grated door, muttering to herself, "This will make a dainty mouthful."

After that, she pokes Gretel with her cane until the girl stirs, pulls the comforter off the bed, and cries, "Get up, you lazy thing, and cook something good for your brother's breakfast. I want him made nice and fat."

Fair is fair. The children want to eat the house that is her body. She wants to take them back into her belly, where they came from in the first place. She'll baste them in the oven with their own juices, she'll put their vigor and energy inside her to flesh out her wrinkles and oil her joints. She'll feast on their youth. Without the supper she gave them, they would have been dead by now anyway.

OUT OF OUR FEAR of crones and the specifically female fear of turn-ing into one, out of our dread of death and also out of unholy desires, we create the fairy-tale witch, who is the opposite of the traditional good woman. Manless, she's masterful rather than obedient, furious instead of meek, particularly venomous against children, whom women are supposed to adore, or at least protect. Gathering into herself the boundless anger suppressed by humans at the outrages life has inflicted on us, she becomes an untamable force, rising on an updraft of fire with appetites young women never dream of.

I turn and burn.
Do not think I underestimate your great concern. . . .
Herr God, Herr Lucifer,
Beware
Beware.

Out of the ash
I rise with my red hair
And I eat men like air.

So wrote Sylvia Plath, a modern poet more than half in love with death.

HANSEL'S DREAM was to be fed. Now, as always in fairy tales, his dream comes truer than true. Not only is he fed; on the witch's orders, he's stuffed with food, plied with the richest, fattiest delicacies, which are brought to him on heaping platters by his sister, who gets nothing but crab shells to eat herself (a strange dish to find in the middle of a forest). Food needn't be wasted on Gretel. She isn't a future meal but a breeder of future meals, an apprentice witch who is forced to provide fodder for the death-witch. Hansel is a Strasbourg goose being readied for the dinner table.

"When he is fat enough I will eat him," the witch declares.

Every morning she visits Hansel in his cage. "Poke your finger through the slats," she demands. "I want to find out how soon you'll be plump enough to eat." Being no fool, Hansel sticks out a bone he has saved from his meal, and the witch, with her dim eyes, thinks it's his finger, which is no fleshier than it was the day before.

More food must be loaded on his plate, she orders, but weeks pass, the bone stays bony, and she can only dream about melting him in her mouth, soft as sweetbreads, brimming with the juice of youth. Once Hansel is inside her, she will be younger than he is, because she will have the rest of his years added on to hers.

How, then, does Hansel, locked in his pen, differ from any of us, locked into our knowledge of what lies ahead? How shall we live in front of the terror that grips us (and only us, burdened by an awareness that animals are spared) when we remember that we must die, and there isn't anything we can do about it? If we measure age by the amount of time left to us, rather than by the number of years that have passed since we were born, Hansel is older than the oldest man in his village.

Seen in this way, the fairy-tale witch in her gingerbread cottage can be recognized as a degraded version of the ancient grain goddess in her roles as both nourisher and devourer, degraded here because she serves her own needs rather than those of the earth. She brings food out of the soil to sustain life, and then in winter folds everything back inside her body with an impartial hand. This is the final phase of the triple-goddess sequence: Maiden, matron, crone. Sowing, ripening, harvesting. Followed by eating.

It's easy enough to picture the goddess in the first two phases: Young and virginal like Mary, shrinking back in awe when the angel Gabriel flies into her bedroom with the news that she is pregnant. This picture we like. Yes, we say, this is the way it must have been in my family. I always knew my mother—magically fertile with me, and yet untouched—would never have gotten into bed with my father and done *that.*

She's fresh as Venus blown to shore on a seashell, naked except for the long golden hair that hides her genitals. Or Marilyn Monroe in *The Seven Year Itch,* standing over a subway grating on a hot summer day with her white skirt billowing up to her waist in a rush of wind when a train passes below.

With equal ease, we see, or used to see, the goddess in her matron stage as Mother of All Living: Isis of Egypt, suckling the infant god Horus on her lap; Diana at Ephesus, covered with rows of breasts that reach from her collarbone to her waist, while from the waist down ranks of animals wait to be nourished by her milk; Mary again, cradling her son in her arm, this time while her milk spurts into his mouth; Sethe, the mother of Beloved in Toni Morrison's novel of the same name.

But the third and last phase of the goddess is one we don't choose to look at head-on. Mortal males arouse our respect, or at least our sympathy, in the ravages of old age (Lear, Prospero, Willy Loman, the Old Man and the Sea), but not females, whether human or divine. Our goddesses have to remain young if we are to worship them. When the Virgin Mary holds the body of her crucified son on her lap, she looks as young and unlined as she did when she bore him. Later, when he raises her to heaven as his Queen in a Cinderella finale, she looks younger than he does. In Egyptian art, when Isis stands beside the throne of her husband-brother, Osiris, ruler of the Underworld, he is bandaged like a mummy, but she is forever youthful as a ray of sunshine.

In our culture, we have never made room for a death goddess, a bloody devourer like the Indian goddess Kali, endlessly eating sacrifices at one end while giving birth at the other. All that we have is a hideous old witch, waiting to make a meal of two children. Or rather, we have a witch waiting to be annihilated herself in a puppet show, while children clap their hands and laugh when she is shoved into her own oven. They have been promised that Death will be put to death for their sake but are relieved to see it happen all the same.

CHILDREN, FOOD, DEATH, whirl after one another like the spokes of a pinwheel. Children eat food. Death eats children. Spinning the other way around, death clears the earth of the generations that clutter it now, making new growth possible, spring crops along with children who grow taller each year. Death fertilizes. Life destroys.

As Greek women chant to the corpse at rural funerals even today while they sample a mixture of seeds, "The earth, your mother, who fed you will eat you now."

In the process of looking at another human being as if he were good to eat, or making a game out of nibbling flesh, or considering a person as if he were food, we come to the border between life and death, and at the same time between self and others. We straddle that border. Women, in particular, never get over their passion for baby flesh. They long to embrace it, hold on to it, keep it for themselves.

"You're delicious," women say to a baby in his carriage. "You're sweet as candy." "I'm going to eat you up," a mother growls in a make-believe threat to her toddler son. She tosses her head like a lion. "Oh no, you're not." The child squeals in delight, flattered by her adoration. "Oh yes, I am." She bends her head down to his belly and inhales his essence. This came out of her belly.

Interpenetration is what we want. Close isn't close enough. What a woman longs for is to penetrate and, even more vividly, to be penetrated, to escape the limitation of being a single body encased in her skin. As in sex: penis in vagina, tongue in mouth, tongue in genitals. Or pregnancy, another body inside hers. This is what she's made for. Food and feeding—filling up the cavities, an emotional need as well as a domestic duty. What a man wants includes nuzzling. Sucking nipples. Penis in mouth. Love bites. For either sex, the kiss is the innocent substitute for a bite, like wine in the place of blood. All acts of intimacy contain an element of eating.

But intimacy carries its own taboos. In our society, we are permitted to know another person, but not too well—no cannibal supper like that of the witch. The point at which intimacy turns into possession is forbidden to us.

WHEN VIEWED FROM OTHER CULTURES, cannibalism looks radically different if it transmits spiritual rather than physical nourishment from the dead to the living descendants. Yanomami people of the Amazon find it horrifying that we put the bodies of our loved ones into the ground and leave them there to rot. They cremate their dead, and some time later grind up the bones and mix them with bananas to make a soup, which each person close to the dead man or woman drinks. "Their souls would be unhappy if they did not find a resting place within their relatives," says a tribesman, who regards us as heartless barbarians for discarding our family members when we are through with them.

If we have only an ounce of a superior being inside us, or a being that is at least superior in youth and vitality, as Hansel and Gretel are more vigorous than the witch, we are no longer hopelessly mortal; we are more than ourselves. This idea lies behind holy sacrifice in ancient cultures and cannibalism, and behind the Christian ceremony of the Eucharist as well.

At the Last Supper, according to the Gospel of John, Jesus took a piece of bread and said, "I am the living bread which came down from heaven: if any man eat of this bread, he shall live for ever: and the bread that I will give is my flesh." He went on, "Except ye eat the flesh of the Son of man, and drink his blood, ye have no life in you. Whoso eateth my flesh, and drinketh my blood, hath eternal life."

When he held up bread, he marked the progress of religion from human sacrifice to animal (the story of Abraham and Isaac), and then from animal to bread, the staff—and stuff—of life. All of us are familiar with transubstantiation: Our bodies change the bread that we eat into flesh, but Jesus promised to transform his sacred flesh into bread that would then become part of our flesh, and his blood into wine. This promise was given at the Last Supper, which was the Jewish Passover meal, referred to in the Gospels as the Feast of Unleavened Bread, where bread (in the form of *matzoh*) and wine are central symbols. The town of Bethlehem, where Jesus was born, can be translated from the Hebrew as *beth,* "house," and *lehem,* "bread"— the house of bread.

At a more pragmatic, worldly level, most of us are cannibals right now, or soon will be, surviving and living longer, fuller lives because we carry parts of other people's bodies inside us. In every major hospital in this country, organs and tissues from corpses arrive daily, chilled as if in picnic baskets. Every cadaver is a potential treasure chest: one heart (to be refrigerated for no more than four or five hours), one pancreas and liver, two kidneys (136,000 of these have been transplanted already), two lungs, veins and arteries, one small intestine, two corneas, skin for burn patients, bone marrow for the treatment of cancer. New vertebrae can be constructed from the patient's own bones, mixed with cadaver bones, sea coral, and putty. Eighty thousand patients are on the national waiting list for body parts right now.

If the witch has cannibal instincts, that's because she represents the death force, but not many of us are prepared to admit that we contain part of another person inside us. We use life—scientifically—in any way we can to foster our own well-being and postpone the day when we will meet the witch.

———

FOUR WEEKS GO BY, moon to moon, and the witch can't wait any longer for her meal, never mind whether Hansel is fat or lean. "Get stirring, lazy girl, and bring water for the cauldron," she says to Gretel. "I intend to cook your brother for dinner. And keep your noise to yourself, it won't do you any good," she adds over the sound of Gretel's wails. "But first, while the water is boiling, I'm going to bake bread. I've already heated the oven and kneaded the dough." The witch and her weeping apprentice stand in front of the oven, which isn't a metal box like a modern one but a brick-lined hole in a stone wall with a wood fire blazing underneath a grate. "Creep in there," says the witch, who has decided that she can have two tasty meals as easily as one—delicate white meat from Gretel in contrast to her brother's juicy dark meat. "You can tell me if the oven is hot enough to put the bread in."

Flames are leaping under the grate. Reading the witch's mind, Gretel says she can't possibly crawl in there, the door is too small. "Why, silly fool, it's so big I can get in myself," the witch says contemptuously, climbing up and thrusting her head into the oven to show her stupid servant how the job should be done. At this, Gretel gives her a mighty shove forward, slams the door shut, and bolts it. The supposedly passive heroine has saved her brother's life.

As soon as the screams of the burning witch die down, Gretel rushes to the stable and unlocks Hansel's pen, after which the two children jubilantly caper back to the witch's house. There they find chests full of jewels and pearls in every corner, which, strangely enough, they hadn't noticed before.

Emeralds and sapphires and pearls. In fairy-tale language, this is our reward whenever we come face-to-face with death in the course of the daily routine and miraculously escape it, bravely escape it because we didn't die of fright during the encounter. When the CAT scan or EKG proves normal (the stitch in the side is only a stitch in the side), when the biopsy comes back benign, when the paramedics arrive in time to administer CPR, we are gripped by a seizure of joy that transcends any other except possibly that of childbirth at the instant the pain stops. Each corner of our lives is filled with treasure—how could we have failed to notice these jewels and pearls before? On every tree the leaves reflect sunlight, as if mirrors have been hung from the branches. The rocks are quartz crystals, the birds fly toward Heaven. The world has been created anew, and we are its center.

Hansel and Gretel stop long enough to hug each other before filling their pockets with gems. Nothing remains for them to do except to find their way home, which proves easier than they would have dreamed. Even the geography of the forest has changed in their favor. After only two hours of walking, they come to a stretch of water where there was no water before. No bridge or boat is at hand, but an obliging duck ferries them across one at a time: a white duck, feathered like an angel, the third and final guardian bird in the story.

Once across the water, they can see their old home. Rushing through the door, they throw their arms around their father's neck, scattering jewels over the floor as they do so. Father adds news of his own: The children's stepmother has died in their absence. The death-witch is dead twice over.

From then on, Hansel and Gretel have everything their own way. Without a stepmother to interfere, Gretel runs a household for her father and brother where there's always enough food to eat, but not too much pushed at them. This feminine Oedipal dream is as close to the heroine's traditional happy ending of marriage as she can come at her age. Together with Hansel, she takes better care of their father than he ever took of them.

"Then all anxiety was at an end," the story concludes, "and they lived together in perfect happiness." We take this to mean perfect oblivion. During the years ahead, we can imagine nature cleverly strewing more pearls and emeralds in their path: love affairs, sex, marriage, children, companionship. Keeping house, keeping busy. Hansel, who was once locked in his pen like an animal awaiting slaughter, must not remain paralyzed by his consciousness of mortality, or he will never satisfy his urge to establish a family. Gretel must see herself as more than the witch's unwilling accomplice in feeding her brother. The jewels in their path focus their attention on the job of perpetuating their bloodline and convince them that witches with ovens no longer exist.

On the other hand, if they, and we, don't feel some sporadic pangs of mortality, we are no more than animals who walk and talk, which is what the witch thought of her captives in the first place.

IN OUR CULTURE, we hold more than one attitude toward death, with 82 percent of all Americans declaring their belief in Heaven, according to a recent poll. In the many images of paradise, the most ecstatic vision is that of the Negro spirituals, which picture Heaven not as a reward for virtue but as the believers' safe house and resting place after worldly woe: "Rocka [sic] my soul in the bosom of Abraham," "Swing low, sweet chariot, comin' for to carry me home," the worshipers sing, like lovers dreaming of consummation.

Our common stance, however, is the opposite: masculine and combative, entrenched in this world. Fight death to the death, we say, in whatever form it takes: the dragon, the Evil Empire, the Matrix or AIDS or cancer. Death is sure to be defeated by the hero— that's the promise we make to ourselves—if not by Luke Skywalker and the Force, then by Gary Cooper as the town marshal, standing alone to face a gunman on a dusty street in *High Noon;* if not by a town marshal, then by two children abandoned by their parents in the woods.

Beyond that, if no hero proves powerful enough, then death will be rerouted by the triumphs of science, unspooling in front of us just fast enough to save us from whatever was supposed to polish us off. Already we have cryogenics, cloning, bionics, open-heart surgery, stem-cell research, transplants, gene therapy, countless ways to engage and conquer death, or at least postpone it, which feels like the same thing.

According to this Western, heroic point of view, life is a line that has high points, low points, and an end point where the line breaks off at the edge of the page. After that, we are destined for either nothingness or final judgment, according to our personal belief. In either case, the story comes to an end.

But there is another, much older approach to death, female rather than male in spirit (though not necessarily in fact), which is based on acceptance and regeneration rather than conflict. This view, in which creation never ends but keeps cycling around, may be what lies behind the myth of Demeter and Persephone in the next chapter, although no one can say for sure what was revealed in their mysteries.

CHAPTER 16

Demeter and Persephone: The Beautiful Mysteries

Life and death hold different meanings for men and for women.

If life implies a life of individual achievement, either success or the hunger for success, as it does for most men in our society, then old age and death can only mean defeat, being conquered instead of conquering.

But if life is seen as women see it—as a state of being in which we move from one level to another—then death is the final transformation from the form we now know, possibly preparing the way for another cycle to begin. In the end, we confront the mystery of who we were (what was our face? the Zen masters ask us) before we were born.

As I said in the Introduction, women are transformers by nature. A woman turns fish from the fish store or pasta from the supermarket into meals for her family. She turns clay into pots, fetuses into toddlers, toddlers into Little Leaguers. As successive links in a pipeline, women serve as conduits who bring human beings out of nowhere into this world and lead others out of it, keeping them company to the brink of the Underworld and then turning back at the last minute, faithful to the experience.

At puberty, a girl sees her own blood for the first time. With every menstrual period that follows, she flushes down the toilet what might, in other circumstances, have become a new life. Eventually, if she is lucky, she gives birth to a child. On the delivery table, she weeps while the umbilical cord is being cut—tears of relief from pain, tears of joy that the baby is healthy and hers, but also tears that transcend sorrow: With her child's first breaths, while her knees are still spread wide, she cannot help but foresee his death at the vanishing point where parallel lines meet.

From that time on, her life is no longer hers. The baby tilts his high chair while she is cooking supper with her back turned. The chair teeters, comes crashing toward the floor. As she lunges to catch it, before her hands touch the floor, she hears in her head a prayer too swift for words: My life, Lord, not his.

At the other end of the life span, when an old person is dying, what happpens? The wife and daughter, or daughter-in-law and sister, take turns sitting by the bed. They lay a damp washcloth on the dying man's forehead; they hold his hands and rub the cold blue soles of his feet and put ice chips between his lips. Serving as midwives for death, they ease the passage from one world to the next. They do this not with any hope of conquering death but in an effort to overcome his fear of leaving this world behind.

And where are the sons and brothers, meanwhile? They are protected by a secret league in which they won't give each other time off from the office for grief, since they haven't the strength to tolerate a situation that they are powerless to change.

———

AFTER MANY TRANSFORMATIONS in my own life, I am now at the age to approach the last in this series. For twenty years I have been a crone, and I have found that crones face a task as strenuous as mothers-to-be in the labor room: learning to breathe under stress.

While I still have time, can I manage to confront the approach of death without quailing? Can I find out how to accept the transformation that is going to take me anyway, with unknown consequences, and if so, can I pass that attitude on to my children as the final instruction I will give them?

Like everyone else, I avoid the task. I busy myself with more manageable things. But once in a while a wind from another world blows straight at me and stirs me to wakefulness, like the first gusts of autumn.

I start gently by making an inventory of my possessions. The silver coffee service goes to my daughter; her father always wanted her to have it. The gold bracelet that I got from my mother-in-law should go to my daughter-in-law, who may decide to give it to her future daughter-in-law someday. The Tibetan tanka is for my older son, the Japanese wooden Bodhisattva statue for the younger. But he won't know anything about our history together. I see myself running up Madison Avenue to catch a bus on a rainy evening with my husband by my side, passing a store window at a fast clip where this statue was displayed, and saying from the shelter of my umbrella, "There. That's what you can get me for our silver wedding anniversary." And that's what I saw on the coffee table when I came downstairs for breakfast that day.

So much for possessions. They will be stripped of their associations of joy, astonishment, indecision, dismay, grief, gratitude, their emotional links to the donors or days that brought them to me, even the practically new ones. They will shed their biographies just as I will shed mine when I die, only they will start fresh, impartial, with their new owners, their surfaces wiped clean in someone else's hands. Not an object that I own could be moved from one room to another, much less discarded, without reflecting some substantial change in my life.

As for the house that I have lived in for fifty years (which resembles me, zealously well kept up but hopelessly outdated), how are my children ever going to find a buyer for a house with a one-car garage?

This is soothing. This takes on the flattering aspect of an indefinitely postponed Christmas where I needn't worry about wrapping the gifts.

I go deeper. What have I done with the more than seven decades that I have been given so far? Borne children (who not only don't need me any longer but may soon have to take care of me). Written some pages for my own relief rather than anyone else's pleasure. Raced a sailboat in strong winds with a spinnaker billowing in front of the bow and waves rolling like whales under the stern, a neat balancing trick, leaving me both exultant and fearful—fearful not of death but of failure. When I am most afraid, I am most alive. The competitive urge carries me along, too fast for comfort, like the wind.

With eyes sharpened by mortality, I see more acutely at this age than I did before. I have moments of gratitude so intense that they almost crush me with sadness, when I say, "I must remember this sight. Give me this one again on my deathbed, that's what I ask." Bulrushes by the waterside turning scarlet in the sunset behind a wooden pier. The first green of spring coursing through the weeping willow's branches, faint as breath on a mirror. The neck of a mallard in the sun. But sights aren't enough. I collect sensations like beads for a necklace. Give me again the moment when I was so overwhelmed by joy in a hotel restaurant that I rushed downstairs to the ladies' room, and the attendant there was the first person to learn that I was engaged to the man paying the check at our table. Give me back that time, and by all means this one: the golden haze that surrounded me for four days after the birth of my youngest child, like the gold-leaf background of a Byzantine painting. I ask to have these with me at the end.

Still, not enough. I brace myself to stare into the mouth of death. In medieval monasteries the monks, who were forbidden to talk otherwise, used to greet one another in passing with "Remember, brother, the hour of your death." We are called on to remember what hasn't happened yet, because that is where our attention is fixed. But what do I know about death, any more than I know about birth and the terror that must have struck me, curled in the womb, when I was carried along with no will of my own, through a narrow pulsing canal, out of darkness into triumphant light and the grasp of a pair of hands larger than I was?

From darkness to light. I may have been given a clue here. Or an analogy. For all I know, this world may be another womb that will discharge me when I reach full term, not without a struggle, perhaps, into a light that will make this one look dim. Maybe I haven't been born up to now; I have just been practicing how to live.

When Socrates was seventy years old, he was charged by his political enemies with impiety and with corrupting the youth of the state, and brought to trial. The court condemned him to death by poison. According to law, he could have requested another penalty— a suitable fine (which his friends would gladly have paid), or exile— but he refused to do so, claiming that he was a public benefactor and should be rewarded by the state instead. In any case, he saw no reason why he should be afraid of death, since he knew nothing about it.

"The hour of departure has arrived, and we go our ways," he said to his judges as he headed for prison and the fatal cup of hemlock. "I to die, and you to live. Which is better, God only knows."

IN A CURIOUS WAY, the myth of Demeter and her daughter is the noble ancestor of "Hansel and Gretel": Both are tales of parenthood and food, involving a Terrible Mother who refuses to feed her children, a superhuman female who holds a baby boy in a fire, a nearly tragic moment of eating the wrong food, and a central figure who is the grain goddess in the days before that goddess was downgraded to a witch living in a house made of bread shingled with gingerbread.

As in "Hansel and Gretel," the principal characters are two generations of females, but in this account no struggle takes place between age and youth. On the contrary, the story gains its thrust from the mother's desperate effort to find her kidnapped child, and the daughter's wish to be found. When the generations are reunited, they forge a relationship that deepens the daughter at the same time that it provides new scope for the mother's energy, giving us a clue to the later stages of a woman's life.

Here, as in the previous chapter, we must bear in mind that each character exists on more than one level. Demeter is the goddess of agriculture, but we see her first as a human female, outraged to find herself being pushed across the border from matron into crone—one of the few deities to have a full biography. Her daughter, the Kore, is transformed from maiden to wife, reigning as Queen of the Dead, but she is also the spirit of youth and renewal, who leaves the misty depths to bring the flowers of spring back to the surface of the earth each year.

AT THE BEGINNING OF THE STORY, which takes place in a mythical time, before the birth of civilization as we know it, a mother and daughter live by themselves in a landscape that never changes—so far as they can tell, will never change—where everything is as clear and certain as morning light. The girl is an only child. For her mother, she's the only child in the world. If others exist, they can be seen far below in the distance, identified only as potential playmates.

The mother is that pre-Homeric deity Demeter, *e metéra* in modern Greek, "the mother": essentially the Great Mother who is found from Neolithic times in all the regions around the Mediterranean. Her daughter, who grows in beauty every day, hasn't come into a name of her own yet but is known as the Kore, which means the Maiden, as if there could never be another. Our first literary record of these two females is the so-called *Homeric Hymn to Demeter,* written by an anonymous author about a century after Homer's work, roughly 2,700 years ago, but the religious ritual that undoubtedly preceded the hymn goes back almost a thousand years further, pre-dating the Trojan War, the biblical Exodus from Egypt, and Western history itself.

From her perch on a rock high above the plains of Nysa in Greece, the goddess overlooked fields rich in gold and green, where there seemed to be no limit to the goodness of the land. No consciousness of time ruffled the air. The goddess produced food for humans and animals without thought, the way the breasts of a nursing mother fill and flow when her baby cries. Like any good mother of a young child, she was aware of her existence chiefly as a bundle of responses to her child's needs.

The only shadow was the maturing beauty of the Kore, which should have put Demeter on guard against what would happen next, but so absorbed was she in her daughter that she made the mistake all fond mothers make: She believed that her child would be hers forever.

One day the Kore, with her slender feet (this is the poet of the Homeric hymn speaking), took it into her head to climb down to the lowlands to join her age-mates—a select group of maidens, including those perpetual virgins Athena and Artemis, along with the "big-breasted" daughters of Ocean—in that most dangerous of all pastimes, picking flowers.

In the meadow, the blooms of many months stood ready for picking without regard to season: crocuses and roses, violets and deep-throated lilies and iris, but these were nothing compared to a single flower like no other seen before or since, a glory, a trick and trap that earth had produced at the request of its reigning god, the lord of the Underworld. (Demeter is not the earth goddess—that is Gaia—but the goddess of what grows on the surface, principally grain.) Here was a narcissus with a hundred heads, each streaming light, with an odor so sweet that it made the sky smile and the salt air of the distant sea soften its tang. Overcome by divine fragrance, the girl reached out both hands and grasped her fate. Like Little Red Riding Hood picking flowers on the primrose path to Grandmother's house, like Beauty shyly asking her father to bring her a rose in winter that could be found only in the garden of the Beast, or Eliza Doolittle selling violets to kind gentlemen for tuppence a bunch, she showed that she, too, was old enough for plucking. Deflowering.

At the moment that the Kore tugged at the narcissus, the earth split open, as if the roots of the flower were all that had been holding it together. Out of the chasm rode the god whom the poet dares not call by name for fear of angering him, but terms He Who Receives So Many, because everyone alive must become his guest sooner or later. Hades, as we call him, or Pluto, King of the Underworld, thundered onto the meadow in a golden chariot drawn by horses as black as coal: King Death, the Beast himself, come up from the depths and smelling of horse sweat. The lord of the averted head he is, with his head set backward on his neck because he looks only toward what was, never forward to what will be. His worshipers turn their faces away when offering pitch-black animals as midnight sacrifices, because who can look King Death in the face and go on living?

Hades grabbed the girl. She screamed as he carried her off. Unexpectedly, she screamed for her father, Zeus, rather than her mother, having just discovered the power of the male but, like all fairy-tale fathers, the god chose to preserve his neutrality by doing nothing. At first, no one heard the Kore, no god or human except the night goddess Hecate (who spent the daylight hours sitting in her cave) and the Sun.

So long as the Kore could see the earth and sea and stars in the sky, everything she had known as a girl—her journey must have taken from day until night—she had hope of seeing her mother again and continued her cries. At last Demeter heard her, tore off her cloak, and rose straight into the air like a hawk on the hunt, circling the earth for nine days without resting, eating, or bathing, carrying a torch in each hand as a sign of her search. On the tenth day, she encountered Hecate, a dark spirit herself, goddess of the moon, ghosts, witches, and crossroads where three roads intersect. Hecate is in charge of dogs that howl in the night. (Kore, Demeter, Hecate. At the beginning of the story: Maiden, matron, crone.) Together, Demeter and Hecate came to the Sun, who alone had seen the act and told the grieving mother what happened: "There is no other god responsible but Zeus . . . who gave her to Hades, his own brother, to be called his wife." The maiden becomes a matron, the matron will soon be transformed into a crone.

When the Beast erupted from the depths, as he must in the maiden's story if the species is to continue, he interrupts the world of females to bring in something new. Let the Beast in, the outraged mother might have said when she heard the all-seeing Sun's report. But not this way. Rape, yes, if it can't be avoided, traumatic but not inconceivable, but not kidnapping, and certainly nothing as dire as marriage. The goddess herself had slept with males when she pleased, and she, too, suffered rape a number of times, but never would she have dreamed of living permanently with a male in his territory, subjecting herself to his control, which is what threatened the Kore. This had been done without notifying Demeter, who learned that she was not all-powerful as she had thought.

In the eyes of Hades and his brothers, who were Demeter's brothers as well, the girl had been properly married off as befit her status. On the day when the roots of the narcissus tore open the earth, bringing Death to the surface to mingle with men, the balance of power shifted, like the Kore herself, away from the realm of the mother and food and toward the realm of the father and sex; from the ancient Great Goddess under one of her many names to the newer religion of the Olympian sky gods, never to shift back again. The male, who used to be nothing more than the mortal son and consort of an immortal goddess, was now the lawgiver and husband.

Zeus was the Kore's father, though not Demeter's husband. In classical Greek society, a father had the right to hand over his daughter to anyone he chose, since marriage was a social and financial contract between father and son-in-law, as is true in patriarchies in many parts of the world today. Marrying a girl to her uncle or other close relative was considered the correct thing to do if a man had no male heir, in order to keep her inheritance within the family, since women could not own property.

Besides, who else would have been an appropriate husband for a virgin goddess? "He is not unworthy as son-in-law among the gods, Aidoneus, The Ruler of Many, your own brother, your own blood," the Sun said to Demeter in an effort to placate her. The world had been divided into three parts among the senior Olympian male gods: Zeus was lord of the sky, Poseidon of the ocean, and Hades of the nether region, with power allocated in terms of three regions of space, in masculine fashion, instead of three segments of time as the goddesses saw it, three stages of women's lives.

Marriage can be considered the promise of a new life cycle for a bride and her parents. Or it can be considered death-in-life, which was often the case in bygone times—not death in the sentimental terms of "death of the maiden," meaning loss of virginity, but death in the form of absence, a void where a daughter used to be. In ancient Greece, women were sequestered in their homes, allowed to travel only for religious festivals and family occasions. If a bride lived at a considerable distance from her parents, she might not see them for months or years, might never see them again if the distance was great. She might die in childbirth—many did, and Greek girls were only thirteen or fourteen when they married, which made repeated childbirths more dangerous. The daughter might be miserable, might be barren or ill, might have lost a child, and her parents would know nothing about it.

As we said before, marriage is a foreign country, from which reports to the homeland, if any, are sparse and guarded. Persephone, who must be called by her own name from now on, had become Queen of the Shades, whose realm Demeter, as a grain goddess, was not allowed to enter. The daughter might as well be dead to her mother.

WITHOUT OUR THINKING MUCH ABOUT IT, the United States was populated by immigrant Persephones, who left behind their mother-

land and crossed an ocean steerage class as brides with ambitious
husbands, or young mothers with one or two children in tow and
plans for more, or even single women on their way to meet men
whom they had arranged through connections to marry. Women
have always served as traveling wombs.

My own mother remarked to me one day in an offhand way that
my great-grandmother may have been one of those picture brides, a
poor Jewish girl from a large family in Switzerland—a housemaid,
my mother hinted—sent mail-order in effect to a Jewish man who
lived in Quincy, Illinois, where there were no other Jewish settlers. I
know only that my great-grandfather, who died when his children
were teenagers, rarely spoke, according to his few friends, while my
great-grandmother was a cheerful soul famous for her coconut layer
cake. I remember her as an old lady (or so she seemed at the time,
though she probably wasn't seventy yet), living in my grandparents'
apartment in New York City. When she died, she wasn't much bigger than I was at the age of six. The two of us were allies in a family
of towering adults. She taught me simple card games, which we
played in a back bedroom, so I wasn't surprised when she visited me
a few weeks after her death. I was sleeping in my grandmother's
apartment when I woke in the middle of the night and saw my great-
grandmother sitting in her rocker with her hands folded placidly in
her lap, which seemed a natural sight. I was the youngest in her line
of descent after all, and I was sleeping in her bedroom.

Three generations back I can remember, and two forward, probably three in the not so remote future. This will make a chain of
those I have touched that will stretch from the Civil War period into
the twenty-second century, with myself as the fulcrum in the middle.
What surprises me, now that I think of it, is that our ghosts are constructed out of such random scraps that float in memory. A coconut
layer cake; a game of Casino played with a child who couldn't read
yet; those doll-like feet in their black laced shoes scurrying into the
kitchen to sterilize her insulin syringe without disturbing the routine
of a household that wasn't hers. So far as I know, no one ever asked

her whether her parents were still alive when she left her country, nor what prompted her to cross an ocean in search of a husband, nor how she survived in a foreign land without any friend who spoke her language. No one asked about the agonies of choice that must have made up her life. Maybe no one dared to.

When I die, no one will be left who remembers her or her daughter.

BEFORE SEPARATION THERE HAS TO BE UNION, whether we remember it or not, or we would have no idea of it. Never mind what Genesis and Hollywood tell us: The primary bond between humans, which all other bonds imitate—in frustration as well as comfort—isn't that of man and woman but that of woman and child. For each of us there was a time when we were pillowed on a woman's arm, not necessarily our mother's since substitutes have always been available. Many of us weren't suckled at all, since breast-feeding was out of fashion from the end of the nineteenth century, when pasteurization and sterilization made bottle-feeding safe, until the breast became morally de rigueur for the upper middle class in the 1970s, reintroduced by the members of the women's movement—ironically, just when women returned to work in droves with breast pumps as standard equipment.

Breast-fed or bottle-fed, one way or another we were held and fed, sometimes hugged in an outburst of ardor, or with the guilt that follows rage, or with the deep, sad suspicion of inadequacy. (Who is worthy to be a parent, after all?) It's even possible that when a woman and a man curl close to each other in bed they want something more intimate than sex. Each finds mother in the heat of the other body and falls asleep.

And yet separation from mother is inevitable, a process that's one thing for a girl, another for a boy, and quite another for a mother, as observers ever since Freud have pointed out. Would Demeter have left her perch and searched the world over if her missing child had been an adolescent god who decided to leave home and strike out on his own? Her daughter, her Kore, on the other hand, was her second self, her built-in companion, bound to remain close to her side forever. Or so she thought.

If the identification between this pair is so close that in sculpture we can't tell Demeter from her child except by the hairstyles, how and when did their separation come about? Not when Hades galloped from the chasm in his golden chariot. By itself, that wouldn't have been enough. The girl wouldn't have been available to him unless she had left her home and ventured down to the meadow with the other maidens, out of earshot of her mother's perch, suddenly aware when she grasped a flower finer than any of her companions had plucked that she had a self and future of her own.

THE SCENE SHIFTS to modern times. My husband and I are sitting at the dining-room table flanking our daughter, a college freshman visiting us for the first time since leaving home—our daughter who is also our guest, looking around the room as though she never saw candles on a table before. Fortunately, the school is only a hundred miles away. A student who lives not too far from here has offered her a ride down and back.

Last spring, she stepped into her beauty with the same certainty and grace that she stepped into a long suede skirt and high-heeled boots this evening. Her complexion cleared up; she swept her hair away from her face as if she had always expected her beauty to arrive on schedule for college registration and had bided her time to show us.

This is the child born under a caul. A magic child, according to old belief. "I hope to goodness you didn't let them steal it in the delivery room," my mother said when I told her. "Sailors pay a fortune to get hold of a caul. You know that, don't you? Keeps them from drowning."

"You haven't finished half your steak yet," I say to this girl who will never die by drowning. What I want more than anything else is to feed her. Put flesh on her bones, while she eats at the family table with the dog stretched out possessively behind her chair.

As I get up to take away the main course, a car horn sounds in the driveway. The driver remains invisible. "I won't be able to stay for dessert," my daughter says politely, with sympathy for us in her tone. "I have to be going home now."

From the tone in which she says it, I know that no matter what it may be—a room in the freshman dorm now; an apartment shared with two other upperclassmen later on, so small that their half-size refrigerator has to stand out in the hall; a studio in the city after graduation; a lover's apartment; a house and garden in the suburbs equipped with a husband, two children, and two cats—whatever and wherever and with whomever it may be, home will never be here at a table with us, never in this house again.

MOTHER PINING FOR her daughter. Daughter moving away from mother, never entirely free from her mother's shadow. Never wanting to be. What has happened to this long-lost love story?

In our culture, until recent times, daughters past puberty could not afford to love their mothers too openly. Heroes and heroines were supposed to be self-made: the self-made man side by side with the self-defined woman, free to choose their occupations, spouses, pleasures, sex practices, lifestyles, habitats, time of childbearing, style of child-rearing. Free to live life as they imagined it.

For a mother to love her daughter is taken for granted ("admire" is a more difficult verb to put into practice). Love, like water, tends to run downhill in this world. Parents love children more than children love parents. Honor thy parents, love thy child. If a daughter of marriageable age loves her mother wholeheartedly (or loves her father "all," as Cordelia's sisters claimed), what can that mean but the submersion of the young woman in the parent? What effect does it have on the daughter's chance for a happy marriage?

To guard against this absorption and make sure that heroines develop the strength to break away from home, storytellers have impressed us with the image of the bad mother who persecutes the teenage girl. Snow White's stepmother, Cinderella's stepmother—

these serve as the unacknowledged agents of transformation, pushing the girl out of her childhood home and into the woods, where transformation to the level of sexual maturity takes place.

The evil mother's opposite, the fairy godmother, is in the dangerous business of granting wishes, but fortunately, godmothers in human form are rarer than we suppose. In any case, godmothers are cautious enough to impose strict conditions—Be home from the ball by midnight, my dear girl, or else!—in order to make sure that the heroine is ready for her transformation.

One obstacle remains: the good, kind mother who gives her daughter no reason to leave home. In the past, this irreproachable female had to disappear at the storyteller's earliest convenience. "And then she had a child as white as snow and as red as blood, and when she beheld it she was so delighted that she died" is the way the Grimms' story of "The Juniper Tree" begins. There are, of course, a few Good Mothers we hear about: The Virgin Mary had a mother whose name we know, as did Demeter and Persephone, but they were part of the prehistoric goddess tradition dating back at least six thousand years. In the current world of the fathers, we have waited a long time for an image of a strong-minded young woman who owed any debt to her mother.

What ever happened to Lear's wife, the mother of Cordelia, for instance? Who mentions the mothers of Jane Eyre, Catherine Earnshaw, Emma Bovary, Dorothea Brooke, Mary Lennox in *The Secret Garden,* Nancy Drew, or Scout Finch in *To Kill a Mockingbird*? (Those last two daughters of widowed lawyers are too young for romance, but they live with their fathers in Oedipal dream homes where the cleaning and cooking are taken care of by paid housekeepers.) The list could go on for pages of motherless girls who suffer heartache for lack of female guidance. Or because of it, like Juliet, whose mother pushes her daughter toward a socially approved marriage resembling her own, while Juliet's bawdy nurse helps her toward passion and death.

BUT THE EMOTIONAL CLIMATE is changing in our own times. Fifteen hundred years after the "Hymn to Demeter" was last sung, we have a few relatively current stories about mothers, as if they, too, might be heroines and motherhood might be a drama of its own. We see Hester Prynne with her "burning blush, and yet a haughty smile," standing on a scaffold with the scarlet letter pinned to her breast and her infant daughter in her arms, that Pearl of great price. After Hester comes Eliza in *Uncle Tom's Cabin,* leaping across the Ohio River from one ice floe to the next while carrying her boy to freedom, followed more than a century later by Sethe, crossing the river in Toni Morrison's *Beloved,* who loves her "crawling-already?" baby so wildly that she cuts the child's throat rather than see her carried back into slavery.

Two slaves and an adulteress. Add Scarlett O'Hara's Mammy (not her ethereal mother, who is obviously slated to die early), along with Ma Joad from *The Grapes of Wrath.* Also Charlotte, the excellent spinner of *Charlotte's Web,* whose magnum opus, by her own reckoning, was her peach-colored egg sac containing 514 eggs, laid even though she knew she would not live to see them hatch. Among mothers, it seems that poor and lower class is generally superior to privileged.

If we acquire more stories about mothers in the future, it will be because motherhood has become a choice, often tragically delayed, rather than a development taken for granted, or else an accident. Only the mother story grows with time, moving from girlhood to death and beyond, instead of the few years of sexuality, romance, and childbirth that have been the core not only of fairy tales but of Western literature in general.

AFTER DEMETER HEARD the Sun's report of her daughter's abduction, she turned up the soles of her feet toward the Olympian gods who had betrayed her (Father Zeus prudently wrapped himself in clouds) and flew down to the cities of men, disguising herself before she landed as an old woman wearing a black veil over her face. How could she have the heart to appear in her godlike beauty when she was suffering as only mortals are supposed to suffer?

She was no longer a primitive fertility goddess who spawns every human and animal on earth without giving them further thought, but rather the single mother with a single child, predecessor of the Virgin Mary in that respect, but capable of rage and revenge as Mary was not. The goddess of the gold sword, as the poet of the Homeric hymn calls Demeter, wasn't the sort to be obedient to the will of a father god, no matter how much he made her child suffer.

Outside the town of Eleusis, which was twelve miles from the center of Athens (but is now part of the city), Demeter landed and sat down to rest near the Virgin's Well. No one could recognize a goddess in this shabby old woman veiled in black, an old servant no doubt from the looks of her, who wore her suffering for the world to see. The uses of homeliness are familiar to beautiful women whenever they feel out of step with the world and choose to be completely, abysmally themselves. Homeliness is allowed to sit by herself in a corner, taking everything in but giving nothing out.

Four young women approached the well, carrying bronze pails. Greeting them, Demeter did what many postmenopausal women do today: She asked for their help in finding a job for her, in this case a job suitable for an elderly woman—nursing an infant, for instance, or making beds. The girls, who were daughters of the local king and queen, were arrested by something in her appearance. "You look like a god," the loveliest of them said. Their mother, Queen Metaneira, had recently given birth to a late-born and long-desired son—surely she would be overjoyed to have such a nurse.

So Demeter was led to the palace, where she sat silent, veiled, refusing to drink anything but barley water as she mourned the loss of her daughter. Seeing a mysterious majesty "as of kings" in the eyes of the stranger, the queen hired her at once to take care of the newborn Prince Demophoon.

No mother expected such a nurse. The goddess never fed the baby from her breast, never fed him at all, and yet he grew like a god. She massaged his skin with ambrosia. She breathed her fragrance over him while he sat on her lap. And every night in secret she held him in a blazing fire, as if he were a stick of wood, to burn away his mortality. The princeling already looked like a young god on the night when his mother, astonished by his growth, spied on the nurse and saw her son lying in the flames.

Metaneira shrieked. Demeter whirled around and threw the child to the ground. (Tenderness is not a virtue of the gods.) Fool, she cried. Imbecile. You have no idea what you are seeing, good or bad. I would have made your son deathless and ageless forever. I would have spared him that pain. But you have put a stop to my work.

(Could this be the scene that was misunderstood thousands of years later and transferred to a supernatural witch, living in a house made of bread, who tried to roast two children in the oven, for her benefit rather than theirs?)

Virtually the same story is told of the Egyptian goddess Isis, another deity who is a giver of grain. When Isis roamed the world in her search for the body of her murdered husband-brother, Osiris, she too paused in her wandering, heavily veiled and dressed in mourning, to take a job as nursemaid for a royal infant. She, too, laid her charge in the fire to cure him of his humanity while she flew around a mysteriously fragrant column in the form of a swallow, until the child's mother interrupted in horror. Her husband's body was inside the column, said Isis, staking her claim to it.

But how are we to understand this baffling incident, which was significant enough to be preserved by two major civilizations? We can only guess, since no scholar has come up with a convincing answer.

In each case, the goddess was thrust out of her earlier role in life, as if she were no more than human. Isis became a childless widow for the time being, Demeter a mother past childbearing who had been robbed of her only child. Human or divine, the mortal part of a female clings to her period of fertility and motherhood, and if that is unavailable, then to a job where she can use her spiritual fertility to nurture those who are not her biological offspring.

In Demeter's divine arrogance, she did not see that she could not overcome the limits of human flesh by imposing immortality on an unconscious being; nor could she take another female's child for her own. Twice she had been displaced from her role as the Mother. She had been robbed of her daughter, the Kore, who might be returned but would no longer be a maiden, nor belong to her. Now she had given up this foster child who lay wailing on the floor. Her mortal self had been transformed into a crone.

The human mother, Queen Metaneira, knew less than the goddess but knew it more sharply. This baby belonged to her. He must stay in her kingdom, as human as she was. She cared less for immortality than for his little finger.

Between the queen and the goddess, the child was left gasping on the ground until his sisters took him in their arms and cared for him, though all night he refused to let those inferior nurses quiet him.

Enraged by the human family's failure to recognize her blessings, Demeter shot up to her godlike stature and threw off her old age. Celestial brightness streamed through the house when she shook her golden hair. Perfume floated from her veils. Metaneira felt her knees buckle.

The next morning, the king ordered the people of Eleusis to build a sumptuous temple on a hill for Demeter, as she commanded, and there she installed herself, far from the gods of Olympus, veiled in black and brooding on her pain. While the wicked witch in "Hansel and Gretel" sought to kill only two children, the goddess of the golden sword was the Good Mother and the Bad Mother rolled into one, so consumed with longing for her child that she determined to kill all human beings on earth.

Thus began the most terrible year the earth had ever known. Barley seeds sprinkled on the soil failed to sprout, because Demeter smothered them where they lay. The cattle struggled to plough the rock-hard fields in vain. When famine threatened to wipe out every member of that pitiful species known as men, Zeus took alarm, but not for humanity's sake. If men perished, no further sacrifices would be offered to the gods, who batten on praise. One at a time, he dispatched every Olympian down to earth to plead with the goddess, who sat in her temple swearing that not a shoot would break through the soil until she saw her daughter's face again.

The male power to seize and strike, for all its thunder, cannot stand up long against the female power to nourish or withhold. Surrendering at last, Zeus sent Hermes (Mercury), the conductor of souls with his winged sandals, down to the Underworld to order King Hades to release Persephone, who would be honored among the gods.

"Smiling grimly," the poet says, Hades promised to bring his wife back to the daylight world, but when she sprang joyfully from their couch he secretly slipped a pomegranate seed, very sweet, into her mouth. The pomegranate (*pomme,* "apple"—the garnet apple), whose organ-red and juicy interior is packed with glistening seeds, grows on trees in Hades' garden, carrying the same double message as Eve's apple picked from the tree in Eden: fertility, seeded with death. (According to primitive taboo, red food belongs to the dead.) The same fruit was the symbol of the mother goddess Hera, as well as Demeter and Persephone.

When Hades drove his queen to the surface, Demeter leaped from her seat and ran from the temple to embrace her daughter. Persephone felt obliged to tell her mother what had happened. My husband tricked me, she said. "He forced me, unwillingly, violently, to eat it." To accept his seed in my body, she meant. (She wasn't the last young woman to offer this excuse.) As a result of eating forbidden fruit, Persephone would never belong exclusively to her mother's world again.

Zeus and the two goddesses were still at war; humankind was in danger. Down from Olympus swooped Rhea, mother of Demeter— three generations of goddesses on the scene—to extend an offer, or order, from Zeus: Persephone would spend a third of the year in her husband's dusky kingdom, but she could return to sunlight for eight months when the earth blooms with flowers, "to the great astonishment of gods and mortal men," as her mother put it. With her daughter restored, Demeter yielded and brought in such a crop of fruits and grains that the fields sagged under the weight.

Seasons had been established in the grain goddess's realm, death and dearth giving way to rebirth. From nothing comes abundance. And the other way around.

THE DAUGHTER RETURNS, a full-blown divinity and wife now, a queen, but all that matters is that she comes back to her mother. The Two Goddesses, they are called, and the religious ritual established in their names a couple of millennia ago is based on this union in which they are like two poles of a battery with a world-energizing current flowing between them. As the Queen of Death, Persephone is ruler of the shades, older and more ghostly than her mother, but she is also the goddess who brings new life to the surface in spring, traveling between two levels of being while her mother remains on the level of physical bodies: grain, matter, mother. *E metéra.*

In the course of human life, a daughter expects to move beyond her mother's experience, familiar with her mother's world in a way that the mother can never be at home in hers. With the passing of years, she becomes her mother's mother as well as her mother's daughter. Eventually, after her mother's death, a new relationship springs up between them, with the mother ageless, or every age at once, while the daughter is finally able to see her as a person as well as a parent: see her at every stage; take into account the historical era and social background, the family and choice of husband and state of health that shaped her while her child thought she was self-created as the wind. Meanwhile, the daughter passes through her own stages of eldering and, in turn, becomes the crone.

I WASN'T WITH MY MOTHER on the night that she died. A young woman, who was working her way through college by taking care of sick people on weekends, had taken my place. Two weeks earlier, I had invited my mother to my house for dinner to celebrate my daughter's birthday, but she wasn't feeling up to the trip to the suburbs, she'd said, which freed the rest of us from guilt: my two sons and son-in-law, as well as my daughter and infant granddaughter. By this time, I was a widow.

Three generations of females in one house again, and the fourth in her New York apartment in a rented hospital bed with railings on the sides. "Can't quite hear you," she said when I phoned her in the afternoon. "Water running in my ears. I may have had another stroke."

"Have you called the doctor?"

"What do you expect him to do about it? Why can't I die when I want to?" Death was one more acquaintance who failed to show up when wanted, like her daughter who visited once a week and stayed only two hours until the parking meter ran out, like her old friends, all of whom had dropped her from their weekly bridge games.

Before dinner my daughter bathed the baby and herself in a few inches of water in the tub in her childhood bathroom, with the baby propped in the V of her legs. (Why hadn't I thought of something so simple? In my day, young mothers bought awkward and dangerous Bathinettes that stood on wobbly legs and had to be filled from a pail.) My grandchild nestled only inches from the bush from which she'd emerged six months earlier, like Moses coming out of the bulrushes, while her mother shampooed her own hair with a hand spray.

"Shall I hold her on my lap while you dry your hair?" I offered after the child had been dried and dressed in a diaper and shirt. As my daughter connected the blower, the baby looked up suspiciously to make sure that her mother didn't plan to escape from the room, but then sat solid on my lap, soothed by the familiar sound.

I am the other woman in your life, I said silently to my granddaughter, your second mother. I am difference and separation and possibility, a binocular view of life. I am risk and strangeness, while your parents offer only identity and safety. I am the past which is mythical, which shifts every time you look at it, while your parents are the demands of the present.

Don't cry, I willed her, pressing her ear against my cheek. My stomach muscles were tense with the fear of being rejected. You have to show your mother you're happy with me, so that she'll let me have a little piece of you. Just wait, you'll see how much fun the two of us will have. We'll be special to each other, because we don't see each other every day.

But the baby made unhappy noises. I wasn't her mother, her whimpering told me. She lifted her feet to raise herself off my lap. Turning off the hair dryer, my daughter scooped her child into her arms and held her in front of the steamed-up mirror. "Who do you see in there?" she asked.

"Ba-by," I expected her to say, as I'd said so often to the infant face in my medicine-chest mirror.

"Mother and child, that's who you see," she answered herself.

Mother and child. I was marked out then as the grandmother, the widow, the crone. For the rest of my life, the crone. A broader, more diffuse view of my role was needed.

WHEN THE BABY had been fed and put to sleep in the Porta-Crib upstairs, the rest of us sat down to eat.

In the middle of the meal, a single sharp cry was heard on the intercom. My daughter sprang to her feet. "Wait a moment," I said. "She may go right back to sleep." I wanted my own child to finish what was on her plate for once. Sure enough, the intercom was silent. A moment later, the phone rang.

"Who'd call at dinnertime?" I asked as I went into the kitchen to answer. It was my mother's attendant, whose name I couldn't remember, saying I'd better come right away. From the tone of her voice, I knew I was too late.

I like to think that the last thing my mother's spirit did, on her way out or up or wherever, was visit her great-granddaughter in the crib, brushing her youngest descendant's cheek and causing her to cry out in her sleep at the instant when they greeted one another in passing, as my great-grandmother had visited me. A family tradition: completing the circuit. I wonder whom I'll visit when my time comes. Perhaps the child of the baby upstairs in her crib.

"I want to call you sooner," the attendant said on the phone, obviously terrified of death or me, or both. "I want to call the doctor and I want to call you, but she say no, she want to die at home." But I shouldn't have needed a call. My mother had told me she'd suffered a stroke. Faced with a choice between mothering my mother or mothering my daughter, I'd chosen my daughter. Love, like water, flows downhill. "You know what she say last thing? Her last words? She say 'I think I'm dying. When I get there, I'm going to tell them what a good girl you been.'"

My birthright. The words I'd waited a lifetime to hear from my mother she gave, in her last minute, to this stranger. Because I wasn't there. Those words, which she must have known would be repeated had been meant as her final reproach to me.

Or is it possible that I'm wrong? Have I misjudged her all these years since her death? As I write this, I wonder if, in the final gratitude of flesh for the touch of flesh, she thought that the hand holding hers must be mine.

I am the same age now that my mother was when she died, which changes everything between us.

IF THE STORY OF Demeter and Persephone was an ordinary story, it would end at the moment when King Death harnesses his immortal horses to the chariot and flies up from the abyss, carrying his bride back to her mother: the reverse of the usual bridal-plot of "Cinderella" or "Snow White." Peace is restored among the gods. The furrows of Attic soil will be crowded with stalks of grain, and humanity—"that weak race of men"—has been saved from extinction.

Sure enough, in later Greek works Demeter is credited with giving the gift of agriculture to mankind at Eleusis. (Presumably, wheat and barley had grown wild before that time.) From the Rharian plain, just outside Athens, it spread to the rest of the world, no small gift in Athenian eyes. Agriculture, as opposed to hunting-and-gathering,

involves increased population; permanent settlements; private own-
ership of land; male domination over women because men have the
strength to clear fields and domesticate large animals; inheritance
from father to son, which means enforced chastity for women; irri-
gation; buildings for storage; calendars; writing. In short, civilization
as we know it.

But this isn't what the poet of the Homeric hymn celebrates. According to him, once the Mother Goddess herself had been initiated
into suffering and the end of suffering, her chief gift to mankind was
spiritual rather than physical: the initiation rites known as the
Eleusinian mysteries, which, in the words of an ancient historian,
held the entire Greek-speaking world together for more than a
thousand years.

"Her beautiful mysteries, which are impossible to transgress, or to
pry into, or to divulge: for so great is one's awe of the gods that it
stops the tongue," the poet describes them. "Happy is that man,
among the men on earth, who witnesses these things." From the
night of sacred initiation until the end of his life, the initiate was
blessedly freed from the fear of death.

Seen in social terms, the Eleusinian rite was the most accessible
of mysteries, open to anyone who could pay the entrance fee,
whether male or female, free or slave, Athenian or foreign, as long as
the candidate had not shed blood and was able to speak Greek
(which distinguished him or her from "barbarians"). On the other
hand, the mystery itself—whatever it was that took place at Eleusis
each year—was never revealed, not by a single one of the hundreds
of thousands, or even millions, of initiates who took part during the
ten centuries that the rites were the centerpiece of Greek civilization.
The worship of the Two Goddesses ended only when Alaric and his
Goths poured through the pass of Thermopylae in A.D. 396, bringing Christianity with them and extinguishing the classical spirit not
only in Greece but in all parts of the Greek-speaking world.

In esoteric religious groups, the mantra is "He who knows does
not speak. He who speaks does not know." Whatever we want to

know about the events at Eleusis is kept hidden from us. What we are allowed to know, or deduce, doesn't tell us anything that matters: On a night in late September, the initiates, who had been fasting for nine days in imitation of Demeter's fast while searching for her daughter, drank a prescribed barley drink (probably hallucinogenic) before they walked in procession from Athens to Eleusis. Arriving in the dark, they danced sacred dances around the well where the goddess had sat, which still stands outside the temple. Pigs were thrown into a pit as a sacrifice to the goddess, reminding us that in prehistoric times the Great Mother was represented by a sow, a prolific animal that produces litters of piglets bearing a startling resemblance to human babies, for whom they must have substituted in archaic rites. (Think of Fern, the farmer's daughter in *Charlotte's Web*, feeding her pretend-baby Wilbur, the doomed piglet, from a baby bottle.)

Fire erupted in the darkness when the door of the sanctuary was thrown open. The high priest cried out that the mistress had given birth to a holy boy, the Queen of the Dead had given birth in the flames. A bronze gong thundered when the priest called on Persephone to come forth, the same clamor that announced the death of Spartan kings. After that came a vision we know nothing about. Some say the goddess responded to the priest's call.

"Thrice blessed are those among men who, after beholding these rites, go down to Hades. Only for them is there life; all the rest will suffer an evil lot," says a character in a play by Sophocles. Among throngs of men and women who were the wittiest, most eloquent, sophisticated, analytical, drunken, and frequently cynical people in world history (including the Roman emperor Augustus and several of his successors), only a few ever mocked the ceremonies, and not even they dared to describe the mystery that apparently could not be divulged, just as the Homeric hymn said.

A good guess is that the vision may have had something to do with a stalk of wheat. After all, it seems impossible that tender shoots should break their way through the winter-packed earth. But they do.

THE UPWELLING OF SPRING that marks new life on earth depends on the Greek goddess being united—fused—with her lost daughter, who rises from the kingdom of the dead. In a similar way, the Christian celebration of Easter reunites the divine father with his murdered son, but a difference exists between the two rites that stems from differences in gender and era.

The Christian passion is the ultimate hero story: a singular event that takes place in historical time, in which a man-god offers himself as a sacrifice in order to redeem humanity from its sins. The miracle happens once and forever. Jesus is crucified once, entombed once, and resurrected once. His Second Coming will put an end to time as we know it, but, meanwhile, those who believe in him are promised eternal life in Heaven.

The Demeter-Persephone story is a passion of another sort, reflecting the female experience of life as a cycle, a series of transformations rather than a line. Far from offering herself as a sacrifice, the Kore is kidnapped and raped, causing grief to her divine mother, who had endured the same ravages herself. At the end of their suffering, when the daughter returns from the Underworld, the Two Goddesses establish their "beautiful mysteries," ending in a vision that each participant must experience personally, as they personally experienced their divine sorrow and pain. Initiation is not a story but a change of being.

An agricultural festival, scholars say, as if that explained everything. Developed from pre-Greek fertility rites. Celebrated at the end of September, which was the time the new crop was planted. If Demeter is the grain goddess, her daughter can be seen as the grain that emerges from the ground four months later, grows tall, with delicate blonde hair rippling in the wind, and is cut down when ripe, leaving seeds behind. A portion of the seeds is stored (in jars buried underground in the ancient era) to produce the next crop, but the new stalks cannot be considered the old ones reborn. The bulk of the crop is beaten, ground up, and turned into flour, no longer recognizable as separate grains. (Ground wheat was known as *kore* in pre-classical Greece.) Through kitchen alchemy, the flour is leavened with yeast and comes out of the oven lighter in substance, as if a living spirit has been infused into it. But transformation doesn't stop there. We eat bread. The bread becomes us: bones, blood, brains, dreams, doubts, musings about mortality.

This is what we find hard to accept, the threshing of our bodies: the prospect of giving up the hard shell of individual existence, the well-armored capital "I" that separates each of us from the others and from the energy of the world.

And maybe this is what the initiates mastered: the surrender of the private self, still wrapped up in its triumphs and troubles, which seemed so important before setting out on the road to Eleusis but mean nothing in the face of death. Maybe this was the lesson of the mysteries.

Within the myth itself, every element undergoes change. Boundaries blur. Sky is reconciled with earth; mother with son-in-law; matriarchy with patriarchy. Winter changes to spring but is sure to change back and harden the earth again.

Each spring the daughter returns, strewing flowers along her path, but we also know her as the Queen of the Dead, whose name—Persephone—means "bringer of destruction." She is the death that fertilizes the flower garden. When she sees her mother again, the daughter is both the older and younger of the two in experience (which happens in human life as well), a wife who will soon bear a child, taking over the role of generation. Demeter, who was first a self-contained matron and then an outraged mother, looks down from a higher level at the end, taking all human beings as her children and nourishing them both physically and spiritually.

If the celebrants of the rite allow themselves to enter, undefended, into this whirlpool of energy, their consciousness may have been transformed so that they were rid of their fear of death from that time on. "We have been given a reason not only to live in joy but also to die in better hope," Cicero reported after his own initiation.

Ever After

Transformation is what we long for when young, what we dread when we are old: those inevitable journeys from the known to the unknown.

The first transformation—birth—must have been the most wracking, which is why we don't remember it. We don't ask to be born—at least most of us assume that we don't ask—but nonetheless we find ourselves squeezed out of the warm womb bath in which nothing exists more foreign than our thumb, no sound but the drum of the mother's heart marking time. Not every life is happy by any means, and yet almost no one would wish not to have been born.

At each later ascent from one level to another, we feel a spasm of fear followed by a flood of hope. From the first time we dare to stand on two feet without support, in danger of falling, to the arrival of puberty; from the blood loss of virginity to that of childbirth, we are reassured by messages from those who preceded us. We are impelled to change. Nothing lasts, but everything returns in another form—that is the message handed down to us.

Eventually, we come to the transformation that nobody ahead of us has come back to tell us about. Perhaps death is no less a miracle than birth, bringing us new perceptions that come to us through more refined senses. With no memory of what we left behind, any more than we now remember the infancy of what we consider to be our distinctive, imperishable selves, we start over again.

A LONG TIME AGO, I used to take my daughter to the movies on a half-price ticket: *Bambi, Pinocchio* in revival. Then my daughter grew up and married and had children, and I took my two grandchildren to the movies half price: *The Little Mermaid. Beauty and the Beast.*

My granddaughters are teenagers now. I step up to the cashier's window at the movie theater and buy three adult tickets for my daughter and her children and one ticket half price. The last for me. I take up half as much space in the world as they do. We see the movie together, but they would have seen it in the same way without me, while I wouldn't be in the theater without them. My granddaughters grow more vivid all the time, and will go down to the meadow soon to pick flowers, while I am growing transparent. They can see the scenery right through me. They will remember the movie, but won't remember that I saw it with them.

Afterward I drive the three of them back to their house, which is much larger than mine. Goodbye, I call from my car as they open the door of the house and go in.

Goodbye. I am your past. But I am also your future.

Acknowledgments

I have been extraordinarily lucky, during the years that I have spent writing this book, to be sustained by editors who have become my friends, and by friends possessed of the sensitivity and expertise of editors.

My thanks go first to my chief editor, Kate Medina, who gave me the greatest gift any editor can give a writer: She prodded me to keep going forward where I was most afraid. In addition, she brought in several younger colleagues, Olga Seham, Frankie Jones, Jessica Kirshner, and Robin Rolewicz, representing different decades in a woman's life, so that as a team we ranged in age from the twenties to my stance, in the seventies. Janet Wygal was an ideal production editor, as sensitive as she was scrupulous.

Arnold Corrigan, my steadfast partner, is in a category all his own. When I began writing this book, I warned him that for two or three years I might be irritable, impatient, even obsessive, and I hoped he would be tolerant. That was twelve years ago. During all that time, his comments have unfailingly expanded the soul of this book and its author.

My friend Kathryn Harrison taught me (when I was already middle-aged) what I should have learned much earlier: that intimate friendship can be as transformative and pervasive an experience as love. I am indebted to her for many of the perceptions in this book.

My special gratitude goes to other talented friends who not only listened to my ideas and enriched them, but also reinforced them by adding anecdotes from their own lives: Dawn Drzal, Rosemary Salomone, Rebecca Straus, and Stephanie von Hirschberg.

Without Anne Kofod I could not have made use of any of the other contributions. What she gave me was the opportunity to write.

Finally—and fervently—I acknowledge the lessons from my teacher, the late Louise M. Welch.

Notes

Introduction *Spinning Straw into Gold*

p. xvi "Rumpelstiltskin" is one of the stories collected by the brothers Grimm and first translated into English in *German Popular Stories, Translated from the Kinder-und-Haus-marchen, Collected by M. M. Grimm, from Oral Tradition,* 1823. I have based this version and all my retellings of the Grimms' tales in this book on *The Complete Grimm's Fairy Tales* (New York: Pantheon Books, 1944, copyright renewed 1972), although I have changed the wording and added details that do not affect the structure of the story.

The tale is known all over Europe. In England, the dwarf is called Tom Tit Tot; in Scotland he is Whuppity Stoorie, in France Ricdin-Ricdon, and so forth through a litany of peculiar names.

For a comprehensive account of attitudes toward hard work in contrast to arbitrary power in European folklore as a whole, and a sympathetic analysis of the dwarf's nature in this story compared with the boastful father and the avaricious king, see Maria Tatar, *The Hard Facts of the Grimms' Fairy Tales* (Princeton: Princeton University Press, 1987), 122–28.

p. xvi **"The dwarf, not the Queen, is the pivot of the story":** Private communication from Cavin Leeman, M.D., Clinical Professor of Psychiatry, SUNY Downstate Medical Center, Brooklyn, New York.

p. xxi **"If, during that time, you can tell me my name":** Names in archaic tales contain a power to command that we still sense today. In many religions, including Judaism, the name of the god must never be spoken because that would imply undue equality, or compel the god to grant the worshiper's request.

p. xxii *"The first day I brew":* These lines are my own rendition of the dwarf's rhyme.

Part 1

p. 4 Nature, which can be thought of as Mother Nature, or the Mother Goddess, is often split into two images: negative and positive.

The Terrible Mother represents death, darkness, the hungry earth that eats its own children, like the jaws of a dragon or sea monster. In fairy tales, she appears as the witch or stepmother who wants to devour Hansel and Gretel.

The Good Mother represents fertility, food, the virgin who bears a holy child and feeds him from her breast. In fairy tales, she is the one who gives birth to a long-awaited baby but dies soon afterward, though she may show up later in the story as a fairy godmother.

There can be no birth without death. Since the Good Mother wants to keep her child safe on her lap forever, I choose to recognize the Terrible Mother—in the form of witch or stepmother—as the transformer who pushes a fertile girl out of the house and starts her on the road toward procreation, new life for old.

For the best account of the Mother Goddess in her many aspects, see Erich Neumann, *The Great Mother,* Bollingen Series (Princeton: Princeton University Press, 1963).

Chapter 1 *Snow White: Breaking Away from Mother*

p. 9 **always three, the magic number:** Myths, religion, fairy tales—all are haunted by the number three.

We hear of three wishes in fairy tales, three witches in *Macbeth,* three Wise Men, three Fates or Norns spinning the thread of human lives, three Furies (but nine Muses, three times three), three sisters or brothers in fairy tales, three days granted to the Queen to discover the name of the helpful dwarf.

On a more abstract plane, we have three divisions of the universe (sky, sea, and Underworld), with three gods to rule them in Greek religion; a Trinity in Christianity; three supreme deities in Hinduism; three divisions of time (past, present, and future); three phases of life (youth, middle age, and old age).

What accounts for the recurring triad? Probably the original link between the prehistoric Mother Goddess and the moon, which passes across the sky in three phases—crescent, full, and waning—linked to time and to the female menstrual cycle.

p. 9 **"Would that I had a child as white as snow":** All quotations come from "Little Snow-White," in *The Complete Grimm's Fairy Tales* (New York: Pantheon Books, 1944, copyright renewed 1972). I refer to the story here as "Snow White."

Essentially the same tale is known from the west coast of Europe to Asia Minor and down into Africa. Two versions appear in Giambattista Basile's seventeenth-century collection of Italian tales, *Il Pentamerone.*

For a Freudian analysis, see Bruno Bettelheim, *The Uses of Enchantment: The Meaning and Importance of Fairy Tales* (New York: Knopf, 1976), 199–215. Maria Tatar, in her fine anthology of tales and criticism, *The Classic Fairy Tales* (New York and London: W. W. Norton, 1999), 74–101, provides a comprehensive overview of different versions and interpretations. She includes Jack Zipes's essay "Breaking the Disney Spell," which explores Walt Disney's identification with the oppressed child, 332–53. Iona and Peter Opie, scholars of children's literature, also discuss Disney's influence in *The Classic Fairy Tales* (London and New York: Oxford University Press, 1974), 228–29.

p. 9 **Together they form a series:** Many stories dwell on the magical combination of colors. In "The Juniper Tree," another Grimms fairy tale, a childless woman is paring an apple in her garden when she cuts her finger and makes the same wish for a child upon seeing drops of blood on the snow.

p. 9　**The Queen has felt a prick:** In an early chapter of *Madame Bovary,* when Dr. Charles Bovary is summoned to a farmhouse for the first time, young Emma, the daughter of the house, is sewing pads for her father's broken leg. "As she sewed she pricked her fingers, which she then put to her mouth to suck them."

p. 10　**the three colors paint a picture of time and growth:** In the medieval color scale of alchemy, black (*nigredo*) stands for the primal matter that the universe gives us to work with, the cinders that are left when everything else burns away, and so it belongs at the beginning as well as at the end of a story. The ultimate aim of the alchemists was gold, which in its highest sense did not signify material wealth but the spiritual transformation of the soul. For details about color symbolism in alchemy, see C. G. Jung, *Psychology and Alchemy* (Princeton: Princeton University Press, 1968).

　　Black, white, and red are the first colors of art, used in the work of cave men: red from blood, white from bone, and black from charcoal. Psychologists now realize that they are also the first colors that infants can distinguish, so the most up-to-date baby toys are made in those color combinations.

p. 10　**the ancient goddess in her triple phases:** The original divine Trinity was probably the goddess seen in three stages as maiden, matron, and crone, representing the creator, preserver, and destroyer of life. In India, her names were Pārvatī, Durga, Kālī. In Greece, she was Hebe the virgin, Hera the wife of Zeus, and Hecate the crone.

　　In later ages, one, two, or all three members of the Trinity became male or asexual, as in Father, Son, and Holy Ghost.

p. 11　**As child psychologist Bruno Bettelheim pointed out:** Bruno Bettelheim, *The Uses of Enchantment,* 66–74.

p. 12　**"Magic Mirror on the wall":** I have used Disney's form of the Queen's question, since this is so well known, but I have reverted to the translation of the Grimms' tale for the mirror's answer and for the following text.

p. 13　**At that, the Queen "turned yellow and green with envy":** Sandra M. Gilbert and Susan Gubar, in *The Madwoman in the Attic* (New Haven: Yale University Press, 1979), 36–43 offer a provocative analysis of the splitting of female identity into two parts: the vigorous and rebellious Queen-stepmother, who is "a plot-maker, a schemer, a witch, an artist, an impersonator . . . witty, wily, and self-absorbed," as opposed to her stepdaughter, the passive angel-virgin, who functions solely as an object of masculine desire. According to the authors, the Queen's hatred of Snow White stems from her desire to obliterate the doll-like side of her own nature.

Gilbert and Gubar interpret the voice in the mirror as that of the King, "the patriarchal voice of judgment that rules the Queen's—and every woman's—self-evaluation."

p. 13 **"Bring me back her lungs and liver":** In Mesopotamia in the first millennia B.C., the lungs and liver of sacrificed animals were sent to the king so that he could read the god's message for himself, says Julian Jaynes in *The Origin of Consciousness in the Breakdown of the Bicameral Mind* (Boston: Houghton Mifflin, 1975), 243–44.

The two organs go together. "Liver and lights" was what pirates longed to cut out of their victims, "lights" being an old-fashioned word for *lungs,* which weigh little. In other words, they wanted the victim's blood supply and breath.

p. 14 **the average age at menarche:** Edward Shorter, *Women, Men, and Bodies* (New York: Basic Books, 1982).

p. 14 **The boar is a ferocious wild animal:** The symbolism of the boar is discussed by Joseph Campbell, *The Masks of God: Primitive Mythology* and *Occidental Mythology* (New York: Viking Penguin, 1968); by Robert Graves, *The Greek Myths* (New York: George Braziller, 1955); and by Robert Bly, *Iron John* (Reading, Mass.: Addison-Wesley, 1990), 210 ff. It is summarized by Barbara G. Walker in *The Woman's Encyclopedia of Myths and Secrets* (San Francisco: Harper San Francisco, 1983).

Adonis, Attis, Tammuz, Odysseus, and the Fisher King are among the many mythical heroes who were pierced in the thigh or groin by the castrating boar.

p. 16 **"If a child cannot permit himself":** Bettelheim, *Uses of Enchantment,* 204.

Chapter 2 *Snow White: Tempted by the Witch's Wares*

p. 23 **As the Greek saying goes:** Quoted by Max Luthi, *Once Upon a Time: On the Nature of Fairy Tales* (Bloomington: Indiana University Press, 1976), 63.

p. 24 **"Children, especially pretty, nicely brought up young ladies":** Moral to "Little Red Riding Hood" by Charles Perrault, *Histoire ou Contes du temps passé. Avec des Moralitez,* Paris, 1697. Translated by Angela Carter, *Sleeping Beauty and Other Favourite Fairy Tales* (New York: Schocken Books, 1982).

p. 28 " **'Things look different'** ": *Walt Disney's Snow White and the Seven Dwarfs* (New York: Harry N. Abrams, 1987).

p. 28 **The dwarfs have been transformed into adorably messy little boys:** The notion of the dwarfs as children who will be supervised by Snow White was found in a silent movie that Disney saw as an adolescent, which, in turn, was based on a play for children written in 1912. Karen Merritt refers to this in "Little Girl/Little Mother Transformation: The American Evolution of 'Snow White and the Seven Dwarfs,' " included in *The Art of the Animated Image,* edited by John Canemaker, Los Angeles American Film Institute, 1994.

p. 29 **"Of course Nana has been trained":** *The Plays of J. M. Barrie* (New York: Charles Scribner's Sons, 1935). *Peter Pan,* stage directions to Act 1.

p. 30 **Peter and the boys keep busy warding off Captain Hook with his iron claw:** Captain Hook, followed by a crocodile with a clock in its belly, can be seen as a shrunken version of the ancient Greek god Cronos (known as Saturn to the Romans), who carries a sickle in his hand, bearded old Father Time himself.

p. 31 The mirror's answer and the remaining quotations come from "Little Snow-White," in *The Complete Grimm's Fairy Tales* (New York: Pantheon Books, 1944, copyright renewed 1972).

p. 35 **the dwarfs lay Snow White in a coffin made of glass:** In a modern replay of this image, Judy Garland, another daughter of a devouring mother, was buried in New York City at the age of forty-seven in a white coffin with a glass top, so that twenty-two thousand mourners could see her as they filed past.

p. 35 **While Snow White lies in the coffin:** In a seventeenth-century version of the story from Giambattista Basile's *Il Pentamerone,* the heroine is only seven years old when she falls into the sleep-death and is buried in seven crystal caskets, one inside the other. She keeps growing like a normal woman, but the caskets grow with her until she is awakened.

Chapter 3 *Cinderella: Surviving Adolescence*

p. 39 For scholarly collections of Cinderella stories from many cultures, along with reflective essays, see Alan Dundes, *Cinderella: A Folklore Casebook* (New

York and London: Garland, 1982); and Neil Philip, *The Cinderella Story* (New York: Penguin Books, 1989).

p. 40 **she's called Cinderbreech or Cinderbottom:** The name "Cinderbreech," later modified to Cinderilla, or Cinderella, appears in the version by Charles Perrault, translated by Robert Samber in 1729 and printed in Iona and Peter Opie's *The Classic Fairy Tales* (London and New York: Oxford University Press, 1974).

p. 40 **She's his only blood kin:** Widows' rights of inheritance were not clearly established in England until the Dower Act of 1833, which means that stepmothers had good reason to feel uneasy in the home.

p. 40 **they strip Cinderella of her pretty clothes:** In the Bible, the jealous brothers of seventeen-year-old Joseph strip him of the radiant coat of many colors that their father, Jacob, gave him before they throw him into a pit and sell him into slavery in Egypt, which is equivalent to Cinderella's drudgery.

Robert Bly brilliantly describes the hero's descent from his pampered childhood to the kitchen in *Iron John* (Reading, Mass.: Addison-Wesley, 1990), Chapter 3.

Cinderella's gray bedgown and wooden shoes are found in the Grimms' version of the story, known as "Aschenputtel" in German.

p. 47 **"What, you go, Cinderella!":** *The Complete Grimm's Fairy Tales* (New York: Pantheon Books, 1944, copyright renewed 1972).

p. 47 **women . . . could expect to die in their twenties or early thirties:** In 1800, in lower Burgundy, women lived an average of only twenty-five years, says Marina Warner. By the end of the century, the average life span had more than doubled, to fifty-two years.

For historical details about family life in general and the position of stepmothers in particular, see Marina Warner's insightful work *From the Beast to the Blonde: On Fairy Tales and Their Tellers* (New York: Farrar, Straus & Giroux, 1994); Maria Tatar, *The Hard Facts of the Grimms' Fairy Tales* (Princeton: Princeton University Press, 1987), and also *The Annotated Classic Fairy Tales,* with her introduction and notes (New York: W. W. Norton, 2002); Robert Darnton, *The Great Cat Massacre and Other Episodes in French Cultural History,* "Peasants Tell Tales" (New York: Basic Books, 1984); and Jack Zipes, *The Brothers Grimm: From Enchanted Forests to the Modern World* (New York and London: Routledge, 1988).

p. 48 **"his wife governed him entirely"**: "Cinderella, or The Little Glass Slipper," as translated by Robert Samber and published as part of *Histories or Tales of Past Times* (London, 1729). Included in Iona and Peter Opie's *The Classic Fairy Tales.*

p. 48 **"No, said the man"**: Grimms' "Cinderella."

p. 49 **In the story "Thousand-Furs"**: This story, which was collected by the brothers Grimm, is known in German as "Allerleirauh."

p. 49 Anne Sexton, private papers quoted by Diane Wood Middlebrook, *Anne Sexton: A Biography* (Boston: Houghton Mifflin, 1991), 174.

p. 51 **"a hundred times handsomer"**: Perrault's "Cinderella."

p. 51 **being interviewed on television by David Frost**: *One on One with David Frost.* Rebroadcast on *Biography*, on A&E.

p. 53 **"bullied and punished me"**: Charlotte Brontë, *Jane Eyre*, first published London, 1847; (London and New York: Penguin Books, 1985), Chapter 1.

Chapter 4 *Cinderella: Stepping into the Dance*

p. 59 **"Well, said her godmother"**: Charles Perrault, "Cinderella, or The Little Glass Slipper," as translated by Robert Samber and published as part of *Histories or Tales of Past Times* (London, 1729). Included in Iona and Peter Opie's *The Classic Fairy Tales.*

p. 60 The official title of the book was *Histoires ou Contes du temps passé. Avec des Moralitez.* (*Histories or Tales of Past Times. With Their Morals*).
    While the book is universally attributed to Charles Perrault these days, it was his son Pierre—eighteen years old at the time—who signed the work. Father Charles wrote copiously on literary questions and was a member of the French Academy, while Pierre was never known to write another word.

p. 61 **"Well, my grandmother she told me"**: "Ashey Pelt," an Irish folktale included by Neil Philip, *The Cinderella Story* (New York: Penguin Books, 1989).

p. 61 **A thousand years ago in China**: A servant named Li Shih Yuan, described as "a cave man" from southern China, told this story to his master, Tuan

Ch'eng Shih, who recorded it around A.D. 850. R. D. Jameson wrote an essay in 1932 entitled "Cinderella in China," which was reprinted by Alan Dundes, *Cinderella: A Folklore Casebook* (New York and London: Garland, 1982). Arthur Waley's translation appeared as "The Chinese Cinderella Story" in *Folk-Lore*, vol. 58 (London: Folklore Society, 1947).

p. 62 **hazel is a magical tree:** Traditions concerning hazel were verified for me by the Royal Forestry Service of the United Kingdom.

p. 62 **"Thrice a day":** "Cinderella," *The Complete Grimm's Fairy Tales* (New York: Pantheon Books, 1944, copyright renewed 1972).

p. 65 **"nimble nurslings of earth":** R. E. Butler's translation of *The Golden Ass* of Apuleius, as edited by Erich Neumann. Neumann also refers to the analogy between Psyche's sorting of seeds and the opening portion of Ovid's *Metamorphoses*. The same test is devised for the Russian and Indonesian Cinderellas, among others.

p. 65 **Ovid's *Metamorphoses*:** Translated by Rolfe Humphries (Bloomington: Indiana University Press, 1955).

p. 66 **in Greece today, women still prepare *kolliva*:** I am indebted to the Press and Information Office of the Consulate General of Greece for these details.

p. 69 **"the old man thought":** Grimms' "Cinderella."

p. 71 **"She must then be very handsome indeed":** Perrault's "Cinderella."

p. 72 **"The shoe or slipper is a . . . symbol of the female genitals":** Sigmund Freud, "The Sexual Aberrations," footnote added in 1910. The essay, included in *The Basic Writings of Sigmund Freud*, translated and edited by Dr. A. A. Brill (New York: Modern Library, 1938), is reprinted in *Three Essays on the Theory of Sexuality*, translated and revised by James Strachey (New York, Basic Books, 1975), 21.

p. 73 **At traditional Jewish weddings today:** The rabbinical explanation is that the shattered glass symbolizes the destruction of the Temple in Jerusalem by the Romans in A.D. 70, but that would scarcely seem an occasion for applause and shouts of congratulation among Jews.

p. 75 **"one-in-herself":** See M. Esther Harding: *Woman's Mysteries: Ancient and Modern* (Boston and Shaftesbury: Shambhala, 1990), 103–5. In ancient times, the great goddesses could be mothers and lovers and still remain *parthenos*, which does not mean "virgin" in the limited physical sense but "autonomous," "self-ruled." Temple prostitutes could be *parthenos*, but lawful wives could not.

p. 78 **"What did you throw those slippers at me for?":** All quotations come from George Bernard Shaw's play *Pygmalion*, first presented in London in 1914, unless otherwise noted, rather than from the Broadway musical *My Fair Lady*, which opened on Broadway in 1956, adapted by lyricist Alan Jay Lerner with music by Frederick Loewe.

p. 83 **"I've grown accustomed to her face":** From the musical *My Fair Lady*.

Chapter 5 *Sleeping Beauty: Going to Sleep a Girl . . .*

p. 89 "wish-maid" and the quotation that follows it come from Richard Wagner's opera *The Valkyrie* (*Die Walküre*), which is part of the *Ring* cycle. The libretto was translated by Stewart Robb and published by Schirmer.

p. 89 **In a Norse saga compiled in the twelfth century:** For information about the twelfth-century *Volsunga-Saga*, and background information on the way in which Wagner changed the old myths, see Jessie L. Weston, *The Legends of the Wagner Drama: Studies in Mythology and Romance* (New York: AMS, 1978).

p. 89 **"You all die at fifteen":** Denis Diderot, *Lettres à Sophie Volland.*

p. 91 **When the change comes, it may be a long-awaited breakthrough:** Marie-Louise von Franz, *The Feminine in Fairy Tales* (Boston and London: Shambhala, 1993), 27.

p. 93 **A man sees sleep as a defeat or a lost opportunity for heroism:** This does not hold true for the old Celtic heroes, like King Bran's companions, who are still under the influence of a Mother Goddess who taught them to value dreams and omens.

p. 97 **And yet we travel deeper than this every night:** Sandra Blakeslee, "Experts Explore Deep Sleep and the Making of Memories," *The New York Times*, November 14, 2000.

p. 98 For the anecdote about Friedrich Kekulé, see R. W. Gerard: "The Biological Basis of Imagination," included in *The Creative Process: A Symposium*, edited by Brewster Ghiselin (New American Library, 1952), 226. Wolfgang Mozart's quotation appears in the *Life of Mozart*, by Edward Holmes, included in the same symposium, 44–45. The authenticity of Mozart's letter has been questioned.

p. 99 **"Ah, if only we had a child!":** This quotation is from the Grimms' "Little Briar-Rose," known as "Dornroschen" in German, *The Complete Grimm's Fairy Tales* (New York: Pantheon Books, 1944, copyright renewed 1972). Charles Perrault's story "La Belle au Bois Dormant" ("The Sleeping Beauty in the Wood"), which preceded the Grimms' by more than a century, is the more elegant text. Earlier versions exist: *Perceforest*, a fourteenth-century French romance, and a tale from Day 5 of Basile's seventeenth-century *Il Pentamerone* both tell of beautiful Princesses who prick their fingers on flax, and fall into enchanted slumbers.

The quotation from the frog comes from the Grimms.

p. 100 **"there were thirteen Wise Women in the kingdom":** Perrault speaks of eight fairies, while the Grimms give us thirteen Wise Women, twelve of whom have been invited and one left out. This is particularly apt, since there were thirteen lunar months consisting of twenty-eight days each in the ancient matriarchal calendar. One month was disinvited, in effect, by the substitution of the patriarchal sun year of twelve months. The moon calendar, with its twenty-eight-day months, still governs a woman's menstrual cycle and pregnancy, which averages 280 days or ten lunar months. As the number of Wise Women tells us, the King-father overlooks sexuality, or chooses to exclude it.

p. 100 **"The King's daughter shall in her fifteenth year prick herself with a spindle":** Grimms' "Cinderella."

p. 101 **"The Princess shall indeed pierce her hand with a spindle":** Perrault, "The Sleeping Beauty in the Wood," (referred to here as "Sleeping Beauty"), translated by Robert Samber in 1729 and printed in Iona and Peter Opie's *The Classic Fairy Tales* (London and New York: Oxford University Press, 1974).

p. 102 **Climbing to the top of the tower, she comes to a little door with a rusty key in the lock:** These details are found only in the Grimms' version.

p. 102 **a locked room stands for the female genitals:** As early as 500 B.C., the locks on storerooms and women's jewelry chests were made in the shape of women's genitals. The owner had to insert the key into the lock and turn it in order to reach the treasure. Elizabeth Wayland Barber, *Women's Work: The First 20,000 Years* (New York: W. W. Norton, 1994), 251.

p. 102 **"Good day, old mother":** Perrault's "Sleeping Beauty."

p. 103 **"What is that, that jumps around so merrily?":** Drop spindles were used for flax until at least the eighteenth century, while spinning wheels, with their spindles fixed in place, rather than jumping around merrily, were used exclusively for wool.

p. 104 **she's about to have her first menstrual period:** Girls no longer swoon at the onset of menstruation, but a century ago fashionable doctors in England reported that because of the mothers' prudery, one quarter of their young patients had no idea what was happening to them when they found themselves losing blood. Often they thought they were hemorrhaging, or imagined they had injured themselves through their secret habit of masturbation. Carroll Smith-Rosenberg reports this in *Disorderly Conduct: Visions of Gender in Victorian America* (New York: Knopf, 1985).

Smith-Rosenberg offers the following quotation from *Transactions of the American Gynecological Society* 25, 1900: "Many a young life is battered and forever crippled in the breakers of puberty; if it crosses these unharmed and is not dashed to pieces on the rock of childbirth, it may still ground on the ever-recurring shallows of menstruation."

p. 105 **"Your Death has entered into you":** Cotton Mather, *The Angel of Bethesda*, Chapter 53. Quoted by Judith Walzer Leavitt, *Brought to Bed* (New York: Oxford University Press, 1986).

p. 105 **two mothers died for every hundred childbirths:** The same rate—expressed as 2,000 maternal deaths for every 100,000 births—still holds true in countries like Afghanistan, where medical care for pregnant women is virtually nonexistent in rural areas. In the United States today, the rate is eight deaths among mothers for every 100,000 births. Sources: UNICEF, World Bank.

Chapter 6 *Sleeping Beauty: . . . Waking as a Woman*

p. 111 Kathryn Harrison, *The Kiss* (New York: Random House, 1997).

p. 114 **With depression . . . incidence is twice as high among women as men:** Andrew C. Leon, Gerald L. Klerman, and Priya Wickramaratne, "Continuing

Female Predominance in Depressive Illness," *American Journal of Public Health* (May 1993).

p. 114 **During the Victorian era there was a tremendous vogue, particularly in England, for hysteria:** The founding text is by Sigmund Freud and Josef Breuer, *Studies on Hysteria,* 1895. For an insightful analysis of hysteria and other forms of nervous illness, see Elaine Showalter, *The Female Malady: Women, Madness and English Culture, 1830–1980* (New York: Pantheon Books, 1985), including the chapter on "Male Hysteria."

p. 114–115 **In the nineteenth century, doctors classified it as a neurological disease:** Jean-Martin Charcot, the great French neurologist of the nineteenth century, firmly believed that hysteria was a neurological disease, common to both genders, that had nothing to do with the uterus. Many doctors were unconvinced, however, and hysteria continued to be associated with women until the early twentieth century, when it was already diminishing in northern Europe.

p. 115 **they were frustrated in their craving for higher education, independence, and work in the outside world:** In 1874, Henry Maudsley warned that the intellectual training of adolescent girls could permanently injure their reproductive systems and brains. See Showalter, *Female Malady.*

Another doctor advised the young woman to "take to her bed from the first signs of a discharge until menstruation was firmly established, months or perhaps years later." From *Transactions of the American Gynecological Society* 25, 1900, quoted by Carroll Smith-Rosenberg, "Puberty to Menopause," in *Disorderly Conduct: Visions of Gender in Victorian America* (New York: Knopf, 1985).

p. 115 **Florence Nightingale, for instance, was an English beauty:** Details about her life, including her relationship with Richard Monckton Milnes, are taken from *Florence Nightingale,* by Cecil Woodham-Smith (New York: McGraw-Hill, 1951). Also see Showalter, *The Female Malady.*

p. 117 **In our era, the identical role is played by eating disorders:** Anorexia was described as early as 1689. In 1873, it was defined as a clinical syndrome among adolescent girls in both England and France. See Hilda Bruch, *Eating Disorders: Obesity, Anorexia Nervosa, and the Person Within* (New York: Basic Books, 1973); and Joan Jacobs Brumberg, *Fasting Girls: The Emergence of Anorexia Nervosa as a Modern Disease* (Cambridge, Mass.: Harvard University Press, 1978).

p. 119 **In a seventeenth-century Neapolitan Sleeping Beauty:** Giambattista Basile, *Il Pentamerone*, Day 5, tale 5.

p. 119 **He carries Talia to the nearest bed and rapes her:** In the movie *Talk to Her*, made by Pedro Almodovar in 2002, not one but two beautiful, unmarried young women, one a bullfighter and the other a ballet dancer, are severely injured and rendered comatose. Both are watched over in their apparently hopeless condition by men who love them. The bullfighter dies. The dancer is tended by a male nurse who becomes madly enamored of her and eventually rapes her. She does not stir when raped but, unlike Talia, miraculously returns to life during the process of childbirth.

p. 120 **"a great league and friendship":** Nineteenth-century translation, quoted by Iona and Peter Opie, *The Classic Fairy Tales* (New York and Toronto: Oxford University Press 1974), 104.

p. 120 **"the branches part like thighs":** Robert Coover, *Briar Rose* (New York: Grove Press, 1996), 1.

p. 121 **two Dutch scientists:** The scientists who saw the "animalcules" were Anton van Leeuwenhoek and Niklaas Hartsoeker. See Thomas Laqueur, *Making Sex: Body and Gender from the Greeks to Freud* (Cambridge, Mass., and London: Harvard University Press, 1990), 171–72.

p. 122 **breast buds, which are considered the first sign of puberty:** Lisa Belkin, "The Making of an 8-Year-Old Woman," *The New York Times Magazine*, December 24, 2000, reporting the findings of Marcia E. Herman-Giddens, Jay Belsky, and Bruce J. Ellis, among others.

Chapter 7 *Sleeping Beauty, American Style*

p. 127 In Basile's seventeenth-century story of Talia, which is half a century older than Perrault's "Sleeping Beauty," the royal rapist spends only a few days with the newly awakened princess and her infants before returning to his own palace, where he keeps his new "league and friendship" secret for good reason: He is already married. His wife, who overhears him talking in his sleep, arranges to have the children and then Talia brought to her on the sly, and instructs her cook to turn them into tasty dishes for supper. This explanation for the older woman's fury is rather more convincing than Perrault's story of a Queen-mother who is jealous of a young daughter-in-law and her children.

Chapter 8   *Beauties and Beasts: Borne on the Back of Desire*

p. 133–134 **"East of the Sun and West of the Moon,":** This is a Norwegian story collected by Peter C. Asbjornsen and Jorgen Moe, first published in Oslo in the mid-nineteenth century in their volume *Norwegian Folk Tales.* It has appeared with variations in numerous collections, including the selection from Asbjornsen and Moe published in paperback (New York and Toronto: Pantheon Books, 1982); *The Blue Fairy Book* edited by Andrew Lang, first published c. 1889 (New York: Dover, 1965); and *Best-Loved Folktales of the World,* selected by Joanna Cole (New York: Doubleday, 1982). I have somewhat changed the wording.

p. 135 "Beauty and the Beast" was written by Madame Jeanne-Marie Leprince de Beaumont, a Frenchwoman who worked in England for fourteen years as a governess. The story was published in 1757 and translated into English five years later. Madame de Beaumont's tale was adapted from that of her countrywoman, Madame Gabrielle-Suzanne de Villeneuve, who meandered through 362 pages to tell the same story.

p. 137 **"the terrible novelty of light":** W. B. Yeats, "High Talk" (his last sonnet), *London Mercury,* December 1938.

p. 141 **the constraints of arranged marriages:** Some historians believe that the implied protest against arranged marriages accounts for the story's popularity in eighteenth-century France. See Marina Warner, *From the Beast to the Blonde: On Fairy Tales and Their Tellers* (New York: Farrar, Straus & Giroux, 1994), 277–80, 293–94.

p. 142 **almost one third of high-school students:** *The New York Times,* October 10, 2000.

p. 146 **"I am greatly obliged to you":** This and the following quotations come from the story "Beauty and the Beast," included in *The Classic Fairy Tales,* by Iona and Peter Opie (London and New York: Oxford University Press, 1974).

p. 148 **asked why an attractive young woman like Anna Freud:** Abram Kardiner, quoted in *Freud's Women,* by Lisa Appignanesi and John Forrester (New York: Basic Books, 1992), 278.

Chapter 9   *Beauties and Beasts: Descending into the Body*

p. 153 **In ancient times . . . a princess named Psyche:** The story of Cupid and
Psyche was written in the second century A.D. by Apuleius, a native of a Roman
colony in North Africa, and included in his novel *The Golden Ass.* The full title
of the work, which is seldom used, is *The Transformations of Lucius, Otherwise
Known as The Golden Ass.* An earlier version of the myth had been current in
Greek.

I have relied on the fine translation of *The Golden Ass* by Robert Graves
(New York: Farrar, Straus & Giroux, 1951). For insights, I am indebted to
Erich Neumann's volume *Amor and Psyche: The Psychic Development of the Fem-
inine,* Bollingen Series LIV (Princeton: Princeton University Press, 1956).

In the seventeenth-century collection known as *Il Pentamerone,* recorded by
Giambattista Basile, the lover first appears as a black slave, but by the light of
the heroine's candle "ebony changed to ivory, caviar into milk."

p. 154 **He was the youthful god of love:** Cupid's proper names, *Amor* in Latin
and *Eros* in Greek, both connote erotic love. Venus is the Roman equivalent of
the Greek goddess Aphrodite, and Jupiter, as king of the gods, is equivalent to
Zeus.

p. 154 **"fierce and wild and of the dragon breed":** This is from the translation
by H. E. Butler. All other quotations come from Robert Graves's translation.

p. 157 *The African Queen* (1951), directed by John Huston, was written by
James Agee and John Huston, based on a novel by C. S. Forester.

p. 161 **the head and hooves of a bull on the body of a human:** Male mythological beasts are often represented as human below the neck with animal
heads on top. Female beasts, on the other hand, are generally put together the
other way around. Mermaids, sirens, sphinxes—all the famous singers and rid-
dlers of sex and the Underworld—along with harpies, have the heads of beautiful women poised on top of animal lower halves. Their bodies define their
menace, but their seduction lies in the voices, irresistible to men, which come
out of their human throats.

The alluring head and torso combined with a sinful lower area is echoed
in Shakespeare's *King Lear,* Act IV: "But to the girdle do the gods inherit, /
Beneath is all the fiend's."

The Walt Disney studio was faithful to this idea in its portrayal of the sea witch in *The Little Mermaid.* Below the waist, Ursula has the tentacles of an octopus.

p. 161 **To the Athenians, he was never a god in the first place:** The god of a conquered people always turns into a monster in the eyes of the conquerors, says scholar Jane Ellen Harrison in her book *Mythology* (New York: Harcourt, Brace & World, 1924).

p. 161 **Baffled and terrifying, the Minotaur waits for the sun hero Theseus:** I have used the legend of Theseus in the Labyrinth as a metaphor for the change in the status of the beast-god, rather than historical fact. Jorge Luis Borges amplifies the legend to stunning effect in his story "The House of Asterion," in *Labyrinths: Selected Stories & Other Writings* (New York: New Directions, 1964). Asterion is the birth name of the Minotaur.

p. 166 **She might listen to the anthropologist Margaret Mead:** Helen E. Fisher, *Anatomy of Love: The Natural History of Monogamy, Adultery, and Divorce* (New York: W. W. Norton, 1992), 297.

p. 168 **"Don't look into my eyes":** This line comes from the movie *Beauty and the Beast,* directed by Jean Cocteau and released in 1946.

Chapter 10 *Beauties and Beasts: Looking Love in the Face*

p. 170 **"Lovely Psyche, darling wife, beware":** This is from *The Golden Ass* by Apuleius, translated by Robert Graves (New York: Farrar, Straus & Giroux, 1951). I have slightly modernized the translation.

p. 170 **"I have so great a desire to see my father, that I shall fret to death":** Madame Leprince de Beaumont's "Beauty and the Beast," included by Iona and Peter Opie in *The Classic Fairy Tales* (New York and Toronto: Oxford University Press, 1974).

p. 175 **"Oh my, he may well be a Troll":** "East of the Sun and West of the Moon." Translation slightly revised.

p. 181 **"What have you done?" he cries. If only she had held firm for a year, he would have been free from a curse:** The same untimely revelation takes place with the genders reversed in the Russian fairy tale "The Frog Princess," in which a human bridegroom cannot resist burning his enchanted bride's animal skin after he sees her as a wonderfully beautiful woman.

p. 186 **"Give me back my Beast!" wailed Greta Garbo:** Quoted in a *New Yorker* film review, November 30, 1992.

PART 2

p. 191 **96 percent of (senior citizens) married at some time in their lives:** Rose M. Kreider and Jason M. Fields, 2001, "Number, Timing, and Duration of Marriages and Divorces: Fall 1996," U.S. Census Bureau, Washington, D.C.

p. 192 **"I was the most commitment-phobic person on earth":** Gina Bellafonte, "Sunday Styles," *The New York Times,* September 30, 2001, quoting Lindsey Gates of New York City.

Chapter 11   *The White Bride and the Black Bride: The Discovery of Two Selves*

p. 193 **Not one person in a hundred knows this story, despite the fact that there are four versions in Grimms' alone:** Variations of the story, known generically to folklorists as "the substituted bride," are found in many parts of the world—in Africa and among widely separated tribes of Native Americans as well as all over Europe. The usurper is a servant girl in one of the best-known examples: the Grimms' story of "The Goose Girl."

p. 193 **she splits in two:** For a masterly, in-depth study of the doubling, substitution, and disguises of bed partners in myths, tales, and movies, see Wendy Doniger, *The Bedtrick: Tales of Sex & Masquerade* (Chicago: University of Chicago Press, 2000). Her introduction to the book begins, "You go to bed with someone you think you know, and when you wake up you discover that it was someone else."

p. 196 **The golden clothes belong to the King:** In a related story, Jane Eyre will feel the same way about the finery that Mr. Rochester wants to buy for her before their wedding.

p. 196 **The coachman-brother is so dazzled by love for his sister:** So important is the brother in numerous versions of the story that some scholars suggest this is a story of aborted incest. In their interpretation, the brother wants to spirit his sister away to be *his* bride, but the stepmother, upholding community morals, intervenes by breaking off communication between them and substituting her own daughter. In that scenario, the stepmother and the Black Bride would be heroines.

See Nicole Belmont, writing in *Mythologies,* compiled by Yves Bonnefoy and prepared by Wendy Doniger (Chicago: University of Chicago Press, 1991), vol. 2, 746–49.

p. 197 **a snow-white duck:** Birds, which are skyborne creatures, at home in two or three elements, often serve as helpers or guardians for young heroes and heroines, as in "Snow White" and "Cinderella," or else they serve as bodies for displaced human souls, as in "The Six Swans," or "The White Bride and the Black Bride." Kindly ducks also appear in "The Three Little Men in the Wood" and in "Hansel and Gretel." The endnote to "Hansel and Gretel" refers to an essay by Margaret Atwood on this subject.

p. 199 **When David Buss, a pioneer in the field of evolutionary psychology:** David Buss, *Evolutionary Psychology: The New Science of the Mind* (Boston and London: Allyn & Bacon, 1999). Eleanor E. Maccoby reports on Buss's work and adds her own insights in *The Two Sexes: Growing Up Apart, Coming Together* (Cambridge, Mass.: Belknap Press of Harvard University Press, 1998). Also see Deborah Blum, *Sex on the Brain: The Biological Differences Between Men and Women* (New York: Viking Penguin, 1997).

p. 199 **scientists from Saint Edward's University in Austin, Texas:** Blum, *Sex on the Brain.*

p. 200 **sociological studies proving that single men with high-status jobs and a superior education:** Robert Wright, "Our Cheating Hearts," *Time,* August 15, 1994, adapted from his book *The Moral Animal: Evolutionary Psychology and Everyday Life* (New York: Pantheon, 1994).

p. 201 **Today, in the lands of the former Mongol Empire:** Dr. Henry Harpending, Distinguished Professor of Anthropology, University of Utah, cited in "We're Not Fully Evolved," *The New York Times,* August 24, 2003.

p. 201 **"A lasting relationship with a woman":** Harpending, "We're Not Fully Evolved."

p. 201 **the age gap is scarcely more than two years:** Carrie Conaway in the *Regional Review,* Q3 2002.

p. 202 **This alternation of desire for two sorts:** Research by Ian Penton-Voak, currently at the University of Bristol, as discussed by Carl Zimmer, *Evolution: The Triumph of an Idea* (New York: HarperCollins, 2001).

p. 203 **Curious games were played in the French countryside:** Nicole Belmont, writing in *Mythologies,* 746.

p. 203–204 **her community might try to palm off a less desirable female:** In the Bible, Jacob, a champion cheater himself, is defrauded by his future father-in-law into toiling for seven years in order to earn the beautiful Rachel as his wife. But on the morning after his wedding he discovers that he has been wed to her homely older sister—"behold, it was Leah!"—who has been slipped under his bedcovers instead. For Rachel, he will have to labor for another seven years. In the Jewish tradition, the younger sister could not be given in marriage before the older one, a problem that is repeated in Shakespeare's *Taming of the Shrew* and its musical version, *Kiss Me Kate.*

p. 209 **Adam's first wife . . . was not Eve but Lilith:** The story of Lilith, whose name appears in the Bible only once and then indirectly, derives from post-biblical Jewish sources. See Mircea Eliade, editor in chief, *The Encyclopedia of Religion* (New York: Macmillan, 1987); Robert Graves and Raphael Patai, *Hebrew Myths: The Book of Genesis* (New York: McGraw-Hill, 1963); and Theodor H. Gaster, *Myth, Legend and Custom in the Old Testament,* vol. 2 (New York: Harper & Row, 1969). The earliest complete version of the legend appears in *The Alphabet of Ben Sira* in the eleventh century, probably of Persian or Arabic origin. See the introduction by Howard Schwartz to *Lilith's Cave: Jewish Tales of the Supernatural,* selected and retold by Howard Schwartz (San Francisco: Harper & Row, 1988).

Chapter 12 *Rapunzel and Jane Eyre: Confronting the Madwoman in the Attic*

p. 216 **depression . . . is more common among married women than among the unmarried:** National Mental Health Association, 2004.

p. 216 **twice as common among women between the ages of fifteen and twenty-four:** *Journal of Consulting and Clinical Psychology* (August 2003), reported in *The New York Times,* March 16, 2004, Science section.

p. 217 "Rapunzel" is known to us from the Grimms' collection of fairy tales, first published in 1812, but its roots can be found in many parts of Europe, where the heroine may be named Fenchelchen (fennel) or Persinette (parsley), rather than Rapunzel (rampion), usually for a fresh herb that a pregnant woman might desire to eat.

In the Grimms' first edition, the sorceress is called a "fairy." Some translations describe her as a witch, but her sole fault seems to be excessive desire to keep the heroine closely confined, which used to be a customary safeguard for well-bred unmarried girls. The words "sorceress" and "enchantress" seem appropriate for the older woman, but I also use the term "mother-witch" for any self-serving mother-daughter relationship.

p. 217 **a bed full of those hardy greens known in English as rampion:** Rampion, or creeping bellflower, is so weather-resistant that if planted in August in northern Europe it will sprout in March or April, while the earth is still bare and winter appetites are starved for greens.

p. 220 **After World War II, French women who had slept with Nazi soldiers:** The same punishment was meted out by the IRA to "betraying sisters" who consorted with British soldiers, as poet Seamus Heaney tells us in his poem "Punishment." The Roman historian Tacitus describes the identical treatment among Germanic tribes.

p. 220 **Joan of Arc was condemned to death:** For details about representations of Joan in the Middle Ages, see Marina Warner's erudite book *From the Beast to the Blonde: On Fairy Tales and Their Tellers* (New York: Farrar, Straus & Giroux, 1994). Also see Warner's *Joan of Arc: The Image of Female Heroism* (New York: Knopf, 1981).

p. 221 **"Tell me, Mother Gothel, why do you think my clothes have become too tight for me?":** Quoted by Jack Zipes, *The Brothers Grimm: From Enchanted Forests to the Modern World* (New York and London: Routledge, 1988), 13. Also see Maria Tatar, *The Hard Facts of the Grimms' Fairy Tales* (Princeton: Princeton University Press, 1987), 18.

p. 224 **She has heard the voice of "the madwoman in the attic":** The book *The Madwoman in the Attic,* by Sandra M. Gilbert and Susan Gubar (New Haven: Yale University Press, 1979), illuminates images of female repression in Victorian literature and analyzes the shadow relationship between the two wives of Edward Rochester. The authors also identify Eyre with "air" and "ire."

p. 225 **"You—poor and obscure and small and plain as you are":** Charlotte Brontë, *Jane Eyre,* first published London, 1847 (London and New York: Penguin Books, 1985), Chapter 23.

Chapter 13   *The Seal Wife: Hungry for Intimacy, Thirsty for Silence*

p. 235 **Early one morning, a fisherman from one of the islands:** This story has been loosely adapted from Thomas Keightley's version of "The Mermaid Wife," in *The World Guide to Gnomes, Fairies, Elves and other Little People* (New York: Avenel Books, 1978). I have combined it with "The Seal's Skin" from Jacqueline Simpson, *Icelandic Folktales and Legends* (Berkeley: University of California Press, 1972); and "The Woman of the Sea," from *Folktales of the British Isles,* edited by Kenneth Crossley-Holland (New York: Pantheon, 1986), adding details of my own invention.

For numerous insights, I am indebted to Barbara Fass Leavy, *In Search of the Swan Maiden: A Narrative on Folklore and Gender* (New York: New York University Press, 1994).

p. 238 **"It is given to them that their sea-longing shall be land-longing":** David Thomson, *The People of the Sea: A Journey in Search of the Seal Legend* (London: Barrie and Rockliff, 1965). Quoted by Barbara Fass Leavy, *In Search of the Swan Maiden,* 37.

p. 238 **a tug as irresistible as the tide:** Behind this story there may lie another, not quite forgotten, of the primal journey from sea to shore undertaken by the species, but also by the individual. All of us spend our fetal months floating in liquid in our mother's womb. And all of us let out a cry—the first sound we hear in this world—when we are forced out of our miniature ocean into a world of solid forms, seized by a pair of hard, huge hands and swaddled in unwanted clothes. But this, too, may be a transformation that we wished on ourselves without remembering it. According to an ancient belief, no baby is born unless its soul makes a choice to be born on earth, at the difficult intersection of biology and free will.

p. 240 **Ibsen's play *A Doll's House*:** Translated by Ralph Fjelde (New York and Scarborough, Ontario: New American Library, 1965).

p. 247 **"I will not, I simply will not":** Details and quotations are taken from Doris Lessing, *Under My Skin: Volume One of My Autobiography, to 1949* (London: HarperCollins, 1994).

p. 251 **"It began when I had picked up a book":** Adrienne Rich, *Of Woman Born: Motherhood as Experience and Institution* (New York: W. W. Norton, 1986), 23.

p. 252 **while still doing four fifths of the housework:** *The New York Times,* December 15, 1996.

p. 252 W. B. Yeats: "The Choice," *Collected Poems* (New York: Macmillan, 1943).

Chapter 14 *Bluebeard's Wife and the Fitcher's Bird: Taking Her Life in Her Hands*

p. 255 **"Here," said Bluebeard to his last wife, "are the keys of the two great rooms":** Quotations come from "The Blue Beard" by Charles Perrault, *Histoires ou Contes du temps passé. Avec des Moralitez,* Paris, 1697, translated into English by Robert Samber (1729). Reprinted in *The Classic Fairy Tales,* Iona and Peter Opie (New York and Toronto: Oxford University Press, 1974).

p. 256 **a barely visible crack in the golden bowl:** *The Golden Bowl* is the title of a novel by Henry James that deals with a flawed marriage.

p. 256 **in this real-life case Katharine Graham:** Katharine Graham, *Personal History* (New York: Knopf, 1997).

p. 256 *The Bloody Chamber:* A modern feminist version of "Bluebeard," this is the title story of Angela Carter's book of stories, published in the United States by Harper & Row (San Francisco, 1980) and Penguin Books (New York, 1987).

p. 259 **"Now the serpent":** Gen. 3:1–3, King James version.

p. 260 "Fitcher's Bird," sometimes called "Fowler's Fowl," appears in *The Complete Grimm's Fairy Tales* (New York: Pantheon Books, 1944, copyright renewed 1972).

   The original German title, "Fichters Vogel," does not seem to have any clear meaning. Marina Warner has suggested in her book *From the Beast to the Blonde* (New York: Farrar, Straus & Giroux, 1994) that it derives from the Icelandic word *fitfugl,* which means "web-footed bird."

   The Icelandic application of the term to water birds was confirmed for me by the Icelandic Society for the Protection of Birds.

p. 261 **Taking the keys in one hand and the egg in the other:** Margaret Atwood has written a perceptive contemporary story entitled "Bluebeard's Egg."

p. 262 **Egg and key:** The same symbols can be seen in the classic egg-and-dart frieze of ancient Greece, which, in turn, derives from Egyptian friezes depicting male and female sex symbols. Barbara G. Walker, *The Woman's Encyclopedia of Myths and Secrets* (San Francisco: Harper San Francisco, 1983), 270–71.

p. 262 **Eggs still represent birth or rebirth:** Long before Christianity, Easter was a spring festival of rebirth in northern Europe, named for the Teutonic goddess Eostre, or Ostara, who is identified with the pagan goddess Astarte. Worshipers colored eggs red to mark the triumph once again of life over death. See Barbara Walker, *Encyclopedia of Myths and Secrets,* 267–68.

Is it possible that the Fitcher's Bird, who carries an egg in her hand, may be a confused remembrance of a woman celebrating Easter? Or is she the goddess herself, instructing her celebrants, "Here is your life. Worship it. Eat it." "Fitcher's Bird" is a German story, possibly an inheritor of the Teutonic tradition.

p. 262 **she reigned as bird goddess:** Prehistoric statues of the goddess commonly show her with a bird's beak and the staring eyes of an owl. See Marija Gimbutas, *The Language of the Goddess* (San Francisco: Harper & Row, 1989); Erich Neumann, *The Great Mother: An Analysis of the Archetype,* especially plates 8, 10, and 14, Bollingen Series XLVII (Princeton: Princeton University Press, 1955).

An impressive statue from classical Boeotia shows a crowned Aphrodite, the goddess of love and fertility, standing upright on the back of a flying goose, not unlike Mother Goose flying on the back of her fowl. Neumann, plate 137.

p. 266 **Psyche, that other great trespasser:** The story of Cupid and Psyche comes from *The Golden Ass,* by Apuleius, translated by Robert Graves (New York: Farrar, Straus & Giroux, 1951).

p. 272 **"I knew a child once who adored her father":** Eleanor Roosevelt, "Ethics of Parents" (unpublished, 1927). Quoted by Joseph P. Lash, *Eleanor and Franklin* (New York: W. W. Norton, 1971), 46.

I have derived the material for this section principally from Eleanor Roosevelt's own writing, especially *This is My Story* (New York and London: Harper & Brothers, 1937); Blanche Wiesen Cook, *Eleanor Roosevelt* (New York: Viking Penguin, 1992); Doris Kearns Goodwin, *No Ordinary Time* (New York: Simon & Schuster, 1994); Joseph P. Lash, *Love, Eleanor* (Garden City, N.Y.: Doubleday, 1982); as well as *Eleanor and Franklin* (New York: W. W. Norton, 1971).

p. 274 **"I did not believe in knowing things which your husband did not wish you to know"**: quoted by Cook, *Eleanor Roosevelt*, 223; also quoted by Lash, *Love, Eleanor*, 67.

p. 276 **she couldn't eat normally, couldn't even take Communion:** Lash, *Love, Eleanor*, 73.

p. 276 **The repeated vomiting may have loosened:** Cook, *Eleanor Roosevelt*, 235.

p. 277 **"I faced myself, my surroundings, my world":** Letter to Joseph P. Lash, written in 1943, quoted by him, *Eleanor and Franklin*, 66.

p. 278 **"a completely colorless echo of my husband and mother-in-law":** Letter to Joseph P. Lash, quoted by him, *Eleanor and Franklin*, 80.

p. 280 **"Can you learn to live?" asks Colette:** Colette, *My Apprenticeships* (1957). Translated by Helen Beauclerk (New York: Farrar, Straus & Giroux, 1978), 84.

PART 3

Chapter 15 *Hansel and Gretel: Life in the Light of Death*

p. 290 **The word *crone* . . . repels us:** The *Oxford English Dictionary* gives a secondary definition of *crone* as "an old ewe; a sheep whose teeth are broken off."
  The term "hag" might conceivably be related to *hagia*, the ancient Greek word for *holy*, as in the church of Hagia Sophia in Istanbul, meaning Holy Wisdom, or *hagiography*, the biographies of saints, but the OED does not recognize this derivation for the word. In any case, it is even less acceptable to women than "crone."

p. 290 **In 1900, the average American woman died at the age of forty-eight:** United States Census Historical Data. The rate of increase was estimated by Dr. James Vaupel of the Max Planck Institute for Demographic Research in Rostock, Germany. *The New York Times*, November 11, 2003, Science section.

p. 295 **"At fifty":** Carolyn G. Heilbrun, "Virginia Woolf in Her Fifties," *Hamlet's Mother and Other Women* (New York: Ballantine Books, 1990), 90.

p. 295 **an afterlife rather than a future:** See *Isak Dinesen: The Life of a Storyteller* (New York: St. Martin's Press, 1982), the excellent biography by Judith Thurman.

p. 295 **"Only when she had lost what had constituted her life":** Hannah Arendt, *Men in Dark Times* (New York: Harcourt Brace Jovanovich, 1968).

p. 295 **"God cannot stand continuance":** Isak Dinesen, "The Monkey," *Seven Gothic Tales* (New York: Vintage Books, 1972).

p. 296 **"little to bite and to break":** "Hansel and Gretel," *The Complete Grimm's Fairy Tales* (New York: Pantheon Books, 1944, copyright renewed 1972). The remainder of the story is adapted from the same source.

   This fairy tale was made into a perennially popular opera for children by Engelbert Humperdinck in 1893.

p. 298 **the woodland birds—which so often serve in fairy tales as guardian spirits or heavenly messengers:** Margaret Atwood, in an essay entitled "Of Souls as Birds," writes with imagination and sensitivity about soul transformation in fairy tales, where brothers are often changed into birds and can return to life as human beings only through the heroism of their sisters. The essay appears in *Mirror, Mirror on the Wall: Women Writers Explore Their Favorite Fairy Tales,* edited by Kate Bernheimer (New York: Anchor Books, 1998), 25–36.

p. 298 **corpses lay in ditches:** Robert Darnton, *The Great Cat Massacre and Other Episodes in French Cultural History* (New York: Basic Books, 1984), 30–31.

   Oddly enough, in the book version of *Peter Pan* by J. M. Barrie, which followed the staging of the play by seven years, Wendy's fate is uncertain at birth: "For a week or two after Wendy came it was doubtful whether they should be able to keep her, as she was another mouth to feed. Mr. Darling was frightfully proud of her, but he was very honorable, and he sat on the edge of Mrs. Darling's bed, holding her hand and calculating expenses, while she looked at him imploringly . . . but at last Wendy just got through."

p. 299 **the hard-hearted parent had been replaced by a stepmother:** Maria Tatar, *The Hard Facts of the Grimms' Fairy Tales* (Princeton: Princeton University Press, 1987), 36–37. The same camouflage of the vicious mother's identity takes place in "The Juniper Tree" and "Mother Holle," among other stories.

p. 302 ***"I turn and burn":*** Sylvia Plath, "Lady Lazarus," *The Collected Poems* (New York: HarperPerennial, 1992).

p. 305 **"The earth, your mother, who fed you will eat you now":** See Chapter 4, the second "Cinderella" chapter.

p. 306 **Yanomami people of the Amazon:** Documentary on the Yanomami, *Nova,* "Warriors of the Amazon," PBS, April 6, 1999.

p. 306 **behind the Christian ceremony of the Eucharist as well:** See C. J. Jung, "Transformation Symbolism in the Mass" (1941), included in *The Mysteries,* papers from the *Eranos Yearbooks,* edited by Joseph Campbell, Bollingen Series XXX, vol. 2 (Princeton: Princeton University Press, 1955), 274–337.

p. 306 **"I am the living bread":** John, 6:51–55.

p. 307 **The town of Bethlehem:** According to tradition, in ancient times Bethlehem was the grove of Adonis, a Greek man-god who died and was resurrected each year in the form of vegetation. See Sir James George Frazer, *The Golden Bough: A Study in Magic and Religion,* abridged (New York: Macmillan, 1922), 346; and Joseph Campbell, *The Masks of God: Primitive Mythology* (New York: Viking, 1959), 299–300.

p. 307 **Eighty thousand patients are on the national waiting list:** *The New York Times,* February 19, 2003.

p. 308 **Emeralds and sapphires and pearls:** In the myths of every culture, heroes who survive encounters with the death spirit become heir to unimaginable riches that were hidden in the enemy's lair: the dragon's hoard of gold; the copper, dried meat, and bear grease stored up by the Dzonokwa, cannibal ogresses of the Pacific Northwest coast. Our heart's desire is kept from us by the figure of death.

p. 310 **with 82 percent of all Americans declaring their belief in Heaven:** Harris poll, 2003, reported in *The New York Times,* December 21, 2003.

Chapter 16 *Demeter and Persephone: The Beautiful Mysteries*

p. 316 **"The hour of departure has arrived":** Plato's *Apology,* translated by Benjamin Jowett (New York: Random House, 1937), Socrates' concluding lines, 423.

p. 317 **_Homeric Hymn to Demeter_:** This is one of a collection of thirty-three poems known as the *Homeric Hymns,* written by anonymous authors between the eighth and sixth century B.C., after the death of Homer but using his diction and meter. I have relied on the translation by Charles Boer (Dallas: Spring, 1970).

p. 318 **the plains of Nysa in Greece:** A number of sources place the abduction at Enna in Sicily, or in Eleusis, or near Cnossus in Crete, among other locations. I have followed the *Homeric Hymn*. Lines are unnumbered.

p. 320 **"There is no other god responsible but Zeus . . . who gave her to Hades":** Quotations come from the *Homeric Hymn*.

p. 326 **"And then she had a child as white as snow":** The Grimms' story of "The Juniper Tree" begins with almost the same words as "Snow White," though the baby in this case is a boy, who will also be subject to his stepmother's murderous rage.

p. 327 **"burning blush, and yet a haughty smile":** Nathaniel Hawthorne, *The Scarlet Letter* (New York: The Modern Library, 2000), 47.

p. 329 The story of "Isis and Osiris," derived from Plutarch's essay, is recounted by Sir James George Frazer, *The Golden Bough,* vol. 1 (New York: Macmillan, 1922).

p. 331 *pomme,* "**apple**"—**the garnet apple:** *Granate* can mean the color garnet or many-grained, holding many seeds.

p. 331 **"He forced me, unwillingly, violently, to eat it":** In Ovid's *Metamorphoses,* Proserpina, as she was called in Latin, picks the fruit herself and eats the seeds because she is hungry—possibly with the desire to bear a child.

p. 335 **Demeter is credited with giving the gift of agriculture:** Similarly, the goddess Isis, who was also a ruler of the Underworld, was credited by the Egyptians with the discovery of wild grains, which her brother-spouse, Osiris, then taught the people to cultivate. Food and worship seem to go together.

p. 336 **the initiation rites known as the Eleusinian mysteries:** There is evidence of a sacred precinct in Eleusis as early as 1500 B.C., which would give a total span of almost two thousand years, but secret initiation rites and a fully developed myth should be attributed to a later century.

For scholarly analyses of the Eleusinian mysteries and the Homeric "Hymn to Demeter," I relied on the following works, among others:

C. Kerenyi, "Kore," included in C. G. Jung and C. Kerenyi, *Essays on a Science of Mythology,* Bollingen Series XXII (Princeton: Princeton University Press, 1949).

C. Kerenyi, *Eleusis: Archetypal Image of Mother and Daughter,* translated by Ralph Manheim, Bollingen Series LXV (Princeton: Princeton University Press, 1967).

Walter F. Otto, "The Meaning of the Eleusinian Mysteries," included in *The Mysteries,* papers from the *Eranos Yearbooks,* edited by Joseph Campbell and translated by Ralph Manheim, Bollingen Series XXX (Princeton: Princeton University Press, 1955).

Helen M. Luke, "The Perennial Feminine," *Parabola,* V, no. 4.

p. 336 **in the words of an ancient historian:** Zosimos, a pagan author of the fifth century A.D. Quoted by Kerenyi in *Eleusis.*

p. 336 **the hundreds of thousands, or even millions, of initiates who took part:** During the Persian War, thirty thousand people from all over the Greek-speaking world reputedly attended the Eleusinian mysteries each year. This number was roughly equal to the entire population of Athens.

p. 338 **The miracle happens once and forever:** Mystics believe that the god is not subject to linear time, so that his death and resurrection are eternally present.

p. 338 **the new crop was planted:** In ancient Greece, fall was the usual season for planting. Wild grain takes longer to sprout than cultivated grain, says Kerenyi, which accounts for the four months that the seeds spent underground. In the area around Athens, crops are harvested in June before the summer drought sets in, but some areas, like the Rharian plains, have two harvests a year.

Index

Spinning Straw
into Gold

What Fairy Tales Reveal

About the Transformations

in a Woman's Life

Joan Gould

A Reader's Guide

A Conversation with Joan Gould

Random House: What was the genesis of *Spinning Straw into Gold*? And how long have you been working on it?

Joan Gould: The quick answer is that I've been sitting in front of a computer and working on this book for twelve years. But in another way, it's been on my mind for sixty years. During my freshman year at college, when I was sixteen, the college awarded a prize for the best term paper by a freshman—a very big deal at the time. I told my adviser that I'd been struck by similarities between heroes in classic myths and comic books. Superman, for instance (who had appeared in print only five years earlier) is sent to our world from the doomed planet Krypton in a rocket ship, to be found and raised by foster parents, just as the infant Moses was rescued from the Egyptians by being put into an ark made of reeds and floated downriver, where the Pharaoh's daughter found him.

No way, said my adviser. I could write on that subject if I insisted, but I'd never win the prize. Why wouldn't I write about Virginia Woolf instead? He was right. I didn't win the prize. It went to a girl who wrote about Virginia Woolf. But the notion stayed with me from then on that the most meaningful themes in our stories—those that we can't forget—change their names and settings over the centuries while their meaning remains intact.

RH: The first sentence in your book reads "What's your favorite fairy tale?" What's the point of such a question?

JG: This may sound like a parlor game, but naming a story on the spur of the moment can be a clue to our childhood dilemmas and our inner selves. The choice will change from one period in our lives to another, even from day to day. Ten women who say that "Cinderella" is their favorite story may be thinking of ten different aspects: the heroine's sense of being excluded from the family group, for instance; the humiliation of looking so much less attractive than her "stepsisters" (who may be her classmates or friends); her rivalry with those stepsisters; or perhaps her problems with her stepmother, who could actually be her own mother, as seen through a resentful teenager's eyes.

Those who choose "Snow White" may be thinking of the scenes with the dwarfs as they appear in the Walt Disney movie—heigh-ho, heigh-ho—while Snow White plays the perfect Cub Scout den mother, hands on her hips, gently correcting their manners and insisting that they wash their hands. In the original Grimms' story, however, the dwarfs, who are the same size as Snow White, are father figures who insist that she must do the housekeeping and cooking if she's to stay in their cottage. Another woman may remember the story as a mother-daughter duel, starting with a mother, still beautiful and sexual, who realizes that her daughter is approaching womanhood and will soon become a Queen in her own right. The mother may not be jealous of the girl's beauty—that's a fairy-tale metaphor—but of the lovers and babies and homes that have not yet appeared in her life, or the doors that are open for her daughter that were never open for her.

RH: You say that on the surface this is a book about fairy tales, but at a deeper level it deals with transformation. What do you mean by "transformation," and what does it have to do with bed-time stories for children?

JG: By "transformation" I mean those fundamental shifts in levels of being that come over us from time to time and leave us wondering how we got to where we are today. We are born to be changed, the stories tell us. We are always on the move from one stage to the next, whether we want to be transformed or not. This is why so many of our favorite tales focus on girls and women, with their built-in and obvious metamorphoses, rather than boys and men.

RH: Could you give some everyday examples?

JG: A girl is a child before puberty and a woman afterward. This is the story of Cinderella, who changes from a kitchen maid scorned by her stepsisters into a beautiful princess; Sleeping Beauty, who bleeds when pricked by a forbidden spindle; and the Seal Maidens, who swim to shore on certain nights and slip out of their animal skins to reveal their beautiful legs and what lies between them.

A woman is one person before she has sexual contact with a male and another person, more alive or less alive, later on. Beauty is more alive when she recognizes her love for the Beast; Daphne is less alive when she changes into a tree in order to avoid being raped by Apollo.

Marriage is a transformation that splits a woman in two. In one part, she's her independent, strong-willed self, like Scarlett O'Hara; in the other part, she's half of a couple, tenderly maternal, like Melanie Wilkes. ("The White Bride and the Black Bride" is the story of this conflict.) A woman is transformed when she's pregnant and again, miraculously, when she becomes a mother. Menopause is a generally unwelcome transformation, signaling age, but becoming a grandmother teaches continuity and difference.

But one thing transformation is not: It's not a magic wand that changes a poor girl's rags to riches, or treats her to an *Extreme Makeover*, both of which are external changes. Real transformation involves rising (or falling) from one level of consciousness to another, usually after a dark period of suffering or sleep.

RH: Do you see "Cinderella" as the drama that all girls go through at puberty?

JG: No, "Cinderella" is just one account—though it's the most popular—of this transformation. We never get tired of the basic plot: *Jane Eyre, Harry Potter,* "The Ugly Duckling," and *A Little Princess* are all about adolescents of superior birth who suffer miserably while living with their foster families but outstrip their oppressors in the end.

But this isn't the only story of the dark passage that leads from childhood through adolescence to adulthood. Cinderella works as a scullery maid until the night when her rags turn into a ball gown that is the outer sign of her natural new splendor, while Sleeping Beauty doesn't work at all. Instead she sleeps; she incubates until the time comes for her to emerge as a woman. Snow White does both: She works while she lives in the dwarfs' cottage, but later she sleeps in a glass coffin. In every case, the heroine has to go through a period of darkness and depression, or else oblivion—a time we call adolescence—before she's ready to become a wife and mother. But the most dramatic transformation, the most erotic, is "Beauty and the Beast" in its hundreds of forms.

RH: Erotic? How can a fairy tale be erotic?

JG: Oddly enough, in a society obsessed with sex, we have forgotten how to value it as the highest energy we know—low as the animals, high and spiritual as the gods. To be intense, sex requires privacy—one male and one female locked together in a castle in the wilderness—the opposite of our contemporary TV mating shows that flaunt sexiness instead of sex. A true beauty-and-beast story has something erotic and terrifying about it, because a virgin's first contact with a hairy, powerful male is bound to be frightening, but it also has a quality of tenderness—because the Beast is shamed by the knowledge of his beastliness.

RH: So the Beast is transformed into a Prince when Beauty says she loves him, and the two of them fly off to his kingdom, where they live happily ever after. Why do all fairy tales seem to end in the same way?

JG: They don't. In fact, I've divided this book into the three phases of a woman's life, following the classic division according to the phases of the moon: crescent moon, full moon, and waning moon. The Maiden's story—I call it "The Age of Attraction"—begins with puberty and ends with love, marriage, and motherhood, because that's the way we keep the species going. But on the Maiden's wedding day the Matron's story begins—I call that phase "The Age of Attachment"—entirely different from the Maiden's but just as full of trials and triumphs. The final phase of a woman's life is the Crone, "The Age of the Spirit," which is the most challenging, giving us the chance to see ourselves retired from the cycle of reproduction, living in the clear, sharp light of mortality.

RH: We've all heard charges from feminists that the old fairy tales are demeaning to girls because the heroines seem to do nothing but lie around and mope until a Prince comes along to save them. What do you think about this?

JG: The idea that fairy-tale heroines are passive creatures who wait for a deliverer is a twentieth-century notion that's out-and-out wrong. Sisters rescue brothers in fairy tales far more often than brothers rescue sisters. Daughters rescue fathers or lovers rather than the reverse. Beauty goes into the Beast's castle prepared to die in order to save her father. Hansel scatters bread crumbs to mark the way out of the woods (men like to serve as pathfinders), but it's Gretel who pushes the witch into her own oven. Cinderella is supposed to be the most passive heroine of all, waiting to be rescued from the ashes. Then why does she run away from the Prince three times in the German version, after dancing with him at the ball?

No, it's not fairy-tale heroines who are passive victims. It's the heroines of the Walt Disney movies, especially the earlier ones, who warble and weep on the sidelines and then accept rescue by a Prince in place of transformation.

RH: So you disapprove of Disney? It seems hard to remember fairy tales in detail except through his movies.

JG: I retell the old stories for just that reason. Walt Disney is the leading mythmaker of our time, to such an extent that his movies and books are the only versions of the stories that most people know. Disney changes what used to be the heroine's story of growth and transformation—in other words, nature magic—into the hero's story of conflict: good against evil, youth against age, masculine courage against the trickiness and cruelty of old witches. It's Disney's patriarchal slant that feminists object to, whether they realize it or not.

In Disney's kingdom, the hero is present from the first reel, infatuating the heroine and ultimately saving her. In traditional stories, he doesn't appear until the end, and then chiefly as a sign of the girl's new maturity—he's a sort of graduation present. With Disney, the heroine isn't transformed; she's rescued. The hero becomes the agent of change. Of course, sixty-five years have passed since the first full-length Disney fairy-tale film, and themes have been altered to suit the times, especially in the new *Beauty and the Beast*, but the old movies are revived for each generation.

RH: Did you keep your own children away from the Disney fairy-tale movies?

JG: Of course not. No one should be deprived of a chance to see the dwarfs marching off to the mines—"We whistle while we work"—or the squirrels cleaning house by sweeping the dust under the rug with their tails. Disney movies are an entertainment form all their own. But Disney isn't enough. His movies and simplified fairy-tale books teach us nothing about the mysterious pain and transcendence involved in growing up. For that, we need the old stories in their traditional form (especially Grimms' and Perrault's), which were what I read to my own children.

RH: But if fairy-tale heroines aren't passive, as you say, why do we hear so much about sleep? Snow White is on display in her glass coffin, either asleep or dead. Sleeping Beauty sleeps for a hundred years after being pricked by a spindle.

JG: Sleep—which is one of the natural paths of inner development—is equated with death by men, who think that only a Prince can bring the heroine back to life by arousing her sexual desire. But women know better. We know that vitally important work goes on in sleep—not only in the drowsiness that we experience during the early months of pregnancy and the tranquil hours of nursing a baby, but during transformation from one physical or emotional stage to the next.

Women often need a time of solitude in which their emotions can catch up with their bodies, especially after the shock of their first encounter with sexuality. For a while, psychological sleep offers a girl or woman escape from situations that overwhelm her, while protecting her from the need to make decisions. This is the message of "Sleeping Beauty." In a more positive sense (and this is a phenomenon that we've all shared in a small way), artists and scientists report that the solution they've been seeking for a problem, or the new line of melody that eludes them, doesn't come to them while they are hard at work at their desks and straining for it, but while they're asleep or day-dreaming.

RH: In modern times, when women are less apt to be repressed, do we still have Sleeping Beauties?

JG: Among my friends, I know a surprising number who were anorexics or bulimics, which are ways of forcibly putting the body to sleep, to the extent that some of them no longer menstruated. They denied that their time had arrived to become mature women. Others went through major depressions, or became addicted to drugs or alcohol. Wherever we look, we can find Sleeping Beauties.

RH: One of the main themes in *Spinning Straw* is the idea that "females are the vehicles of transformation in this world." Do you think that older women can relate well to younger women today, and vice versa? Do women from each generation confront the same issues, or has society changed so much as to render the experiences very different?

JG: Of course society has changed radically in recent decades, but I think that the changes of the past thirty or forty years have brought the generations closer together rather than further apart. Girls of fifteen have babies, and so do women in their forties, even fifties. Women in their seventies dress in jeans and sweat shirts like their granddaughters, go hiking and camping and have love affairs and divorces. Older women remember how hard it is to work full time, and young women, just starting their careers, look forward to being homemakers as well—as soon as they have the time. The younger generation hasn't shocked its elders since the 1970s, now that sexuality has been pretty well divorced from reproduction, and the older generation no longer seems dreary, thanks to improvements in medicine and beauty care. Even our popular culture has melded. Because of modern technology, young folks have seen *I Love Lucy* and heard the Beatles sing "I Want to Hold Your Hand." The past is wrapped up in the present.

So what can old women teach young women? Only this: Watch. Stay awake. Busy as you are while you're working and dating, or during the years of child-rearing when it's a small victory to find the time to brush your teeth, try to be aware of the transformations going on around you and because of you. Before you know it, the child you left at the kindergarten door this morning will be working in his office, too busy to take his mother's phone calls. Miracles are passing through you. When you become a Crone (like me), you'll be surrounded by silence and time, in which you'll look at young mothers with their children and see the energy—I almost said radiance—streaming from them.

RH: Now it's your turn, Joan, to tell us—what's your own favorite fairy tale?

JG: When I was young, I think my favorite was the Greek myth of the goddess Demeter and her daughter, Persephone. I thought this was because the pretty girl picking flowers was kidnapped by Hades, King of the Underworld, and became the Queen of the Dead. The mysteries of the spirit world fascinated me. Then one day, when my mother was old and sick and bitter, and I was telling her this story for lack of anything else to talk about, it occurred to me that I'd never known the real reason for my preference. I was caught by the story of a mother so in love with her daughter, her only child (as I was), that she defied the gods and made the whole world suffer for her loss. This was more than I thought my mother would do for me.

But in recent years I've often had "Beauty and the Beast" in mind. For thirty-five years I was a racing skipper, sailing a small boat on Long Island Sound in calms and storms, without any member of my family on board. (I still sail, but I no longer race.) It seems to me that we've lost too much of the wilderness in ourselves as well as in our surroundings, so that we have few occasions when we can be fully conscious of our bodies, with an occasional jolt of fear to remind us that we are fragile but present on the starting line anyway, like our boats. I tend to admire good male skippers (when I began to sail there were no other females in our area racing without their husbands). I respect boat owners who not only sail and race as I do but also have enough knowledge of aerodynamics to judge the cut of a sail and the rake of a mast, which is beyond me. Often these skippers are dull socially, like "poor Beast," hot-tempered and difficult, but with a rare physical intelligence.

I didn't choose to marry a Beast, however. I married a landlubber hero who never chose to set foot in a boat but let me go right on racing my own—and I never wanted anyone else.

Questions for Discussion

1.   Many myths and fairy tales focus on change and transformation. What are some examples of this from the book? Is the importance of change an issue for women only, or are men faced with similar issues? Discuss change as a central theme in a woman's life, and explore some of the ways it has affected your own life.

2.   Are you currently a maiden, matron, or crone? Do you find that your experiences in this phase of life are similar to those in the book? After reading about the phase you are currently in, do you look at your life in a different way? Was there something unexpected in the

book that helps explain an aspect of your life you had not previously been able to understand fully?

3.   Although fairy tales and myths are at the heart of Joan Gould's exploration of the three phases of a woman's life, she also draws on contemporary examples from popular books, movies, and television to illustrate the roles of Maiden, Matron, and Crone. Think of some examples from movies or books you have cared about that illustrate these phases. Now think of your favorite heroine from one of these works. What is her personal story of transformation?

4.   Psychological sleep is a major theme in this book. Can you identify any period in your life when you were sufficiently awake to follow your usual routines but felt emotionally paralyzed, unable to make decisions that would move your life forward?

5.   When you think of your own Cinderella stage, what part of your body caused you the most embarrassment? Did it affect your image of yourself as a woman? Who played the haughty stepsisters in your life—classmates, friends, or relatives? Were you able to learn anything from them? Was your mother critical of your looks, like Cinderella's stepmother, or was she supportive?

6.   In many ways, the section on the Crone is the most powerful and beautiful. This is the stage in which a woman will do the most important and independent work of her life—the work of the spirit. Why is this section the shortest of the three, and why does it have the fewest stories? Does this section of the book in any way change your view of the future?

7.   You were probably familiar with many of the stories in *Spinning Straw into Gold* before reading the book. Did you first encounter these fairy tales in the Disney versions or in the traditional form? Did you understand them in a different way after reading *Spinning*

Straw into Gold? Which stories gave you the most insight into your own life? Were any of them stories you read here for the first time?

8. Joan Gould discusses very openly the aspects of a woman's life that are deeply hidden within fairy tales, often revealing quandaries that all women share but do not discuss. What are some of these secrets? Did you find the revelations in the Black Bride/White Bride section surprising? Do you think Gould accurately explores the conflicts within a woman between her role as an individual and as a wife and mother?

9. Look at your own life and some of the major events that are on the horizon for you. How has *Spinning Straw into Gold* helped you to understand what you can expect over the next few years? What are the issues that you will soon be facing?

10. Finally, what is your favorite fairy tale, and why? After reading *Spinning Straw into Gold*, has your choice changed? If not, do you have a better understanding of what this particular story reveals about your personal journey and transformation?

Joan Gould is available to speak to book groups in person or via speakerphone.

Website: www.joangould.com
E-mail: joan@joangould.com

JOAN GOULD's work has appeared in many publications, including *The New York Times*, for which she has written numerous columns. Her last book, *Spirals: A Journey to the Center of a Woman's Life*, was a family memoir. She lives in Rye, New York.

Printed in the United States
by Baker & Taylor Publisher Services